Intimate Economies of Immigration Detention

International migration has been described as one of the defining issues of the twenty-first century. While a lot is known about the complex nature of migratory flows, surprisingly little attention has been given to one of the most prominent responses by governments to human mobility: the practice of immigration detention.

Intimate Economies of Immigration Detention provides a timely intervention, offering much needed scrutiny of the ideologies, policies and practices that enable the troubling, unparalleled and seemingly unbridled growth of immigration detention around the world. An international collection of scholars provide crucial new insights into immigration detention, recounting at close range how detention's effects ricochet from personal and everyday experiences to broader political-economic, social and cultural spheres. Contributors draw on original research in the US, Australia, Europe and beyond to scrutinise the increasingly tangled relations associated with detention operation and migration management. With new theoretical and empirical perspectives on detention, the chapters collectively present a toolbox for better understanding the forces behind and broader implications of the seemingly uncontested rise of immigration detention.

This book should be of great interest to those who study political economy, economic geography and human mobility across borders, as well as policy makers interested in immigration.

Deirdre Conlon is a Lecturer in Critical Human Geography at the University of Leeds, UK. Her research examines immigration enforcement and detention in policy and practice, their effects on migrant (in)security, citizenship and everyday life, as well as the wider reverberations of immigration control.

Nancy Hiemstra is Assistant Professor of Migration Studies at Stony Brook University in New York, USA. Her research analyses the geopolitical and socio-cultural reverberations of restrictive immigration policies and practices in the United States and Latin America, with a focus on US detention and deportation.

Routledge Frontiers of Political Economy

Intimate Economies of Immigration Detention

Critical perspectives

Edited by Deirdre Conlon and Nancy Hiemstra

LONDON AND NEW YORK

First published 2017 by Routledge

2 Park Square, Milton Park, Abingdon, Oxfordshire OX14 4RN
52 Vanderbilt Avenue, New York, NY 10017

Routledge is an imprint of the Taylor & Francis Group, an informa business

First issued in paperback 2019

British Library Cataloguing in Publication Data
A catalogue record for this book is available from the British Library

Library of Congress Cataloging in Publication Data
Names: Conlon, Deirdre. | Hiemstra, Nancy.
Title: Intimate economies of immigration detention : critical perspectives /
edited by Deirdre Conlon and Nancy Hiemstra.
Description: London ; New York : Routledge, 2017.
Identifiers: LCCN 2016010438| ISBN 9781138900660 (hardback) |
ISBN 9781315707112 (ebook)
Subjects: LCSH: Emigration and immigration—Government policy. |
Emigration and immigration—Economic aspects. | Immigrants—
Government policy. | Detention of persons.
Classification: LCC JV6038 .I66 2017 | DDC 365/.45—dc23LC record
available at https://lccn.loc.gov/2016010438

ISBN: 978-1-138-90066-0 (hbk)
ISBN: 978-0-367-87291-5 (pbk)

Typeset in Times New Roman PS
by diacriTech, Chennai

Contents

Illustrations

Figures

Tables

Contributors

Mario Bruzzone is a doctoral candidate in the Department of Geography at the University of Wisconsin–Madison, USA. His dissertation concerns the localised economic and political processes of transit migration through Mexico. In addition to chapters in several books, his work has been published or is forthcoming in *Antipode* and *Cultural Geographies*.

Dr. Kate Coddington is a Lecturer in the Geography Department at Durham University, UK. Her work focuses on borders, migration, and postcolonial governance structures in the Asia-Pacific region. She has published related work in *Progress in Human Geography, Social and Cultural Geography, Geography Compass, Tourism Geographies, Journal of the Indian Ocean Region,* and *SHIMA: The International Journal of Research into Island Culture.*

Deirdre Conlon is a Lecturer in Critical Human Geography at the University of Leeds, UK. Her research examines immigration enforcement and detention in policy and practice, their effects on migrant (in)security, citizenship, and everyday life, as well as the wider reverberations of immigration control. Her current work, with Nancy Hiemstra, examines internal (micro)economies in the US detention system. She is co-editor of *Carceral Spaces: Mobility and Agency in Imprisonment and Migrant Detention* (Ashgate, 2013) and has published in *Annals of the Association of American Geographers, Citizenship Studies,* and *Environment and Planning D: Society and Space,* and in several edited volumes.

Caroline Fleay is Senior Lecturer at the Centre for Human Rights Education, Curtin University in Western Australia. She conducts research into the experiences of people seeking asylum in Australia and has been a regular visitor to Western Australian immigration detention centres and an active campaigner for refugee rights over the past fifteen years. Her publications in this field include the monograph *Australia and Human Rights: Situating the Howard Government* (2010) and a range of journal articles and reports that explore the impacts of public policy on people seeking asylum.

Michael Flynn is the Executive Director of the Global Detention Project, an interdisciplinary research center based in Geneva, Switzerland, that investigates the use of detention as a response to international migration. His research has been supported by the Geneva International Academic Network, the Swiss Network for International Studies, the Pew International Journalism Program, and the Fund for Investigative Journalism. Flynn holds a BA in Philosophy from DePaul University and an MA and PhD in International Studies from the Graduate Institute of International and Development Studies in Geneva.

Nick Gill is Professor of Human Geography at the University of Exeter, UK. He has written widely about geography and immigration control and his current research considers the legal geographies of refugee claim determination throughout Europe. He is the author of *Nothing Personal? Geographies of Governing and Activism in the British Asylum System* (Wiley-Blackwell, 2016).

Alexandra Hall is a Lecturer in Politics at the University of York, in York, UK. She has conducted research into the everyday production and experience of security within immigration detention and the rise of smart border targeting systems in the UK and Europe. She is the author of *Borderwatch* (Pluto Press, 2012).

Nancy Hiemstra is Assistant Professor of Migration Studies at Stony Brook University in Stony Brook, New York, USA. Her research analyses the political and socio-cultural reverberations of restrictive immigration policies in the United States and Latin America, with a focus on US detention and deportation policy and practice. Her current work, with Deirdre Conlon, examines internal (micro)economies in the US detention system. She has published related work in *Annals of the Association of American Geographers, Antipode, Environment and Planning D, Geographica Helvetica*, and *Geopolitics*.

Malene H. Jacobsen is a PhD candidate at the Geography Department, University of Kentucky, USA. She wrote her MA thesis on the topic of asylum seekers' everyday life within the Danish asylum system. Her research interests center broadly around issues of forced migration, subaltern geopolitics, and state practices within and across national borders. Her dissertation research focuses on the transnational dimensions of forced migration between Jordan and Denmark.

Anitta Kynsilehto holds an Academy of Finland Postdoctoral Research Fellowship at the Tampere Peace Research Institute, University of Tampere, Finland. Her research explores gender and global mobilities, undocumented mobilities, and knowledge practices and politics in mobile forms of solidarity across borders. Her work has appeared in *Environment and Planning A, Body &*

Society, International Studies Perspectives and *European Journal of Cultural Studies*.

Matthew Lowen is the Associate Program Director for the American Friends Service Committee (AFSC) of Arizona, USA. He holds an MA in Geography from the University of Arizona, where his research gave specific attention to carceral geographies of solitary confinement and popular representations of maximum-security prisons. While at AFSC Arizona, he has authored numerous reports on conditions of confinement, such as *Buried Alive: Solitary Confinement in Arizona's Prisons and Jails* (2007), *Lifetime Lockdown: How Isolation Conditions Impact Prisoner Reentry* (2012), and *Still Buried Alive: Arizona Prisoner Testimonies on Isolation in Maximum-Security* (2014).

Lauren Martin is a Lecturer in Human Geography at Durham University, UK. Her research explores the commodification of border enforcement, the politics of family and intimacy in US immigration controls, and the legal geographies of detention. She has published in *Progress in Human Geography, Environment and Planning A, Geopolitics, Gender, Place & Culture, Space and Polity, Antipode*, and *Geography Compass.*

Vanessa A. Massaro is a Visiting Assistant Professor of Geography at Bucknell University, USA. Her research draws on mixed quantitative and ethnographic methods to explore the way spatially segregated racial minorities, particularly African Americans, navigate the intersection of racism with broader forces of economic injustice. Her work has been published in *Gender, Place, and Culture, Geopolitics, Geography Compass*, and *Territory, Politics, Governance.*

Julia Morris is a doctoral candidate in Social Anthropology at the University of Oxford, UK and a research student at the Centre on Migration, Policy and Society (COMPAS). Julia's research looks at the creation of a refugee legal and development system for the Republic of Nauru, examining the transnational social and commodity networks that go into projects grounded in legal epistemologies. She is completing her thesis under a research fellowship at UC Berkeley's Center for the Study of Law & Society. She has a forthcoming article in *Global Networks* on the international detention rights movement.

Alison Mountz is Professor of Geography and Canada Research Chair in Global Migration at the Balsillie School of International Affairs at Wilfrid Laurier University and the 2015–2016 William Lyon Mackenzie King Visiting Professor of Canadian Studies at Harvard University. She publishes widely on detention and recently authored *Seeking Asylum: Human Smuggling and Bureaucracy at the Border* (University of Minnesota) and two forthcoming monographs: *The Enforcement Archipelago: Hidden Geographies and the Death of Asylum* and *Boats, Borders, and Bases: Race, the Cold War, and the Rise of Non-Citizen Detention in the United States* (co-authored with Jenna Loyd).

Eeva Puumala is a postdoctoral researcher at the University of Tampere, Finland. Puumala's work focuses on questions of agency, seeking asylum and the creation of the figure of the asylum seeker. She has published in a number of journals including *International Political Sociology, European Journal of Cultural Studies, International Studies Perspectives* and *Review of International Studies*. Currently she is in the process of completing a book manuscript, *Asylum Seekers, Sovereignty and the Senses of the International: A Politico-Corporeal Struggle*, with Routledge.

Dora Schriro is the Commissioner of the Connecticut, USA Department of Emergency Services and Public Protection, a state enforcement agency that includes the state police, homeland security and emergency management. Over her career, she has lead public safety agencies in three American states and two cities. Dr. Schriro also served as Special Advisor to Department of Homeland Security Secretary Napolitano and was the first Director of the Immigration and Customs Enforcement Office of Detention Policy and Planning. During her tenure at DHS, she authored *A Report on the Preliminary Assessment of ICE Detention Policies and Practices: A Recommended Course of Action for Systems Reforms*, DHS's template for improving the nation's immigration detention system. Schriro currently serves as a commissioner on the boards of the ABA Commission on Immigration and the Women's Refugee Commission.

Jill M. Williams is an Assistant Research Social Scientist and Director of the Women in Science and Engineering Program at the Southwest Institute for Research on Women at the University of Arizona, USA. Her research employs a feminist geopolitical framework to explore contemporary border enforcement policies and their effects, paying particular attention to discourses and practices of humanitarianism. Her work has been published in *Political Geography, Geopolitics, Geography Compass*, and *The Geographical Journal*.

Foreword

On the importance of intimate economies

Alison Mountz

This is a groundbreaking collection. Its contributors will challenge you, their reader, to contend with the intimate economies of detention: with the mundane, the insidious, the monotonous, the salacious, the abhorrent. Prepare yourself to experience sadness and anger, revelation and frustration. The authors use carefully researched empirical evidence to prove beyond doubt that the detention of non-citizens is big business, cleverly bundled into life's 'little things', like bed space and overpriced ramen noodles, all the while capitalising on life's biggest things, like freedom and attachment to family. They show with heartbreaking detail and incisive analysis just how these little things add up to billions of dollars, pounds and euros of profit and just how far these profits reach.

If detention is big business, it is also small business. Sustained scrutiny of intimate economies of detention reveals them to be at once place-specific and global, what Geraldine Pratt and Victoria Rosner (2006) call 'the global intimate'. Research findings on the investments in and returns on intimacy challenge more general assertions that transnational corporations are the only groups profiting from detention. It is true that privatisation of incarceration continues apace, damaging people on the inside who generate profits for those on the outside. It is also true that there is much more to the story.

In order to determine what more there is to the story, these essays link the intimacies of detained people – their bodies, their labour, their everyday lives – to the intimacies of profit, or what Conlon and Hiemstra (2014) call 'internal micro-economies'. In one sense, these are simple equations. Hunger demands food. The hungry person deprived of liberty works for a pittance. This business of working to buy food, buying food to eat, sustaining the body to labour, requires production, provision and payment. Deprivation is equated with need, desire and despair for work, even work that pays $1 per day.

Although simple, these are also hidden equations. How many US residents, for example, know that approximately 400,000 non-citizens were detained in their midst over the course of a year and that companies are turning a profit from their 'voluntary work'? The intimate economy pervades our contemporary landscape. While often 'hidden in plain sight', detention facilities have become ubiquitous, as have their attendant economies.

And what kind of economy is the intimate economy? As the ensuing essays reveal, it is multifaceted, multi-scalar capitalism applied to the art of confinement. First, governments pay corporations and each other (for example, federal to county agencies in the US) for the construction and management of facilities. They pay for each unit of space, broken down in this economy as 'beds', an economy of possibilities that many have argued drives the detention and deportation machinery, assigned the mandate of filling these beds. Corporations such as Serco, Geo Group, Corrections Corporation of America and G4S compete for bids to run facilities.

But bodies, too, factor into these equations. Non-citizens are exploited outside *and* inside of carceral spaces for their labour. As editors and authors, Deirdre Conlon and Nancy Hiemstra are committed to exposing 'circuits of exploitation and wealth accumulation' through which bodies are dispossessed. They show how people placed in detention are deprived of liberty and mobility and subjected to commissaries and 'voluntary work'. Both of these force them into economies designed to capitalise on need and boredom.

The collective weight of the empirical evidence in this book shifts thinking away from the primary rationale for detention: that detention acts as deterrent, dissuading future unauthorised migration. Evidence simply makes it more believable that the dramatic rise in construction, policy, criteria and scope for detention globally relates to the tremendous and hideously easy profits to be made.

For several years, the dominant economic narrative used to explain the rise in detention of non-citizens has been privatisation. A key contribution of this collection is a strategic and important shift *beyond* the rhetoric of privatisation. Transnational corporations still have their place in the analysis. But the focus on intimate economies expands the field, enabling deeper understanding of the forces driving the massive expansion in detention over the last two decades. This shift builds on feminist thought designed to include activities once excluded from consideration of what counted as economic. The authors are able to show not only *that* detained bodies are dispossessed and commodified, but *how* these processes occur within detention through accumulation by dispossession. People themselves are dispossessed through their removal from communities where they live and work; whereas accumulation from their labour is funneled through detention facilities and the entities that run them and reap their profits.

The material dimensions of detention unearthed through this shift in scale to the intimate are revolting. They needed to be written, and now they need to be read and contended with, widely. Details from the mundane lives of people detained are striking: that people can keep only wedding rings; that they work for one fifteenth of minimum wage, but pay five times as much for basic food supplies as the average customer at the average grocery store. Hiemstra and Conlon adroitly lay out the workings of this capitalist infrastructure in the US detention system.

Julia Morris also writes about the process of accumulation through what she calls 'ethical capitalism'. In her analysis, she shifts attention from corporations that run facilities to the human rights campaigns designed to improve detention, arguing that they too are imbricated in its expansion. While much contemporary scholarship tackles the humanitarian rhetoric associated with the fine line between rescue and enforcement (for example, Williams, 2016), Morris shifts some of the blame to the role of non-governmental organisations and their academic experts, from the immigration detention complex to what she calls 'the detention improvement complex'. Morris shows how 'ethical capitalism' advances through efforts to create standards and norms to protect human rights.

From human rights to labouring bodies, the depth of this collection lies with its richly textured understandings of intimacy. The word opens a field of possibilities elucidated in each essay. In the Australian context (in chapters by Kate Coddington and Caroline Fleay), intimacy means simultaneous erasure and disclosure. On the one hand, private contractors, government agencies and people who run detention centres enact the erasure of those on the inside. Simultaneously, those same people, along with a limited number of visitors, also witness their perpetual disclosure, forced through enclosure. Coddington and Fleay flesh out these intimate processes and economies of erasure and witnessing in discussion of their work in northern Australia.

Fleay, Coddington and other scholars in this book politicise the affective response to witnessing intimate economies of detention. They are motivated by moral, emotional and political forces to act in response to the research they do, underscoring that the writing of this collection is an important and pressing political intervention with local, national and transnational implications for activism, policy and scholarship. They understand intimate economies as hidden geographies and work to bring these into broader political purview.

The contributors also think materially. They will tell you the mundane details of entering facilities and associated paperwork. They report the costs of items in the detention centre's commissary alongside its hours. They also offer important interventions for the more policy-oriented reader, such as histories of national detention policy, the details of contracts with private entities to run facilities and careful consideration of how to understand the broad range of people involved in this work who, as Michael Flynn cautions, move well beyond the binary of 'state' and 'non-state actors'. Lauren Martin maps the complex history of legislation, policy and the construction of facilities in the United States. She also offers incisive conceptual considerations: how we should think through these practices and processes through which detention becomes what Michel Foucault calls a technology of government. Martin identifies family as the latest target of the US government to control intimacy.

This collection offers an array of feminist interventions. One involves disruption of the division between economic and social reproduction, with body and family as entities that bear the burden of social reproduction. Like Martin, Jill Williams and Vanessa Massaro study the intimacies of US family detention, focusing on social reproduction through migrant care networks, the sphere where the carceral state has offloaded social reproduction to advance detention as a capitalist project. Alex Hall offers another feminist intervention. Drawing on research in the UK, she analyses intimate economies through affective and visual registers, arguing persuasively that the economic and the intimate are coproduced.

Also working in England, Nick Gill observes the need to 'take account of various intimacies', juxtaposing them to understand what is happening both intimately at the scale of the body that experiences sexual assault and globally, where these assaults are carried out by the same companies (such as Serco) that are running facilities around the world. He suggests that the intimate and the economic should not be entangled as they are in detention, because this entanglement puts at greater risk the health of those detained. Gill notes, 'Immigration detention centres are global sites of profit making that inevitably "affect, and are shaped by, intimate relations"' (Wilson, 2012, p. 42) in profound ways because detention centres render their inhabitants reliant on profit-motivated relationships for their most personal and intimate needs.'

For some authors, understanding intimate economies means a focus on the everyday. Malene Jacobsen, for example, explores how 'pocket money' – small cash allowances provided for asylum seekers – shape their precarity in Denmark. Like their counterparts detained in the US system and forced to use the commissary, they too must find ways to survive on means that are 'not enough'. Kynsilehto and Puumala, working in Finland, also study detention through the lens of everyday life. They draw on interview data to 'reflect on how the status of detainee affects their self-conceptions and relations to others, how the everyday is lived, the past remembered and the future planned beyond their current status'. Whereas Jacobsen's participants live precariously outside of detention, Kynsilehto and Puumala trace materially the lived spaces *inside* detention. The result of intimate research in both pieces is the narration of intimate economies by those who live them, albeit in distinct locales and ways.

Matthew Lowen writes of the crushing lived precarity of Operation Streamline, a program along the Mexico-US border designed by US Customs and Border Patrol to expedite the legal process to 'remove' thousands of people detained for entering the US without authorisation. Lowen finds intimacy in the techno-bureaucratic spaces of criminalisation. His rendering of a legal process through its intimate spaces is moving and infuriating. Mario Bruzzone explores the geographical spread of such enforcement practices beyond sovereign territory in order to understand how interior and exterior detention regimes operate in concert to restrict and contain human mobility. He explains how this happens at and well beyond the border to produce diverse migrants as a class of workers subjected to deprivation, precarity, exploitation and violence across intimate economies.

Issues outlined in each national context addressed in this book resonate in others. As such, the project succeeds in showing that intimate economies *are* the global intimate, at once highly localised, experienced by and enacted upon the body; and global in reach, a new economy of detention with no respect for the very borders that render those on the inside so vulnerable. The collection is global in scope, but the problem is even more global in scope with material infrastructure to detain growing in transit areas and borderlands not represented in this collection, such as Indonesia, Malaysia, Guatemala and Libya. Furthermore, states of the Global North not necessarily represented in this book are also expanding their capacity to detain. One example is Canada. Until recently, Canada was known for its progressive, humanitarian approach to asylum seekers. Of late, Canada, too, has been increasing capacity to detain and shutting down paths to asylum. Capacity to detain has also grown across the European Union, and it remains to be seen whether temporary reception centres set up to house asylum seekers associated with the 2015 surge in arrivals from Syria and beyond will evolve into carceral spaces, a classic historical trajectory through which detention centres merge.

This collection utilises diverse methodological and conceptual approaches to reach deeper understandings of detention, from archival and ethnographic research, legal analysis and access to information requests, to Bruzzone's use of Mezzadra and Nielson's (2013) border method. This range of approaches enables a comprehensive portrait as well as strategic interventions into detention economies that build on political economy and feminist scholarship.

To conclude, I encourage you to read on, and share this book with others. This collection has been written and assembled by the scholars who are leading a new field of study and political work. Its contributors are international and interdisciplinary. Some label this field detention studies (Martin and Mitchelson, 2009), while others conceptualise it as carceral studies (Moran et al., 2013). Some would call the work participatory research, public scholarship or scholar activism. What matters far more than categorisation is the collective commitment to confront rather than turn away from ethically and politically challenging research. Read on knowing that you are reading some of the best, most innovative and important work in the field on a topic that lingers, a haunting capitalist infrastructure whose intimate economies do not promise to disappear any time soon.

References

Conlon, D. and Hiemstra, N. 2014. Examining the everyday micro-economies of immigrant detention in the United States. *Geographica Helvetica* **69**, pp. 335–44.

Martin, L. L., and Mitchelson, M. L. 2009. Geographies of detention and imprisonment: interrogating spatial practices of confinement, discipline, law, and state power. *Geography Compass* **3**(1), pp. 459–77.

Mezzadra, S. and Neilson, B. 2013. *Border as method, or, the multiplication of labor*. Durham: Duke University Press.

Moran, D., Gill, N. and Conlon, D. eds. 2013. *Carceral spaces: mobility and agency in imprisonment and migrant detention*. Farnham Surrey: Ashgate.

Pratt, G. and Rosner, V. 2006. Introduction: the global and the intimate. *Women's Studies Quarterly* **34**(1/2), pp. 13–24.

Williams, J. 2016. The safety/security nexus and the humanitarianisation of border enforcement. *Geographical Journal*. **182**(1), pp. 27–37.

Wilson, A. 2012. Intimacy: a useful category of transnational analysis. In Pratt, G. and Rosner, V. eds. *The global and the intimate: feminism in our time*. New York: Columbia University Press, pp. 31–56.

Acknowledgements

We would first like to thank the contributors to this volume, for sharing their inspiring and important work, their attention to detail, and for doing an unprecedented job meeting deadlines. We are grateful to Alison Mountz and Dora Schriro for engaging with the contributions in incisive ways and for augmenting the collection with their insights. Special thanks to Dominique Moran and Robert Vanderbeck for providing timely feedback on the *Introduction* to the collection, and to Steve Borsak and Roger Hiemstra for assistance in the final stages. Our thanks, also, to the editorial team at Routledge for all their assistance in preparing this book.

We each (Deirdre and Nancy) wish to acknowledge the other for the vision, enthusiasm, inspiration, and commitment to collaboration this project has nurtured. We are enormously thankful to others who have supported us in countless ways. *Deirdre:* I am indebted to friends and family and grateful to colleagues at Saint Peter's University and the University of Leeds who have provided support along the way. Foremost, my thanks to my comrade and partner Steve and daughter Sadie who are there for me in myriad ways with life('s)work, *céad míle maith agaibh. Nancy*: I am grateful to family, friends, and colleagues at Stony Brook University and elsewhere for support in myriad forms. Above all, I thank my husband Sean for his unflagging support and confidence in me, and my children Kian and Saskia, whose hugs and laughter renew my energy and keep me smiling.

Finally, we dedicate this collection to detained immigrants everywhere. It is our fervent hope that it contributes in at least small ways to the disruption and dismantling of detention regimes, from intimate to global scales.

1   Introduction

Intimate economies of immigration detention

Deirdre Conlon and Nancy Hiemstra[1]

International migration has been described as one of the defining issues of the twenty-first century (Betts, 2015). The movement of people across borders has profound social, cultural, economic and geopolitical ramifications. While a vast literature explores the complex nature, scope and significance of migratory flows, surprisingly little attention has been given to one of the most prominent responses by governments to human mobility: the practice of immigration detention. This volume is grounded in the conviction that immigration detention – often hidden from public view – requires scholarly attention equal to that given to the more visible and better known dimensions of international migration. The contributions to this volume together offer a timely intervention in a developing field of inquiry, providing much needed scrutiny of the ideologies, policies and practices that gird the troubling, unparalleled and seemingly unbridled growth of immigration detention. While previous scholarship has examined the growth in detention at the macro level, a distinctive characteristic of this volume is its attention to micro-level processes. Through careful consideration of the *intimate economies* of immigration detention – that is, the complex systems of micro and macro relationships that enmesh in the realisation of detention and lived experiences of being detained – the contributors collectively prise open the concealed worlds of immigration detention, shedding necessary light on the costs and implications of an increasingly prevalent form of human confinement.

Intimate economies of detention expansion

Immigration detention is growing exponentially in disparate sites around the world, in terms of overall numbers as well as capacity, as Alison Mountz notes in the Foreword to this volume. In the United States, for instance, the detention system has grown by 75 per cent since 2003, so today an average of 33,000 migrants are detained on a daily basis and over 400,000 annually" (Detention Watch Network [DWN], 2015; see also Miroff, 2010). In the United Kingdom, the number of migrants detained annually increased by a total of 10 per cent between 2010 and 2014, to approximately 29,000 (Home Office, 2014), with the capacity to detain up to 3,915 people per day (Migration Observatory, 2015).

Australia detains approximately 8,400 individuals per year, with as many as 3,624 people in custody per day in 2014 (Australian Government Department of Immigration and Border Protection, 2015). Across European Union member states, 570,660 individuals were held in various types of detention centres in 2011 (Migreurop, 2013).[2]

These trends promise to continue in response to recent upswings in migration flows. Current turmoil, particularly in the Middle East, has resulted in a 47 per cent increase in asylum applications in European states in the one-year period between 2013 and 2014 (UNHCR, 2015). Recently, there has been a notable increase in US/Mexico border crossings particularly by women and unaccompanied children from Central America. The standard state response to such developments entails expanding the capacity to detain people. As destination countries such as the US, UK, Australia and EU member states aim to stop migrants from ever entering their territorial borders, they push for immigration detention in transit countries (Hyndman and Mountz, 2008) as well as offshore (Mountz and Loyd, 2014; Mountz, 2013). We therefore see detention systems developing in, for example, Mexico, Turkey, Nauru, Indonesia and Central American and North African states.

Detention has thus become a primary response to human mobility in a substantial – and growing – swath of countries across the world. Detention policies and practices develop, travel and vary from region to region (Nethery and Silverman, 2015; Ceccorulli and Labana, 2014), revealing detention to be flexible and adaptable to a range of geographic and political contexts (Mountz et al., 2013; Loyd et al., 2012; Hall, 2012; Martin and Mitchelson, 2009). The range of specific rationales given by states for detaining immigrants include: to verify identity, to examine requests to enter a state, to 'house' asylum seekers at various stages of a request for refuge, and in order to deport persons whose immigration status is deemed irregular. Common to each of these situations is that for migrants whose status is in question in some way, free movement is curtailed, day-to-day activities are circumscribed or monitored, and liberty is restricted (see Aierbe and Baylac, 2013). While immigration detention originated as an 'improvised response' (Migreurop, 2013, p. 81) to migration flows and governments often frame it as an administrative procedure, it is simultaneously a fundamental tool for managing migration, securing borders, asserting sovereign power and assuaging conservative and capricious voters.

There is a growing body of interdisciplinary scholarship as well as advocacy sector research examining the driving role of *privatisation* in contemporary human mobility and, specifically, the global expansion of immigration detention. Attention to privatisation and migration broadly considers the influence of private actors and institutions. Salt and Stein (1997), Kyle (2000), Castles and Miller (2003), Spener (2009), and Mountz (2010), for instance, call attention to the range of legal and illicit intermediaries that are involved in facilitating migration. In their edited collection, Gammeltoft-Hansen and Nyberg Sorensen (2013) examine privatisation as it intersects with different dimensions of the migration process including state actors and practices; border enforcement; the security industry; and informal as well as clandestine networks. In doing so, they highlight the complexity of migration in the current era. Hernández-León (2008, p. 154) refers to the constellation of agents involved in facilitating migration as constituting the 'migration industry'. Clochard and Rodier highlight the growth of 'opportunities' for private groups across European states in what they describe as a 'border security economy' (2013, p. 69). Another body of scholarship examines privatisation and immigration enforcement, with attention to matters of security (Fernandes, 2007; Bigo, 2002), devolution (Coleman, 2009) and the impact of localised immigration controls in the US (Varsanyi, 2008). Golash-Boza (2009) describes the private actors involved in implementing immigration policies in the US as forming the 'immigration industrial complex', which functions with similar logic and dynamics to the prison and military industrial complexes.

There can be little doubt that privatisation has been key to the 'geometric expansion of immigration detention' (Doty and Wheatley, 2013, p. 427). In the US private prison companies operate 62 per cent of detention beds (DWN, 2015). The UK boasts the largest number of privatised migrant detention centres in Europe with 73 per cent of detainees held in privately run facilities (Mason, 2013) while Australia's entire immigration detention system is run by private companies (Mason, 2013; Flynn and Cannon, 2009). Additionally, a wide array of services – including food services, medical care and transportation – within both private and government-operated detention facilities are subcontracted to private as well as non-profit entities (Conlon and Hiemstra, 2014; Mitchelson, 2014; Tyler et al., 2014; Doty and Wheatley, 2013; Feltz and Baksh, 2012; Dow, 2004). As Flynn and Cannon observe, privatised detention 'encompasses a diverse range of relationships, including the contracting of services to non-governmental organisations and differing configurations of private ownership and operation of detention facilities' (2009, p. 3). All in all, privatisation ensures 'profits for the companies involved while incentivising the incarceration of immigrants' (DWN, 2015, p. 1). Prior research illuminates detention privatisation at the macro level, for instance, attending to large-scale corporate involvement; government daily 'bed rates'; the influence of political lobbying in the expansion of detention; and the devolution of government operations to local authorities and third sector entities.

To date, there has been limited scrutiny of the deep and broad impacts of detention, privatisation and devolution at the micro level, that is to say within and around detention centres and as they affect the internal operation, day-to-day experiences, social fabric and wider dynamics of immigration detention. *Intimate Economies of Immigration Detention: Critical perspectives* brings together an international collection of scholars whose work engages these pressing issues. In addition to offering insight into detention systems in specific geographic contexts, the contributions to this volume deepen understanding of the ramifications of the expansion and proliferation of immigration detention regimes around the world by examining the manifold ways that detention reverberates in individual, social, cultural, political and economic spheres. As a whole, we conceptualise these chapters as exemplifying an approach that illuminates the 'intimate economies' of immigration detention. While this 'intimate' perspective may appear jarring in the context of detention regimes, we contend that it is not only important, but essential to the critical study of immigration detention.

Ideas connected to 'intimate economies' of detention evolved out of a themed session focusing on 'micro economies' of detention at the Annual Meeting of the Association of American Geographers (Tampa, Florida, April 2014) organised by the co-editors. This session sparked substantial interest from conference participants for the ways in which it pushed analysis beyond that fostered by typical macro-scale approaches. As conversations continued and ideas developed, we recognised the additional potential of an 'intimate' frame for identifying and scrutinising the range of micro-scale processes and practices where privatisation and devolution have taken hold and impact detention, as well as their overlap with the macro scale. An intimate lens, we suggest, is powerful precisely because it conveys attention to the personal at close range, while simultaneously allowing multiple approaches to and perspectives on the study of immigration detention.

The polyvalence – and critical utility – of intimacy is evident in the distinct yet overlapping interpretations employed by chapters in this volume. Some contributors draw on work that engages closely with the inside and inner workings of immigration detention. In this sense, intimacy invokes a sense of the physical closeness and knowledge that develops between entities in near proximity (see Berlant, 1998, 2000). Contributions thus evoke intimacy associated with being familiar and proximate to detention. In addition, chapters demand intimate attention – understood to refer to focused scrutiny – to the broad and growing networks of relations and practices that comprise detention. They also expose various ways – from deeply personal and problematic spheres to detached, remote and profit-focused realms – in which detention is experienced and its effects materialised. Our framing thus draws inspiration from Pain and Staeheli, who characterise intimacy as 'a set of spatial relations [...] a mode of interaction [... and] a set of practices' that extend from the 'proximate, personal and interpersonal' to 'spatial relations that are distant, interactions that are global, and practices that traverse institutional and national realms' (2014, p. 345).

An intimate *economic* lens draws on Wilson (2012), who proposes that intimate economies describe aspects of life that are typically excluded from considerations of 'the economic', yet are linked to processes of production and exchange in complicated ways and through complex relationships. An intimate economic perspective on immigration detention, then, also allows for attention to the increasingly tangled associations between government and corporations; private, public and non-profit sectors; and how the ensuing webs influence ideology, policy, practice and experiences related to detention. Framing these investigations vis-à-vis intimate economies thus augments calls from geographers and other social scientists to attend to the ways in which the ties of intimacy register and reverberate beyond the personal and the everyday at scales from the domestic to the global (Pratt and Rosner, 2006). An intimate economic approach to detention, therefore, entails analyses of production and social reproduction, or what Katz describes as the 'messy, fleshy stuff of everyday life' (2001, p. 711), yet also takes account of the ricochet beyond individual, subjective, and proximate spheres to social, cultural, political and economic realms beyond detention (see Conlon and Hiemstra, 2014).

Engaging and exposing the intimate

Together, the contributions to *Intimate Economies of Immigration Detention: Critical perspectives* provide crucial, critical insights into detention by scrutinising at close range the increasingly complex, tangled and proximal relations between the multiple actors subject to and involved in operating and managing immigration detention. The volume includes an array of perspectives and brings together original work from scholars and advocates whose research examines detention in the US, UK, Australia, Finland and Denmark, as well as case studies from Mexico, Central America, South Korea, Libya and the United Arab Emirates. Contributors productively extend both understandings and the significance of an intimate lens on immigration detention by engaging in various ways with 'intimate' and 'intimate economies'.

The volume is organised in two parts. The first part, *Engaging the intimate*, contains chapters that foreground frameworks, concepts and tools for examining immigration detention. Each of these chapters, while empirically grounded in a specific place or problem of immigration detention, puts forth a groundbreaking approach to the study of detention, carefully situated within an intimate economic perspective.

Part I opens with Michael Flynn's critical intervention on how privatisation in detention is frequently conceived. Drawing on 'limit cases' of detention from North Africa, South Korea, Gulf States and the Middle East, the chapter identifies an expanding range of non-state actors who are implicated in detention systems. This chapter offers significant insights for thinking about what analytical tools are needed to track the range of forms that detention now takes as well as efforts to monitor accountability. Flynn's empirically based conceptual analysis also sets the tone for chapters that follow, each of which adds complexity to the ways we understand detention, its expansion, and privatisation.

In Chapter 3, Lauren Martin focuses on the expansion of family detention in the US to argue that practices of 'discretion', 'contracting' and 'commodification' gird detention privatisation and become a technology of government that controls migrant life. This conceptualisation facilitates insight into the complex 'messiness' of the detention system where 'nominally distinct economic logics of financial gain and political logics of deterrence and enforcement are entangled' (p. 33), and pushes understandings of who becomes economic actors in detention. The chapter engages concepts of 'industry' and 'assemblage' as tools for analysing detention privatisation and, in doing so, offers an important response to some of the critiques of the 'migration industry' and 'immigration industrial complex' as concepts.

Julia Morris (Chapter 4) argues that international humanitarian organisations are imbricated with maintaining and expanding detention regimes. Attentive to ideological and policy level shifts that prop up detention and extend its privatisation under the guise of 'moral capitalism', Morris observes that so-called reforms in the name of international human rights are consistent with rather than oppositional to detention as capitalist accumulation strategy. The chapter shows how a veritable industry has emerged out of the emphasis on 'humane' detention, and illustrates how 'moral capitalism' functions to sustain rather than question detention. Importantly, the chapter also highlights the role academics and professionals play in this process.

In Chapter 5, Caroline Fleay draws on her research and activism as an independent visitor to the remote Curtin Immigration Detention Centre in Western Australia to theorise how 'bearing witness' can work as an alert to abuses within the detention system and, therefore, contribute to affecting change. Fleay identifies myriad negative effects of privatised detention, but also suggests that intimate spaces within the confines of detention prove crucial to contesting privatisation and detention more broadly. Significantly, this chapter indicates that personal connections also lead staff within detention facilities to 'bear witness' in ways that can lead to covert or overt assistance of detainees. Bearing witness can thus be understood as a valuable tool for contesting privatisation and the growth of detention in Australia and beyond.

Jill M. Williams and Vanessa A. Massaro, in Chapter 6, use a feminist analytic approach to develop an incisive analysis of the ways family detention and related migration management measures in the United States reverberate beyond detention facilities and their operators. As relatives, volunteers and non-governmental organisations are increasingly called upon to fulfil basic everyday needs for families released from detention, US Immigration and Customs Enforcement (ICE) effectively externalises costs associated with social reproduction. Simultaneously, Williams and Massaro suggest, the 'inside' and 'outside' of detention are made more proximate, as actors involved in care and assistance become more intimately entwined and, unwittingly, they allow ICE to evade responsibility in ways that facilitate the continued expansion of detention.

Chapter 7, by Mario Bruzzone, proposes a new conceptual framework, in which contemporary detention has both *internal* and *external* regimes, through a close reading of spaces exterior to the US-Mexico border that are simultaneously extensions and manifestations of the border. The chapter scrutinises the bureaucratic logic of the US strategy 'prevention through deterrence', arguing for re-conceptualising detention as 'spatial unfreedom' along a time-space continuum that extends beyond formal detention centres. The chapter also discusses the work of Mezzadra and Neilson (in their book *Border as Method*) alongside the work of JK Gibson-Graham to think through how border regimes spill over and beyond sites of detention to configure migrants' experiences in Mexico as well as how they govern differential processes of class formation.

While also theoretically grounded, chapters in the second part, *Exposing intimate economies*, foreground case studies from the US, Europe and Australia.

Through empirically rich, nuanced approaches, contributions provide compelling, in-depth analyses of the driving factors and embodied consequences of detention privatisation and devolution in specific sites and spaces.

Part II opens with Nancy Hiemstra and Deirdre Conlon's analysis of the intimate micro-economies that operate within US detention facilities. Chapter 8 knits together a feminist perspective on the intimate with David Harvey's concept of accumulation by dispossession to present an incisive account of 'circuits of dispossession' that flourish in detention, teasing out relationships between persistent deprivation of detainees' everyday needs, detention facilities' commissary systems, and 'voluntary' work programmes. Hiemstra and Conlon demonstrate how these relationships spatially fix detainees as captive consumers and coerced labourers, arguing that these intimate economic relationships effectively commoditise and dispossess detainees while securing demand for and expansion of detention.

In Chapter 9, Kate Coddington examines the fascinating case of Darwin, Australia, at one point the 'capital of detention' in that country. The chapter 'braid(s) together a dense array of connective strands of analysis' (p. 153) to illuminate an intimate economy of detention that is both deeply embedded and has far-reaching effects. Coddington highlights Darwin's isolation, the transience and marginalisation of the local population, and historical and contemporary processes of colonialism, to argue that simultaneous factors of ambiguity and erasure led to the development of detention in Darwin. By pairing analysis of local intimacies with global processes, the chapter's carefully detailed framework offers a model for exploring how and why detention takes root in disparate places around the world.

In Chapter 10, Malene H. Jacobsen draws on ethnographic research in Denmark's open detention system to present a critical perspective on the ways the cash allowance system permeates migrant life. She argues the 'pocket money' system produces dependency and vulnerability as well as shapes asylum seekers' everyday spatiality. In particular, Jacobsen emphasises how the Danish detention system – through the *aktivering* or activities programme – serves the political and economic interests of the Danish state. Like other contributions, this chapter highlights the importance of feminist scholarship for analyses that explicate the ways the political economy and politics of resistance fuse with subjective experience and everyday life.

Nick Gill's contribution (Chapter 11) employs the concept of intimacy in novel ways to explore how the presence or absence of various intimacies impacts the physical and mental health of immigration detainees in the UK. Gill argues that the economic goals of privatised detention undermine intimate contact with support networks while exposing detainees to unwanted heteronormative intimacy and uneven power relations, and also curtail possibilities for public scrutiny and accountability. The chapter calls for an approach to 'intimacies in the plural' (p. 183) and concludes that detention centres are dangerous places that exacerbate vulnerability and exploitation and damage detainee health.

In Chapter 12, Matthew Lowen provides a moving and troubling account of Operation Streamline, an immigration enforcement policy in the southwest United

States that literally criminalises migrants en masse. Using a series of vignettes from Streamline courtroom proceedings to frame the chapter, Lowen presents a penetrating depiction of how politicians and lobbyists, for-profit companies intent on expanding detention, and policies that criminalise migrants are conjoined. In addition to exposing the intimate ties between government, politics and economics, the chapter calls attention to the importance of various types of activism, ranging from direct confrontation to legal advocacy, which can filter through and disrupt the injustices of this system in unanticipated ways.

Anitta Kynsilehto and Eeva Puumala sketch the contours of Finland's nascent detention system in Chapter 13. In comparison with other European states, Finland has a very low number of asylum seekers (and detainees), largely due to its narrow focus on the economic interests of the state when making asylum decisions. Until very recently, Finland has also differed from other states in the *lack* of privatisation in immigration detention, but there are indications that under pressure to expand, this stance toward privatisation is changing. Drawing on ethnographic research with detainees, the chapter scrutinises how anxieties around sovereignty, national cultural imaginary and geopolitical relations within the EU become inscribed in material and corporeal realities for immigrants.

Alexandra Hall's chapter, the last in the collection, pays special attention to the role of spectatorship, or watching and looking, in the intimate spaces of immigration detention. Through a case study of employees of a UK detention centre, Hall draws on feminist film analysis techniques and psychoanalytic theory regarding the male/imperial gaze to understand what detention officers' practices of watching detainees reveal about security and border practices. In addition to illustrating the utility of incorporating feminist theories of vision and watching into studies of immigration detention and border security practices, the chapter explores the gendered nature of detention as reflection *and* producer of larger security regimes.

Exploding the intimate

Each of the chapters in this volume contributes to theorising detention as a complex system of exploitation that goes beyond macro-economic considerations, such as profit and loss or the state–private sector relationships involved in the immigration industrial complex, to consider intimate economies that enmesh with and exacerbate the impacts of detention. Contributions draw upon diverse theoretical and methodological frameworks including Marxist-humanist political economy, post-structuralist insights on governmentality, and feminist epistemologies and methods. Authors consider the increasing number and range of actors and spaces that are implicated in detention regimes. They disrupt simplistic associations that, for instance, pair 'open' systems of detention with fairness or privatised detention as always being more problematic than state owned or operated facilities. They examine intimacies that operate inside detention; in open as well as closed systems of confinement; in association with adjunct policies to detention (deterrence and Operation Streamline, for instance); and that manifest as part of a structurally and geographically exterior system that nonetheless halts or confines migrants in a carceral social state. Contributions elucidate the role of activism and research in the detention regime. They are careful not to reproduce 'storybook' representations of either; instead authors consider the challenges associated with these realms while also making clear the need to redouble efforts to undermine ideologies and practices that enable detention expansion. In these and other ways, each chapter articulates as a central concern the processes through which detention interlocks with practices, policies and systems that objectify, dehumanise and criminalise migrants.

We began this introductory chapter with the claim that critical attention to immigration detention is of equal importance as critical attention to human migration. We conclude with the claim that this book's intimate economic perspective shows that detention is not just a consequence of 'crises' of human migration;[3] detention is also a *cause* of continued migration. Attention to the intimate economies of detention reveals that migration across borders and detention are tightly linked. While migration is typically interpreted as a matter of concern for only destination, origin and transit countries, the intimate perspective on the global phenomena of detention provided in this volume forces recognition that all migrations and responses to them are interconnected. That is, government leaders are not motivated to look beyond local or national factors driving migration to larger systemic reasons as long as there are institutionalised responses like immigration detention from which multiple sectors of the population stand to benefit in various ways. By bringing attention to the growth and reverberations of immigration detention through a focus on intimate economies, this volume challenges us to think deeply and critically about what we already know about detention. It also contributes to identifying and addressing larger global trends of forced migration across national borders. Thus, *Intimate Economies of Immigration Detention: Critical perspectives* not only provides a framework for critical understanding and analysis of detention regimes; its significance lies in addressing, more broadly speaking, the causes and consequences of migration.

Notes

1 Both authors contributed equally in the writing of this chapter and editing of contributions to the volume.
2 This number includes the 27 states that were members of the EU in 2011; the 28th member state of Croatia joined the EU in 2013.
3 As Mountz and Hiemstra (2014) have argued, the portrayal and interpretation of migration as a crisis is often mobilised by states to justify extreme responses (like detention) and to solidify and expand power.

References

Aierbe, P. and Baylac, S. 2013. Developing open and closed camps in Europe and beyond. In: Clochard, O. for Migreurop. ed. *Atlas of migration in Europe: a critical geography of migration policies*. Oxford: New Internationalist, pp. 82–5.

Association of Visitors in Detention (AVID). 2014. *In Touch*. January 2014. London: AVID [Online]. Available from: www.aviddetention.org.uk [Accessed 10 October 2015].

Australian Government Department of Immigration and Border Protection. 2014. *The year at a glance 2014-2015* [Online]. Available from: www.border.gov.au/about/reports-publications/reports/annual/immigration-2014-15/the-year-at-a-glance [Accessed 6 February 2016].

Berlant, L. 1998. Intimacy: a special issue. *Critical Inquiry* **24**(2), pp. 281–8.

Berlant, L. 2000. *Intimacy*. Chicago: Chicago University Press.

Betts, A. 2015. Human migration will be a defining issue of this century. How best to cope? *The Guardian*, Opinion. 20 September [Online]. Available from: www.theguardian.com/commentisfree/2015/sep/20/migrants-refugees-asylum-seekers-21st-century-trend [Accessed 16 January 2016].

Bigo, D. 2002. Security and immigration: toward a critique of the governmentality of unease. *Alternatives* **27**, 63–92.

Bosworth, M. 2014. *Inside immigration detention*. Oxford: Oxford University Press.

Castles, S. and Miller, M. 2003. *The age of migration: international population movements in the modern world, third edition*. New York: Guilford Press.

Ceccorulli, M. and Labana, N. 2014. *The EU, migration and the politics of administrative detention*. Oxon: Routledge.

Clochard, O. and Rodier, C. 2013. The border security economy. In: Clochard, O. for Migreurop. ed. *Atlas of migration in Europe: a critical geography of migration policies*. Oxford: New Internationalist, pp. 69–71.

Coleman, M. 2009. What counts as the politics and practice of security, and where? Devolution and immigrant insecurity after 9/11. *Annals of the Association of American Geographers* **5**(99), pp. 904–13.

Conlon, D. and Hiemstra, N. 2014. Examining the everyday micro-economies of migrant detention in the United States. *Geographica Helvetica* **69**(5), pp. 335–44.

Detention Watch Network (DWN). 2015. *Banking on detention: local lock-up quotas and the immigrant dragnet* [Online]. Available from: www.detentionwatchnetwork.org/sites/default/files/Banking_on_Detention_DWN.pdf [Accessed 29 January 2016].

Doty, R.L. and Wheatley, E.S. 2013. Private detention and the immigration industrial complex. *International Political Sociology* **7**(4), 426–33.

Dow, M. 2004. *American gulag: inside US immigration prisons*. Berkeley, CA: University of California Press.

Feltz, R. and Baksh, S. 2012. Business of detention. In J. Loyd, Mitchelson, M. and Burridge, A. eds. *Beyond walls and cages: prisons, borders and global crisis*. Athens, GA: University of Georgia Press, pp. 143–51.

Fernandes, D. 2007. *Targeted: homeland security and the business of immigration*. NY: Seven Stories Press.

Flynn, M. and Cannon, C. 2009. *The privatisation of immigration detention: towards a global view*. Global Detention Project working paper. Geneva: GDP [Online]. Available from: www.globaldetentionproject.org [Accessed 6 February 2016]

Gammeltoft-Hansen, T. and Sørensen, N.N. eds. 2013. *The migration industry and the commercialization of international migration*. Oxon: Routledge.

Golash-Boza, T. 2009. The immigration industrial complex: why we enforce immigration policies destined to fail. *Sociology Compass* **3**(2), pp. 295–309.

Hall, A. 2012. *Border watch: cultures of immigration, detention and control*. London: Pluto.

Hernandez-Leon, R. 2013. Conceptualizing the migration industry. In T. Gammeltoft-Hansen and Sorensen, N.N. eds. *The migration industry and the commercialization of international migration*. New York: Routledge, pp. 24–44.

Hernandez-Leon, R. 2008. *Metropolitan migrants: the migration of urban Mexicans to the United States*. Berkeley, CA: University of California Press.

Home Office. 2014. *Immigration statistics: October to December 2014* [Online]. Available online from: www.gov.uk/government/statistics/immigration-statistics-october-to-december-2014 [Accessed 10 October 2015].

Hyndman, J. and Mountz, A. 2008. Another brick in the wall? Neo-refoulement and the externalization of asylum in Australia and Europe. *Government and Opposition* **43**(2), pp. 249–69.

Katz, C. 2001. Vagabond capitalism and the necessity of social reproduction. *Antipode* **33**(4), pp. 709–28.

Kyle, D. 2000. *Transnational peasants: migrations, networks, and ethnicity in Andean Ecuador*. Baltimore, MD: The Johns Hopkins University Press.

Loyd, J., Mitchelson, M., and Burridge, A. 2012. *Beyond walls and cages: prisons, borders and global crisis*. Athens, GA: University of Georgia Press.

Martin, L. and Mitchelson, M. 2009. Geographies of detention and imprisonment: interrogating spatial practices of confinement, discipline, law and state power. *Geography Compass* **3**(1), pp. 459–77.

Mason, C. 2013. *International growth trends in prison privatisation*. Washington DC: Sentencing Project.

Migreurop. 2013. *Atlas of migration in Europe: a critical geography of migration policies*. Oxford: New Internationalist.

Migration Observatory. 2015. *Immigration detention in the UK: Briefing*. Migration Observatory, University of Oxford [Online]. Available from: www.migrationobservatory.ox.ac.uk [Accessed 6 February 2016].

Miroff, N. 2010. Controversial quota drives immigration detention boom. *The Washington Post*. 13 October [Online]. [Accessed 20 September 2014]. Available from: www.washingtonpost.com/world/controversial-quota-drives-immigration-detention-boom/2013/10/13/09bb689e-214c-11e3-ad1a-1a919f2ed890_story.html [Accessed 20 September 2014].

Mitchelson, M.L. 2014. The production of bedspace: prison privatization and abstract space. *Geographica Helvetica* **69**(5), pp. 325–33.

Mountz, A. 2010. *Seeking asylum: human smuggling and bureaucracy at the border*. Minneapolis, MN: University of Minnesota Press.

Mountz, A., Coddington, K., Catania, T. and Loyd, J. 2013. Conceptualizing detention: mobility, containment, bordering, and exclusion. *Progress in Human Geography* **37**(4), pp. 522–41.

Mountz, A. 2013. Shrinking spaces of asylum: vanishing points where geography is used to inhibit access to asylum. *Journal of Human Rights* **19**(3), pp. 29–50.

Mountz, A. and Hiemstra, N. 2014. Chaos and crisis: dissecting the spatiotemporal logics of contemporary migrations and state practices. *Annals of the Assocation of American Geographers* **104**(2), pp. 382–90.

Mountz, A., and Loyd, J. 2014. Transnational productions of remoteness: building onshore and offshore carceral regimes across borders. *Geographica Helvetica* **69**(5), pp. 389–98.

Nethery, A. and Silverman, S. 2015. *Immigration detention: the migration of a policy and its human impact*. Oxon: Routledge.

Pain, R. and Staeheli, L. 2014. Introduction: intimacy-geopolitics and violence. *Area* **46**(4), pp. 344–60.

Pratt, G. and Rosner, V. 2006. Introduction: the global and the intimate, *Women's Studies Quarterly* (special issue) **34**(1/2), pp. 13–24.

Salt, J. and Stein, J. 1997. Migration as business: the case of trafficking. *International Migration* **35**(4), pp. 467–94.

Spener, D. 2009. Some critical reflections on the migration industry concept. Self-published [Online]. Available from: www.trinity.edu/dspener/clandestinecrossings/indexa.htm [Accessed 20 May 2016].

Tyler, I., Gill, N., Conlon, D., Oeppen, C. 2014. The business of child detention: charitable co-option, migrant advocacy and activist outrage. *Race and Class* **56**(1), pp. 3–21.

UNHCR. 2015. *Asylum applications in industrialized world soar to almost 900,000 in 2014* [Online]. Available from: www.unhcr.org/5512c51e9.html [Accessed 13 February 2016].

Varsanyi, M. 2008. Rescaling the 'alien', rescaling personhood: neoliberalism, immigration and the state. *Annals of the Association of American Geographers* **98**(4), pp. 877–96.

Wilson, A. 2012. Intimacy: a useful category of transnational analysis. In Pratt, G. & Rosner, V. eds. *The global and the intimate: feminism in our time*. New York: Columbia University Press, pp. 31–56.

Part I
Engaging the intimate

2   Detained beyond the sovereign

Conceptualising non-state actor involvement in immigration detention

Michael Flynn

Introduction

Over the course of the last two decades, immigration detention has taken on increasing prominence across the globe. In the past detention appears to have been used largely as an *ad hoc* tool by wealthy countries, but practices have steadily matured, domestic laws refined to clarify when detention measures can be applied, new bureaucracies created to manage burgeoning detainee populations, and a growing number of countries – particularly in developing regions – cajoled into adopting this practice to help keep migrants and asylum seekers from reaching their intended destinations (Flynn, 2014).

As immigration detention has ripened and expanded, various socio-economic forces have impacted its evolution. For instance, human rights advocacy appears to have played a role in spurring states in some regions, particularly in Europe, to incorporate relevant norms regarding the treatment of detainees into their detention regimes (see Morris, this volume). One result of this has been that most countries in the region now use specialised facilities rather than prisons (Flynn, 2013). Rights advocacy has also led to a growing number of civil society groups and international organisations becoming involved in providing services and in some cases (like France) operating directly inside detention centres (Fischer, 2011).

Mounting political pressure to restrict migration and increasing adherence to neoliberal economic models have conspired to help spur additional innovations. For instance, the perceived need to quickly ramp up detention capacity was exploited by private prison entrepreneurs in the United States to pressure immigration authorities to allocate funds in the mid-1980s for establishing that country's first privately run immigration detention centre. Since then, other countries, particularly in the Anglophone world, have invited private prison companies to manage their immigration detention facilities, raising questions about legal accountability at detention centres and the social forces promoting growth in this practice (Flynn and Cannon, 2009).

As a result of these and other developments explored in this chapter, the phenomenon of migration detention, as with the larger issue of global migration management, today involves a large variety of non-state actors. As Betts (2013, p. 59) writes: 'While global migration governance is usually understood to be state-centric', it is in fact 'polycentric, involving a range of public and private actors' (see also Geiger and Pécoud, 2010; Martin, this volume).

Yet, the significance of the involvement of these actors in immigration control remains severely understudied. Most scholarship has focused on the increasing privatisation of detention operations and the impact this has on policy-making (for instance, Conlon and Hiemstra, 2014; Menz, 2013). While these are important subjects of study, they are part of a larger socio-political phenomenon. Who exactly is involved in the expansion of detention? To what extent is their involvement a result of the growing associations between official and private actors? And how does knowledge of these issues influence our understanding of immigration detention?

This chapter seeks to address these questions by developing concepts that can comprehensively account for the full range of non-state actors involved in immigration detention and help assess the consequences of their work in this area. By applying the concept of 'intimate economies' that undergirds this volume – that is, by scrutinising the complex nature of particular detention situations to reveal hidden or underappreciated processes that help sustain detention as a tool of immigration control – this analysis seeks to encourage a broader consideration of the role that private actors, including non-profits, play in shaping and nurturing this practice. Sharpening and clarifying our concepts can also improve empirical analyses of this issue and allow us to be systematic in our efforts to track detention trends. Finally, with improved clarity about the actors involved in depriving migrants and asylum seekers of their liberty, we can better assess who should be held to account when rights are disregarded and people abused.

The following section situates the subject of this chapter within the broader discussion of immigration detention, advancing an overall definition of immigration detention and demonstrating how standard notions of this practice can overlook the role of non-state actors. The chapter then introduces a set of limit cases that provide concrete examples of how various non-state actors have become entangled in detention operations, yet whose activities raise questions about the meaning of immigration detention. The ensuing section attempts to deepen our conceptual understanding of the relationship between non-state actors and immigration detention. The chapter then concludes with an assessment of the broader significance of non-state actor involvement in detention, in particular with respect to accountability.

Non-state immigration detention?

As a relatively recent phenomenon in much of the world, immigration detention is often not clearly understood, and the concept is widely contested as numerous scholars and human rights advocates have advanced differing definitions. These efforts have resulted in divergent ideas, leading to considerable confusion over what exactly amounts to immigration detention. Further complicating matters, states frequently seek to define certain detention activities in ways that obfuscate the real nature of their practices (Grange, 2013). A recent Oxford study of national detention regimes that was prepared for the UN Working Group on Arbitrary Detention found that many countries 'have no express legal threshold for determining whether a person has been "detained"', which means determinations for what amounts to immigration detention can be effectively arbitrary (Oxford Pro Bono Publico, 2014, p. 18). Thus it is critically important from the outset to establish some clarity on the overall meaning of immigration detention before considering how actors traditionally not associated with this practice can be brought into the frame.

The Global Detention Project[1] (GDP), an interdisciplinary research centre based in Geneva, Switzerland, employs a concise definition of immigration detention, which this chapter proposes applying (and testing) in its analysis of non-state-actor involvement in this practice: 'The deprivation of liberty of non-citizens for reasons related to their immigration status.' By assessing the strengths and weaknesses of this definition vis-à-vis the phenomenon of non-state actor involvement in detention, we can clarify how non-state actors upset conventional concepts of detention and obscure the consequences of the growing use of this practice.

Like most definitions of immigration detention that have been proposed by scholars, the GDP's suffers from an important weakness: it is entirely state-centric. The concepts of citizenship and status both imply the existence of a sovereign power that can either grant or retract such qualities. Yet, as this chapter explores, the deprivation of liberty of migrants and asylum seekers often takes place in venues that occupy a grey area of state authority. This fact complicates any effort to develop a fully comprehensive definition of immigration detention that encompasses the actions of actors who are not formally a part of the state.

On the other hand, as Phillip Alston has pointed out, 'negative, euphemistic terms' like non-state actor 'do not stem from language inadequacies but instead have been intentionally adopted in order to reinforce the assumption that the state is not only the central actor, but also the indispensable and pivotal one around which all other entities revolve' (Alston, 2005, p. 3). Following Alston, we could argue that immigration detention is only possible as a distinct form of deprivation of liberty because of the existence of the Westphalian state system. And while legal scholars have sought to apply international human rights law to non-state actors (for example, Clapham, 2013), the state should always be considered responsible if abuses of detainees occur on their territory or as a result of their command, regardless of the peculiarities of a detention situation or the fact that relevant law is still being developed (Gammeltoft-Hansen, 2013, p. 144).

Thus, any definition of immigration detention will by necessity be permeated by the notion of state power. This form of deprivation of liberty is girded by the existence of official actors who are empowered by the laws of a state to confine non-citizens on the basis of specific legal grounds. This sovereign power then engages in intimate associations with actors who are not formally a part of the state, contracting them to undertake specific detention-related activities. Who are these actors?

To answer this question, we need to identify the limits of the meaning of immigration detention. This will improve our ability to observe the variety of phenomena and actors that it encompasses as well as to understand the degree to which standard concepts of this activity fail to adequately capture all its complications, particularly in light of the increasing range of private and civil society actors who are implicated. We may not be able to find a single, unifying concept that accounts for all custodial arrangements involving migrants and asylum seekers, but by systematically interrogating our concepts we can see where our ideas fall short and also winnow out activities that arguably do not amount to immigration detention.

An important aspect of the GDP's definition is that it does not distinguish between asylum seekers, irregular migrants, stateless people or refugees. Instead, it intentionally fits all of these categories into a single cohort – 'non-citizen'. In many countries there is little effort to separate asylum seekers from irregular migrants within detention regimes. What is more, 'reception centres' and so-called shelters can sometimes resemble detention centres in all but name (Gallagher and Pearson, 2010). Thus, while there is a clear rationale for assessing differences in the legal frameworks that treat asylum seekers and undocumented migrants, when analysing migrant detention regimes it is preferable to view all non-citizens as a single group.

The definition is also meant to encompass both criminal incarceration and administrative detention. Discussions about immigration detention tend to focus on administrative detention (that is, detention to undertake legal procedures that are not part of the criminal process) because in most countries immigration violations are considered 'civil' rather than criminal matters, and thus detention for status-related reasons usually takes the form of an administrative process. A narrow focus on administrative detention, however, fails to capture a critical aspect of contemporary detention regimes: that many countries charge irregular migrants with criminal violations stemming from their status. Nevertheless, although it seems clear that any definition of migration-related detention should include both criminal and administrative forms of detention, this chapter focuses generally on administrative detention because the vast majority of people confined for status-related reasons are placed in civil detention.

This definition also implies a carefully circumscribed meaning of 'deprivation of liberty'. Some scholars have sought to define detention broadly to include 'restriction of movement or travel within a territory in which an alien finds him or herself' (Helton, 1989). On the other hand, in the landmark case *Amuur v. France* (1996), the European Court of Human Rights held that 'Holding aliens in the international zone does indeed involve a restriction upon liberty, but one which is not in every respect comparable to that which obtains in centres for the detention of aliens pending deportation'. More recently, the Optional Protocol to the UN Torture Convention (OPCAT), adopted in December 2002, provides a definition of deprivation of liberty that avoids some of the pitfalls in the formulations discussed above and – importantly for this volume – acknowledges the complex economies of immigration detention by including private actors in its conceptualisation. Article 4.2 of the Protocol states that 'deprivation of liberty means any form of detention or imprisonment or the placement of a person in a public or private custodial setting which that person is not permitted to leave at will by order of any judicial, administrative or other authority'.

What these competing definitions underscore is the confusion that often surrounds discourse on immigration detention. From both policy and scholarly perspectives, it is important to carve out the phenomenon from these divergent ideas to enable comparative assessment. This chapter thus proposes defining deprivation of liberty as 'forcibly imposed confinement within an enclosed space'. At the heart of this definition is the notion of coercion. As Guild (2006) writes: 'The common feature of places of detention … is their coercive nature.' Many scholars have underscored this aspect of immigration detention as an important corrective to more lax characterisations of detention centres as being 'open' or 'closed', which are commonly used terms (Flynn, 2012). Incorporating the concept of physical imposition or coercion into our definition of deprivation of liberty provides an important marker for identifying sites of detention. In other words, only facilities that physically prevent people from leaving ought to be considered detention centres; facilities that do not share this quality should not be considered detention sites.

A final important dimension of the GDP's definition of immigration-related detention is the concept of 'status'. Generally, unless they have committed unrelated breaches of the law, detained non-citizens have been taken into custody as a result of complications stemming from their residence status (see also Cornelisse, 2010, pp. 8–22). This is critically important to keep in mind when discussing non-state actors and the intimate economies of immigration detention. While there will be clear cut cases in which we see private-sector actors performing functions at the behest of the state, there are also cases where the particular roles of non-state or civil society actors undermine the underlying rationale of the detention itself, thus raising questions about whether such situations amount to immigration-related detention.

Non-state actors at the limits of immigration detention

This section presents four cases involving actors who are neither for-profit prison contractors nor official state agencies engaging in the deprivation of liberty of non-citizens. To what extent are these actors acting on behalf of or substituting for sovereign power? How do these cases challenge our notions of immigration detention? And which cases should be considered part of the intimate economy of immigration detention?

CASE I. In 2009, the International Centre for Migration Policy and Development (ICMPD), a Vienna-based international organisation comprised of 15 Member States from Europe that assists in the development of migration management programmes, launched a two-year project titled 'Strengthening

Reception and Detention Capacities in Lebanon' (STREDECA). The project aimed to develop 'Lebanon's capacities to manage its mixed migration flows post interception and/or apprehension' (ICMPD website). Partners on STREDECA – which was funded by France, Switzerland, Italy and the Netherlands – included Caritas Lebanon, the UN High Commissioner for Refugees (UNHCR), and Lebanon's General Security, the state security apparatus that oversees implementation of Lebanon's detention policies and operates the country's immigration detention centre (GDP, 2014).

According to the ICMPD, the project 'evaluated essential national infrastructure and enhanced national institutional capacities for the reception and detention of irregular migrants and asylum seekers in line with international human rights standards' (ICMPD website). However, several years after STREDECA was launched, there continued to be severe criticism of the conditions at its detention centre, which is located in a former parking garage under a highway in Beirut. The facility includes an office for Caritas, which is reminiscent of a practice in French detention centres (*centres de rétention*). Called the Caritas Lebanon Migrants Centre (CLMC), the office has received repeated criticism from other civil society groups, who accuse Caritas of abetting illegal detention. Caritas, however, claims that it is the sole NGO proving assistance to detainees (GDP, 2014).

The STREDECA project was part of a larger initiative called the 'Dialogue on Mediterranean Transit Migration' (MTM), which involves national governments from across the Mediterranean, Europol, the EU border control agency Frontex, UNHCR, the International Organisation for Migration (IOM) and the European Commission, among other supra-national entities. As one scholar writes, 'The MTM is a textbook example of migration management. The composition of participants brings together states, representatives of different state institutions, as well as intergovernmental organizations with diverging interests' (Kasparek, 2010, p. 134).

STREDECA is a striking example of how detention has become a key element of international migration management initiatives involving a range of state and non-state actors. These efforts have increasingly drawn international organisations (IOs) into the detention orbit, including those with rights-based mandates like UNHCR. However, IOs that have no treaty-based mandate – like the ICMPD and the IOM – have been the main actors in this regard. The IOM has helped manage offshore detention facilities for Australia, provided capacity-building initiatives for detention officials in numerous countries, and worked with the EU to fund detention operations in countries on the periphery of Europe (Georgi, 2010; Grange, 2013). Likewise, there are increasing numbers of civil society groups and non-profit charities operating in detention facilities or providing basic services to detainees. The Italian Red Cross has for many years helped operate that country's *centri di identificazione ed espulsione* (GDP, 2012a). As noted previously, France's *centres de rétention* include offices inside the facilities for NGOs who provide various forms of assistance to detainees (La Cimade website). And a host of non-profits in the United States have been contracted to provide services in detention centres and jails that house immigration detainees (GDP, 2012b).

CASE II. The Incheon International Airport in Seoul, South Korea, is equipped with a secure 'waiting room' that is reportedly operated by an 'Airlines Operators Committee' comprised of various airlines and staffed by private security guards hired by the airlines. Arriving passengers who are deemed inadmissible by Korean authorities are taken to this facility to await removal by one of the airlines.

According to an account of this facility provided by a South Korean lawyer to the Global Detention Project:

> When people are not admitted to entry at the airport, they are taken to the waiting room until they are deported. … The facility remains locked and secured by private security guards employed by the Airline Operators Committee, most of whom do not speak English and are known for their mistreatment to detainees. Detainees are fed chicken burgers three times a day for their meals and their requests for medical service are often neglected.
>
> (Kim, 2014)

Although the Korean attorney said that the waiting room appears to ultimately be under the 'control of the immigration office of Korean government', a US attorney representing a US client who had been detained at the facility claimed in an email to the GDP that a Korean airlines manager told her firm that the facility was wholly operated by Korean Airlines and Asiana Airlines. She added that people detained at the facility 'have a single shower, no soap, no towels and no laundry facilities and they are being kept locked up by airlines who have no legal authority to hold them' (Cornell, 2013).

The Incheon airport case is indicative of a much larger global phenomenon involving the privatisation of immigration controls resulting from the application of 'carrier sanctions', in which private transport companies are held accountable for people they transport who are refused admission at their destinations (Rodenhäuser, 2014). These sanctions can lead to the detention of passengers by these companies, which is explicitly foreseen in legal provisions contained in many national immigration laws. For example, Article 7 of Ireland's *Immigration Act 2004* provides:

> The master of any ship arriving at a port in the State may detain on board any non-national coming in the ship from a place outside the State until the non-national is examined or landed for examination under this section, and shall, on the request of an immigration officer, so detain any such non-national, whether seaman or passenger, whose application for a permission has been refused by an immigration officer, and any such non-national so detained shall be deemed to be in lawful custody.

Similarly, Article 5(3) of Malaysia's *Passports Act 1966* provides that any person who unlawfully attempts to enter Malaysia 'may be conducted across the frontier or placed on board a suitable vessel by an immigration officer, police officer or officer of customs, and may be lawfully detained on board the vessel during the period that the vessel is within Malaysia or the territorial waters thereof' (UNHCR, 2016).

CASE III. Following the 2011 uprising in Libya and the subsequent armed conflict there, numerous parts of the country were taken over by armed groups or militias, who assumed many of the functions of the previous local authorities. In some cases, immigration detention centres, which often hold asylum seekers from sub-Saharan countries who have been sent back to Libya after being inter-dicted at sea by the Italian Navy, fell under the control of these militias. To this day, militias continue to operate some of these facilities (GDP, 2015).

A 2014 briefing from Amnesty International (AI) reported on a visit to an immigration detention centre near Gharyan, some 80 kilometres south of Tripoli:

> The center is run by the 9th Brigade, a militia nominally under the control of the Ministry of Defense. The center has not yet been handed over to state authorities. Although outside of direct state control, Libyan security agencies cooperate with the 9th Brigade, meaning that refugees, asylum-seekers, and migrants continue to be brought to the facility on a regular basis.
>
> (AI, 2014)

During AI's visit there were approximately 1,250 migrants at the centre, includ-ing 20 unaccompanied children who were detained alongside adults. There were detainees from Chad, Egypt, Eritrea, Niger, Somalia and Sudan. The facility was comprised of metal hangars that were in 'freezing conditions' and provided no access to the outside. In addition, the centre did not have a functioning sewage system and lacked clean drinking water. Detainees claimed 'that their shoes had been confiscated to prevent escapes and many reported ill-treatment, including beatings with metal bars or plastic tubes, being forced to roll over in dirty water while being kicked by the guards with their boots, and being intimidated by guards shooting at the ceiling inside the hangars' (AI, 2014).

CASE IV. Gulf countries are notorious for their kafala sponsorship system for migrant labourers. Described by human rights advocates as a form of modern-day slavery, the kafala system gives employers almost complete control over all aspects of migrants' lives, including their freedom of movement. Once a migrant accepts a contract and receives a residency permit, he or she is contractually bound to the employer, who becomes responsible for this person for the duration of employment, which prompts many employers to confiscate workers' passports to prevent them from absconding or illegally switching jobs (HRW, 2014).

> The abuse of female domestic workers is often particularly egregious and can include rape and beatings at the hands of employers as well as forced confine-ment inside the home. In a 2014 report on domestic workers in the United Arab Emirates, Human Rights Watch collected testimony from dozens of workers that attested to these abuses. In one case, a 35-year-old Filipina worker named Mabel L. told HRW that her employer confiscated her passport, forced her to work 20-hour days, withheld her salary, physically and verbally abused her,

and kept her locked inside the house. 'He slapped me, beat me, and kicked me. I couldn't walk. He beat me on my left hip.'

(HRW 2014, p. 54)

Although domestic courts in UAE have ruled that passport confiscation is illegal and government ministries have said the practice is unlawful, according to HRW the practice 'persists largely because of the nature of the kafala (visa sponsorship) system. This holds sponsors liable for workers who "illegally" switch employers, thus incentivising them to control their workers' (HRW 2014, p. 39).

All four of these cases challenge our standard notions of the meaning of immigration detention, raising a number of related questions: To what extent are these actors acting on behalf of or substituting for sovereign power? Do these cases all amount to immigration detention? And which cases should be considered part of the intimate economy of immigration detention? The next section seeks to address these questions by questioning our notions of the meaning of non-state actors and their roles in the 'migration industry'.

Conceptualising the role of non-state actors

An important lacuna in the GDP definition of immigration detention, which is underscored in the cases discussed above, is that it implies – rather than specifies – detaining actors. By implication, it is the state that is supplying both the legal justification for detention decisions and the force necessary to carry out such decisions. Yet, as we have seen, a plethora of actors not directly associated with any state apparatus has become involved in the confinement of migrants and asylum seekers. To assess the role of non-state actors in immigration detention, several strands of academic literature can be referred to, including legal studies on non-state actors and the international human rights regime, the burgeoning scholarship in immigration studies on the 'migration industry', and post-structural discourse emerging from the work of Giorgio Agamben.

A good place to start is to define what we mean by non-state actor which, like the concept of immigration detention, has been hotly debated. Alston (2005, pp. 15–16) argues that the 'most comprehensive' definition is the one proposed by Josselin and Wallace (2001, p. 3), which provides that non-state actors include all organisations that are 'largely or entirely autonomous from central government funding: emanating from civil society, or from the market economy, or from political impulses beyond state control and direction'. This definition also holds that such actors be engaged in transnational activities and that they be at least partly devoted to influencing political outcomes.

At first blush, this definition would appear to be adequate for our purposes. Arguably, it encompasses private companies, NGOs, and international organisations. However, in light of the limit cases discussed above, we might argue that the requirement of being a transnational actor is overly restrictive. We would be hard pressed to characterise private individuals who are empowered by the state to confine migrant workers in their homes as international actors. Similarly, many of the service-providers in prisons and detention centres used to hold migrants and asylum seekers are local companies that do not operate internationally. Also, as Alston states (2005, p. 16), this definition is 'endlessly debatable, as the very first criterion illustrates: what level of governmental funding, support, or encouragement might disqualify a group as a non-state actor?' This question is also relevant with respect to GONGOs[2] as well as international organisations, which to a certain extent operate as surrogates of states, which make up these organisations' membership. (The IOM and ICMPD present particular dilemmas because they have no treaty mandate and thus arguably never operate 'beyond state control or direction'; it is just not the direction of a single state.)

Literature from immigration and refugee studies can provide additional clarity. For instance, scholars have conceptualised the various ways in which states – often motivated by the effort to evade normative restrictions like *non-refoulement* of refugees – have sought to share the burden of immigration control policies and to employ non-state actors to assist in the 'remote control' of migrants and asylum seekers (Zolberg, 1999). Examples include imposing sanctions on transport companies that carry aliens and establishing cooperative agreements with neighbouring states and sending countries, as well as the 'devolution' of certain roles to private entities.

According to Lahav and Guiraudon (2000, p. 58), these efforts can be arranged on a 'playing field' that runs along two intersecting axes: public-private and domestic-international. In the domestic sphere, we find some states delegating responsibility for apprehending migrants to local police forces (public) and increasingly using for-profit companies (private) to run detention centres. In the international sphere, states pressure airlines (private) to verify whether travellers have proper travel documentation and arrange with third countries (public) to manage migration movements (i.e. by establishing readmission agreements).

In this chapter, we are concerned with those actors whose activities fall within the private-domestic and private-international sections of this schematic. Even with this broad scheme in place, there are complications. For instance, is it accurate to describe the operations of international organisations as belonging to a 'private' sphere of activities? And how are we to treat detention activities that do not directly involve state authorities and thus fall outside this model?

Recent scholarship on the 'migration industry' contributes more useful concepts. Definitions of the migration industry tend to focus on for-profit actors who facilitate human mobility, particularly with respect to labour migration, in order to make a profit. Thus, for instance, Hernández-León (2008, p. 154) has characterised this industry as 'the ensemble of entrepreneurs who, motivated by the pursuit of financial gain, provide a variety of services facilitating human mobility across international borders'. Building on the work of Hernández-León, Nyberg Sørensen and Gammeltoft-Hansen (2013) have sought to expand the conceptual framework of the migration industry to comprise actors who restrict immigration (for instance, 'control providers' like private prison companies) as well as private actors who are not profit-motivated, like NGOs involved in the 'rescue industry' who assist migrants. This leads Nyberg Sørensen and Gammeltoft-Hansen to redefine the migration industry as 'the array of non-state actors who provide services that facilitate, constrain, or assist international migration' (2013, pp. 6–7).

This conceptualisation of the migration industry provides a promising framework for analysing the involvement of non-state actors in immigration detention regimes. It is not constrained by geographic scope (domestic or international); it does not focus narrowly on profit-driven enterprises; and it encompasses both the facilitation of migration as well as migration control, including interdiction, detention and deportation. Also, returning to the limit cases discussed above, it seems that all the actors identified in those cases arguably fit with this definition. Militias and rebel groups, private households, international organisations and even private companies acting as custodial agents all fit within the scope of this formulation. This begs the question, however: should the detention of immigrants and asylum seekers by each of these actors be considered 'immigration detention'?

To answer this question, we must return to the GDP's definition of immigration detention: 'The deprivation of liberty of non-citizens for reasons related to their immigration status.' As discussed previously, immigration detention is by its very nature a matter of the state. Remove the state from the equation, and we have some other form of deprivation of liberty (i.e. kidnapping, ransom, illegal incarceration, trafficking). Can a private individual hold an asylum seeker in immigration detention? What about an armed group operating outside any legal mandate? Or a private company that uses its airplanes or ships to lock up passengers denied entry in the state? All of these actors can of course be involved in 'facilitating, constraining, or assisting international migration', but if they are not operating on behalf of the state when they confine someone, then we should probably not consider its activities as amounting to immigration detention.

In other words, immigration detention requires an element of lawfulness. It must be provided for in domestic law. And yet, if this is the case, then some scholars would apparently contend that immigration detention does not exist at all – in fact, that it cannot exist because it represents an inherent absence of rights.

A predominant contemporary scholarly discourse on immigration detention revolves around the paradigm of the 'camp'. This discourse is largely informed by the work of the Italian philosopher Giorgio Agamben (1998) and his concepts *homo sacer* – which denotes depoliticised life as opposed to the political life of the citizen – and *zones of exception*, which are typified in his discourse using the term 'camp'. Agamben argues that politics is constructed around notions of those who belong within the rights-conferring institutional arena of the state and those who do not. The latter become the object of state power through the absence of rights in *zones of exception*. Through this dichotomy, sovereignty is exercised by inclusive exclusion (Flynn, 2015).

Numerous scholars have sought to employ Agamben's concepts in their characterisations of immigration detention regimes. For instance, one scholar writes that Agamben's paradigm of the camp is 'materialised' in the Nazi extermination camps as well as contemporary airport transit zones and the more notorious detention centres in Australia and the United Kingdom (Walters, 2010). These efforts have elicited sharp criticism. Levy writes that 'Agamben and his enthusiastic followers lack any proportionality when they distastefully lump together varieties of refugee camps, Auschwitz, and even gated communities' (Levy, 2010, pp. 100–101).

More importantly for the purposes of our current study, Agamben-inspired post-structuralist arguments can fail to specify actors who are involved in the creation of detention centres and who operate within this field, which leads them to posit a functionalist argument susceptible to teleological thinking. Outcomes thus become social causes. Detention centres play a central logic in the underlying dialectic of the state – its power to extend freedoms and rights, and ultimately to define human life is premised by denying the same to others. This circular thinking is evident when post-structuralists like Rajaram and Grundy-Warr (2004, p. 26) argue that 'the enclosure of certain human beings [is] not an anomaly of the logic of contemporary sovereignty, but a normal outcome of this logic'. A key problem with this type of analysis is that 'disembodied notions of the state and sovereign power substitute the role and intentions of actors for changing laws used to classify sets of people as illegal, to construct systems of control, and to operate detention centers' (Flynn, 2015).

Thus, if we accept these critiques and regard immigration detention, properly understood, as a function of the state that exists because a set of actors adopt and/or implement established rules – and not as a result of a state of exception or absence of rights purportedly inherent in the logic of sovereignty – then it follows that our conceptualisation must have at least two key facets: actors and state authority. Thus, adapting Nyberg Sørensen and Gammeltoft-Hansen's definition of the migration industry, we could argue that *non-state actors involved in immigration detention include the array of actors not formally part of any official state apparatus who in agreement with the state provide services that facilitate the state's objective of depriving non-citizens of their liberty for reasons related to their immigration status.*

With this conceptualisation in mind we can return to our limit cases to determine which may be considered a part of the intimate economies of immigration detention. Case I clearly fits the profile as the STREDECA project in Lebanon, which involves an amalgam of entities – including local NGOs, international organisations and national authorities – engaged in a detention-related project funded by foreign governments who want to restrict migrants and asylum seekers. This type of externalisation activity has been widely noted in academic works assessing the policies of recipient countries like Australia and the United States. In the process these countries have enlisted a range of actors – not all of whom necessarily aim to make a profit – thereby broadening the intimate economy of global immigration detention efforts.

Case II on the airline companies at Seoul's Incheon Airport also appears to meet the necessary criteria. It has some similarities to the STREDECA case insofar as it represents a form of detention that seems aimed in part at preventing people from officially reaching or remaining inside the border. These detention activities have emerged as a result of a country's laws and occur at the behest of state authorities, even if the custodial relationship between the detainees and the state appears to be tenuous, thereby calling into question whether this particular instance of deprivation of liberty is within the framework of our formal definition of immigration detention. Nevertheless, this particular manifestation of 'carrier sanctions' calls to mind the work of political geographers like Mountz (2004, p. 341) who have demonstrated how states create 'detached geographies of detention' inside their borders and beyond that limit asylum seekers ability to access relevant legal processes.

Case III involving militias in Libya is markedly different from the previous two but nevertheless seems to fit our criteria. The militias have stepped into the vacuum of authority created by internal armed conflict, acting as a de facto sovereign power. While they are not technically a state, they act as surrogates because they carry out a function that had been mandated by the presumably temporarily absent official state authority. Arguably this is a case of immigration detention, though one which represents a rather peculiar variation of the intimate economies of detention.

Case IV on the kafala system appears to be the sole outlier. It is clear that people in this system face a form of confinement to which they are susceptible because they are foreigners whose treatment is provided for in law. However, although there is often collusion between authorities and private individuals in the abuses suffered by these workers and the law puts the workers under the responsibility of private individuals (thereby making them de facto custodial authorities), it is difficult to argue that this detention occurs at the behest of the state or for immigration reasons. Nevertheless, the kafala system serves as a useful limit case for trying to conceptualise where the intimate economy of immigration detention begins and ends.

Conclusion

This chapter contends that any study of the intimate economies of immigration detention requires expanding our understanding of the range of actors involved in this practice. To date, the major focus of studies on the outsourcing of detention regimes has been private for-profit prison companies. However, as this chapter has endeavoured to demonstrate, a host of other actors has been pulled into the orbit of immigration detention, ranging from international organisations and local NGOs to airline companies and militias.

This chapter has interrogated our understanding of immigration detention and non-state actors to encourage a more comprehensive consideration of the role that private actors, including nonprofits, play in shaping and in some cases nurturing national immigration detention regimes. This in turn can improve our analyses of the political economy of immigration policymaking and implementation. Additionally, sharpening and clarifying our concepts can improve empirical analyses and allow us to be systematic in our efforts to track trends in the global detention phenomenon.

Underlying all these issues is the fundamental question of who is accountable when rights are violated in detention. As Gammeltoft-Hansen (2013, p 144) writes, 'By its very design the migration control industry brings about certain responsibility and accountability gaps, which risks further undermining human rights of migrants and refugees.' Countries cannot be left off the hook simply because they shift certain responsibilities to private companies or other non-state actors. At the same time, new actors involved in immigration control efforts must not be allowed to argue that they are merely acting on the orders of a country and thus not liable for abuses occurring under their watch. The multifaceted nature of these situations can lead to confusing attributions of responsibility.

A case in point is the impact of 'carrier sanctions', which were briefly discussed in the case of the detention room operated by privates airlines at the airport in Seoul and which have been the subject of considerable academic attention (Rodenhäuser, 2014; UK Refugee Council, 2008). The effort to block asylum seekers from boarding planes or entering national territory has resulted in private companies serving as de facto arbiters of asylum as airlines are pressured to deny passage to certain people, which can lead to violations of *non-refoulement*. On the one hand, as scholars have noted, state responsibility in such cases can be interpreted narrowly so that the state is not held accountable for the rejection of asylum seekers on another state's territory; however, it may be impossible to hold the airline accountable for a violation, particularly in extraterritorial cases (Rodenhäuser, 2014; Reinisch, 2005).

Many of the cases discussed here – in particular those that can be categorised as immigration-related detention – arguably merit pursuing 'shared accountability', a legal concept that 'recognises that more than one entity may be responsible for the same wrongful act' (Majcher, 2015, p. 54). Numerous scholars have sought to apply this concept to human right violations that involve a range of actors working alongside or at the behest of state authorities, including international organisations and private companies, as well as cases involving public-private partnerships (Clarke, 2014).

Nevertheless, significant legal hurdles remain and states continue to try to insulate themselves by 'creating the appearance that migration control is ... private and thus external to the state itself' (Gammeltoft-Hansen, 2013, p. 145). To break through this conundrum, it is important to insist on the ties between the actions of non-state actors and the state, and to carefully circumscribe those activities that can be termed immigration-related detention. Critically assessing the multifarious aspects of the 'intimate economies' of immigration detention is one modest step in that direction.

Acknowledgements

The author would like to thank Deirdre Conlon, Matthew Flynn, Mariette Grange, Nancy Hiemstra and Izabella Majcher for their helpful comments and suggestions.

Notes

1 About the Global Detention Project: www.globaldetentionproject.org/about/about-the-project.html
2 Government-Organised Non-Governmental Organisations

References

Amuur v. France. 1996. European Court of Human Rights. Judgment of 25 June 1996.

Alston, P. ed. 2005. *Non-state actors and human rights*. Oxford: Oxford University Press.

Agamben, G. 1998. *Homo sacer: sovereign power and bare life*. Stanford: Stanford University Press.

Amnesty International (AI). 2014. Amnesty International's submission to the Council of Europe Committee of Ministers: *Hirsi Jamaa and Others v. Italy* (Application No. 27765/09). Amnesty International. Ref: B1525. 11 February 2014.

Betts, A. 2013. The migration industry in global migration governance. In: Gammeltoft-Hansen, T. and Nyberg Sørensen, N. eds. *The migration industry and the commercialization of international migration*. New York: Routledge, pp. 45–63.

Clarke, L. 2014. *Public-private partnerships and responsibility under international law*. New York: Routledge.

Clapham, A. 2013. *Human rights and non-state actors*. Cheltenham: Edward Elgar Publishing.

Conlon, D. and Hiemstra, N. 2014. Examining the everyday micro-economies of migrant detention in the United States. *Geographica Helvetica* **69**(5), pp. 335–44.

Cornelisse, G. 2010. *Immigration detention and human rights: rethinking territorial sovereignty*. Leiden: Martinus Nijhoff Publishers.

Cornell, L. 2013. Email message to the Global Detention Project. 9 December 2013.

Fischer, N. 2011. Monitoring detention: the control of immigration detention in France and the role of human rights organizations. Paper prepared for the Workshop 'Europeanization of Exclusion Policies and Practices', University of Neuchâtel, 16–17 June 2011.

Flynn, Matthew. 2015. Bureaucratic capitalism and the immigration detention complex. Unpublished paper. Delivered at the 14th Annual Conference of the International Social Theory Consortium. Cambridge University. 18–19 June 2015.

Flynn, Michael. 2014. There and back again: on the diffusion of immigration detention. *Journal on Migration and Human Security* **2**(3), pp. 165–97.

Flynn, Michael. 2013. Be careful what you wish for. *Forced Migration Review* **44**, pp. 22–3.

Flynn, Michael. 2012. Who must be detained? Proportionality as a tool for critiquing immigration detention policy. *Refugee Studies Quarterly* **31**(3), pp. 40–68.

Flynn, M. and Cannon, C. 2009. *The privatization of immigration detention – Towards a global view: Global Detention Project Working Paper No. 1*. Geneva: GDP [Online]. Available from: www.globaldetentionproject.org/fileadmin/docs/GDP_PrivatizationPaper_Final5.pdf [Accessed 11 February 2016].

Gallagher, A. and Pearson, E. 2010. The high cost of freedom: a legal and policy analysis of shelter detention for victims of trafficking. *Human Rights Quarterly* **32**, pp. 73–114.

Gammeltoft-Hansen, T. 2013. The rise of the private border guard. In: Gammeltoft-Hansen, T. and Nyberg Sørensen, N. eds. *The migration industry and the commercialization of international migration*. New York: Routledge, pp. 128–51.

Geiger, M. and Pécoud, A. 2010. *The politics of international migration management*. New York: Palgrave.

Georgi, F. 2010. For the benefit of some: the International Organization for Migration and its global migration management. In: Geiger, M. and Pécoud, A. eds. *The politics of international migration management*. Basingstoke: Palgrave, pp. 45–72.

Global Detention Project (GDP). 2015. *Libya immigration detention profile* [Online]. Available from: www.globaldetentionproject.org/countries/africa/libya [Accessed 28 January 2016].

Global Detention Project (GDP). 2014. *Lebanon immigration detention profile* [Online]. Available from: www.globaldetentionproject.org/countries/middle-east/lebanon [Accessed 28 January 2016].

Global Detention Project (GDP). 2012a. *Italy immigration detention profile* [Online]. Available from: www.globaldetentionproject.org/countries/europe/italy [Accessed 28 January 2016].

Global Detention Project (GDP). 2012b. *A survey of private contractor involvement in U.S. facilities used to confine people for immigration-related reasons* [Online]. Available from: www.globaldetentionproject.org/publications/survey-private-contractor-involvement-us-facilities-used-confine-people-immigration [Accessed 28 January 2016].

Grange, M. 2013. *Smoke screens: is there a correlation between migration euphemisms and the language of detention? Global Detention Project Working Paper No. 5.* Geneva: Global Detention Project [Online]. Available from: www.globaldetentionproject .org/sites/default/files/fileadmin/publications/Smoke_Screens_-_the_language_of_ immigration_detention_v10.pdf [Accessed 11 February 2016].

Guild, E. 2006. *Report for the European Parliament: Directorate General internal policies of the Union: a typology of different types of centres in Europe.* Brussels: Centre for European Policy Studies.

Hernández-León, R. 2008. *Metropolitan migrants: the migration of urban Mexicans to the United States.* Berkeley: The University of California Press.

Helton, A. 1989. The detention of refugees and asylum seekers: a misguided threat to refugee protection. In: Loescher, G. ed. *Refugees and international relations.* Oxford: Oxford University Press.

Human Rights Watch. 2014. *'I already bought you': abuse and exploitation of female migrant domestic workers in the United Arab Emirates* [Online]. Available from: www .hrw.org/sites/default/files/reports/uae1014_forUpload.pdf [Accessed 28 January 2016].

International Centre for Migration Policy and Development (ICMPD). MTM: Completed Projects [Online]. Available from: www.icmpd.org/Completed-Projects.1624.0.html [Accessed 28 January 2016].

Josselin, D. and Wallace, W. eds. 2001. *Non-state actors in world politics.* New York: Palgrave.

Kasparek, B. 2010. Borders and populations in flux: Frontex's place in the European Union's migration management. In: Geiger, M. and Pécoud, A. eds. *The politics of international migration management.* London: Palgrave Macmillan, pp. 119–140.

Kim, J. 2014. Email correspondence with Michael Flynn (Global Detention Project). 4 February 2014.

La Cimade. 2016. *Histoire* [Online]. Available from: www.lacimade.org/nous-connaitre/ histoire/ [Accessed 28 January 2016].

Lahav, G. and Guiraudon, V. 2000. Comparative perspectives on border control. In: Andreas, P. and Snyder, T. eds. *The wall around the West.* Lanham: Rowman & Littlefield, pp. 55–80.

Levy. C. 2010. Refugees, Europe, camps/state of exception: 'into the zone', the European Union and extraterritorial processing of migrants, refugees, and asylum-seekers (theories and practice). *Refugee Survey Quarterly* **29**(1), pp. 92–119.

Majcher, I. 2015. Human rights violations during EU border surveillance and return operations: Frontex's shared responsibility or complicity? *Silesian Journal of Legal Studies* **7**, pp. 45–78.

Menz, G. 2013. The neoliberalized state and the growth of the migration industry. In: Gammeltoft-Hansen, T. and Nyberg Sørensen, N. eds. *The migration industry and the commercialization of international migration.* New York: Routledge, pp. 108–27.

Mountz, A. 2004. Embodying the nation-state: Canada's response to human smuggling. *Political Geography* **23**, pp. 323–45

Nyberg Sørensen, N. and Gammeltoft-Hansen, T. 2013. Introduction. In: Gammeltoft-Hansen, T. and Nyberg Sørensen, N. eds. *The migration industry and the commercialization of international migration*. New York: Routledge, pp. 1–23.

Oxford Pro Bono Publico. 2014. *Remedies and procedures on the right of anyone deprived of his or her liberty by arrest or detention to bring proceedings before a court: a comparative and analytical review of state practice*. University of Oxford Faculty of Law [Online]. Available from: http://ohrh.law.ox.ac.uk/wordpress/wp-content/uploads/2014/05/2014.6-Arbitrary-Detention-Project.pdf [Accessed 11 February 2016].

Rajaram, P. and Grundy-Warr, C. 2004. The irregular migrant as homo sacer: migration and detention in Australia, Malaysia, and Thailand. *International Migration* **42**(1), pp. 33–64.

Reinisch, A. 2005. The changing international legal framework for dealing with non-state actors. In: Alston, P. ed. *Non-state actors and human rights*. Oxford: Oxford University Press, pp. 37–92.

Republic of Ireland. *Immigration Act 2004* [Online]. Available from: www.inis.gov.ie/en/INIS/Immigration_Act_2004.pdf/Files/Immigration_Act_2004.pdf [Accessed 28 January 2016].

Rodenhäuser, T. 2014. Another brick in the wall: carrier sanctions and the privatization of immigration control. *International Journal of Refugee Law* **26**(2), pp. 223–47.

UK Refugee Council. 2008. *Remote controls: how UK border controls are endangering the lives of refugees*. London: UK Refugee Council.

UNHCR. 2016. *Malaysia: Act No.150 of 1966, Passports Act* [Online]. Available from: http://www.refworld.org/docid/3ae6b5204.html [Accessed 28 January 2016].

Walters, W. 2010. Deportation, expulsion, and the international police of aliens. In: De Genova, N. and Peutz, N. eds. *The deportation regime: sovereignty, space, and the freedom of movement*. Durham: Duke University Press, pp. 69–100.

Zolberg, A. 1999. Matters of state: theorizing immigration policy. In: Hirschman, C., Kasinitz, P. and DeWind, J. eds. *The handbook of international migration: the American experience*. New York: Russell Sage Foundation, pp. 71–93.

3 Discretion, contracting and commodification

Privatisation of US immigration detention as a technology of government

Lauren Martin

Introduction

Until 2014, US immigration officials did not detain families indefinitely as a rule. The Immigration and Naturalization Service (INS) first contracted with Berks County in March 2001, to hold up to 84 parents and children traveling with insufficient documentation while their asylum claims were processed, but the vast majority of arriving noncitizen families were released on their own recognizance or with bond. Policy changes in 2004 and 2005 created new categories of detainable people, and the new Bureau of Immigration and Customs Enforcement (ICE) opened the T. Don Hutto Family Residential Facility in 2006 to hold families subject to mandatory detention under the new rules (see Martin, 2012). The Obama Administration released all families from Hutto in 2009 as part of a broader detention system reform, but was careful to retain its *discretion* to detain families. In the summer of 2014, ICE encountered an unprecedented rise in undocumented children and families: 49,959 unaccompanied children and 52,326 family units were apprehended that year, mostly in the Rio Grande Valley of Texas (US Immigration and Customs Enforcement, 2014, 2). In response to what became known as the 'child migrant crisis', ICE opened a 532-bed facility for families in Artesia, New Mexico.

The Artesia family detention centre was built at a border patrol training facility, 200 miles from the nearest city with immigration legal services. ICE implemented a no-release policy and an expedited immigration court procedure, with the goal of quickly deporting detained families. A volunteer lawyer network quickly formed to represent families (Manning, n.d.), and multiple lawsuits followed, charging the immigration agency with violating the right to claim asylum, children's access to residential facilities, intimidation, lack of access to legal services, blanket detain-and-deport decisions regardless of individual circumstances, and refusal to release documents about detained families (*M.S.P.C v. Johnson*, 2014; *American Immigration Council et al. v. DHS*, 2014). With legal pressure mounting against detention procedures at Artesia, ICE closed the facility in the fall of 2014 and transferred families to facilities in Karnes County and Dilley County, Texas. These two facilities are owned by the two largest private corrections firms in the US, GEO Group and the Corrections Corporation of America, respectively. While GEO's facility was built as a 'civil detention centre' for low-risk detainees in 2012, the South Texas Family Detention Center has been constructed specifically for families. At 2,400 beds, the South Texas facility is the largest detention centre in the United States. All three of the family detention centres opened in 2014 were contracted quickly and without competitive bidding, a process that ICE defends as necessary to respond to large influxes. The role of ICE's authority to contract with private sector partners relied upon, in this case, the expediency of crisis to justify a drastic expansion of detention as a spatial practice of immigration control (Mountz and Hiemstra, 2014).

Because of family detention's fast expansion, and growing evidence of private corrections corporations' large lobbying expenditures, much of the popular and academic analysis has focused on collusion between private firms and migration policy-makers. While much blame is laid at private corporations' feet, family detention's story shows how nominally distinct economic logics of financial gain and political logics of deterrence and enforcement are entangled. This chapter argues that the private-public boundary itself is a *technology of government*, a distinction that enables certain practices, material arrangements and logics. I focus on three processes through which 'state' and 'private' actors codify formal relationships with each other: discretion, contracting and commodification. Through the example of family detention, however, I show how messy and *ad hoc* these relationships can be and that processes of discretion, contracting and commodification challenge the divisions between market and state, private and public, and political and economic actors. To better account for this messiness, I approach the boundary between public and private as a technology of government that enables immigration officials to control migrant life in particular ways. By emphasising the practices that make detention privatisation possible, this conceptual approach is at once flexible enough to account for the messiness of migration control on the ground and precise enough to critique exclusionary arrangements of power.

The following analysis is based on interviews with advocates and attorneys; visits to T. Don Hutto and Karnes City detention centres in 2010, 2011 and 2015; participant observation of the campaign to close Hutto from 2008 to 2010; and analysis of detainee testimonies and media, journalism, non-governmental reports, legal cases and government documents pertaining to family detention between 2009 and 2015. The chapter will first review contemporary approaches to the privatisation of immigration enforcement, then explain how understanding private-public boundaries as a technology of government opens up wider frames for these relationships. The third section works through some examples of discretion, contracting and commodification to show how the public-private boundary is put to work to allow the expansion of family detention. The concluding discussion draws further inspiration from anthropological and sociological studies of the economy to elaborate a nuanced approach to political economies of enforcement.

Unpacking privatisation

Studies of immigration enforcement have focused a great deal on political rationalities, legal frameworks, and discursive productions of 'illegal immigrant', 'alien', 'migrant' and 'refugee'. Recently, research has drilled down into banal and embodied practices of policing, detention and deportation, which has revealed highly variable detention conditions, ad hoc policing and transfer practices, and lasting physical and emotional effects of deportation (Conlon and Gill, 2013; Hiemstra, 2013; Mountz et al., 2013; Williams and Boyce, 2013; Coleman and Kocher, 2011; Conlon, 2011; Mountz, 2010; Coutin, 2010; Gill, 2009). Scholars have problematised policy discourses and elite framings of immigration through ethnographic approaches that emphasise the interconnectedness of human living and the intimacies of everyday life. While much of this work notes the prevalence of private prison and security companies in policing, processing, detention and deportation practices, less work has problematised the process of marketisation of immigration enforcement at the same level of detail (a gap that this volume goes far to address). There are, however, some important efforts to provide an analytic frame for these political economic relationships across sociology, anthropology, geography, political science and international relations. Two key terms, 'industry' and 'assemblage', have dominated this emerging literature, deployed in distinct, but sympathetic, ways to conceptualise the complicated relationship between immigration control and non-state actors. Here I review this work, focusing on the implications industrial and assemblage conceptualisations have for analysing privatisation as a political process.

Migration, enforcement and illegality as industry

Analyses of the political economy of immigration enforcement, especially the privatisation of detention in the United States, have revolved around various formulations of 'the immigration industrial complex' (Doty and Wheatley, 2013; Golash-Boza, 2009a, b; Fernandes, 2007; Welch, 2002). These studies have tracked campaign donations from the private corrections sector to politicians (Saldivar and Price, 2015); the 'revolving door' between immigration and corrections agencies and private prison companies (Golash-Boza, 2009a, b; Welch, 2002); media pundits' exaggerated claims about immigration rates and terrorist threats (Golash-Boza, 2009a); the merging of counter-terrorism and immigration enforcement (Saldivar and Price, 2015); and the role of private corrections representatives in drafting immigration legislation (Doty and Wheatley, 2013). The broad claim behind arguments for an 'immigration industrial complex' is that private sector, media and immigration agencies emphasise enforcement, albeit to different ends, and this produces a 'convergence of interests' that supports the continued expansion of immigration detention in privatised facilities.

Focusing on immigration detention, Doty and Wheatley (2013) elaborate four specific components of the immigration industrial complex: (1) the immigration law apparatus in the US; (2) prison corporations; (3) ideas and worldviews of neoliberal commercialisation, deterrence and criminalisation; and (4) lobbying, donation, and policy-making networks. This four-part complex forms a 'massive, multifaceted, and intricate economy of power, which is composed of a wide-spread, diverse, self-perpetuating collection of organisations, laws, ideas, and actors' (Doty and Wheatley, 2013, p. 438). This economy of power is nei-ther purely economic nor purely political. It includes profit-oriented manage-ment knowledge, but also lobbying and campaign donations that seek to build the kind of personal connections that lead to contracts (Fernandes, 2007). The immigration industrial complex is not, then, a closed entity, but a compilation of networks sustained by multiple discourses, embodied practices, material infra-structures and legal regimes.

Corporations are not, however, the only actors seeking to profit from the migration process, which has provoked some migration scholars to situate immi-gration control within a larger set of migration-related economic networks. Hernandez-Leon (2013) argues that migration studies has largely neglected the role of profit-seeking in migration's facilitation, regulation, control and insti-tutionalisation, and proposes the concept of 'the migration industry' to capture the entrepreneurial motivations of many actors across migration trajectories. He is most concerned with how 'financial gain' motivates migrants, facilitators and a range of service providers alongside mutual aid and familial obligation. For Hernandez-Leon, profit-seeking and mutual aid are not mutually exclusive; rather, we should recognise that not only do migrants move in and out of dif-ferent roles in the migration process, but that they have overlapping economic desires. This approach displaces profit-seeking from enterprises like corporations or smuggling networks, showing that profit-seeking is one of many economic rationalities and can be performed by anyone.

Gammeltoft-Hansen and Sørensen (2013) expand Hernandez-Leon's defini-tion of the migration industry to include 'control providers' and non-profit 'rescue industry' organisations. For them, facilitation, control and rescue form three (often overlapping) prongs of the migration industry with varying degrees of 'horizon-tal' and 'vertical' market integration. Their primary concern is to begin to tease out how economic rationalities are imbricated with migration decisions at every part of the facilitation and management process. In particular, they argue that state migration policies form an important part of the background context in which facilitators, rescuers and migrants themselves operate. As states gather informa-tion about migration pathways and people smuggling networks, facilitators influ-ence migration management policies carried out by states, and private operators profit from the performance of state migration control procedures. Migration bro-kers, both licit and illicit, make a premium from increased enforcement, and states respond to creative migration strategies with ever-more technological fixes.

For Andersson (2014) it is precisely this migration-enforcement feedback loop that is productive and that makes 'the illegality industry' a useful frame. Through his multi-sited study of migration in Africa and the Mediterranean, Andersson argues that the illegality industry works not just through economic relationships between agencies, contractors, facilitators and travelers, but through discursively producing 'the migrant' as a category and 'illegality' as a condition, and threat as a quality of both. The term refers to economic, geographical and symbolic elements of migration management in order to allow analytical flexibility: 'it foregrounds interactions among humans, technology, and the environment; it highlights how illegality is both fought and forged in material encounters; and it allows for the consideration of a dispersed "value chain," or the distinct domains in which migrant illegality is processed, "packaged," presented, and ultimately rendered profitable' (Andersson, 2014, p. 15). Like Gammeltoft-Hansen and Sørenson's 'migration industry', Andersson's 'illegality industry' emphasises the interrelatedness of actors across apparent boundaries of public, private, legal, illegal, state and non-state. Like US scholars studying the immigration industrial complex, Andersson seeks to show how discursive categories produce migration as a particular kind of problem and the large amounts of money circulating between actors seeking to manage migration in various ways. All of these conceptualisations of industry seek to show that economic, social and symbolic relationships are bound up with each other.

Across this work, there remains ambiguity about what, precisely, economic or profit-seeking practices are, where they begin and end, and to what extent profit-seeking behaviour or private firms' motivations explain migration policy-making. Spener (2009) argues that most social scientists use the term 'industry' figuratively rather than analytically; it operates more as a metaphorical comparison than a full-fledged theoretical category. When, for example, are migrants treated *like* commodities and when are migrants actually priced, exchanged and circulated? In many of the analyses cited above, framing human mobility as an industry has also implied a corporate structure of integration, valuing real estate, and creating markets that can narrow analysis of heterogeneous governmental practices to a single economic logic, namely a profit-oriented capitalist one. Spener argues that industrial figures of speech are, in fact, useful if we acknowledge them as such, and then turn our analysis to the specific types of activities, relationships and circulations that produce human mobility. For studies of the intimate economies of detention, it is important to analyse not only the material processes of commoditisation, marketisation, embodied labour and legal practices, but also to problematise the work that these terms do, as metaphors or as efforts to frame political relationships in new terms. Here I turn to another approach to the same problematic: the assemblage.

Migration governance as assemblages

Research in security studies and international relations has traced the imbrication of finance and security, but has conceptualised these new governmental arrangements not as an industrial complex but as an assemblage. The empirical content of this research is similar to the research reviewed above, in that it traces former officials' private sector enterprises and major governmental contracts with multinational data management and security analysis firms. Coming from international relations and political science, much of this work has focused on state security agencies and contractors, however. Analyses of security-economy assemblages have emphasised shared ways of knowing space and time over sectoral interests, preferring to focus on the proliferation of certain knowledge practices instead of personal relationships between public and private sector actors.

For critical security studies and international relations scholars, the blurring of boundaries between state and economy has produced new legal and spatial formations of sovereignty. In her analysis of anti-terrorist financing policies, de Goede (2012) shows that speculative risk analysis practices from the financial sector were picked up by security professionals seeking to *preempt* the next terrorist attack. Preemptive security practices and financial speculation both require a particular disposition towards the future and its unpredictability, a conception of uncertainty, possibility and emergence that allows for multiple forms of intervention with little evidence (Amoore, 2013). And because governments awarded counter-terrorism risk analysis contracts to some of the world's largest financial and accounting firms, the connection is material and monetary. Moreover, security professionals in North America and Europe use banal monetary transactions in the banking sector to track everyday mobilities and associations, so that economic activity itself becomes a medium of security knowledge (Amoore and de Goede, 2008).

In addition, US dominance in the private security sector has become an *economic development* concern for EU policy-makers, so much so that some EU-level agencies seek to establish a 'European civil security market' (Hoijtink, 2014). This market is supposed to bridge defense and individual security sectors and has focused on hard- and software interoperability, or making data shareable across platforms. The European civil security market came to be through a series of EU-level research funding schemes, which recruited expertise from private sector security firms for recommendations on how to build a civil security market (Bigo and Jeandesboz, 2010) These examples do not fit neatly into narratives of public sector privatisation because state, supra-national, non-governmental and corporate organisations worked together in a wide variety of capacities, with different contractual obligations. In addition, shared understandings of uncertainty and emergence are harder to capture by focusing on the public or private ownership of security activities.

For many of these scholars, European security governance is best conceptualised as an *assemblage* to grapple with the contingent agreements between different actors. Focused on the growing role of private security companies throughout the world, Abrahamsen and Williams argue for a 'global security assemblage', 'a complex and multilayered arrangement in which global capital, transnational private security, state authorities, local police, and international police advisers are integrated in the planning and provision of security' (2009, p. 8). This distribution of tasks traditionally left to sovereign state governments changes the substance and composition of sovereign power. De Goede argues for a 'finance-security assemblage', 'not so much a tightly drawn sovereign power but an apparatus in which diverse and sometimes contradictory elements come together to ʒic of governing that works through an appeal to uncertain futures'

(2012, p. xxii). Also concerned with both public-private cross-pollination and the shared spatiotemporal calculations of possible futures, Amoore (2013) argues that contemporary security practices indicate an 'alliance' between economy and sovereignty, a sharing of knowledge practices, measurement techniques and authority. In this 'moving complex', economy and sovereignty 'resonate' and 'infiltrate' each other, rather than sorting neatly into separate spheres.

There are two important points to draw from this work. The first point is that private sector participation in public service provision is rather unexceptional in the context of neoliberal state restructuring. Non-governmental organisations operate youth detention facilities, hospitals, charter schools, public school testing and audits, infrastructure construction, security in public buildings, and a host of food, physical plant and personnel services. Abrahamsen and Williams (2009) argue that the privatisation of security needs to be located in relation to broader transformations of governance that have reworked spatialities of public and private, global and local, state and non-state power. For example, Doty and Wheatley (2013) understand the United States' growing reliance on private prison firms as part of a broader trend towards the 'privatisation of sovereignty functions', such as surveillance, immigration responsibilities, risk analysis and policing. As Lahav has argued, enrolling third-party actors like airlines and freight companies has allowed state agencies to extend control without expanding bureaucracy, producing 'reinvented forms of state sovereignty and exclusion' (1998, p. 678). Responsibility for migration control has been rescaled 'up', 'out' and 'down' in ways that do not curtail state power to manage population movement, but reduce political costs to European states while increasing their flexibility in controlling migration. Not the attenuation of state power once presumed by globalisation scholars, outsourced sovereignty functions like security and migration controls are indicative of changing governance arrangements and the blurring of key liberal legal dichotomies of public and private, state and market, national and international (Abrahamsen and Williams, 2009). In the case of migration control, outsourcing usually enables states to extend policing powers.

The second point is an analytical one. The economy-security assemblage approach shifts focus from the boundary-crossing of public and private to the techniques, technologies and calculations that produce regimes of truth about security, mobility and economy. This thread of research focuses on what Miller and Rose describe as *technologies of government*:

> The actual mechanisms through which authorities of various sorts have sought to shape, normalize and instrumentalize the conduct, thought, decisions and aspirations of others in order to achieve the objectives they consider to be desirable. ... apparently humble and mundane mechanisms which appear to make it possible to govern: techniques of notation, the invention of devices such as surveys and presentational forms such as habits; the inauguration of professional specialisms and vocabularies; building design and architectural forms – the list is heterogeneous and is, in principle, unlimited.
>
> (Miller and Rose, 2008, p. 32)

In the context of immigration detention, technologies of government include head counts; facility audits; quality assurance measures; handbooks and protocols; entrance-way metal detectors; visitation regulations; dining hall menus and their development; ID checks for detained persons, staff and visitors; building designs and flow charts; per-bed economic analyses; real estate valuation of facilities; private correction firms' stock price valuation and credit ratings; corrections as an academic discipline and profession; and the myriad legal frameworks governing imprisonment, labour, state facilities, contracting and administrative practice. For Miller and Rose (2008), technologies of government make political rationalities capable of being realised, and so these technologies not only enumerate, define, hierarchise and order noncitizens as both individuals and populations, but also establish and reproduce certain forms of authority, expertise and knowledge. In other words, detention's calculative practices create the conditions of possibility for particular forms of immigration detention, for the choice of contracted prisons over residential ones, for detention as a policy choice for vulnerable populations, and for legal relief options available to detained noncitizens.

Technologies of government normalise detention as a migration policy, and they do so, in part, by creating relationships. Like all economic transactions – capitalist and otherwise – exchange creates social bonds and networks of circulation (Appadurai, 1988). These relationships require work and continual maintenance, some of which occurs through repetition, rituals and reciprocity of exchange. Supported by the material landscape of detention, the very real durability of a detention centre and contractual obligations that create a distinct timeline for particular relationships, outsourcing detention requires and sustains networks that attain their own momentum. Contracts, for example, make relationships between government agencies and service providers durable into the future. This ability to create durable networks, alliances and infrastructure allows certain relations of power to calcify, to become sedimented in time and space. As Povinelli (2011) has argued, the management of time and the ability to create durable relationships is a key axis of social regulation. And so to understand how people become detainable, and how detention continues to be a favoured policy option, we must attend to the contracts that establish enduring relationships between actors, and to the forms of authority and knowledge practices that authorise contracting. More to the point, the practice of contracting relies upon and reproduces a particular formulation of 'public' and 'private', and managing the boundary between them is a critically important technology of government in the US immigration detention system.

Here I return to family detention to show how 'privatisation' relies upon three specific technologies of government: discretion, contracting and commodification. These technologies rely upon different legal norms, but are made to work together. What I will show is that immigration law's specific formulation of discretion is not so exceptional, but makes use of administrative norms at work throughout the executive branch. ICE's administrative discretion is crucially important to ICE's ability to form Intergovernmental Service Agreements (IGSAs) with county governments, who can then contract detention centre management to companies or other organisations. This administrative discretion is, however, a bit different from its prosecutorial and executive discretion. These contracts not only link these actors in relationships that endure for the length of the contract, but they also do the political work of translating detention into a range of services that can be priced. Thus, contracts authorise monetary exchanges that sustain these relationships, and translate detention into a series of exchange values, an abstraction that conceals the violence of detention and the political questions of sovereignty, right to mobility and due process embedded in it (Mitchelson, 2014). Focusing on what makes privatisation possible, I analyse how discretion, contracting and commodification are distinct technologies of government that are made to work together. In the concluding discussion, I discuss how this approach opens up broader understandings of economic practice.

Outsourcing family detention: discretion, contracting and commodification

Legally defined discretion over immigration enforcement is a critical legal technology of government for immigration agencies in the United States, and crucial to enabling the fast growth of outsourced immigration and border enforcement. US immigration officials practice discretion in three important ways. First, they have prosecutorial discretion, which allows immigration prosecutors a degree of autonomy in deciding who to prosecute. This allows them to focus resources on particular groups of noncitizens (such as violent criminals) or to provide relief to other groups (such as 'deferred action' for noncitizens who entered the US as children). Second, they have administrative discretion to grant parole to detainees based on flight risks assessments. Third, immigration officials have executive discretion to decide what tools and practices, such as biometric passports and workplace raids, are necessary to enforce immigration legislation. Many of these policies are subject to Congressional funding, and Congress can set certain demands or limitations, such as requiring ICE to have 34,000 beds available to detain noncitizens. Administrative discretion has become a common legal tool throughout federal government policy-making to make government more efficient. Based on legal precedent (*Chevron U.S.A. v. NRDC*, 1984), courts defer to executive agencies because they are accountable to the voting public (via the presidential office) and this accountability forces those agencies to work in the best interests of affected populations (Neuman, 2006). With respect to immigration, conservative legislators argued that migrants' multiple appeals of their deportation decisions led to inefficiency in achieving deportation goals (Neuman, 2006). Protected by judicial deference to executive agencies, an ICE officer's decision-making process about who to detain, why, where and for how long is exempt from federal court review. Thus, discretion's overlapping legal norms allowed ICE to expand its authority to detain, to define who is eligible for detention, and to choose what forms of detention are appropriate.

ICE implemented the first permanent family detention policy in March 2001 at the Berks County Family Shelter Care Center near Reading, Pennsylvania (Berks hereafter), a location close to major airports in the New York City area. The facility was built as Berks Heim (German for *home*), a nursing home for indigent elderly people in the county. When a new elderly care facility was built in the late 1990s, the county looked for ways to use the old building. Berks County contracted with then-Immigration and Naturalization Services (INS) to hold non-citizen detainees in the county jail. County officials charged far more for detainee beds than it paid for county prisoners, allowing it to support further county operations. A family detention facility, however, had to meet the standards of care for minors laid out in a 1997 lawsuit, *Flores v. Meese*. Because other INS detention facilities were modelled on prisons rather than residential centres, INS faced a contradiction between court-mandated conditions for children and the actually existing conditions of its own facilities. Berks filled this gap, allowing INS to detain some families without violating children's entitlements. With these procedures in place, the county maintained around 84 persons in detention, primarily asylum-seeking families arriving without identity documentation.

The terrorist attacks of 11 September 2001 heightened concerns over cross-border migration, and in 2003, the Department of Homeland Security (DHS) was founded, absorbing and reorganising 27 agencies including immigration, citizenship and border enforcement (Martin and Simon, 2008). In 2004 and 2005, DHS expanded Expedited Removal, a provision in immigration legislation allowing summary deportation, from ports of entry to areas between ports of entry and maritime areas. In other words, DHS changed how it applied legislative categories, and in doing so, made a much larger set of noncitizens subject to mandatory detention, also required by immigration legislation. At the time, expanding detainability re-asserted the contradiction between immigration detention conditions and children's protections: families who had not been subject to mandatory detention before now fell into that category. This move limited ICE officers' discretion to release families with Notices to Appear in immigration court. To address this gap in detention capacity, and to deter more families from attempting entry, ICE entered into an IGSA with Williamson County, Texas, to detain families at the T. Don Hutto Family Detention Center (Hutto hereafter) in 2006.

The Corrections Corporation of America (CCA) built the T. Don Hutto Correctional Facility in 1995, as a medium-security facility for federal male inmates. Williamson County sub-contracted with CCA to provide the family detention services stipulated in its IGSA with ICE. CCA made no changes to Hutto's disciplinary procedures or physical appearance to accommodate its new population, and in 2007 advocates sued DHS under a previous class action settlement, *Flores v. Meese* (1997). As the ICE Field Office Director explained during the legal proceedings against family detention at Hutto:

> In our IGSAs, our contractual arrangement is with the local government, the entity, state, county or local entity that has the facility. The county or whoever

we have that contractual arrangement with, it's their choice who operates that facility for them. And that's the matter for the county in this case and CCA.

(Bunikyte et al. v. Chertoff et al. Deposition of Immigration and Customs Enforcement Field Office Director Marc Moore)

The ICE-CCA-Williamson County triumvirate became particularly complex during and after the lawsuit, as the federal court held ICE liable for its noncompliance with Flores, ICE held Williamson County liable for completing stipulated changes at Hutto, and Williamson County directed CCA to complete those changes:

> More importantly, the IGSA is between the County and ICE, and Williamson County, TX is responsible for performance under the terms of the agreement. As background, Williamson County was issued a change order under the IGSA on 2/16/2007 to make improvements to the facility to bring it more in-line with a non-secure facility required for ICE Residential Facilities. The Contracting Officer's Technical Representative authorized improvements and ICE is in the process of negotiating a final price for these changes with CCA. However, any changes to the IGSA should be directed by CCA through Williamson County, and then to the ICE Officer, as that's who the agreement with ICE is with.
>
> (Email from Anthony Gomez, ICE Deputy Assistant Director, Office of Acquisition Management, and Removal Operations to Hal Hawes, Assistant to Williamson County Attorney, April 5, 2007)

In most cases, CCA then sub-contracted with other private firms for painting, bath fixture replacement, fence removal, installing new child-safe doors, social services and education (Email Correspondence from Damon Hininger, CCA on file with author), and ICE outsourced inspections to a private firm, as well. This created some confusion, as the functional relationships between ICE, CCA and Williamson County did not cohere with the legal hierarchy of contracted responsibilities. Ultimately, Williamson County Commissioners' Court agreed to delegate authority to CCA, allowing ICE and CCA to negotiate Hutto's changes directly (Email Correspondence between Ashley Lewis, ICE Head of Contracting Activity and Gary Mead, Assistant Director of ICE Detention and Removal Operations, June 8, 2007). Thus, IGSAs and contracts produce complicated networks of liability, monetary circulation and oversight.

The Obama Administration released Hutto's families in 2009, filling the empty beds with adult women. From 2009 to 2014, ICE returned to its previous policy of issuing Notices to Appear to most families, and Berks remained the only family detention facility. In 2013 and 2014 Customs and Border Patrol (CBP) and ICE faced an unprecedented increase in arriving unaccompanied children and families. In 2013, CBP apprehended 21,553 unaccompanied minors and 7,265 minors and adults traveling as families; in 2014, CBP apprehended 49,959 unaccompanied children and 52,326 family members, as also discussed by Williams and Massaro (this volume) (US Immigration and Customs Enforcement, 2014).

Concerned about reports that people smugglers told children and families that the US would not detain them, ICE opened a 672-bed family detention centre in the border patrol training facility in Artesia, New Mexico. In addition, ICE implemented a detain-and-deport policy for all families held there (Carcamo, 2014; Preston, 2014a) and produced public advertisements about the dangers of crossing (Arnold, 2014). Artesia is 200 miles from the nearest city, and the facility was closed to visitors for over a month, including human rights representatives and lawyers. Policies on communication, legal orientations and basic child welfare practices changed frequently (Detention Watch Network, 2014). ICE closed Artesia in December 2014 after a class action lawsuit charged due process violations (Preston, 2014b; *M.S.P.C. v. Johnson*, 2014).

In the meantime, ICE renegotiated existing IGSAs with Karnes County, Texas, and Eloy County, Arizona, to open two more family detention centres. Karnes County and ICE have an IGSA for the Karnes County Residential Center that is similar to Williamson County's, but Karnes County contracts with GEO Group, the second largest private prison company in the US after CCA. Opened in 2012 as a 'civil detention center', the facility held adult males until August 2014, when ICE began holding families there. The facility was built as a model facility for low-risk detainees like asylum seekers, and was touted as a significant step towards a civil model of immigration detention in the United States (US Immigration and Customs Enforcement, 2012). Within months, multiple reports of sexual assault emerged from the facility, and lawyers filed a legal complaint (Mexican American Legal and Educational Defense Fund, 2014).

Despite CCA's lacklustre performance at Hutto, ICE worked with CCA to open the South Texas Family Residential Facility in Dilley County, Texas, in December 2014. While it opened with 480 beds, it has since expanded to 2,400 beds. In what ICE calls a 'creative response to a difficult situation', Eloy, Arizona, facilitates the 'pass-through' IGSA between ICE and CCA for the facility, even though the facility is located in Dilley County (Burnett, 2014). While Eloy houses another CCA detention centre, the county is 931 miles from the South Texas facility, departing from ICE's usual habit of working with counties in which detention centres are housed. To establish the centre, ICE revised its IGSA with Eloy County, rather than establishing a new one with the Dilley County government. Eloy County passes ICE's payment of $290 million to CCA, and CCA compensates Eloy $438,000 for this service. In this arrangement, Eloy County officials seek financial gain by expanding their existing contract with ICE; for their part, ICE avoids time-consuming negotiations with a new county and lengthy competitive bidding requirements for contracting with the private sector. Thus, ICE's executive discretion enabled the creative revision of Eloy County's IGSA, through which Eloy County expanded its financial relationship with CCA. As technologies of government, discretion and contracting were made to work in ways that allowed ICE to expand family detention quickly and outside of 'normal' bidding and negotiations. The service obligations and financial remunerations created by these contracts connect federal and county actors and companies in durable networks, relationships that allow firms to guarantee shareholders revenue over time.

Given the high involvement of non-state firms in the US detention (and criminal justice) system, commodification is integral to the operation of IGSAs, contracts and ICE's ability to quickly expand and contract detention capacity. Intergovernmental Service Agreements price detention in 'bed days' (one person per bed per day) and include additional billable services of transportation, guards and detainee work programmes (e.g. ICE's IGSA with Karnes County). Thus, pricing detention transforms policy aims into a priceable commodity, through per diem payment rates per bed or per migrant. These contractual relationships circulate money between federal, county and non-state actors, forming networks of people working to reproduce detention. As Conlon and Hiemstra (2014) show, commissaries, communication and bartering form additional economies within detention centres, so that detainees themselves become sources of income for contractors, through 'bed day' payments, labour and profit on everyday comfort items. Detention centre 'privatisation' produces overlapping circuits of exchange and a complex web of consumers, clients, service providers, and governmental agencies. In these economies, the boundaries of public and private do not fit neatly into profit-oriented and non-profit groups. Public counties seek monetary gain; detainees are commodities, labourers and traders; and private companies enact disciplinary measures formerly reserved for sovereign governments. ICE's administrative, prosecutorial and executive discretion and IGSAs' extra-market flexibility allow state and non-state actors to expand and contract migration control practices outside of democratic processes and public oversight.

Conclusion

ICE can and does contract directly with CCA and GEO Group to run other immigration detention facilities, and so we must ask what these ICE-county-company arrangements facilitate. What strategies, knowledge practices and legal tactics make family detention possible? What forms of authorisation enable it, and how is family detention maintained, rolled back and expanded once again? In July 2015, a federal court judge ruled that any form of family detention violates *Flores v. Meese* and gave ICE until October to comply with her order to release families (*Flores v. Johnson*, 2014). DHS attorneys appealed the decision, and have applied for childcare facility licenses to bring the Dilley and Karnes facilities into compliance with *Flores*. In October, advocates filed a temporary restraining order on the licensing process, and legal organisations have documented expedited deportation for asylum-seeking families in both facilities (*Grassroots Leadership v. Texas Department of Child and Family Services*, 2015; American Immigration Law Association, 2015). Legal rulings on 'children's special vulnerability' give federal courts more opportunities to intervene in ICE's discretion, contracting and commodification of family detention than adult detention (see Martin, 2011), but these rulings can also be used to legitimise and authorise detention practices. In this chapter, I have argued that discretion, contracting and commodification enabled ICE to implement family detention at Berks, expand it to Hutto, roll it back to

Berks, expand it to Artesia, and replace Artesia with the Karnes and Dilley facilities. These three processes are integral to the 'privatisation' of detention, but understanding them as technologies of government opens up analysis of the active and enthusiastic participation of state agencies in commodifying and contracting out state services. Particular legal formulations of ICE's discretion over immigration enforcement marked out its authority to develop, implement and revise IGSAs with, in this chapter, county governments. These county governments entered into IGSAs for financial gain in the form of tax revenue (from employees) and pass-through payments. Eloy and Karnes Counties contract detention services out to private corrections firms, and this public-public-private arrangement allows all parties to avoid lengthy competitive bidding processes. The IGSAs and contracts themselves detail the price ICE will pay for detaining people, with education, transportation and additional costs for families individually detailed separately. This commodification process is not performed solely by for-profit companies; counties and federal agencies also detail the costs of providing government services in order to develop budgets, accounting procedures and transparency of public spending. Pricing these services has become a normal technology of governing.

My goal here has been to destabilise the association between private actors and profit motives, and between public agencies and policy aims. As private and non-state actors become increasingly active in the everyday work of controlling human mobility and closing borders, our theoretical analysis of migration control's socio-technical arrangements is vitally important to our ability to provide meaningful critique. Here I want to draw out four important analytical points that follow from conceptualising privatised family detention as technologies of government. First, anyone can be an economic actor, regardless of their location in the public or private sector. As the examples above demonstrate, county government managers seek revenue streams to fund county activities, to provide employment and to provide tax revenue. They value county-owned real estate, liabilities and budgets, even while they do not report to shareholders in the same terms as private corporations. Following from Spener (2009), 'financial gain' is a more flexible description of the economic logics at work across public and private sectors in immigration detention. To fully appreciate how and why detention endures as an immigration control – and asylum prevention – strategy, we must be just as attuned to counties' financial incentives to maintain detention as an immigration policy as to those of for-profit firms.

The second point is that discretion, contracting and commodification do political work. Together, they inscribe detention (and imprisonment more broadly) in a marketised regime of value, in which value is calculated, exchanged and circulated according to rules governing commerce, corporations and public-private partnerships. What was once a fundamental sovereign right – the right to deny liberty – exercised by state officials has been translated into a service commodity, an amalgam of expertise, real estate and labour. As such, it is not valued as an ethical or disciplinary practice oriented towards remaking men's souls (as analysed by Foucault, 1995), but in terms of real estate values, long-term profitability and stock prices. Translating detention and imprisonment into a marketised regime of value requires certain abstractions (Mitchelson, 2014) and these abstractions *depoliticise* incarceration as a policy practice to many of the actors involved in its daily operations.

The third point is that commodification is a political process, only ever partial and often refused by the humans and beings subjected to commodification. For Appadurai (1988, p. 41), commodities are 'complex social forms and distributions of knowledge' that move in and out of commodification. Commodification produces new socio-technical arrangements that translate things into exchange values, circulate them and insert them in a particular regime of value, a discursive regime of shared understandings about what things *are*, what they *mean*, how they relate to each other and what they say about the person who owns them (see Appadurai, 1988; Callon, 1998). These valuations rely upon calculative practices like headcounts, centre capacity quotas, bed day pricing, oversight mechanisms, accounting, shareholder annual reports, migration population data, enforcement outcome expectations, and so on. Interrogating how these come to be linked up – and the authority that enables them to come together in particular forms – allows us to trace a broader range of relationships that enable the reproduction of detention as an enforcement strategy.

The fourth point is that 'privatisation' processes work to solidify certain boundaries between public and private, and these boundaries also work to delimit who may act as political subject, where, and on what terms. As Appadurai argues, people disagree about values and rules of exchanging commodities, and it is in these tensions between value, exchange and commodity that 'politics ... links value and exchange in the social lives of commodities' (Appadurai, 1988, p. 57). Likewise, Radin (1996) argues that human commodities are only partially commodified because their humanity places a moral limit on our willingness to view them solely in terms of money. Moreover, many commodified beings exceed the exchange relations in which they are placed; in short, they rebel (Collard, 2014). Detention centres are lively, peopled places, and the people detained in them are highly capable of disrupting their order, which in turn negates companies' ability to sell detention centre space. For example, prisoners in a US Bureau of Prisons Criminal Alien prison in Willacy, Texas, overtook guards and controlled the facility for almost two days in February 2015, destroying the tent-like buildings that held them and rendering the facility unusable (Tyx, 2015). Detained mothers launched two hunger strikes at Karnes, refusing to work and send their kids to the school (Planas, 2015), and these protests were met with threats of separation. These refusals of commodification create their own politics, and their own publics, by asserting their right to be and act politically, despite families' designations as undocumented and deportable. And so the boundary between public and private is itself a site of struggle.

Focusing on technologies of government allows us to reframe the privatisation of detention in a way that points to more diffuse geographies of complicity in imprisonment as a political project. What is perhaps exceptional about detention's commercialisation is that the deprivation of liberty, or the right to imprison a private citizen, has long been a privileged – and highly restricted – right of liberal sovereign states. Next to the right to take life, the right to deny liberty is a right to a form of physical violence and state control that is quite different from state obligations to provide social benefits like education, healthcare, unemployment assistance and housing. In fact, the individual's relationship to the state is mediated by complex legal regimes stipulating the grounds, timing and conditions in which a state may confine a person. Enrolling non-state actors in this kind of state violence, however, inscribes detention and incarceration in different regimes of value; processes of marketisation and commodification work to revalue the denial of liberty, translating it from an issue of sovereign and individual rights to the right to accumulate wealth, the ability of markets to provide efficient services, and the responsibility of states to both secure national territory and rule efficiently. We need a conceptualisation of privatisation that accommodates a diverse range of financial relationships, actors, logics and calculative practices to ground a critique of detention and incarceration beyond a profit motive, to trace the complex geographies of participation in an exclusionary regime of value.

Acknowledgments

Thanks to Deirdre Conlon, Nancy Hiemstra and Eeva-Kaisa Prokkola for their constructive feedback and support for developing the ideas in this chapter.

References

Abrahamsen, R. and Williams, M.C. 2009. Security beyond the state: global security assemblages in international politics. *International Political Sociology* **3**(1), pp. 1–17.

American Immigration Lawyers Association. 2015. Letter to USCIS and ICE Concerning Due Process Violations at Detention Facilities. 24 December [Online]. Available from: www.aila.org/advo-media/aila-correspondence/2015/letter-uscis-ice-due-process [Accessed 29 January 2016].

Amoore, L. 2013. *The politics of possibility: risk and security beyond probability*. Durham, NC: Duke University Press.

Amoore, L. and de Goede, M. 2008. Transactions after 9/11: the banal face of the preemptive strike. *Transactions of the Institute of British Geographers* **33**(2), pp. 173–85.

Andersson, R. 2014. *Illegality, Inc.: clandestine migration and the business of bordering Europe*. Oakland, California: University of California Press.

Appadurai, A. 1988. Introduction: commodities and the politics of value. In Appadurai, A. ed. *The social life of things: commodities in cultural perspective*. Cambridge: Cambridge University Press, pp. 3–63.

Arnold, R. Government's warning not deterring all immigrants. 2014. KPRC Houston. August 6 [Online]. Available from: www.click2houston.com/news/how-are-american-tax-dollars-being-used-for-texas-border-crisis/26968928 [Accessed 11 September 2015].

Bigo, D. and Jeandesboz, J. 2010. *The EU and the European security industry: questioning the 'public-private dialogue'*. Oslo, Norway: INEX Policy Brief.

Burnett, J. 2014. How will a small town in Arizona manage an ICE facility in Texas? *National Public Radio* [Online]. Available from: www.npr.org/2014/10/28/359411980/how-will-a-small-town-in-arizona-manage-an-ice-facility-in-texas [Accessed 22 January 2015].

Callon, M. 1998. Introduction: the embeddedness of economic markets in economics. In Callon, M. ed. *Laws of the markets*. Oxford: Blackwell, pp. 1–57.

Carcamo, C. 2014. Nearly 300 women, children deported from immigration detention centers. *Los Angeles Times* [Online]. Available from: www.latimes.com/nation/nationnow/la-na-nn-ff-new-mexico-immigration-deportation-20140821-story.html [Accessed 10 September 2015].

Coleman, M. and Kocher, A. 2011. Detention, deportation, devolution and immigrant incapacitation in the US, post 9/11. *The Geographical Journal* **177**(3), pp. 228–37.

Collard, R. 2014. Putting animals back together, taking commodities apart. *Annals of the Association of American Geographers* **104**(1), pp. 151–65.

Conlon, D. 2011. A fractured mosaic: encounters with the everyday amongst refugee and asylum seeker women. *Population, Space and Place* **17**(6), pp. 714–26.

Conlon, D. and Gill, N. 2013. Gagging orders: asylum seekers and paradoxes of freedom and protest in liberal society. *Citizenship Studies* **17**(2), pp. 241–59.

Conlon, D. and Hiemstra, N. 2014. Examining the everyday micro-economies of migrant detention in the United States. *Geographica Helvetica* **69**(5), pp. 335–44.

Coutin, S.B. 2010. Confined within: national territories as zones of confinement. *Political Geography* **29**(4), pp. 200–8.

de Goede, M. 2012. *Speculative security: the politics of pursuing terrorist monies*. Minneapolis: University of Minnesota Press.

Detention Watch Network. 2014. Expose and close: Artesia Family Residential Center, New Mexico [Online]. Available from: www.detentionwatchnetwork.org/sites/detentionwatchnetwork.org/files/expose_close_-_artesia_family_residential_center_nm_2014.pdf [Accessed 11 September 2015].

Doty, R.L. and Wheatley, E.S. 2013. Private detention and the immigration industrial complex. *International Political Sociology* **7**(4), pp. 426–43.

Fernandes, D. 2007. *Targeted: Homeland Security and the business of immigration*. New York: Seven Stories Press.

Foucault, M. 1995. *Discipline and punish: the birth of the prison*. New York: Knopf Doubleday Publishing Group.

Gammeltoft-Hansen, T. and Sørensen, N.N. eds. 2013. *The migration industry and the commercialization of international migration*. Oxon: Routledge.

Gill, N. 2009. Governmental mobility: the power effects of the movement of detained asylum seekers around Britain's detention estate. *Political Geography* **28**(3), pp. 186–96.

Golash-Boza, T. 2009a. A confluence of interests in immigration enforcement: how politicians, the media, and corporations profit from immigration policies destined to fail. *Sociology Compass* **3**(2), pp. 283–94.

Golash-Boza, T. 2009b. The immigration industrial complex: why we enforce immigration policies destined to fail. *Sociology Compass* **3**(2), pp. 295–309.

Hernandez-Leon, R. 2013. Conceptualizing the migration industry. In T. Gammeltoft-Hansen and Sorensen, N.N. eds. *The migration industry and the commercialization of international migration*. New York: Routledge, pp. 24–44.

Hiemstra, N. 2013. 'You don't even know where you are': chaotic geographies of US migrant detention and deportation. In Moran, D., Gill, N. and Conlon, D. eds. *Carceral spaces: mobility and agency in imprisonment and migrant detention*. Farnham Surrey: Ashgate, pp. 57–76.

Hoijtink, M. 2014. Capitalizing on emergence: the 'new' civil security market in Europe. *Security Dialogue*. **45**(5), pp. 458–75.

Lahav, G. 1998. Immigration and the state: the devolution and privatisation of immigration control in the EU. *Journal of Ethnic and Migration Studies* **24**(4), pp. 675–94.

Manning, S. n.d. Ending Artesia. *Innovation Law Lab* [Online]. Available from: https://innovationlawlab.org/the-artesia-report/ [Accessed 4 September 2015].

Martin, L. and Simon, S. 2008. A formula for disaster: the Department of Homeland Security's virtual ontology. *Space and Polity* **12**(3), pp. 281–96.

Martin, L.L. 2012. Governing through the family: struggles over US noncitizen family detention policy. *Environment and Planning A* **44**(4), pp. 866–88.

Martin, L. 2011. The geopolitics of vulnerability: children's legal subjectivity, immigrant family detention and US immigration law and enforcement policy. *Gender, Place and Culture* **18**(4): pp. 477–98.

Mexican American Legal and Educational Defense Fund. 2014. RE: complaints regarding sexual abuse of women at Karnes County Residential Center [Online]. Available from: http://www.maldef.org/assets/pdf/2014-09-30_Karnes_PREA_Letter_Complaint.pdf [Accessed 11 September 2014].

Miller, P. and Rose, N. 2008. *Governing the present: administering economic, social and personal life*. Cambridge: Polity Press.

Mitchelson, M.L. 2014. The production of bedspace: prison privatization and abstract space. *Geographica Helvetica* **69**(5), pp. 325–33.

Mountz, A. 2010. *Seeking asylum: human smuggling and bureaucracy at the border*. Minneapolis, MN: University of Minnesota Press.

Mountz, A. Coddington, K., Catania, T. and Loyd, J. 2013. Conceptualizing detention: mobility, containment, bordering, and exclusion. *Progress in Human Geography* **37**(4), pp. 522–41.

Mountz, A. and Hiemstra, N. 2014. Chaos and crisis: dissecting the spatiotemporal logics of contemporary migrations and state practices. *Annals of the Association of American Geographers* **104**(2), pp. 382–90.

Neuman, G.L. 2006. Discretionary deportation. *Georgetown Immigration Law Journal* **20**, p. 611.

Planas, R. 2015. Mothers launch a second hunger strike at Karnes City Family Detention Center. *Huffington Post*. April 14 [Online]. Available from: www.huffingtonpost.com/2015/04/14/detention-center-hunger-strike_n_7064532.html [Accessed 11 September 2015].

Povinelli, E.A. 2011. *Economies of abandonment: social belonging and endurance in late liberalism*. Durham, NC: Duke University Press.

Preston, J. 2014a. As U.S. speeds the path to deportation, distress fills new family detention centers. *New York Times*. August 5 [Online]. Available from: www.nytimes.com/2014/08/06/us/seeking-to-stop-migrants-from-risking-trip-us-speeds-the-path-to-deportation-for-families.html?_r=0 [Accessed 21 January 2015].

Preston, J. 2014b. Detention center presented as deterrent to border crossings. *New York Times*. December 15 [Online]. Available from: www.nytimes.com/2014/12/16/us/homeland-security-chief-opens-largest-immigration-detention-center-in-us.html?hp&action=click&pgtype=Homepage&module=second-column-region&region=top-news&WT.nav=top-news&_r=1 [Accessed 21 January 2015].

Radin, M.J. 1996. *Contested commodities: the trouble with trade in sex, children, body parts, and other things*. Cambridge, MA: Harvard University Press.

Saldivar, K.M. and Price, B.E. 2015. Private prisons and the emerging immigrant market in the US: implications for security governance. *Central European Journal of International and Security Studies* **9**(1), pp. 28–53.

Spener, D. 2009. Some critical reflections on the migration industry concept. Self-published [Online]. Available from: www.trinity.edu/dspener/clandestinecrossings/related%20articles/migration%20industry.pdf [Accessed 22 January 2016].

Tyx, D.B. 2015. Goodbye to tent city. *Texas Observer*. March 26 [Online]. Available from: www.texasobserver.org/south-texas-prison-riot-willacy-county-economic-future/ [Accessed 11 September 2015].

US Immigration and Customs Enforcement. 2012. ICE opens its first-ever designed-and-built civil detention center. *Press Release*.

US Immigration and Customs Enforcement. 2014. ICE Enforcement and Removals Report Fiscal Year 2014. Washington, D.C.: Department of Homeland Security.

Welch, M.D. 2002. *Detained: immigration laws and the expanding I.N.S. jail complex.* Philadelphia: Temple University Press.

Williams, J. and Boyce, G.A. 2013. Fear, loathing and the everyday geopolitics of encounter in the Arizona borderlands. *Geopolitics* **19**(4), pp. 895–916.

Legal Cases

American Immigration Council et al. v. DHS. 2014. Case No. 14 CV 8403.

Bunikyte et al. v. Chertoff et al. 2007.0 Case No, 1:07-cv-00765-SS.

Chevron U.S.A Inc. v. Natural Resources Defense Council, Inc. 1984. 467 U.S. 837.

Flores v. Meese. 1997. Case No. CV 85-4544-RJK(Px).

Flores v. Johnson. 2014. Case 2:85-cv-04544-DMG-AGR.

Grassroots Leadership v. Texas Department of Child and Family Services. 2015. No. D-1-GN-15-004336.

M.S.P.C. v. Johnson. 2014. Case 1:14-cv-01437.

4 In the market of morality

International human rights standards and the immigration detention 'improvement' complex

Julia Morris

Introduction

In response to the increasing use of immigration detention worldwide, 'improving' detention has become a dominant focus of state and non-state actors. Nation states, non-governmental organisations (NGOs), intergovernmental organisations (INGOs), and academic researchers all focus on ameliorating increasingly restrictive policies through humanitarian-based solutions that 'enhance' facility standards. There is a proliferation of international legal and regulatory mechanisms that seek to reform detention, buttressed by the institutionalisation of a detention rights movement geared towards reforming the practice.

This chapter considers how the global market for immigration detention operates through and with the support of the international human rights regime. I argue that the detention rights movement facilitates and at times is a central part of the development of new markets aimed at providing a humane standard of detention care. This is tightly linked to the growth of what Barry (2004) terms 'ethical capitalism'. While Barry uses the term to refer to the ethicalisation of business, I use this concept to move beyond emergent concerns with human rights on the part of business. Instead, I take 'ethical capitalism' to denote 'softer' forms of accumulation at large, defined by the institutionalisation of human rights rule making, the proliferation of NGOs *and* business and corporate social responsibility norms. Attention to wider capitalist developments, I suggest, assists understanding the degree to which human rights frameworks enable a bipartisan consensus on the appropriate response to detention. It also emphasises that rights-driven structures are not immune to state power and global capital despite operating under a humanitarian ethics.

The chapter builds on recent scholarship that shows how international human rights policy and practice are imbricated in the expansion of detention. Flynn (2013, p. 8) underscores the detrimental consequences of promoting human rights norms when it comes to immigration detention, arguing that rights advocates have influenced the evolution of regimes by providing 'normative cover' to detention practices. In examining the role of the International Organization for Migration (IOM), Ashutosh and Mountz (2011) question new spaces of governance enabled by its contracting into what were once sovereign functions. Similarly, Tyler, Gill, Conlon and Oeppen (2014) look at the role of NGOs in neoliberal projects, showing how a preoccupation with economic survival incentivises NGOs to enter more explicitly into the private detention market. In studying the relationship between western aid and security, Duffield (2001) refers to a 'liberal complex' to denote new governance networks that bring together state and private sector actors in different ways. These strategic complexes are the effect of neoliberal economic reforms. Under an agenda of state outsourcing and devolution, humanitarian action has radically transformed into a 'new humanitarianism', which abets political and security objectives at the expense of 'markets above morality' (Duffield, 2001, p. 260).

While most analyses focus on one particular sector, I explore the convergences between the spectrum of state and non-state actors who come together to 'improve' the practice of immigration detention, or what some have referred to as the immigration industrial complex (Hiemstra, 2013). Much like 'the prison industrial complex' (Davis, 2003), the immigration industrial complex refers to these overlapping bureaucratic, economic and political interests motivating the expansion of migration enforcement. I use the term 'detention improvement complex' to better signpost the development turn, in which state and non-state actors unite around 'humane' forms of detention. Markets *with* morality more aptly describes this 'improvement' complex, where state and non-state actors converge through reform rule making and operational practice. While punitive policies remain in place, the moral sentiments of 'transnational humanitarianism' (Ticktin, 2014) reflect a new form of governance, which unites all manner of institutions. This is part of a trend that can be seen within the trajectories of neoliberal capitalism, in which moral discourses have come to characterise the expansion of capitalist accumulation (Hopgood, 2008). My chapter takes a further step back, drawing rights rule makers onto the commercial map. INGOs and NGOs are not apolitical structures of authoritative rules and principles nor do they only provide discursive legitimation for entrenched state practices. Commercial and performance-based concerns play an important part in all of these organisations, some firm-like leviathans in their own right. This chapter thus contributes to the volume's concept of 'intimate economies' by demonstrating how human rights as a legal and rhetorical framework, manned by organisational workforces, are central to, and are themselves, professionalised accumulation strategies. 'Intimate economies' perfectly captures the new moralistic economic orders. Importantly, the concept illuminates the commercial nature of NGO and INGO workforces who embody and advance human rights rule-making practice.

The chapter begins by setting detention reforms within the context of neoliberalism, before providing a brief overview of the human rights frameworks that have acquired global precedence around immigration detention. This detention rights agenda is commonly referenced as the ideal framework for addressing detention. I illustrate its dissemination with reference to the work of the United Nations High Commission for Refugees (UNHCR) and the International Detention Coalition (IDC). UNHCR and IDC are the dominant organisations focused on detention, aligned through a Memorandum of Understanding (MOU) in June 2013. As such, they provide a lens from which to view the promotional networks that help reform agendas acquire such mainstream visibility. Importantly, a focus on UNHCR and IDC also highlights the economic rationalities behind human rights–based organisational approaches and rule making. Following this, I turn to look at the different industry sectors that come together in the service of detention reform. I detail how new forms of 'ethical capitalism' sustain detention, moving on to examine the politics of academic expertise in enacting neoliberal agendas and consolidating detention rights frameworks. Through these mappings, I argue that human rights policies and practices bring together diverse actors. They help authorise, and are themselves part of, the immigration detention industry.

Detention reforms in the context of neoliberalism

The institutionalisation and industrialisation of immigration detention reforms is best set within the wider socio-economic trends of neoliberal structural adjustments. Broadly, neoliberalism is a form of political-economic governance that posits markets and private capital as the preferred model for achieving efficiency and greater resource dispersal (Dardot and Laval, 2014). As a policy framework, neoliberalism dismantled the Keynesian welfare state and strengthened free-market enterprise, liberalising trade, and outsourcing state functions. This concept describes the changing role of the state in the governance of society and how the ensuing political and economic transformations open up new spaces for capital.

Drawing on Foucault's (1991) work on governmentality and biopower, post-structural perspectives of 'neoliberalism as governmentality' critique the idea of neoliberalism as a monolithic and hegemonic project (Barry, Osborne and Rose, 1996; Brown, 2003; Hall, 2011). While neoliberalism may mean less government, it does not follow that there is less governance. Instead, regimes of power and knowledge are highly dispersed and conducted through the practices of a range of actors. Rather than leading to a 'hollowed out state' (Rhodes, 1994), the trend of non-state actors taking over governmental functions reasserts state power, regulating socio-economic flows out of state hands and through the networked participation and management of non-state actors. This challenges the overly simplified notion of the state as the sole possessor of power.

The political tendency of outsourcing and privatising public services is fully evidenced across the global detention industry. As part of the efficiency and 'improvement' rationale, detention services are delegated to a range of private sector organisations. Contracts to manage detention centres and provide related services are lucrative. A number of corporate bodies, NGOs, INGOs, universities, and research institutes have found financial success from the tendering process. At the same time, new profit-based structures draw further convergences between diverse actors (Wallace, 2003). Previously differentiated practices are subsumed by market economic imperatives. This humanitarian squeeze is manifest across a range of sectors as organisations battle it out for coveted funding pools. Individuals must prove the value of their work and show 'impact' to financiers by choosing project-oriented programmes that lead to rapid and quantifiable outcomes.

To analyse what the neoliberalisation of detention means in practice, I draw on fifteen months of fieldwork conducted principally between Europe, the United States and the Asia Pacific region throughout 2014 and 2015, in which I came into substantial contact with many of these central detention rights players. I attended UNHCR's NGO Consultations and Detention Strategy launch, and IDC's Member Conference, all in Geneva in June 2014. I also attended Detention Watch Network's Washington D.C. member meeting and the Asia Pacific Consultation on Refugee Rights held in Bangkok, in addition to research in Australia and the Republic of Nauru. I conducted interviews and spent time with most of the major UN institutions, international NGOs, and commercial firms whose work intersects with immigration detention. I signed up to listservs and attended academic and detention rights industry conferences as well as working groups focused on a humanitarian response to the practice. My research shows that the creation of new financial and governmental spaces through international human rights law connected to detention leads to the harmonisation of diverse actors. It also illuminates the economic rationalism behind organisations that shape 'ethical' human rights frameworks (see Morris, forthcoming 2016). These financial/legal spaces create broad social and semantic terrains that propagate the rationality of detention rights reforms, and, in so doing, adds to and tightens the cogs of the detention 'improvement' complex.

Developing international 'human rights' standards for immigration detention

The institutionalisation of international human rights standards around immigration detention is a recent trend. Following the signing of the Universal Declaration of Human Rights (1948), United Nations policymakers created several human rights treaties relevant to the issue of immigration detention. In addition, a number of organisations incorporated immigration detention as a part of their agenda or under the broader remit of confinement. For example, Red Cross has long been active in inspecting detention centres and working for institutional improvements. However, detention rights were a somewhat patchy field with little in the way of transnational harmonisation. No law or organisation specifically addressed the practice and there was little international effort to apply human rights norms to immigration detention. In fact, intergovernmental institutions purposely skirted around the issue of immigration detention, fearing that addressing practices of immigration security and control would encroach on the territorial sovereignty of states (Cornelisse, 2010).

This all changed in the 1990s. As detention centres grew in number and popularity worldwide, United Nations staff began to concentrate on addressing immigration detention issues through a focus on 'improvement'. Previously, the *UN Standard Minimum Rules for the Treatment of Prisoners* (1955) and its offspring the *Council of Europe Standard Minimum Rules* (1973) had found appeal as frameworks for institutional improvement. They were compiled by fans of the popular British penal reform movement, propelled by such organisations as the Howard

League and later Penal Reform International and the Prison Reform Trust, who worked to improve and bring about new forms of containment for people held under criminal law. Industry professionals contended that the European custodial standards for prisons did not address the special circumstances of immigration detention. Both were written at a time when few states had constructed dedicated immigration detention centres. Using the Minimum Rules and its constituent international legal treaties as a blueprint, UNHCR and affiliates attempted to regulate state practice by making explicit human rights rules connected to detention. The authors were contracted refugee and human rights professionals, some of whom had worked for refugee legal and social work agencies and in detention centres. They were also firm advocates of the refugee system, seeking distance from criminals and economic migrants to leverage for their industry and promote its internationalisation. They devised the first guidelines related to immigration detention in 1995, revised them in 1999, and in 2012 released them in their latest form as the 'Detention Guidelines'.

UNHCR's Detention Guidelines best define the international normative framework for immigration detention. The point of the standards is to promote a benchmark of accreditation for detention centres. They describe who should be in facilities and what centres should be like. As per UNHCR's wider organisational focus, its human rights standards specifically relate to people presenting as 'a refugee'. They focus on addressing the issue of detention within the framework of the 1951 Refugee Convention, which sets out the basis of who constitutes 'a refugee' in relation to persecution on the grounds of 'race, religion, nationality, membership of a particular social group or political opinion' (Convention Relating to the Status of Refugees, 1951).

The Guidelines develop a detention 'improvement' framework that revolves around proportionality and detention conditions (see Figure 4.1). First, to be lawful, detention must pass tests of reasonableness, necessity and proportionality. The proportionality test is central to the human rights framework within which state detention policies are set (Wilscher, 2011). This test measures the degree to which the deprivation of a person's liberty is justifiable to the ends established in law, providing a forum for 'reasoned' analysis of an individual's detainability. The trend to a proportionality analysis is evident throughout the Guidelines, which focus on exempting *some* people from detention. 'Proportionality' and 'arbitrariness' have become popular phrases for organisations in the sector to leverage for the exclusion of people who present as refugees from detention centres, as well as designated 'vulnerable' groups such as single women, under eighteens, and others with special medical or psychological needs. Under the 'proportionality' rationale, UNHCR staff undertake detention monitoring inspections and encourage other NGOs and lawyers to follow suit. Their aim is to identify and ensure that the right people are held in places of confinement, advertising the distinction between refugee and non-refugee populations (for instance, the 'economic migrant' and 'criminal'), and streamlining detention towards those others who are, as UNHCR rulebooks see it, legitimately detainable.

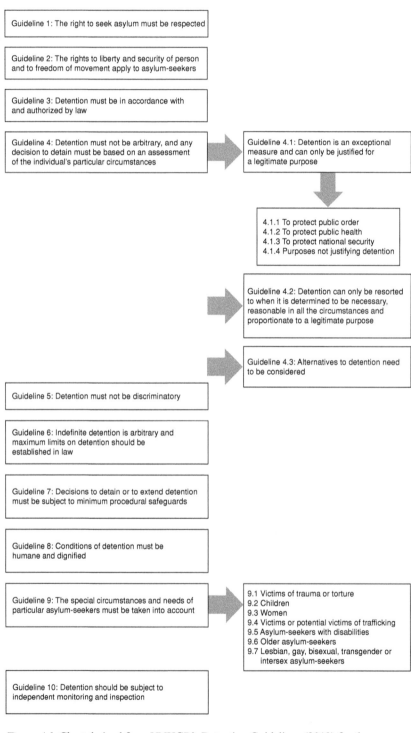

Figure 4.1 Chart derived from UNHCR's Detention Guidelines (2012) for the applicable criteria and standards relating to the detention of asylum seekers

Second, the Guidelines specifically address the conditions of detention. Under the standards, it is stated that 'detention can only lawfully be in places officially recognised as places of detention. Detention in police cells is not appropriate' (UNHCR, 2012, p. 29). The standards go on to detail:

> Detention of asylum-seekers for immigration-related reasons should **not be punitive** in nature … appropriate medical treatment must be provided … asylum-seekers in detention should be able to make regular contact (including through telephone or internet, where possible) and receive visits … the opportunity to conduct some form of physical exercise through daily indoor and outdoor recreational activities needs to be available … the right to practice one's religion … access to reading materials … education and/or vocational training.
>
> (2012, p. 29–31)

They later emphasise, '**Appropriate medical treatment must be provided where needed**, including psychological counselling' (2012, p. 30, emphasis in the original).

UNHCR's Detention Guidelines draw on the primary international conventions protecting human rights, as cited below, all of which are extensively relied upon and propounded as international blueprints for 'humane detention'. Depending on whether states have ratified the Convention, these international instruments are often integrated into national detention standards. The UN Convention Relating to the Status of Refugees (1951), the Convention on the Rights of the Child (1989) and the Convention on the Elimination of All Forms of Discrimination Against Women (1979) are the main international legal mechanisms integrated within the proportionality aspect of state detention standards. These instruments help define who should and should not be detained. In addition, the United Nations' International Covenant on Civil and Political Rights (1966) and the Convention against Torture and Other Cruel, Inhuman and Degrading Treatment or Punishment (1987) are widely used legal frameworks that focus more specifically on a 'humane' standard of detention.

International human rights frameworks carry important weight as nodes within the detention 'improvement' complex. As others well demonstrate, material documents give authority and are central 'techniques' (Riles, 2011) in the production of institutional knowledge and epistemic communities. Transnational rights frameworks are not stand-alone rules but bring organisations into alliance, advance infrastructural 'improvements', *and* provide workload and revenue for rule makers and overseers. The detention rights agenda proliferates out through global regulatory machinery recently connected to or set up specifically for detention. UNHCR has helped bureaucratise and circulate detention 'improvements', recruiting 'Detention Focal Points' internationally. The aim of these appointed individuals and teams is to liaise with state authorities, participate in detention working groups, disseminate detention 'improvement' guides to local NGOS, and 'improve' detention conditions through better resources and the removal of 'persons of concern' to UNHCR. In tandem, international monitoring bodies oversee detention facilities to ensure compliance with human rights standards. In recent years there has been a cottage industry of international monitoring bodies that adjudicate whether states' detention systems are compliant with human rights standards or assess the degree to which states respect the human rights of detained individuals.[1]

Paradoxically, the core rights agenda of all of these international human rights standards is that a 'humane' standard of care is essential to state immigration detention regimes. These regulatory frameworks do not address the root cause of people's distress as detention itself. Rather, they contradictorily attempt to 'improve' the practice, in effect offering a panacea for softening detention's effects. Simultaneously, rights rules forge an industry of 'ethical capitalism', even as INGO rulemakers exist as part of the 'improvement' industry themselves. Detention 'improvements' are heralded as the agenda that states should strive for in their regimes. In response to advocates' calls that immigration detention is incompatible with human rights, states have worked with reformers to set up rights-based frameworks that remedy these criticisms. State judicial practices and human rights organisations draw upon international detention guidelines and their normative convention frameworks in their policies and practices. Rather than reducing detention, state agencies use these guidelines as a regulatory basis for 'good detention practice'. They develop minimum 'quality' standards, which define the rules through which detention centres and their related contracterd organisations or 'service providers' are governed.[2]

The emphasis on 'humane' conditions, the need for states to keep criminal justice and immigration practices separate, and the unlawfulness of detention for 'vulnerable' categories of people has resulted in the entrenchment of immigration detention in a number of other clear ways. In order to ensure 'improved' detention systems, the global trend is for states to construct entirely new facilities specifically for immigration detention that meet human rights compliance.[3] In addition, states channel funds into developing services for the provision of religion, education, work, recreation and health care amongst other services. The private sector is instrumental in this regard. Commercial and non-governmental entities, from construction firms to medical and educational practitioners, help in the facilitation of 'humane' centres. So too, the emphasis on 'vulnerability' and 'refugee' assessment means that states now have vast populations of single men who fall outside of the designated categories. Heteronormative assumptions about who merits inclusion and can expect to be protected – or not – become more entrenched. The need to prove 'credible fear' and present oneself as 'a refugee' through the circumscribed definition of the 1951 Convention has become paramount. This has resulted in the construction of a global industry of recognition including UNHCR, government and private sector involvement (Fassin and Rechtman, 2009). Legal tribunals and consultants, advocacy organisations, healthcare professionals and migration agents all provide assistance and legal training to determine if individuals are 'refugees' or help them to present themselves as such. Similarly, refugee law is an established profession in many states worldwide.

In addition to defining human rights standards and thought practices around detention, UNHCR is a dominant player within the detention rights fiseld. The organisation plays a key role in defining detention governance frameworks. This has segued the dominant rights legislative focus to the rationality of 'improvement' and the humanitarian figures of the 'asylum seeker' and 'refugee'. The widespread dissemination of the Detention Guidelines and authority of international organisations in the field often has the effect of pulling others into its agenda. Many NGOs operate in accordance with international human rights law, as much as demonstrating an alliance with human rights frameworks bolsters organisational funding bids.

UNHCR's own reasons for the immigration detention policy directions it has taken are deeply tied into its makeup and need to prove financial viability. It is both an organisation set up around a refugee protection mandate and one dependent on external funding and effectively shareholder-style performance-based assessment (see Morris, forthcoming 2016). UNHCR's budget is based on global needs assessment (GNA). Office staff in each regional and administrative protection division put forward the assessed needs of their persons of concern on a biennial basis. The Executive Committee (ExCom), consisting of 20–25 UN Member States, then approve UNHCR's budget and programme priorities for the following year, with budgets added by the High Commissioner to meet 'emergency situations'. Following ExCom's approval, the majority of the budget is then sourced by annual global fundraising appeals from member states, NGOs, INGOs, corporations, foundations and individuals worldwide. UNHCR's policy frameworks are driven by the need to assert the refugee agenda and make and care for more people as refugees, in what one UNHCR representative described as 'promoting our people' (per author interview with UNHCR representative). So too, as an organisation made up of states, UNHCR confers its moral authority and legitimacy within the constraints of the Westphalian frame of territorial sovereignty and the political structures of international relations and interests. This is what Cornelisse (2010, p. 26) aptly refers to as the 'blind spot of human rights protection'. As per the epochal rise of neoliberal audit cultures, short-term and performance-based contracts are now the norm in UNHCR. Pragmatism and effectiveness of aid delivery are essential. Staff must demonstrate the value of their work through an increasingly performance indicator–led culture. 'It's all about results based management and proving how many people we can service', one UNHCR representative commented. The performance culture is linked into funding rationales, in terms of being able to easily prove the agency's work to donor states. But it has dramatically affected the organisation as a whole through recruitment, staff socialisation and policy directions.

The power of UNHCR's detention reformism cannot be underestimated as it draws other organisations into its normative focus. NGOs are a central part of UNHCR's work, leading to convergences between organisational approaches. A number of NGOs implement UNHCR's work in the field, furthered through training, organisational collaboration, conferences, media, detention rights databases and other transnational fora. UNHCR representatives are more often than not in attendance at detention rights meetings, in the hope of putting 'asylum seekers', 'refugees' and the Guidelines on the table. This creates social and semantic terrains that institutionalise and propagate the rationality of detention rights reforms and the dual pillars of proportionality and improved conditions. The next section examines the spread of the detention rights agenda through the work of the dominant NGO, the International Detention Coalition. I look at how detention 'improvement' frameworks gain incremental authority as an important aspect of the 'ethical capitalist' or softer profit-making economy.

Disseminating 'human rights' standards

The International Detention Coalition is the premier international organisation focused on immigration detention and the major spokesperson for the NGO detention community. The Coalition began as an informal network of civil society groups at UNHCR's NGO Consultations. They wanted to bring together the scattered organisations involved in detention into a separate detention rights NGO. With the support of major funding bodies such as the Ford Foundation and Open Society Institute, the network became an incorporated NGO in 2009. The organisation has grown exponentially as a secretariat and network in recent years, largely on the success of their 'end child detention', 'detention alternatives' and 'detention monitoring' campaigns. As part of its team, IDC now counts a broad base of full and part-time staff, a Governance and Finance Committee, external researchers and partners, offices in Australia, Mexico, Malaysia and Germany, and over three hundred and fifty members in sixty countries. In 2011, IDC recorded a total revenue of $AU410,171.24 (IDC, 2011a).[4] With the growth in detention and success of the detention reform agenda, by 2014, just three years later, IDC's revenue had more than doubled to $AU1,029.855 (IDC, 2014).

IDC staff describe their role as advocating for greater respect for the human rights of detainees. Their organisational 'vision statement' is 'envisioning a world without *unnecessary* immigration detention' (2015, italics author's own). To achieve this goal, they promote the use of international and regional human rights standards and principles, working with governments to provide 'pragmatic', 'solutions-based' strategies around detention. In 2011, IDC published their 'Legal framework and standards relating to the detention of refugees, asylum seekers and migrants' (IDC, 2011b). The Framework sets out the organisation's position on detention, substantiated through international law, standards and guidelines.

UNHCR's Detention Guidelines (2012) are used by IDC in their legal framework. Like UNHCR's Guidelines, proportionality and conditions also form the core of these ten standards. Notably, Standards Two, Three and Four focus on not detaining vulnerable individuals, children and asylum seekers. Standard Five reinforces the need for detention to be necessary and proportionate to the objective of identity and security checks. Standard Eight highlights that no one should be subject to *arbitrary* detention, which is to say that detention is acceptable for some people. Standard Nine emphasises the 'humane' detention agenda, that conditions of detention must comply with basic minimum human rights standards.

The Coalition works with governments in advocating for detention 'improvements' around these standards. Legal advocacy is crucial to IDC's work. This includes lobbying for changes in law, policy and practice that promote the 'human rights' of those affected by immigration detention. Specifically, IDC focuses on encouraging states to 'improve' their immigration detention practices by tactically negotiating with governments. At times, this involves playing them off of each other in order to achieve reforms. An IDC representative presented their work as follows:

> Our role is to show governments what other countries have done in terms of legislative reform … we highlight what other countries are doing well and we encourage governments to follow suit and we talk about the benefits that these good policies and practices have brought about for these countries … it's a matter of determining which country you promote that example to.
>
> (per author interview with IDC representative)

They also use multilateral regional consultative processes to forge contacts with government representatives and exert influence on them to ratify and implement human rights treaty provisions. Incremental funds are put into what IDC staff term 'capacity building'. Through their work and that of their members, IDC staff encourage more states to (1) end child detention, (2) set up alternatives to detention, and (3) improve rights and conditions and monitor places of immigration detention.[5] For example, in 2009 US-based NGOs and UNHCR brought IDC together with US Immigration and Customs Enforcement (ICE) at a time when ICE was 'looking for new ways to humanise their detention system' (Hoatson, 2014, p. 13). IDC then helped ICE develop a computer software risk assessment and screening package. Nationally rolled out in January 2013, the detention management tool is used by law enforcement to assess the humanitarian risk and vulnerabilities that merit whether a person should be detained or released. 'Detention', IDC proudly claims 'is now seen by ICE as being reserved for those who really warrant it' (Hoatson, 2014, p. 13).

In addition to this direct governmental advocacy, IDC has been instrumental in network and capacity building around detention under human rights standards. IDC and UNHCR signed an MOU with the aim of joint advocacy and campaigning to 'improve' detention standards through UNHCR's Global Detention Strategy. This collaboration has been inordinately helpful for IDC in securing funding as much as it has cemented the ethical capitalist 'improvement' agenda. As well as enhancing IDC's international presence and ability to participate in international relations, the partnership has allowed for the exponential spread of the human rights ethos in detention regimes. This overlays with the work that IDC does in 'capacity building' with regional NGOs. IDC organises numerous workshops that focus on training NGOs in working with governments around 'improving' detention. For example, in April 2015 IDC organised workshops at the Association of

Southeast Nations (ASEAN) Civil Society Conference. The workshop focused on practical skills-based training with sessions on detention standards and visiting places of detention.

The economisation of immigration detention and human rights is of course an integral part of the neoliberal project. The substitution of NGOs for state punitive policy rule making and the emergence of a market in detention 'improvement' are all hallmarks of intensified financialisation. As 'detention rights' organisations assist in devising and implementing reforms or enter into explicit state contracts they become industrially embedded in detention, functioning, as Gramsci (1971) would have it, as forms of civil society hegemony. 'Intimate economies' illuminates the complex and convoluted relations at play in detention 'improvement' regimes. In IDC's case, their policy work circulates the 'improvement' agenda through governmental networks as much as it helps the organisation find its growth in the detention reformism sector. The next section considers the consequences of detention rights advocacy. It takes a closer look at the expansion of more externalised nodes of the detention 'improvement' complex through the help of rights-based reforms.

The detention industry and the rise of ethical capitalism

The emergence of a fully fledged industry around immigration detention is a recent trend. In response to the growth of immigration detention worldwide, and tendencies towards state privatisation and outsourcing, the 1990s and 2000s saw the eruption of NGOs, INGOs and commercial enterprises focused on immigration detention. Some organisations manage detention centres and their related services. Barnardos, Group 4 Securicor (G4S), Jesuit Refugee Services, Red Cross, Save the Children and Serco are some prominent international players that have operated in the industry. Others, such as IOM, UNHCR and IDC advise or help state agencies 'improve' their immigration detention operations and tasks. There has also been a dramatic influx of organisations and individuals that provide welfare programmes to facilities.

The 'ethical capitalist' vogue of instrumentalising human rights frameworks and cross-sector collaborations is most obvious in the commercial field. Business and humanitarianism now go hand in hand, with both the growth of the ethical business model and the partnerships between firms, INGOs and NGOs. Following the dramatic surge of commercial enterprises worldwide, human rights became an organisational priority for business in the 1990s (Weissbrodt and Kruger, 2003). Concerns had been raised over the destructive effects of businesses, and firms were under pressure to integrate ethics and values into their corporate strategies. Subsequently, international institutions also sought to keep in step with the growth of private businesses, focusing their efforts on ensuring corporate compliance through a number of 'best practice' documents.[6]

The major private firms involved in managing detention centres all have elaborate human rights guidelines, ethical codes and compliance measures in place that draw on international frameworks or their rhetorical power. I spoke with many firms operating across the immigration detention arena. All underlined the importance of these measures. While NGOs have the advantage of emphasising their 'not for profit' status, commercial firms require detailed ethics codes and proof of community engagement for securing successive contracts. Tendering processes are elaborate and competitive. The increase in regulatory scrutiny of controversial working contexts pressures corporations to socially engage and make themselves more accountable. Contracts carry with them extensive clauses devoted to proving regulation and accountability, demonstrating how potential operational risks will be addressed. This helps minimise disruption to company activities, drive productivity rates and fulfil obligations to shareholders. It also provides an ethical gauze to entrenched capitalist practices of confinement.

The effect of this is in full evidence in the immigration detention industry. Serco is the multinational corporation headquartered in the UK that holds the contracts to manage both British and Australian detention centres. The AU$1.67 billion Australian contract is the world's largest single detention contract, covering management of the entirety of Australia's mainland and community detention facilities. Serco runs a number of community-based partnerships, environmental programmes, and 'employee and detainee wellness and engagement initiatives' across its estate, many of which are through its non-profit Serco Foundation launched in 2012.

Other corporate contractors have been more directly involved with human rights frameworks. The private security provider G4S was pivotal in the genesis of the International Code of Conduct for Private Security Service Providers in 2013 (ICoC). Building on the Montreux Document, which focuses on monitoring providers in armed conflicts, the ICoC sets out a series of standards for firms to follow based on international human rights and humanitarian law. G4S cites both their inclusion as an ICoC signatory and recently launched human rights policy and guidance framework – conceived with University of Oxford ethicists – as evidence of their high standards. The framework aims to align the company's human rights practices with the UN Guiding Principles on Business and Human Rights.

This humanitarian turn does not translate to the elimination of violence. In fact, serious incidents have occurred across all of these companies' histories. When it comes to immigration detention, G4S is infamously known for previous involvement in managing Australia's offshored detention centres. Amongst a string of cases, February 2014 saw catastrophic riots at the Manus Island Processing Centre, in which one person was killed and seventy-seven injured with the assistance of G4S and Salvation Army employees (Cornall, 2014). Serco has been plagued by incidents throughout their facilities, from sexual misconduct, riots, self-harm, suicide and preventable deaths to a leaked Serco memo that detailed the escalating 'culture of self harm' (O'Keeffe, 2011). Such problems are not isolated to commercial firms; they can be found amongst all detention and prison managerial contractors: commercial, non-governmental and state. Salvation Army is but one high profile example of a 'philanthropic' organisation operating in detention that encountered a wave of problems before the loss of their Australian contract in 2014. A number of other NGOs run the many community detention models upheld by rights institutions as 'humane' alternatives. Despite instrumentalising the rhetoric and imagery of humanitarianism, I found throughout my fieldwork that self-harm and mental health issues also continued in these NGO-run 'alternative detention' models.

Unfortunately, incidents like these are testament to the fact that despite even the best of intentions to soften the impacts of their work, the context in which these organisations operate can only ever lead to human abuse and suffering. As has oft been pointed out, humanitarian work that aims to alleviate suffering can instead paradoxically sustain the action that causes it and often do more harm than good (Terry, 2002). Yet rather than addressing detention and immigration policies as the cause of these harms, governments and rights rule makers emphasise and profit from constructing mitigational strategies as a solution.

The politics of academic authority

As I have argued, the ascendancy of human rights policies and rhetorical frameworks has allowed for, and been a part of, a detention improvement industry. NGO and commercial enterprises are essential to these reforms. But, in tandem with NGO and corporate mechanisms of governance, it is important to recognise that the emergence and consolidation of detention rights policies are also advanced through academic expertise. A brief analysis of the neoliberal shifts within academic institutions and formation of scholarly detention networks illustrate these moves. In addition to assisting in the legal construction of human rights standards, academics conduct 'improvement' interventions themselves or help enhance organisational credentials. In elaborating the transatlantic dissemination of the prison as commonsense institution, Wacquant (1999, p. 344) refers to a 'scholarly whitewash' and 'politological pidgin', whereby dramatic discourses around criminality and penal rigour are academicised and fed into the logic of bureaucratic intervention. In studying the authority of scientific expertise in risk regulation, Jasanoff (1990) finds that expert elicitation is a common practice in the absence of sufficient data. Governments often attempt to shield fundamentally political choices behind the findings of technical experts. Just as scientific facts are constructed through assemblages of authority (Latour, 1987), academic alliances help extend and stabilise the ideological precedence of governing rationalities. In recent years these trends have been extended into the immigration detention context.

Immigration detention 'improvements' have been given sustained academic focus. A large body of research calls for the need to remedy the inhumane and everyday banality of detention in line with international human rights standards. This is combined with a legal positivist scholarship that incorporates a human rights analysis. Such research evaluates national laws and policies and urges legal realignment with international human rights norms and obligations. Others have extended these detention 'improvement' moves concretely by conducting research projects in detention centres with state border agencies. They marry academic data collection with policy recommendations for operational 'improvements'. Such reformist approaches or, as Garland (1985) terms it, 'penal welfare complexes', are often an intrinsic part of criminology and social work-based disciplines, many of which are governed by state-defined policy frameworks and have a history of institutional engagement. However, new modes of governance have also affected the production of knowledge in academic environments (Walters, 2003). Neoliberalism's market-based reforms have driven an intellectual shift as academics are increasingly subject to research performance management. This academic corporatism results in economically advantageous choices for what is taught and who teaches it. It leads to calls for 'public engagement' and 'application', whereby academics must sell themselves and their universities as being of public utility. Throughout my fieldwork, I found that researchers enhance their institutional and personal credibility through the marketability of immigration detention research. Detention research is a valuable commodity, particularly when it produces information from *inside* institutions. As a result, a certain kind of knowledge is produced about immigration governance and policies that aligns with dominant interests of reform not rollback. Ending detention is marginalised as radical or idealistic.

Collaborations between organisations and academics are an important part of strengthening immigration detention 'improvement' agendas. Commercial partnerships with universities, policy think-tanks that function as covert commercial impact enterprises, and evidence-based research commissioned by government agencies are all strategies used for legitimating or 'improving' immigration detention systems. In the international detention rights field, IDC heads the NGO-academic 'improvement' movement. IDC focuses on bringing together an academic network of researchers and institutes working on detention. The Coalition engages academics in writing briefing papers that proclaim the effectiveness of detention 'improvement' measures and are used in their lobbying work with governments. In an interview, an IDC official explained:

> I've been asking around and getting a list of academics that are working in the detention space ... big names, these sorts of folks ... I've already reached out to a number of these individuals and/or organisations to say hey we want to work with you ... join us in writing briefing papers ... So we're going to be putting out one briefing paper a month. And I've got about five or six academics lined up at the moment that are interested in working with us on various aspects ... the plan is to turn them into policy documents and use them in our government engagement.
>
> (per author interview with IDC representative)

According to IDC, the academic hook proves an effective means of leveraging policy makers and strengthening the improvement complex. It is an essential part of 'laying the foundations for all the work we do for government engagement to this day' (IDC personal interview, 2014). The neoliberalisation of detention 'improvements' is still in its infancy and certainly not always a neatly aligned process. Calling into question seemingly benign 'ethical' rules and practices shores up the complex relations underpinning 'intimate economies'.

Conclusion

Neil Smith (2007, p. 3) referred to the 'mitigation industry' to describe the development of new markets focused on ameliorating environmental destruction. He detailed how the production of nature entered an additional phase of 'green capitalism' that opened up more powerful spaces of accumulation. Rather than an anti-capitalist movement, liberal environmentalism deepens the penetration of nature by capital, operating as an industrialised system in and of itself, but also providing the highly profitable energy industry with the presentational appeal of environmentalism. This chapter argues that immigration detention 'improvements' do not represent a disjuncture from dominant political strategies of governance. Instead, they parallel the trend of global capitalism to adopt more creative and bipartisan modes of accumulation. This ethical industry and moral veneer is unlikely to transform global politics and capitalist dynamics in ways that might foster more meaningful social change.

In considering the emergence of institutional overlap around the detention industry, this chapter suggests that scholarship has not gone far enough in unpacking the extent of non-state actors involved in performing state functions and critically assessing the implications of human rights–based policies on detention's expansion. The footprints of market capital extend far beyond contracted organisations but into the halls of human rights rule makers and markets. Bringing together global governance and human rights frameworks is an important means of moving towards an actor network approach that reconceptualises the complexity of human and material assemblages involved in detention reforms. It is also a key step in assessing how we as academics play a part in the industrialisation and professionalisation of detention and 'ethical capitalist' frameworks. Academic scholarship certainly plays a role in this 'production of "illegality"' (De Genova, 2002, p. 419), helping cement governmental categorisations both discursively and through more direct policy and legislative enhancement. Rather than questioning how discursive formations serve as mechanisms of governance, academics can overly fetishise the law and instead legitimise the expansion of detention states.

While some see advocating for 'improved' conditions in detention as a step towards humanising and ending detention, this chapter has argued that rights-centred reforms, on the contrary, enhance and are themselves opportunities for capital accumulation. As Davis (2003) and others have warned when discussing the 'prison industrial complex' and 'double-edged sword' of prison reform (Feeley and Rubin, 2000), generating changes that produce a better incarceration system can instead contribute to its bureaucratisation and financialisation. Calls to 'improve' can reinforce a situation where development and market-based reforms become an alternative to addressing the structural problems undergirding incarceration systems themselves. Rather than concentrating on the expansion of immigration control, detention reforms help in their regulation and create additional profit opportunities for an 'improvement' complex of human rights rule makers, investment, and infrastructure projects.

An array of state and non-state actors converge under the rationality of 'improvement'. As well as building a vast, inescapable industry, state and non-state actors profit from and disseminate the reformist ethos by making recommendations for facility 'improvements', asserting the high standards of their organisational services or advocating for and legally codifying human rights norms. 'Ethical capitalism' may be promoted as a means of softening the destructive impacts of capitalist development or criticised as a humane facade for unrelenting exploitation. Yet, in either case, human rights frameworks and institutions have had a significant impact on providing capital with an opportunity to profit from both human incarceration and its mitigation. Taken together, all of this work has helped to strengthen governance by putting institutional machinery in place that establishes more investment conditions for the detention 'improvement' enterprise.

Notes

1 The UN Working Group on Arbitrary Detention, Committee on Prevention of Torture and other Cruel, Inhuman or Degrading Treatment (CPT), the Special Rapporteur on torture and other cruel, inhuman or degrading treatment or punishment, the Subcommittee on Prevention of Torture and other Cruel, Inhuman or Degrading Treatment (SPT), and the NGO, the Association for the Prevention of Torture (APT) are some of the many international bodies that focus on monitoring conditions and the proportionality of people's detention. If states have ratified the Optional Protocol to the Convention against Torture (OPCAT), national monitoring bodies are also established. Many states now have Ombudsman monitoring bodies in place, often trained or advocated for by European human rights institutions and state governments.
2 'Service provider' is the terminology commonly used by many governments and organisations themselves to denote any outsourced supplier of provisions or management, irrespective of their commercial or non-profit status.
3 See for example a description of the Australian government's funding of detention standards in Indonesia with the help of IOM and UNHCR (Nethery, Rafferty-Brown and Taylor, 2013) and U.S. Immigration and Customs Enforcement 'Performance-Based National Detention Standards' (2011).
4 $AU 1.00 = $US 0.70 or GBP £0.49 (currency exchange calculated 24 January 2016).
5 See Gill (2013) and Klein and Williams (2012) for a critique of 'detention alternatives'. These normally encompass electronic monitoring systems or securitised community detention models. Gill argues that these are forms of 'punitive mobility' that give illusions of freedom, yet are run by the same industry actors as detention facilities.
6 See for example the United Nations Global Compact and the UN Sub-Commission on the Promotion and Protection of Human Rights 'Norms on the Responsibilities of Transnational Corporations and Other Business Enterprises with Regard to Human Rights' (2003).

References

Ashutosh, I. and Mountz, A. 2011. Migration management for the benefit of whom? Interrogating the work of the International Organization for Migration. *Citizenship Studies* **15**(4), pp. 21–38.
Barry, A. 2004. Ethical capitalism. In: Larner, W. and Walter, W. eds. *Global governmentality: governing international spaces*. New York: Routledge, pp. 195–211.

Barry, A. Osborne, T. and Rose, N.S. eds. 1996. *Foucault and political reason: liberalism, neo-liberalism, and rationalities of government*. Chicago: University of Chicago Press.

Brown, W. 2003. Neo-liberalism and the end of liberal democracy. *Theory and Event* **7**(1), pp. 1–29.

Cornall, R. 2014. Review into the events of 16-18 February 2014 at the Manus Regional Processing Centre. Report to the Secretary, Department of Immigration and Border Protection. 23 May 2014. [Online]. Available from: www.border.gov.au/ReportsandPublications/Documents/reviews-and-inquiries/review-robert-cornall.pdf [Accessed 30 November 2014].

Cornelisse, G. 2010. *Immigration detention and human rights: rethinking territorial sovereignty*. Boston: Martinus Nijhoff Publishers.

Dardot, P. and Laval, C. 2014. *The new way of the world: on neoliberal society*. New York: Verso.

Davis, A. 2003. *Are prisons obsolete?* New York: Seven Stories Press.

De Genova, N.P. 2002. Migrant 'illegality' and deportability in everyday life. *Annual Review of Anthropology* **31**(1), pp. 419–47.

Duffield, M. 2001. *Global governance and the new wars: the merging of development and security*. London: Zed Books.

Fassin, D. and Rechtman, R. 2009. *The empire of trauma: an inquiry into the condition of victimhood*. Princeton: Princeton University Press.

Feeley, M.M. and Rubin, E.L. 2000. *Judicial policy making and the modern state: how the courts reformed America's prisons*. Cambridge: Cambridge University Press.

Flynn, M. 2013. Be careful what you wish for. *Forced Migration Review* [Online]. Available from: www.fmreview.org/detention/flynn [Accessed 10 February 2016].

Foucault, M. 1991. Governmentality. In: Burchell, G., Gordon, C. and Miller, P. eds. *The Foucault effect: studies in governmentality*. Chicago: University of Chicago Press, pp. 87–104.

Garland, D. 1985. *Punishment and welfare: a history of penal strategies*. Gower: Ashgate Press.

Gill, N. 2013. Mobility versus liberty? The punitive uses of movement within and outside carceral environments. In: Moran, D., Gill, N. and Conlon, D. eds. *Carceral spaces: mobility and agency in migrant detention*. Farnham: Ashgate, pp. 19–35.

Gramsci, A. 1971. *Selections from the prison notebooks*. Translated by Q. Hoare and G. Nowell Smith. New York: International Publishers.

Hall, S. 2011. The neo-liberal revolution. *Cultural Studies* **25**(6), pp. 705–28.

Hiemstra, N. 2013. 'You don't even know where you are': chaotic geographies of US migrant detention and deportation. In: Conlon, D., Gill, N. and Moran, D. eds. *Carceral spaces: mobility and agency in migrant detention*. Farnham: Ashgate, pp. 57–76.

Hoatson, L. 2014. Evaluating the impact of the International Detention Coalition [Online]. Available from: http://idcoalition.org/wp-content/uploads/2014/12/IDC-Evaluation-2014.pdf [Accessed 15 December 2014].

Hopgood, S. 2008. Saying 'no' to Wal-Mart? Money and morality in professional humanitarianism. In: Barnett, M. and Weiss, T.G. eds. *Humanitarianism in question: politics, power, ethics*. Ithaca: Cornell University Press, pp. 98–123.

International Detention Coalition. 2011a. IDC Member Report [Online]. Available from: http://idcoalition.org/wp-content/uploads/2015/07/IDC12-Annual-Report-v5-Web-1.pdf [Accessed 15 January 2014].

International Detention Coalition. 2011b. Legal framework and standards relating to the detention of refugees, asylum seekers and migrants [Online]. Available from: http://idcoalition.org/wp-content/uploads/2011/07/IDC-Legal-Detention-Framework-Guide_Final.pdf [Accessed 15 January 2014].

International Detention Coalition. 2014. IDC Member Report [Online]. Available from: http://idcoalition.org/publications/2014-annual-report/ [Accessed 15 January 2014].

Jasanoff, S. 1990. *The fifth branch: science advisers as policymakers.* Cambridge: Harvard University Press.

Klein, A. and Williams, L. 2012. Immigration detention in the community: research on the experiences of migrants released from detention centres in the UK. *Population, Space and Place* **18**(6), pp. 741–53.

Latour, B. 1987. *Science in action: how to follow scientists and engineers through society.* Cambridge: Harvard University Press.

Morris, J. 2016. Forthcoming. Power, capital and immigration detention rights: making networked markets in global detention governance at UNHCR. *Global Networks.* Available from: http://onlinelibrary.wiley.com/doi/10.1111/glob.12124/full.

Nethery, A. Rafferty-Brown, B. and Taylor, S. 2013. Exporting detention: Australia-funded immigration detention in Indonesia. *Journal of Refugee Studies* **26**, pp. 88–109.

O'Keeffe, P. 2011. Nightmare on Christmas Island: Serco's Australian Detention Center. CorpWatch [Online]. Available from: www.corpwatch.org/article.php?id=15664 [Accessed 20 April 2014].

Rhodes, R.A.W. 1994. The hollowing out of the state: the changing nature of the public service in Britain. *The Political Quarterly* **65**(2), pp. 138–51.

Riles, A. 2011. *Collateral knowledge: legal reasoning in the global financial markets.* Chicago: University of Chicago Press.

Smith, N. 2007. Nature as accumulation strategy. *Socialist Register* **43**, pp. 19–41.

Terry, F. 2002. *Condemned to repeat? The paradox of humanitarian action.* Ithaca: Cornell University Press.

Ticktin, M. 2014. Transnational humanitarianism. *Annual Review of Anthropology* **43**, pp. 273–89.

Tyler, I., Gill, N., Conlon, D. and Oeppen, C. 2014. The business of child detention: charitable co-option, migrant advocacy and activist outrage. *Race & Class* **56**(1), pp. 3–21.

United Nations High Commissioner for Refugees. 2012. Detention guidelines: guidelines on the applicable criteria and standards relating to the detention of asylum-seekers and alternatives to detention [Online]. Available from: www.unhcr.org/505b10ee9.html [Accessed 15 January 2014].

United Nations Treaty Series. Convention relating to the status of refugees. Geneva, 28 July 1951 [Online]. Available from: www.refworld.org/docid/3be01b964.html [Accessed 25 January 2016].

US Immigration and Customs Enforcement. 2011. Performance-based national detention standards [Online]. Available from: www.ice.gov/doclib/detention-standards/2011/pbnds2011.pdf [Accessed 30 March 2014].

Wacquant, L. 1999. How penal common sense comes to Europeans. *European Societies* **1**(3), pp. 319–52.

Wallace, T. 2003. NGO dilemmas: Trojan horses for global neoliberalism? *Socialist Register* **40**, pp. 202–19.

Walters, R. 2003. *Deviant knowledge: criminology, politics and policy.* Cullumpton: Willan Publishing.

Weissbrodt, D. and Kruger, M. 2003. Human rights responsibilities of businesses as non-state actors. In: Alston, P. eds. *Non-state actors and human rights.* New York: Oxford University Press, pp. 315–50.

Wilsher, D. 2011. *Immigration detention: law, history, politics.* Cambridge: Cambridge University Press.

5 Bearing witness and the intimate economies of immigration detention centres in Australia

Caroline Fleay

There are multiple private contractors with lucrative contracts to provide services in Australian funded immigration detention centres. These sites, located within Australia and offshore on Nauru and Papua New Guinea's Manus Island, detain those who arrive to Australia without a valid visa on an indefinite basis. The vast majority are asylum seekers who arrive by boat, detained under Australia's mandatory detention policy.

This chapter highlights some aspects of the intimate economies of privatisation in the immigration detention network in Australia through exploring visits to immigration detention centres by those independent of the system. I draw in particular on my visits to the Curtin Immigration Detention Centre (IDC) in the remote northwest of Australia throughout 2011. Encounters with contracted organisations and their employees during these visits are highlighted to explore the complexities of the privatisation of operations in a detention environment. I emphasise the critical importance of 'bearing witness', which refers to attending to and acting in response to the experiences of another, with a focus on the acts of some private contractor employees who enable visitors to bear witness as well as those employees who bear witness themselves.

This chapter's perspective on intimate economies of immigration detention helps to explore impacts of privatisation at the individual level that have not yet been interrogated, including the development of relationships between people who are detained and those employed within the detention network, and those who visit. Including a focus on the people employed to carry out 'the daily work' of the state also helps to interrogate assumptions that the state is a 'coherent body politic' (Mountz, 2004, p. 326) by highlighting the role played by employees' perceptions and actions in how state policy is experienced by those detained (Bosworth, 2014; Hall, 2010; Hiemstra, 2014).

For the visitor to a remote site of immigration detention, intimacy is an apt word given how few people independent of the immigration system are able to get to these sites and the intensity of the sense of isolation from the broader community that is experienced by those detained. Intimacy is often understood

> as a quality emergent from intense, long-standing interpersonal connection. Intimacy requires, as necessary conditions, long periods of face-to-face contact;

expressions of affect; and the mutual disclosure of a person's emotional state, desires, dreams, and individual life story.

(McKay, 2006, pp. 476–77)

Here I use 'intimate' to describe relationships in IDCs that may develop in a shorter space of time than the usage of the term outlined above suggests. Intimacy can emerge from a connection and emotional engagement with another when visiting an IDC. Given the isolation of remote detention centres, the presence of relatively few independent visitors, and the sense of urgency that may be experienced when the mental harm of indefinite and long-term detention becomes acute, intimacy can emerge relatively quickly. There may also be less of a mutual disclosure in the development of this intimacy, given there is usually a much stronger need for those detained to disclose their emotional state than those who are not. A sense of intimacy and commitment can develop between the visitor and some of those detained. It can also develop between an employee and those detained.

This chapter's exploration of the intimate economies of privatisation commences with an overview of the mandatory detention policy in Australia and the limits of independent monitoring within the detention network. This is followed by a discussion of the privatisation of detention operations and its implications beyond the intimate. Independent visits to detention centres are then explored as a form of monitoring that can be understood as bearing witness, as well as some of the implications of the privatisation of detention centre operations on acts of bearing witness that were evident during visits to the Curtin IDC. This includes the enabling acts of bearing witness by some of the private contractor employees as well as their own such actions.

Mandatory detention in Australia and the limits of monitoring

Australia has a legal and policy framework that allows for the indefinite immigration detention of non-citizens who arrive to the country without a valid visa. Mandatory detention was enshrined via 1992 legislation in response to asylum seekers coming to Australia by boat. It was intended to act as a deterrent for future asylum seekers and effectively discriminates between asylum seekers arriving by boat and those by plane (Viviani, 1996, pp. 20–1). Mandatory detention continues to allow all asylum seekers arriving without a valid visa to be detained until their protection claims are finalised, unless the Minister for Immigration exercises his/her discretion under this legislation to allow for their earlier release. For thousands of asylum seekers detained over the past twenty years, this has meant long periods of indefinite detention in prison-like conditions in facilities established by the Australian Government, both within Australia and on Nauru and Manus Island.[1] Research highlights that long-term immigration detention has resulted in despair and mental health issues, including incidences of self-harm and some suicides, and that the treatment of such anguish in detention is largely futile (Newman et al., 2013; Silove et al., 2001; Steel et al., 2004).

Many of these sites are in remote locations and there is limited monitoring provided by formal state and non-state bodies across this detention network that is systematic, transparent and independent. There are also few civil society groups and individuals with the capacity to assume a monitoring role given the financial resources needed to engage in systematic monitoring by organisations independent of the government. Other barriers to monitoring include the reliance on the Australian Government and its contracted managers to gain access to sites of detention and the added barrier of territorial sovereignty for bodies seeking access to sites of detention on Nauru and Manus Island. Confidentiality conditions further inhibit some forms of monitoring, such as the confidentiality agreements that the members of the Minister for Immigration's advisory group on detention sign with the Australian government. This group provides advice to the Minister and the Department of Immigration on how conditions and policies of detention should be improved and the confidentiality agreements mean the group's members are limited in their capacity to make their concerns public (Fleay, 2015).

The lack of systematic, transparent and independent monitoring of Australia's immigration detention network elevates the role of others who can gain access to IDCs, including independent visitors. They can play a monitoring role through gaining access to a detention centre, developing relationships with those detained and responding to what it is they are witnessing. However, given the privatisation of many operations within the Australian detention network, the act of visiting includes having to navigate the procedures and practices of a government department as well as multiple private contractors.

Privatisation of immigration detention in Australia

The privatisation of a range of operations within Australia's immigration detention network since 1997 has had impacts at the intimate level and beyond. At the broader level, privatisation has facilitated an expansion of the detention network. Detention centre management functions have been outsourced since 1997 to private corporations in all Australian funded sites of detention. Corporations with particularly lucrative contracts include Serco Australia, which has been responsible for the management operations of all of the IDCs in Australia since 2009. By 2013 its immigration detention contracts with the Australian Government totalled $1.8 billion (Hall, 2013). In February 2014 the Australian Government awarded Transfield Services, another private corporation, a 20-month $1.2 billion contract to provide support and welfare services on Nauru and Manus Island (Australian Stock Exchange, 2014).

Other functions within the detention network that are contracted and subcontracted to a range of operators are health, catering, cleaning and security services. Contractors include International Health and Medical Services, which provides health services throughout the detention network, and non-government organisations such as the Salvation Army (until February 2014) and Save the Children Fund, who have provided humanitarian support services in the detention facilities on Nauru and Manus Island. Other non-government organisations have also been contracted to provide mental health support services in IDCs in Australia.

Over the past four years, Serco, Transfield and other contracted organisations have acted to provide the capacity for greater numbers of asylum seekers to be held in prison-like conditions at the times when the Australian Government sought to expand its immigration detention network. For example, in attempts to address the mental harm that results when people are detained on an indefinite basis for long periods of time, or at least be seen to address it, the Australian Government has been able to contract International Health and Medical Services and non-government organisations instead of closing the detention centres to remove the source of the distress. This highlights the Australian Government's dependence on the services that such organisations can provide in order to implement its detention policy (Loewenstein, 2013, p. 15).

That non-government organisations are willing to provide health and welfare services within the immigration detention network, despite the increasing number of reports that highlight the harmful impacts of long-term immigration detention on mental health, also reflects the neoliberal political and economic contexts within which these organisations navigate. For some non-government organisations, government contracts significantly contribute to their economic viability. But the consequences of accepting government funding can impact the ability and willingness of these organisations to criticise the government policy landscape they work within.

This was illustrated in the Australian context in a 2004 survey of 290 non-government organisations. Seventy per cent of organisations surveyed that received government funding noted that this 'at times restricts their ability to comment on government policy' and many reported they faced 'implicit pressure to censure themselves' (Maddison and Hamilton, 2007, pp. 91–2). Ninety per cent of the organisations surveyed also believed 'that dissenting organisations risk having their funding cut' (Maddison and Hamilton, 2007, p. 95). Kamat observed a similar 'process of professionalisation and depoliticisation of [non-government organisations] at the grassroots' in a range of countries and points to the neoliberal policy context as the main cause (2004, p. 167).

A more recent survey of advocacy and support non-government organisations in the UK highlights a similar story. The study found that accepting government funding in an effort to secure economic viability serves to divert 'resources away from oppositional forms of practice' (Tyler et al., 2014, p. 4). In relation to accepting contracts to provide services within the immigration detention network, research participants reported that this was 'fundamentally eroding the capacity of advocacy organisations to effectively protest the deleterious effect of border-control mechanisms on migrants' lives' (Tyler et al., 2014, p. 4). It is likely that this is also the case for non-government organisations in Australia that currently accept government funding.

Scrutiny of the economic realm at close range highlights other significant impacts of privatisation in the immigration detention network. At the intimate level, privatisation has added another layer of procedural complexity for independent visitors to IDCs and their efforts to bear witness.

Independent visiting as an act of bearing witness

Visits from individuals who are independent of the immigration detention system can provide a form of monitoring and be understood as an act of bearing witness to the impacts of mandatory detention. Bearing witness involves attending to the expressions of the experiences of another, and using this as a starting point for action (Cody, 2001).

> Witnessing has both personal and political consequences for those who are unable to enjoy human rights. Firstly, it reassures such persons that they have not been abandoned. Secondly, witnessing acts as testimony from which action can begin.
>
> (Zion et al., 2012, p. 73)

Witnessing an abuse thus means to become responsible for taking action in response (Peters, 2001, p. 708).

This implies that a commitment has been made to those who are in detention that some form of action will be taken in response to what is witnessed. Such a commitment suggests a sense of felt-responsibility, an emotional response that propels an imperative to take action on behalf of people whose ability to do so is severely limited. This is an understanding of emotions as being 'central to reason' and an important component of decision making as they can 'help us to identify injustices' and propel us to act in response (Jeffery, 2011, pp. 143, 173).

The development of intimacy that can accompany visits to an IDC, particularly one that is in a remote location, resonates with Mammad Aidani's (2013) observations on conducting research with refugees. He argues that 'one must commit to the other by "having the other-in-one's-skin"' (Levinas, 1999, p. 161, quoted in Aidani, 2013, p. 213). The decision to commit is based on an emotional response to sitting and listening to the experiences of those detained in a remote IDC. Similar to Richard Rorty's argument that listening to 'sad and sentimental stories' can move us to action (2001, p. 257), a sense of intimacy and moral outrage, 'an action-orientated emotion', can rapidly develop (Thomas and McGarty, 2009, p. 119). This can be accompanied by a commitment that deepens with further visits, and a continuous reflection on what actions should be taken in response to what is witnessed. This includes a consideration of what forms of action are likely to broaden this sphere of felt-responsibility (Tait, 2011, p. 1227).

While such visits can provide an opportunity for an additional form of immigration detention monitoring, they are not without ethical concerns. The findings of studies that reflect on the ethics of research with refugees or detainees are instructive here. For example, how the researcher (or visitor) understands detention experiences given issues of language, culture and gender needs to be considered (Bosworth, 2014, p. 84), as well as how asylum seekers are represented (Cody, 2001).

Relationships between visitors and those detained can also be characterised by imbalances of power. However, visitors who bear witness can offer a form of agency to people in detention who, while often incredibly resilient, are deprived of much of their agency by the detention system (Fleay and Briskman, 2013).

Bearing witness is a collaborative endeavour. Intimate relationships involving trust, commitment and regular communication can develop between the visitor and some of those detained. These relationships can further deepen the visitor's sense of felt-responsibility to advocate on behalf of these individuals, in addition to actions taken on behalf of the collective. It can also involve collaborative acts with some of those employed within the IDC who similarly experience emotional responses and act in a manner consistent with this understanding of bearing witness.

Along with a number of others from outside the detention system, I spent many hours visiting the remotely located Curtin IDC throughout 2011 (see Figure 5.1). Situated 2,300 kilometres north of Perth, the city where most of Western Australia's population resides, this site detained up to 1,400 men at any one time throughout 2011.[2] All were asylum seekers who arrived to Australia by boat. Many were held for more than 18 months behind the large electrified fences of IDCs, most of this time at Curtin (see Figure 5.2). During this time there were very few visitors to the IDC who were independent of the Department of Immigration and the multiple private contractors. My first visit was in January with friends and refugee advocates Nina Boydell and Ishaq Ali Mohammadi, as Ishaq knew some of the men detained at Curtin. Over three days we remained inside the IDC each day for periods between four to eight hours.

Figure 5.1 The long road leading to Curtin Immigration Detention Centre: the entrance is just beyond the horizon (January 2011)

Source: Author

It was a profound experience. The isolation of the place meant that the 1,200 men it held at that time were largely hidden from the rest of Australia. The gratitude expressed by hundreds who came to talk with us during those few days was very moving and their obvious isolation from regular visitors and legal support was alarming. At this time, all of the men detained at Curtin IDC had fled Afghanistan and most were members of the long-persecuted Hazara ethnic group. Hundreds approached us with many questions about Australian asylum seeker policies, what life was like in Australia and if we knew when their refugee claim would be processed.

The intensity of this visit was such that we all returned for a visit spanning seven days later that year and maintained regular contact with some of the men detained by email and telephone. I returned for three other visits throughout the year, each involving many hours inside the IDC over four-day periods, two of these with fellow academic Linda Briskman. These visits informed a research project that explored the impacts of immigration detention on those detained at Curtin IDC through adopting an ethnographical approach and interviews with some of the men after their release.

Up until the last visit in November 2011, when access to the men detained became much more restricted, we were able to spend many hours inside the detention centre at a table under one of the few trees in the main compound, talking with whoever wished to join us while a Serco employee sat nearby but usually out of earshot. On several of the earlier visits, a Department of Immigration official escorted us on a 'tour' of the detention centre. Men from Afghanistan, and then from Pakistan, Iran and Sri Lanka as the year progressed, would tell us during our visits about how worried they were for their families who remained in dangerous or insecure circumstances. Many asked for assistance with understanding written communications they had received from the Department of Immigration about their refugee claim. Some of the men we got to know well and who had strong English language skills became interpreters for others. As the year progressed, the deterioration of the mental and physical health of many men became painfully evident with each visit. By early 2012, most of the men who had been detained at Curtin IDC for more than 18 months had been released and recognised as refugees. Some of them requested that I more fully document their detention experiences upon their release and interviews were subsequently conducted (Fleay and Briskman, 2013).

Actions we took as a result of what we witnessed and were told included disseminating our concerns about the impacts of lengthening periods of immigration detention to the Minister for Immigration, Members of Parliament, parliamentary inquiries, the media, public forums and refugee advocacy groups. It also included providing emotional and advocacy support to those detained with whom we developed close relationships.

Privatisation and access to bear witness

In addition to the extensive interactions with the men detained, we had multiple interactions with a range of private contractor employees and the occasional Department of Immigration official. An independent visitor has to navigate a web of government and private contractor procedures, as described below, in order to gain and maintain access with those detained. Visiting also involves negotiating the discretionary practices of primarily the private contractor employees. While some employees exercised their discretion to further enable visitors' acts of bearing witness, and engaged in such acts themselves, throughout 2011 the procedural web that accompanies privatisation served to further distance those detained from independent visitors.

Most of our interaction with procedures and employees at Curtin IDC centred around access. Visitors have to negotiate the entry procedures of the detention system as well as engage with private contractor employees to gain and maintain access. In 2011, gaining access to Curtin IDC involved first faxing a completed Serco Visitor Form outlining our contact details and the names of men we wished to visit, and then making phone calls until visit approval was confirmed.

Entry procedures upon arriving at Curtin IDC included passing through multiple checkpoints where our photo identification and visit booking would be checked. After placing most of our belongings in a locker, including mobile phones and cameras, those items we were permitted to take into the detention centre, as well as ourselves, were scanned through security screening machines. Then we would be escorted to a visiting area in the main detention compound with a Serco employee who would sit nearby until they were relieved by another employee. Although the length of time these procedures took and what we were allowed to take into the IDC depended on the discretion of who was working in this area at the time, entry procedures remained largely consistent throughout the year.

Figure 5.2 Looking through the fences surrounding the main compound of the Curtin Immigration Detention Centre (January 2011)

Source: Author

What varied considerably were the procedures and exercise of employee discretion once inside the detention centre. As the year wore on, the extent of access inside Curtin IDC became increasingly restricted. For example, by September 2011 restrictions were placed on the numbers of hours visitors could stay in the detention centre. Prior to this, visits could last much of the day and into the evening inside the main detention centre compound. In September we were told by Serco employees in the entrance building that we would need to leave the IDC during lunch hours, despite having brought lunch to share with those detained who had become our friends. Restrictions were also imposed on how late we could stay inside the main compound during morning and afternoon visits. It was difficult to determine whether the Department of Immigration or Serco led the restrictions, and to what extent they were the result of the discretionary practices of Serco employees who were responsible for implementing access procedures.

By November access procedures had dramatically changed. This followed media reports on the impacts of long-term immigration detention in Australia, including at Curtin IDC (for example, see ABC, 2011), growing concerns expressed by monitoring bodies and refugee advocates, and increasing protests within IDCs. It was not until we arrived at the IDC that we were told we would not be allowed to enter the main compound and sit where anyone could come and speak with us. Instead, we were taken to a room outside the main compound and only some of the few men whose names we had included on our Visitor Form were arranged to join us. When we challenged this, and on the second day presented Serco employees with a list of 70 names of others who also wished to visit with us, we were told that we should have let Serco know prior to our visit that we wished to speak with so many. Despite pointing out that we could not have done so given we had no knowledge of the procedure change, access continued to be restricted in this way throughout the four days of the visit. This was distressing for us and we were told by the few we were permitted to visit that the others who had missed out were upset at being denied the opportunity of spending time with some of the few visitors to the IDC.

On at least some occasions, it appeared that restrictions of access were driven by either Serco management procedures or the discretionary practices of Serco employees, rather than directives from the Department of Immigration. For example, during one visit I was asked by one of the men detained I had gotten to know well to meet with him and his migration agent just prior to his Independent Merits Review interview. The outcome of this interview would determine whether the negative decision issued by the Department of Immigration six months earlier on his refugee claim would be upheld or not. My friend was highly anxious leading up to this interview and a Department of Immigration official agreed with our request that I could meet with him and his migration agent for one hour prior to the interview to help him prepare.

Upon arrival at the entrance building to the IDC the next morning, the Serco employees on shift were sympathetic to my request and, following their procedure, asked their manager to grant me permission to attend the meeting.

This was declined despite my explanation of prior approval. After more than 40 minutes, approval was gained following the intervention of an employee of another private contractor who enabled my contact with the IDC Department of Immigration manager, who then contacted Serco management. I was finally escorted through the entrance by another Serco employee but then told the meeting was being held in a distant part of the complex and that a vehicle was not available to get me there. Understanding my predicament, he allowed me to run unaccompanied along a road next to the main compound to make the meeting, contrary to procedures that visitors were to be escorted.

When I arrived where the meeting was to be held, a Serco employee allowed me to join my friend and his migration agent and left us alone. After ten minutes, however, the Serco employee returned and said that I did not have permission to be there and asked me to leave. My explanation of having permission was not accepted and I asked him to give me a few more minutes given the distress that my friend was in with his review interview about to commence. Several minutes later, the Serco employee returned and informed me that I did have permission after all and so I remained until my friend commenced his interview to help try to calm him.[3]

This example, and the tightening restrictions on access inside the IDC, illustrates how the web of procedures and discretionary practices of employees of an operational system that involves government and multiple private contractors can work to further distance those detained from independent visitors. While some private contractor employees were willing to exercise their discretion to further enable access on some occasions, others acted consistent with tightening procedures or used their discretion to impede access beyond procedural limits. Access was ultimately gained and maintained in relation to my friend's meeting; however, it involved a bewildering and time-consuming series of encounters with private contractor employees about procedures that were mostly unclear. Interviews with some of the men upon their release illustrate further examples of such confounding procedures and practices and the distressing impacts they can have on those detained (see Fleay and Briskman, 2013).

Ascertaining what the procedures actually were inside the Curtin IDC, and who had responsibility for establishing them, remained a challenge in the face of such variable practices, even when a Serco employee offered us an explanation about restrictions placed on access. This resonates with studies into privately operated prisons that highlight how accountability issues can be confounded when there is a complex web of operational contracting and subcontracting (Bacon, 2005, p. 24). A Human Rights and Equal Opportunity Commission report into the investigation of the treatment of children in immigration detention raised similar concerns after both the Department of Immigration and the private company contracted to operate many of Australia's IDCs attempted to avoid responsibility when reports of human rights abuses emerged (2004). Restricted levels of transparency due to privatisation within the immigration detention network are also evident beyond the intimate level. Commercial-in-confidence clauses in contracts between the Australian Government and contracted organisations mean that it is exceedingly difficult to access information in relation to costs and other operational matters (Loewenstein, 2013, pp. 14–24).

That a number of procedures, and the discretionary practices of some private contractor employees, impeded the access of those detained to several of the very few visitors to Curtin IDC highlights that the men's needs were not prioritised in these decisions. While there is little research into the privatised operations in Australian IDCs, studies into social service contracting that suggest 'the rights of individuals are overwritten by profit margins' and concerns for compliance may be instructive here (Kandasamy and Soldatic, 2016, forthcoming). Reports of worker unrest within Australian IDCs suggest cost minimisation practices within Serco operations (ABC News, 2014), as do reports from 2011 that employee numbers in IDCs remained relatively constant despite increasing numbers of asylum seekers being detained (Loewenstein, 2013, p. 18). The impacts of this were evident to at least some of the men detained at Curtin IDC who told us that the demeanour of employees would generally harden towards the end of their lengthy rostered weeks on site. However, it was also evident that some private contractor employees at Curtin IDC were willing to go beyond such constraints and exercise their discretion to collaborate with those detained, and sometimes with visitors, in acts of bearing witness.

Private contractor employees and bearing witness

Some private contractor employees enabled our attempts to bear witness. Such discretionary practices included a collaborative effort during one of the visits when we had access to the main compound. We became aware at this time of the Department of Immigration's refusal to facilitate access to a lawyer for anyone detained who had received a negative decision on their protection claim from the Department as well as from an independent reviewer.[4] Any asylum seeker in detention in this situation was simply given a list by the Department of organisations to contact for help with finding a lawyer to consider whether there was any merit in challenging the independent reviewer's negative decision in court. For many at Curtin IDC there were significant communication barriers to making this contact including limited English language skills, and limited Internet and telephone access.

A number of men approached us who had no understanding of these procedures and great anxiety about their cases. We also had little understanding of the procedures but we did have the benefit of knowing lawyers in Perth. Upon speaking with a lawyer by phone after one of our daily visits, and printing the appropriate forms that were then sent to us by email, we took them to the IDC the next day. Working with some of the men we knew well, we set up an impromptu 'clinic' that involved our friends directing the men needing lawyers to us and helping to interpret as we enabled them to complete the necessary forms to access a lawyer. When it was clear that we would need further advice from a lawyer to ensure the forms were completed correctly, several private contractor employees proceeded to quietly collaborate with our efforts. They further enabled the 'clinic' by surreptitiously facilitating our contact with the lawyer in Perth and offering any further support. For some hours we sat at the table under a tree working with our friends and ensuring that the growing piles of paper on the table were not blown away in the breeze.

The efforts of this collaboration enabled access to lawyers for some of the men detained, as did the efforts of a number of other visitors to Curtin IDC at this time. There were further instances during our visits in 2011 where attempts to address some of the impacts of mandatory detention on those detained were similarly collaborative between ourselves, those detained and some of the private contractor employees. Towards the end of 2011, however, it became increasingly difficult to engage in such collaborations as access became restricted.

Other actions were taken by a number of private contractor employees to do what they could within the detention system to at least assist some of the many men whose mental health was deteriorating, including advocating for their early release. Interviews with some of the men after their release also highlighted the importance of the emotional support that was provided to them on a regular basis by these employees. In a number of cases, contact was maintained between the men and these employees after release, reflecting the intimacy of the relationships that had developed.

These examples illustrate that some private contractor employees were willing to use their discretion to act in ways consistent with bearing witness. These range from relatively minor acts such as 'looking the other way' to allow visitors' access to a particular area of the detention centre, to working with visitors and others to both raise awareness of and address some of the consequences of mandatory detention. These were largely covert actions and are analogous to the 'deviant' acts of social workers outlined by Carey and Foster, particularly those they identified as 'minor, hidden, subtle, practical, shrewd or moderate acts of resistance' (2011, p. 578).

These acts did not necessarily address the need for systemic change, perhaps reflecting that 'great energy and time are required to change large systems' and, in the meantime, people continue to suffer 'waiting for the system to change' (Fine and Teram, 2013, p. 1324). Witnessing this suffering, particularly when relationships between an employee and some of the men detained had developed that are indicative of the levels of intimacy outlined earlier, can propel advocacy efforts that seek to subvert the system on behalf of particular individuals. Acting in ways that are 'somewhat subversive' could also be a coping mechanism for working within a difficult environment such as an Australian IDC (Briskman et al., 2012, pp 42–3) when such a commitment to those detained is felt.

But such acts do not preclude collaborative efforts that go beyond the subversive and covert. More overt acts by employees within Australian funded IDCs are also evident. Despite the confidentiality agreements that all employees within the detention network are required to sign, employees, particularly those from private contractors, have spoken to media sources about their concerns for the safety and welfare of detained asylum seekers over the past few years. This includes some of those employed at Curtin IDC (for example, see ABC, 2011). More recent examples include 9 identified and 22 unidentified past and present Salvation Army employees who released a public statement in July 2013 describing the recent riot in the Nauru site of detention as 'an inevitable outcome from a cruel and degrading policy' (Isaacs, 2014, p. xviii). Past and present private contractor employees on Manus Island, some identified and some not, have also made public comments condemning the inhumane conditions inside this site of detention (for example, see ABC, 2014). Such overt acts, as well as subversive covert acts, indicate that some employees within the privatised immigration detention network experience action-orientated emotions that propel them to go beyond the bounds of their contract, consistent with bearing witness.

However, it is not argued here that private contractor employees are necessarily more likely to engage in actions consistent with bearing witness than government employees. Such acts might have been evident if none of the IDC operations were privatised. Proximity to those detained may be one component in the explanation for such covert and overt acts. One study of employees in sites of immigration detention found that those in operational roles in the UK who interacted with people detained on a daily basis were more likely to see them as individuals than employees who did not have this level of contact (Bosworth, 2014, p. 206). Through proximity there may be a greater capacity for emotional responses that propel acts to challenge the system or at least seek to mitigate its impacts at the intimate level. As in the UK, within Australia's network of detention centres it is the employees of private contractors who have more of this proximity than those employed by the government.

But clearly proximity is not the only component as not all employees respond in this way. Other studies highlight how state and systemic portrayals of asylum seekers can play a powerful role in shaping employees' responses to those detained. Hall (2010) explored the role of emotion in how employees responded to detainees in a UK site of immigration detention. While some examples of empathy and compassion were evident, fear and contempt were found to be the dominant emotions guiding employee responses, underpinned by their associations of those detained with being 'illegal', 'abusers' of the system or having 'failed' to have their protection claims recognised (Hall, 2010, p. 894). Gill concluded that the discretionary practices of employees are steered by the presentation of asylum seekers through the detention system in the UK 'in damaging and defamatory ways, thereby depicting them as a population that is deserving of particular treatments' (2009, p. 229). Hiemstra similarly found that employees in the US detention system 'are disciplined through the constant repetition of narratives in which immigrants are immoral and untrustworthy' (2014, p. 571).

There are no such published studies to date in relation to the attitudes and practices of Australian-funded immigration detention employees, except in relation to healthcare providers (see Briskman et al., 2012). There are also limits to what can be concluded from my encounters with some of the private contractor employees at Curtin IDC that are outlined here, and interviews with employees were not conducted as part of the research project that developed during these visits. However, given the existence of consistent state narratives in Australia over much of the past two decades that have justified the detention of asylum seekers (Cameron, 2013), the findings of the above UK and US studies may be instructive. These studies suggest that the discretionary practices of employees within Australian-funded sites of detention consistent with acts of bearing witness are likely to be more the exception than the rule.

Conclusion

While privatisation adds another layer of procedural and discretionary practice complexity for independent visitors to navigate in relation to access in IDCs in Australia, sometimes an employee's exercise of discretion can serve to enable acts of bearing witness. Some private contractor employees acted to further our efforts as visitors to bear witness to the impacts of detention at Curtin IDC, and acted themselves both covertly and overtly to increase the visibility of the impacts of immigration detention and advocate on behalf of those detained.

These discretionary practices offer some hope that acts at the intimate level of detention by private contractor employees can serve to mitigate some of the impacts of detention on those detained. However, as suggested by other studies, their prevalence is not likely to be commonplace given the existence of state narratives that justify the detention of asylum seekers. Their prevalence may also now be further limited with the passage of the *Australian Border Force Act* in May 2015 that imposes the severe penalty of two years imprisonment for 'the unauthorised disclosures of information' by those employed with Australia's immigration detention network (Parliament of Australia, 2015). In addition, the broader implications of the privatisation of operations in Australian-funded IDCs outlined above must also be considered. These go beyond the intimate to the terrain of government policy and highlight that the introduction of contracted corporations and non-government organisations into the system of immigration detention in Australia has effectively enabled the expansion of the detention network. It also serves to limit protests about the impacts of detention from the organisations that are contracted to provide services.

In the midst of such an enabling environment of detention, the discretionary practices of private contractor employees that enable acts of bearing witness, and act to bear witness themselves, are imperative. Further studies on their prevalence within the Australian detention network are required with a view to understanding the limitations on these acts as well as the prospects for their facilitation. Such studies may contribute to a greater understanding of how systems of immigration detention may be further challenged in Australia as well as other countries.

Acknowledgements

I would like to acknowledge Linda Briskman for her valuable comments on an earlier draft and Nancy Hiemstra and Deirdre Conlon for their very helpful editing suggestions

Notes

1 The Howard Coalition Government negotiated agreements with Nauru and Papua New Guinea in 2001 to establish sites of immigration detention on their territory in return for increased Australian aid assistance (Briskman et al., 2008, pp. 104–5). While these sites were closed in 2008 after the election of the Rudd Labor Government, they were re-established by the Gillard Labor Government in 2012 following an increase in boat arrivals.
2 In 2013, families, including children, were also detained at Curtin IDC in a compound separate from the men. Since August 2014, the Department of Immigration has reported that no one is detained at Curtin IDC (see https://www.immi.gov.au/About/Pages/detention/about-immigration-detention.aspx).
3 After a five-hour interview with the Independent Merits reviewer, and six more months, he finally received the decision that he was recognised as a refugee.
4 During 2010–11, the primary protection visa grant rates of the Department of Immigration dropped to 38 per cent for asylum seekers who arrived by boat from 74.3 per cent the previous year. After independent review procedures were completed for the negative decisions, protection visa grant rates for 2010–11 and 2011–12 increased to 95.3 and 91.3 per cent, respectively (Department of Immigration and Border Protection, 2013, p. 30). Positive judicial review outcomes for some of the decisions that remained negative after independent review led to further positive decisions.

References

ABC. 2011. *Four corners: asylum* [Online]. 24 October. Available from: www.abc.net .au/4corners/stories/2011/10/20/3344543.htm [Accessed 20 December 2014].

ABC. 2014. *Four corners: the Manus solution* [Online]. 28 April. Available from: www.abc.net.au/4corners/stories/2014/04/28/3991401.htm [Accessed 20 December 2014].

ABC News. 2014. Serco workers in strike talks amid dispute over detention centre pay and staffing levels. *ABC News* [Online]. 28 January. Available from: www.abc.net.au/news/2014-01-28/serco-workers-in-strike-talks/5221554 [Accessed 2 May 2015].

Aidani, M. 2013. Face to face: ethics and responsibility. In: Block, K., Riggs. E. and Haslam, N. eds. *Values and vulnerabilities: the ethics of research with refugees and asylum seekers*. Toowong: Australian Academic Press, pp. 207–20.

Australian Stock Exchange. 2014. Transfield Services receives Letter of Intent for Department of Immigration. ASX Statement [Online]. 24 February. Available from: www.asx .com.au/asxpdf/20140224/pdf/42mxphql8ldk1y.pdf [Accessed 10 February 2016].

Bacon, C. 2005. The evolution of immigration detention in the UK: the involvement of private prison companies. RSC Working Paper No. 27. University of Oxford Refugee Studies Centre.

Bosworth, M. 2014. *Inside immigration detention*. Oxford: Oxford University Press.

Briskman, L., Latham, S. and Goddard, C. 2008. *Human rights overboard: seeking asylum in Australia*. Carlton North: Scribe.

Briskman, L., Zion, D. and Loff, B. 2012. Care or collusion in asylum seeker detention. *Ethics and Social Welfare* **6**(1), pp. 37–55.

Cameron, M. 2013. From 'queue jumpers' to 'absolute scum of the earth': refugees and organised criminal deviance in Australian asylum policy. *Australian Journal of Politics and History* **59**(2), pp. 241–59.

Carey, M. and Foster, V. 2011. Introducing 'deviant' social work: contextualising the limits of radical social work whilst understanding (fragmented) resistance within the social work labour process. *British Journal of Social Work* **41**, pp. 576–93.

Cody, W.K. 2001. The ethics of bearing witness in healthcare: a beginning exploration. *Nursing Science Quarterly* **14**(4), pp. 288–96.

Department of Immigration and Border Protection. 2013. Asylum Trends Australia 2012–2013 Publication [Online]. Available from: www.immi.gov.au/media/publications/statistics/immigration-update/asylum-trends-aus-2012-13.pdf [Accessed 26 January 2016].

Fine, M. and Teram, E. 2013. Overt and covert ways of responding to moral injustices in social work practice: heroes and mild-mannered social work bipeds. *British Journal of Social Work* **43**, pp. 1312–29.

Fleay, C. 2015. Monitoring immigration detention in Australia: the prospects and limitations of securing independent scrutiny. *Australian Journal of Human Rights* **21**(1), pp. 21–46.

Fleay, C. and Briskman, L. 2013. The hidden men: bearing witness to mandatory detention in Australia. *Refugee Survey Quarterly* **32**, pp. 112–29.

Gill, N. 2009. Presentational state power: temporal and spatial influences over asylum sector decision makers. *Transactions of the Institute of British Geographers*. **34**, pp. 215–33.

Hall, A. 2010. 'These people could be anyone': fear, contempt (and empathy) in a British Immigration Removal Centre. *Journal of Ethnic and Migration Studies* **36**(6), pp. 881–98.

Hall, B. 2013. Serco profits rise as detention contracts hit $1.86bn. *The Sydney Morning Herald* [Online]. 20 April. Available from: www.smh.com.au/action/printArticle?id=4206299 [Accessed 20 December 2014].

Hiemstra, N. 2014. Performing homeland security within the US immigrant detention system. *Environment and Planning D: Society and Space*. **32**, pp. 571–88.

Human Rights and Equal Opportunity Commission. 2004. *A last resort? National inquiry into children in immigration detention* [Online]. Available from: www.hreoc.gov.au/human_rights/children_detention_report/index.html [Accessed 20 December 2014].

Isaacs, M. 2014. *The undesirables: inside Nauru*. Richmond: Hardie Grant Books.

Jeffery, R. 2011. Reason, emotion, and the problem of world poverty: moral sentiment theory and international ethics. *International Theory* **3**(1), pp. 143–78.

Kamat, S. 2004. The privatisation of public interest: theorising NGO discourse in a neoliberal era. *Review of International Political Economy* **11**(1), pp. 155–76.

Kandasamy, N. and Soldatic, K. 2016 (forthcoming). The impact of government contracts in refugee resettlement services. *Social Policy and Administration*.

Levinas, E. 1999. *Alterity and transcendence*. New York: Columbia University Press.

Loewenstein, A. 2013. *Profits of doom: how vulture capitalism is swallowing the world*. Melbourne: Melbourne University Press.

Maddison, S. and Hamilton, C. 2007. Non-government organisations. In: Hamilton, C. and Maddison, S. eds. *Silencing dissent*. Crows Nest: Allen & Unwin.

McKay, D. 2006. Book review. *Women's Studies Quarterly* **34**(1&2), pp. 476–80.

Mountz, A. 2004. Embodying the nation-state: Canada's response to human smuggling. *Political Geography* **23**, pp. 323–45.

Newman, L., Proctor, N. and Dudley, M. 2013. Seeking asylum in Australia: immigration detention, human rights and mental health care. *Australasian Psychiatry* **21**(4), pp. 315–20.

Parliament of Australia. 2015. *Australian Border Force Bill* [Online]. Available from: www.aph.gov.au/Parliamentary_Business/Bills_Legislation/Bills_Search_Results/Result?bId=r5408 [Accessed 12 June 2015].

Peters, J.D. 2001. Witnessing. *Media, Culture and Society* **23**, pp. 707–23.

Rorty, R. 2001. Human rights, rationality and sentimentality. In: Hayden, P. ed. *The philosophy of human rights*. Saint Paul, MN: Paragon House, pp. 241–57.

Silove, D., Steel, Z. and Mollica, R. 2001. Detention of asylum seekers: assault on health, human rights and social development. *The Lancet* **357**(9266), pp. 1436–37.

Steel, Z., Momartin, S., Bateman, C., Hafshejani, A., Silove, D.M., Everson, N., Roy, K., Dudley, M., Newman, L., Blick, B., and Mares, S. 2004. Psychiatric status of asylum-seeker families held for a protracted period in a remote detention centre in Australia. *Australian and New Zealand Journal of Public Health* **28**(6), pp. 527–36.

Tait, S. 2011. Bearing witness, journalism and moral responsibility. *Media, Culture and Society* **33**(8), pp. 1220–35.

Thomas, E.F. and McGarty, C.A. 2009. The role of efficacy and moral outrage norms in creating the potential for international development activism through group-based interaction. *British Journal of Social Psychology* **48**(1), pp. 115–34.

Tyler, I., Gill, N., Conlon, D. and Oeppen, C. 2014. The business of child detention: charitable co-option, migrant advocacy and activist outrage. *Race and Class* **56**(1), pp. 3–21.

Viviani, N. 1996. *The Indochinese in Australia 1975–1995: from burnt boats to barbecues*. Oxford: Oxford University Press.

Zion, D., Briskman, L. and Loff, B. 2012. Psychiatric ethics and a politics of compassion: the case of detained asylum seekers in Australia. *Bioethical Inquiry* **9**, pp. 67–75.

6 Managing capacity, shifting burdens

Social reproduction and the intimate economies of immigrant family detention

Jill M. Williams and Vanessa A. Massaro

In the spring of 2014, United States Immigration and Customs Enforcement (ICE) began dropping off busloads of migrant families at Greyhound bus stations in the cities of Phoenix and Tucson, Arizona each week. The families, who had entered the country without authorisation in either south Texas or Arizona, were composed primarily of women and small children, and were largely from Central America (El Salvador, Guatemala and Honduras). In order to qualify for release, families first went through a screening process to assess any threat they posed to national security, after which they were required to provide the name, phone number and address of the person with whom they were going to be staying in the United States. They were then released with a notice to appear at an immigration office near their destination within fifteen days, at which time their case would receive further processing and evaluation.

ICE released families with little in the way of knowledge or resources to aid their travels. Most had no idea where they were, how to negotiate US transportation networks, and had little if anything in the way of basic necessities (e.g. food, diapers, toiletries) or money with which to procure them. In response to the crisis this created for these families, networks of volunteers emerged in the two cities to step in and provide basic services for those released. Volunteers collected and distributed donations of food, clothing, medicine and diapers and worked in shifts each day greeting families at bus stations, and helping them to contact family members in the US, purchase bus tickets and arrange overnight hospitality for those who were unable to schedule same-day travel.

While the practice of unceremoniously releasing immigrant detainees at bus stations was not a new phenomenon – this had been common practice for a number of years in southern Arizona for those migrants who were released from detention pending further processing of their immigration cases – the proliferation of families was new. The sudden appearance of families reflects shifts in the demographic composition of unauthorised migrants apprehended by the US Border Patrol in the southwest US during this time. Between fiscal years 2013 and 2014, when only one immigrant family detention facility with less than 100 beds existed in the US, the number of immigrant family units apprehended along the southwest border increased by 361 per cent from 14,855 to 68,445[1] (US Border Patrol, 2014). This increase gravely challenged the capacity of existing immigrant processing and detention infrastructure, meaning that ICE had few options for dealing with the influx of family units. In turn, the proliferation of families released at bus stations in southern Arizona emerged as an impromptu or 'on the fly' (Mountz, 2010, p. 20) governmental response to the material reality of an immigrant detention landscape ill equipped to deal with changing migratory patterns.

While this improvised practice importantly freed families from the confines of prison-like detention centres, the process of release adopted by ICE was haphazard in many regards, and created a number of new vulnerabilities and challenges for these families. In this chapter, we draw on ethnographic research with immigrant service providers in southern Arizona and policy analysis to connect this case with a broader understanding of the intimate economies of immigrant detention. In particular, we draw on work in the field of feminist political geography to shift attention to social reproduction – as in the reproduction of both individuals on a biological level and the reproduction of capitalist social relations. We examine social reproduction as an intimate economic realm through which the daily lives and well-being of unauthorised migrants is managed. In doing so, we define intimate economies as the relations of exchange through which the most personal aspects of migrants' lives are managed. Through this focus on intimate economies and social reproduction, we show that in as much as the networks of care that developed fill certain gaps of vulnerability left (or created) by the state, it is necessary to think critically about the way in which these networks support larger neoliberal and carceral logics that drive immigrant detention more broadly. In doing so, we argue that paying attention to the 'other' side or the 'outside' of detention is necessary for understanding both the political economies shaping detention and their effects on the migrants involved. Moreover, by drawing on work in the fields of feminist geopolitics and political economy, we suggest that a feminist analytic framework is particularly well equipped to grapple with understanding the intimate economies that shape contemporary struggles over family detention.

In what follows, we first draw on work in the fields of feminist geopolitics and political economy to outline a feminist analytic approach appropriate for understanding the relations of exchange that govern immigrant family detention and release. We then provide an overview of the role ideas of the family and childhood have played in shaping US immigration law and policy and contemporary detention practices. Next, we turn to a discussion of a series of events surrounding family detention and release practices in southern Arizona in 2014 and 2015. This attention illustrates the embedded neoliberal logics in contemporary detention practices and the related shifting of responsibility for migrant care and well-being away from the state and onto a whole suite of non-governmental actors and migrant familial and social networks.

A feminist analytic of the intimate economies of family detention and release

Work in the fields of feminist geopolitics and feminist political economy has drawn attention to the need to shift analysis to the unexpected and often unrecognised sites and scales at which political and economic processes play out. In this section, we review some of the relevant work in these fields to sketch out an analytic framework for understanding the intimate economies and reverberating effects of contemporary immigrant family detention and release in the US southwest. The resulting framework (1) re-scales analysis to the intimate sites of the body, family and community in order to see how geopolitical and geoeconomic policies affect the everyday realities of differently situated populations; (2) disrupts overly simplistic notions of political subjectivity that assume an undifferentiated political subject, instead attending to the way in which subjectivity shapes state policies and practices; and (3) highlights how struggles over social reproduction (namely, who is responsible for ensuring a basic level of care and daily survival) are part and parcel of larger political economic processes.

Traditional examinations of geopolitical processes such as border and immigration enforcement have focused on the formal policy realm and policy-makers. This masculinist approach to the study of international politics serves to obscure the role women and other marginalised populations play in shaping geopolitical relations in both formal and informal ways (Enloe, 1993, 2000; Dalby, 1994; Dowler and Sharp, 2001). In turn, beginning in the early 2000s, feminist scholars began calling for a re-scaling of analysis under the umbrella term feminist geopolitics (Dowler and Sharp, 2001; Hyndman, 2004; Dixon and Marston, 2011; Massaro and Williams, 2013). Rather than focusing analysis on the global or national scale and the formal sites of political (in)action, feminist scholarship re-scales analysis to the intimate sites of the body and home, drawing attention to the back and forth reverberations through which geopolitical policies materialise over time and space. For example, Hyndman's (2008) discussion of the geopolitics of mobility shifts attention from national or global security to human security. In re-scaling discussions of transnational migration away from nation-states and to the very bodies of those individuals who are affected by geopolitical policies, Hyndman highlights how efforts to render states more secure often function to make marginalised human populations increasingly insecure. Similarly, Smith's (2012) discussion of intimate geopolitics draws attention to how geopolitical struggles over territoriality are waged on and through the very intimate lives of people as issues of marriage and reproduction are conduits through which territorialities are maintained and contested (see also Yuval-Davis, 1998).

The traditional macro scaling of geopolitical analysis goes hand-in-hand with assumptions about political subjectivity that are central to liberal political theory, which assumes an undifferentiated and universal political subject through which and on which laws and policies act uniformly. However, feminist, queer and critical race scholars (among others) have disrupted this overly simplistic understanding of politics. Instead, critical perspectives draw attention to the way in which state policies both produce different forms of subjectivity and affect differently situated populations in uneven ways. For example, Eithne Luibheid's (2002) examination of US immigration law and policy highlights the way in which different forms of sexual subjectivity are produced and regulated through immigration and border enforcement policies (see also Luibheid and Cantu, 2005). Far from a coherent, undifferentiated universal political subject, immigration law both produces different forms of subjectivity and serves to regulate the transnational movement of different subjects, allowing for some to move more freely across national borders than others (e.g. Hyndman, 2000, 2008; Sparke, 2004, 2006; Rygiel, 2008; Sharma, 2008). In turn, attending to the ways in which state laws and policies produce and regulate different forms of subjectivity is a key task of feminist and other critical scholars as they grapple with the uneven (and often unjust) operation of state power.

While feminist interventions in geopolitics have challenged the scale and scope of analysis, feminist insights have also importantly challenged the field of political economy. Marston (2000), for example, calls for more attention to processes of social reproduction, in addition to production, in our efforts to understand the operation of capitalism (see also, Katz, 2001; Mitchell, Marston and Katz, 2004). Similar to the re-scaling of analysis in the field of geopolitics, a shift to examine social reproduction draws attention to the way in which capitalist economic systems are reproduced and contested in the mundane spaces of everyday life. As Marston notes, social reproduction 'entails both the reproduction of the social relations that maintain capitalism as well as the reproduction of the material bases upon which social life is premised' (Marston, 2000, p. 233). Rather than existing outside of or separate from capitalism, social reproduction is vital to the operation of capitalist economic and social systems, sustaining them materially, biologically and ideologically. Thus, attention to the sites and specificities of social reproduction, that is the 'fleshy, messy, and indeterminate stuff of everyday life', offers important insights into understanding broader processes of global capitalism (Katz, 2001, p. 710).

Not insignificantly, social reproduction has traditionally been contained and understood at the site of the family. Historically, it has largely been through familial relations of care that the labour force is reproduced, making the family a less visible, yet nevertheless indispensible part of the production of value (Sawicki, 1991; Hennessey, 1993). However, the rise of the welfare state in the twentieth century and related struggles over adequate wages shifted how social reproduction was conceptualised in the US (as well as elsewhere). Struggles over social welfare programmes and wage rates are instances where who is responsible for ensuring the fiscal and human resources necessary for social reproduction to be carried out are negotiated. Whereas the rise of the welfare state was indicative of a move to make the state more involved in ensuring adequate resources for social reproduction to take place, the neoliberal era (1980s–present) has been characterised by a rolling back of the welfare state, re-siting responsibility for social reproduction at the level of the individual, home and community (Katz, 2001; McDowell, 2004). Discourses of personal responsibility that define the neoliberal era reverberate into the private sphere and intimate aspects of life as social welfare programmes dwindle and real wages for most workers fall. In turn, individual families and formal and informal community networks emerge to fill in the gaps left by the state.

Moreover, ideologies that locate responsibility for social reproduction on both the individual and the family additionally work to encourage and justify a broad prison industrial complex. Mandatory detention and incarceration policies couched in discourses of personal responsibility have been key drivers of the expansion of immigrant detention and related carceral landscapes more broadly (Benavie, 2009). Ironically, this rise in detention places detainees within the confines of state-run or state-financed detention centres, in theory placing the state in the position of ensuring (either directly or by proxy) the daily survival and well-being of those detained; this includes the most intimate aspects of their lives from personal hygiene to mental and physical health (Conlon and Hiemstra, 2014). Ultimately though, this reflects an emphasis on maintaining social relations of capitalism – particularly through warehousing surplus bodies (Katz, 2007; Gilmore, 2007) – much more than an emphasis on maintaining material well-being.

As Conlon and Hiemstra (2014) and others (Mountz, 2011; Urbina, 2014) have documented, public and private detention centres routinely deny immigrant detainees adequate food, clothing, hygiene products, and medical care – the basics of everyday life. Detainees therefore rely on family and friends outside detention to provide the funds necessary to purchase additional items at commissaries that charge exorbitant markups on basic goods. In limiting the basic goods provided to detainees, detention centres both reduce expenditures and create demand for commissary goods; at the same time, responsibility for ensuring the basic well-being of detainees is shifted onto migrant familial and social networks and negotiated through the commissary system. As we will show, similar processes are reflected within the context of detainee release where the state abdicates responsibility for ensuring the well-being of migrants, instead shifting this responsibility to uncompensated networks of non-profit organisations and the social networks of migrants. Through an examination of the intimate economies of detention and release, we trace a shifting of care responsibilities and thus illustrate how detention and the logics undergirding it reverberate beyond detention centres. However, before exploring immigrant family detention and release practices in more depth, the next section first contextualises these practices in relationship to the role ideas of family and childhood have played in shaping US immigration law and policy.

The family and the shifting landscape of immigrant detention in the US

'The family' holds a special place in US immigration law and policy. As Catherine Lee (2013) discusses, even in times of the most exclusionary and racist immigration policies, exceptions have been made to allow for families to form, reunite and stay together. The privileged place of the family in immigration law is tied to a nationalist, patriarchal notion of ideal citizens that immigration policies (re)produce and mobilise and which buffers against the free flow of 'deviant' bodies and subjectivities across transnational space. For example, under the Gentleman's Agreement of 1907 between Japan and the US, the wives and children of Japanese male labourers were allowed to immigrate despite the exclusion of Japanese immigrants more broadly. This exception allowed for already present Japanese men to create 'proper' nuclear families while limiting the perceived threat of inter-racial unions to the national community (Luibheid, 2002). Over a century later, family unity continues to remain a cornerstone of US immigration policy, making it much easier for legally married individuals and biological family members to migrate than other populations.

Despite the exceptional place afforded families in US immigration law and policy, family units (narrowly defined as minors and their biological parent(s) or legal guardian(s)) *that arrive without authorisation* have presented a conundrum for immigration agencies and related governmental bodies for decades. The 'problem' of unauthorised families represents a growing gap between cultural ideologies regarding childhood innocence and the dominant carceral logics and nationalist frameworks through which immigration enforcement policies and practices are designed and implemented. Since the early 1990s and most notably since 2001, immigration enforcement policies have been based on a framework of criminalisation whereby unauthorised migrants – both those who enter without authorisation and those who become unauthorised after overstaying visas – are framed (legally and ideologically) as criminals, resulting in and justifying the rapid expansion of immigrant detention as a primary aspect of enforcement throughout the US (see Lowen, this volume). The criminalisation of migration and migrants has been made possible by overarching neoliberal ideologies of personal responsibility that disregard the larger structural factors that compel unauthorised migration. These ideologies frame unauthorised migrants as irresponsible lawbreakers who should be held responsible for their independent decision to forego legal migration routes. In turn, the detention of unauthorised migrants has expanded rapidly since the 1990s as policy-makers attempt to use mandatory detention policies as a mechanism to deter unauthorised migration (Martin, 2011, 2012a).

However, discourses of personal responsibility and criminality that serve to justify the detention of adult migrants in prisons or prison-like detention centres during the processing of their immigration case do not stick well to children. Children inhabit an exceptional space in the US imaginary and it is precisely this exceptionality that complicates the detention of families. As Martin (2011) and others (Bosniak, 2013) have discussed, children are framed as non-agential objects who cannot be held fully responsible for their 'illegal' status and are thus deserving of different detention standards.[2]

Founded in cultural ideologies of childhood innocence, the exceptional status of child migrants has ultimately been codified in US law through a series of legal determinations and legislation. In 1997 a legal settlement known as *Flores v. Meese* put in place special requirements for juvenile immigrant detention. In addition to stipulating that juveniles are not to be detained with an unrelated adult for more than 24 hours and setting time limits on how long children can be detained generally, the settlement also set guidelines for the treatment of children in immigration custody (Martin, 2011). While this legislation was specifically intended to protect unaccompanied child migrants (particularly those at risk for human trafficking), it did not differentiate between children traveling alone and those in the presence of a biological parent or legal guardian. In turn, this settlement has largely shaped family detention practices. The linking of children with their adult parents/guardians limits how families can be detained; the literal presence of children buffers the ability of the state to detain families.

The cultural ideologies that take a more sympathetic stance towards child migrants and the subsequent legal codification of exceptional standards for the detention of child migrants has resulted in family detention being relatively rare in the history of US immigration policy. In fact, the first immigrant family detention centre was not opened until March of 2001; before this time families were largely released while their immigration cases were being processed (Martin, 2012a, 2012b). The first family detention centre, the Berks County Family Residential Centre in Pennsylvania, was designed as a 'non-secure residential facility' that aimed to provide a way to both maintain family unity and keep families under the watch of immigration officials while they were undergoing immigration proceedings. The establishment of this centre was part of larger efforts by immigration enforcement agencies to contain unauthorised migrants during the processing of their immigration cases in order to more effectively deport those who were unsuccessful at establishing the right to stay in the country. While the Berks County facility provided some detention space for family units, its limited capacity (less than 100 beds) set a structural limitation on the expansion of family detention. In turn, even after the opening of this facility, the majority of families were released pending their immigration hearings (Women's Commission for Refugee Women and Children and Lutheran Immigration and Refugee Service, 2007). However, shortly after the opening of the Berks County facility, the events of 9/11 shifted governmental approaches to unauthorised migration and migrants, including the expansion of family detention.

As scholars of immigration and border enforcement have illustrated, the events of 11 September 2001 and subsequent launching of the US-led 'War on Terror' have made immigration and border enforcement an issue of national security (Bigo, 2002; Hyndman and Mountz, 2007; Jones, 2011, 2012; Segura and Zavella, 2007; Mountz, 2012; Mountz et al., 2012; Nevins, 2010; Sparke, 2006). The post-9/11 formation of the Department of Homeland Security (DHS) resulted in the unprecedented allocation of resources to immigration and border enforcement. Moreover, unauthorised migrants were reframed as potential terrorist threats, justifying greater and greater policing and detention practices both at the territorial edges of nation-states and within as the geographic reach of immigration policing was extended (Coleman, 2007, 2009; Coutin, 2010; Mountz, 2011; Mountz et al., 2012;

Mountz and Hiemstra, 2012; Hiemstra, 2012; Puar, 2007; Varsanyi, 2008). Whereas historically children and families were treated 'more favourably' than other migrants, in what follows we detail how the events of 11 September 2001 led to shifts in the ideology and practice of family detention. These shifts illustrate the way in which cultural ideologies of childhood innocence are mediated by discourses of terrorism and the imperative of national security, resulting in the expansion of family detention to unprecedented levels.

In the post-9/11 context in which border enforcement was linked with terrorism prevention, officials problematised informal policies of releasing families. Specifically, DHS officials argued that allowances for children and families could result in prospective migrants (and implicitly potential terrorists) 'renting' children to accompany them on their crossings in order to ensure timely release if they were apprehended (Women's Commission for Refugee Women and Children and Lutheran Immigration and Refugee Service, 2007). In response, DHS sought a new policy whereby both adults and the children traveling with them were detained. However, the lack of sufficient family detention bed space made this policy impossible to enforce without separating family units. In turn, the separation of parents from their children became systematic as children were placed with the Office of Refugee Resettlement and their parents were detained in immigrant detention centres or state or county jails.

Upon discovering DHS's policy of separating parents and their minor children, members of Congress issued a statement directing DHS to end this practice of creating unaccompanied minors. DHS was given three suggested courses of action: 'to release families through existing programs, use alternatives to detention, or to house families in appropriate detention spaces where parents and children could be kept together' (Women's Commission for Refugee Women and Children and Lutheran Immigration and Refugee Service, 2007, pp. 5–6). DHS chose the most restrictive of the three options and began expanding family detention capacity with the 2006 opening of the T. Don Hutto Family Residential Facility in Texas. The expansion of family detention capacity allowed DHS to abide by Congressional directives while also avoiding releasing family units. This choice to expand detention to include families implicates immigration policies in a rising prison industrial complex in which detention is always the logical endpoint (Davis, 2005; Gilmore, 2007; Loyd, Mitchelson and Burridge, 2012). Moreover, this signals a slight shift in how immigrant children and families were conceptualised in immigration policy. The post-9/11 linking of immigration enforcement to national security has served to justify family detention in ways not previously realised (Martin, 2012a, 2012b). However, at the same time and as will be discussed further below, the detention of families (in particular children) has received consistent criticism from a variety of constituencies and has come under greater scrutiny of late as familial and childhood exceptionality is invoked to argue for the end of family detention.

While the Hutto Facility aimed to meet the 'special needs' of immigrant children while also fulfilling governmental mandates to detain adult immigrants, it nevertheless quickly came under intense criticism from immigrant rights advocates. In March of 2007, the American Civil Liberties Union (ACLU) filed a lawsuit against ICE on behalf of a number of juveniles housed at the facility. The lawsuit argued that the detention centre did not comply with the standards set forth in *Flores v. Meese* regarding the detention of minors, namely that minors should not be detained in prison-like conditions because doing so could result in long-term psychological trauma. This lawsuit was not successful at ending family detention as federal attorneys argued that the 'rights' of children to not be detained was superseded by the 'need' to detain their adult parents in order to ensure national security (Martin, 2011). In turn, family detention was framed as the only logical way to both avoid family separation and uphold national security objectives. While the lawsuit was not successful in establishing the right to family release, it did result in a settlement that aimed to transform the spatial ordering of Hutto into more 'home-like' conditions and also required monthly review, parole, bond and release decisions for each family in order to avoid indefinite detention (Martin, 2011, p. 491).

Although the legal challenge failed to eliminate the facility, in 2009 the facility stopped detaining families, releasing or deporting all of those previously detained there. This shift was publicly framed as a result of the more 'civil' immigration policy adopted by the newly elected Obama administration; large-scale family detention was framed as 'an example of immigration and homeland-security policy gone astray' (Martin, 2012b, p. 885). However, this shift was also the outcome of the shifting demographic characteristics of immigrant detainees; the profitability of immigrant detention hinges on balancing demand for certain types of detention space with the costs associated with providing the services required by different populations. Two years before family detention was ended at Hutto, the facility transitioned half of the bed space from family detention to female detention. While the exact driver of this shift is not publically stated, it is likely that the additional burdens and costs (both fiscal and in terms of public image) associated with detaining children combined with shifting migratory patterns and associated demands for detention space influenced institutional decisions regarding detention practices at Hutto.

Hutto's shift away from family detention in 2009 left, once again, only one family detention centre in the United States with less than 100 beds – the Berks County facility. In turn, the influx of family units in early 2014 left ICE, CBP and related agencies 'scrambling to respond' (Prendergast, 2014). A chaotic geography (Hiemstra, 2012; Mountz and Hiemstra, 2014) of transfers emerged as many who entered the country in south Texas were transferred to Arizona for initial processing, before being released at local bus stations. This spontaneous practice was the result of uneven resource allocations and shifting migratory patterns along the US-Mexico border. Between 2013 and 2014 the number of individuals apprehended in the Rio Grande Border Patrol Sector in south Texas increased nearly 300 per cent, surpassing the Tucson Sector as the locus of apprehensions. However, the Rio Grande Sector was unprepared to deal with such a dramatic increase in apprehensions and lacked the infrastructure necessary to quickly and effectively process individuals and families. Immigration enforcement officials in Texas turned to Arizona as the geographic site of greater resources and, in turn, ideal location to send family units for processing. In the late spring and early summer of 2014, thousands of families and unaccompanied minors were bussed hundreds of miles from Texas to detention and processing facilities in Arizona (Galvan, 2014). While this strategy partially solved the problem of capacity – providing greater infrastructure to carry out the initial processing of immigration cases – the Tucson Sector also lacked detention centres equipped to house family units, resulting in the continuous release of families throughout the summer and fall of 2014 and into 2015.

In what follows we further explore the processes through which immigrant families were managed and released in southern Arizona during this time, paying particular attention to the shifting relations of social reproduction that shaped how migrant care was managed. In exploring the intimate economies through which the daily lives and well-being of migrants is managed, we show how the burdens (fiscal and otherwise) associated with providing basic care and resources were shifted away from state agencies and to non-governmental organisations, local volunteers, and the familial and social networks of migrants. In doing so, we highlight the need to attend to the transformations in relations of social reproduction that are central to contemporary practices of immigrant detention and release.

Shifting burdens, mobilising resources

'To release this many women and children without tickets or even information on how to purchase tickets is clearly a health and safety threat to an already vulnerable population' – local Tucson volunteer (Carrasco and Trevizo, 2014).

In the spring of 2014, awareness grew among immigrant rights advocates that ICE was releasing large numbers of families at the local Greyhound bus station and that these families were generally being released with little in the way of basic resources. In turn, a loose network of volunteers formed to fill in the gaps left by state agencies and provide much-needed assistance. In Tucson, local volunteers, mostly from local intentional and religious communities, visited the Greyhound station nightly, providing essential services; the first task of volunteers was often providing the basic necessities of life – food, water, clothing, shelter – to the families released, as one volunteer commented, 'the first thing they say when they get off the bus is they are hungry' (Fausett and Belson, 2014). In addition, volunteers helped families navigate the US bus system and provided overnight accommodations for families unable to obtain same-day bus tickets.

Not surprisingly, the physical and emotional toll of dealing with hundreds of individuals daily eventually strained the loose network of volunteers that initially formed in Tucson. By early June, an established social service provider stepped in and volunteered to take over the aid effort, naming the endeavour the Angelitos Project.[3] Information sessions and trainings were held for volunteers, drawing hundreds of individuals interested in knowing more about the unusual situation and how they could help. At the same time, those involved mobilised their social networks to spread the message of need beyond the local community. As a result, donations poured in from across the country. In a short period of time, vast amounts of used clothing, shampoo, soap and other hygiene products, diapers, colouring books and children's backpacks filled storage rooms at both the Greyhound station and multiple off-site locations. Collectively, these steps marked the beginning of a non-governmental effort to ensure that the basic needs of families were being met in the face of a state apparatus that seemed to have little concern for their well-being once they were released from formal custody.

By August of 2014 an agreement was reached between the Angelitos Project and ICE to begin dropping families off at an alternative location rather than the Greyhound station. This alternative facility provided a more comfortable environment for families, giving them an opportunity to contact family members, shower and rest before beginning the next leg of their journey. This agreement to shift the location of migrant release away from the bus station was largely informal, but still one to which ICE quickly acquiesced. This arrangement ultimately solved a public relations sore point for ICE while absorbing the costs and responsibilities for migrant families. In the period leading up to this agreement, news reporters were frequenting the bus stations, interviewing migrants and volunteers about their experiences both with migration and in detention. Many of the media reports focused on the irresponsibility inherent to ICE's treatment of the families – namely, poor care while in detention and release without adequate resources or services (Fausett and Belson, 2014; Galvan, 2014). In turn, moving the release of migrants away from the bus station, to a facility whose location was not widely known or shared with the media served to shield ICE from negative media reports, while also placating citizens, local politicians and Greyhound staff that were pressuring the agency to stop dropping off families at the bus station.

However, this is not to suggest that the movement of release and service provisioning away from the bus station was not beneficial to migrants. For example, moving the provisioning of services out of the chaotic environment of the bus station provided an opportunity for volunteers to offer individuals basic legal information and lists of free legal services near their final destination. While individuals were given documents upon their release from detention that included information on where they were to appear for their next hearing and the type of programme they were released on, these documents were most often only in English and largely incomprehensible to the families (largely Spanish and indigenous Mayan language speakers) (Trevizo, 2015). Informal legal briefings by volunteers served as an opportunity to explain documents to families and provide them with information on accessing free legal services.

The simple act of getting to their final destination and reuniting with family or friends often presented a significant challenge to released families. Because families typically lacked government-issued identification documents which are necessary for airline travel, they relied on cross-country buses as their primary means of transportation once released from federal custody. However, bus tickets are a financial challenge for many families. Tickets from Tucson to common destinations in Florida, Georgia, New York and California (all between 500 and 2,500 miles away) often ranged from $200–300 per person with children over the age of two requiring individual tickets; this means that tickets for a family of three could cost nearly $1000. With little to no money, released families relied upon family members and extended social networks in the US to pull together the large sums of money necessary to finance their bus trip. The process of buying tickets could take from a couple of hours to a couple of days, depending on the availability of their family's financial resources and the ability of a family member to get to a local Greyhound station to buy a ticket on their behalf. During this time, individuals were provided with accommodation, food and clothing through the Angelitos Project.

As this section illustrates, throughout the summer and fall of 2014, a series of shifts occurred whereby responsibility for the basic care and well-being of migrant families was shifted (like the families themselves) away from state agencies and onto non-governmental agencies, individual volunteers and migrant familial and social networks. In the next section we further unpack what these shifts tell us about the intimate economies of immigrant family detention and the larger neoliberal and carceral landscapes of which they are a part.

The carceral state, responsibility and the intimate economies of social reproduction

It is useful to consider this case in the context of social reproduction on one hand and the ongoing growth of the prison industrial complex on the other, both of which are shaped by neoliberal discourses and associated policies that transfer care responsibilities away from the state and onto individuals, families and communities. The current case of immigrant family release we have outlined above is reflective of and reinforces larger state practices of providing minimal resources within detention centres and outsourcing responsibility for ensuring social reproduction to non-governmental organisations, individuals and familial and social networks. This process importantly opens up new opportunities for wealth creation. In the context of immigrant detention, wealth creation can happen both through the creation of new markets (e.g. created demand for basic goods and services discussed by Conlon and Hiemstra, 2014), as well as the gradual siphoning off of profits through various formal and informal cost-saving measures.

We see here that within the context of release, state agencies provide minimal services to released families, placing the responsibility to provide for migrants' basic needs onto familial and social networks, non-profit organisations and volunteers. In doing so, they reinforce the model at work inside detention centres where migrants' families and friends outside detention must transfer funds to cover commissary purchases. When families are released from detention, the financial resources of their families and friends are strained as hundreds of dollars are spent on bus tickets and the resources of sympathetic US residents are mobilised to fuel the stream of donations and volunteer labour necessary to provide basic services for families. For example, by the fall of 2014, nearly 200 volunteers were part of the migrant family support network in Tucson alone. These volunteers offered their time, energy and, at times, homes, to assist families without any form of monetary compensation. Moreover, donations of food, clothing, hygiene products, diapers and other goods poured in to support the work of the Angelitos Project at such a fast rate that three 200 square foot off-site storage units had to be rented to supplement the already existing on-site storage capacity.

While in other contexts, the outsourcing of immigration management services often includes a formalised agreement and compensation to NGOs for providing certain services – for example, the International Organization for Migration (Tyler et al., 2014) – in this particular context the agreement between ICE and the Angelitos Project was largely informal and uncompensated. ICE did not provide the Project with any funds to finance the services provided to migrants and communication between ICE and Project personnel was often lacking. It was not unusual for volunteers to manage 20–30 people in a single evening with little warning. In practice, this meant that the Angelitos Project served as a mechanism to transfer responsibility (financial and otherwise) for migrant care away from state agencies and onto the networks of care mobilised by both the Angelitos Project and migrants.

State practices of releasing migrant families without resources or support is made possible by the vast networks of care that emerge to fill the gaps left by the state. In this context, state agencies are allowed to transfer the costs associated with providing migrant families with the basic goods and services required for their daily survival onto an assemblage of non-profit organisations and migrant social and familial networks. The profitability of detention centres relies upon adequately balancing demand for detention space and managing resources in order to maximise the profit margin per detainee. While not providing adequate food, clothing and hygiene products fuels demand for costly commissary products, releasing immigrants as quickly as possible and with as few resources as possible serves to limit expenditures on both labour and goods. In turn, donated goods and volunteer labour fill the gaps left by haphazard release practices that place immigrant families in situations of produced vulnerability upon their release.

Conclusion

In this chapter, we have expanded how we understand the intimate economies of immigrant detention through an examination of the shifting relations of migrant care and the role these networks of care play in reinforcing both neoliberal and carceral logics. We have shown first that non-profit organisations, individuals and migrant familial and social networks of care can quickly form to fill the gaps of vulnerability left by the state and ensure the daily survival and well-being of released families. However, these networks also, inadvertently, serve to bolster overarching neoliberal and carceral logics that drive immigrant detention more broadly by shielding ICE and related state agencies from negative media attention and allowing for the burdens associated with providing for released migrants to be shifted away from state agencies.

Our analysis further illustrates that understanding contemporary detention practices requires attending to the space 'outside' detention centres and processes of immigrant release. This attention sheds light on the broad-reaching impacts of a carceral state, impacts that reverberate beyond the walls of detention centres. In drawing attention to the practices of immigrant release alongside detention, this chapter works to unravel overly simplistic binaries of inside/outside, detained/ free. As this case illustrates, the detention industrial complex does not only affect those who are kept within the confines of detention centres. Rather, impromptu and haphazard practices of release enroll a whole suite of actors into the processes and practices of providing basic assistance to immigrant families. Finally, this analysis suggests that an explicitly feminist analytic that re-scales analysis to the intimate sites of the body, family and community and attends to the way in which cultural ideologies of social and political subjectivity affect the uneven operation and application of state policies and practices can usefully complicate how we understand contemporary immigrant detention practices.

Attention to daily life, social reproduction and intimate economies is necessary for revealing the neoliberal and carceral logics that justify both migrant detention and mass incarceration more broadly. Such attention reveals that processes of managing migrants through both detention and subjective release mark the ongoing contradiction of carceral logics. Detention and control imply a responsibility for those in custody, yet we consistently see the externalising of the necessary practices and costs of social reproduction. An attention to social reproduction highlights the networks of care that sustain migrants while also revealing the problematic logics of security that drive the expansion of migrant detention. Moreover, as we have done here, a feminist attention to social reproduction and everyday life (Katz, 2001) reveals the way in which the effects of immigrant detention reverberate over space and scale.

As this book goes to press, struggles over immigrant family detention in the US continue. Throughout the summer and fall of 2014, a number of private prison corporations were given contracts to open new family detention centres in Texas. In July, $879 million of the $3.7 billion supplemental appropriations requested by the Obama administration were earmarked for increasing governmental capacity to detain and remove family units (The White House, 2014), funding the construction of up to 6,300 family detention beds across the country (Grassroots Leadership, 2014). In turn, the Corrections Corporation of America was contracted to open a 2,400 bed family detention facility in Dilley, Texas, the largest of its kind in US history (Sakuma, 2014). This facility began detaining families in November of 2014. However, widespread media attention regarding the subpar standards at these centres, in combination with legal challenges to the legality of detaining families with children, threaten both the expansion and continuation of family detention (Carcamo, 2015; Kim, 2015). In the summer of 2015, federal judge Dolly Gee ruled that Obama administration practices of detaining families violated the terms of the 1997 Flores agreement and further issued an order that all children be released without unnecessary delay along with their parents unless the person posed a flight risk or a threat to national security. How exactly this ruling will affect the widespread detention of immigrant families remains to be seen, as the administration continues to look for legal and procedural loopholes to enable the continued detention of families. While these battles are waged in federal courts and behind the closed doors of policy makers, families continue to be released and arrive at the doors of the Angelitos Project as the number of families apprehended in the first three months of fiscal year (FY) 2016 (October–December 2015) outpaced that of FY 2015 by 131 per cent (US Border Patrol, 2015).

While it remains to be seen what will become of immigrant family detention in the US, the above discussion of release practices illustrates the importance of continuing to examine the way in which practices of detention and the economic and cultural logics that shape them transcend detention centres and affect the most intimate aspect of migrants' daily lives and well-being. Understanding the ebbs and flows of immigrant detention in the US and beyond requires attending to what happens both within the walls of detention centres and when families are released from them.

Notes

1 ICE and CBP define family units as biological parents or legal guardians traveling with children under the age of 18.
2 Importantly, this framing of child migrants as innocent and non-agential is often mobilised by migrant advocates in order to argue for more sympathetic policies towards child migrants. However, this inadvertently serves to reinforce discourses of personal responsibility and free will that justify the criminalisation and widespread detention of adult migrants.
3 The names of this project and parent organisation have been changed at the request of the agency involved.

References

Benavie, A. 2009. *Drugs: America's holy war.* New York: Routledge.
Bigo, D. 2002. Security and immigration: toward a critique of the governmentality of unease. *Alternatives* **27**, pp. 63–92.
Bosniak, L. 2013. Arguing for amnesty. *Law, Culture and the Humanities* **9**(3), pp. 1–11.
Carcamo, C. 2015. US policy change may enable speedy release of detained immigrant families. *LA Times* [Online]. Available from: www.latimes.com/nation/la-na-immigration-family-detention-20150624-story.html [Accessed 13 July 2015].
Carrasco, L. and Trevizo, P. 2014. Border crosser surge in Texas crowds Tucson bus station. *Arizona Daily Star* [Online]. Available from: http://tucson.com/news/local/border/border-crosser-surge-in-texas-crowds-tucson-bus-station/article_13d822c7-9ed3-5f36-84ff-0c07975394a8.html [Accessed 13 July 2015].
Coleman, M. 2007. Immigration geopolitics beyond the Mexico-US border. *Antipode* **9**(1), pp. 54–76.

Coleman, M. 2009. What counts as the politics and practices of security, and where? Devolution and immigrant insecurity after 9/11. *Annals of the Association of American Geographers* **99**(5), pp. 904–13.

Conlon, D. and Hiemstra, N. 2014. Examining the everyday micro-economies of migrant detention in the United States. *Geographica Helvetica* **69**, pp. 335–44.

Coutin, S. B. 2010. Confined within: national territories as zones of confinement. *Political Geography* **29**(4), pp. 200–8.

Dalby, S. 1994. Gender and critical geopolitics: reading security discourse in the new world disorder. *Environment and Planning D: Society and Space* **12**, pp. 595–612.

Davis, A. Y. 2005. *Abolition democracy: beyond empire, prisons, and torture*. New York: Seven Stories Press.

Dixon, D. and Marston, S. 2011. Introduction: feminist engagements with geopolitics. *Gender, Place, and Culture* **18**(4), pp. 445–53.

Dowler, L. and Sharp, J. 2001. A feminist geopolitics? *Space & Polity* **5**(3), pp. 165–76.

Enloe, C. 1993. *Sexual politics at the end of the Cold War*. Berkeley: University of California Press.

Enloe, C. 2000. *Maneuvers: the international politics of militarizing women's lives*. Berkeley: University of California Press.

Faussett, R. and Belson, K. 2014. Faces of an immigration system overwhelmed by women and children. *New York Times* [Online]. Available from: www.nytimes.com/2014/06/06/us/faces-of-an-immigration-system-overwhelmed-by-women-and-children.html?_r=0 [Accessed 13 July 2015].

Galvan, A. 2014. Migrants dropped off at bus stations in Arizona. *Associated Press* [Online]. Available from: http://news.yahoo.com/migrants-dropped-off-bus-stations-arizona-211927493.html [Accessed 13 July 2015].

Gilmore, R. 2007. *Golden gulag: prisons, surplus, crisis, and opposition in globalizing California*. Berkeley: University of California Press.

Grassroots Leadership. 2014. *Facts about family detention* [Online]. Available from: http://grassrootsleadership.org/facts-about-family-detention [Accessed 20 December 2015].

Hennessey, R. 1993. *Materialist feminism and the politics of discourse*. New York: Routledge.

Hiemstra, N. 2012. Geopolitical reverberations of us migrant detention and deportation: the view from Ecuador. *Geopolitics* **17**(2), pp. 293–311.

Hyndman, J. 2000. *Managing displacement: refugees and the politics of humanitarianism*, Minneapolis: University of Minnesota Press.

Hyndman, J. 2004. Mind the gap: bridging feminist and political geography through geopolitics. *Political Geography* **23**(3), pp. 307–22.

Hyndman, J. 2008. Conflict, citizenship, and human security: geographies of protection. In: Cowen, D. and Gilbert, E. eds. *War, citizenship, territory*. New York: Routledge, pp. 241–57.

Hyndman, J. and Mountz, A. 2007. Refuge or refusal: the geography of exclusion. In: Gregory, D. and Pred, A. eds. *Violent geographies: fear, terror, and political violence*. New York: Routledge, pp. 77–92.

Jones, R. 2011. Border security, 9/11 and the enclosure of civilisation. *The Geographical Journal* **177**(3), pp. 213–7.

Jones, R. 2012. *Border walls: security and the war on terror in the United States, India, and Israel*. London, Zed Books.

Katz, C. 2001. Vagabond capitalism and the necessity of social reproduction. *Antipode* **33**(4), pp. 709–28.

Katz, C. 2007. Banal terrorism: spatial fetishism and everyday practice. In: Gregory, D. and Pred, A. eds. *Violent geographies: fear, terror, and political violence*. New York: Routledge, pp. 349–61.

Kim, S. 2015. Officials revise immigrant detention policy [Online]. Available from: www .politico.com/story/2015/06/obama-immigrant-detention-policy-revision-119377.html [Accessed 13 July 2015].

Lee, C. 2013. *Fictive kinship: family reunification at the meaning of race and nation in American immigration.* New York: Russell Sage.

Loyd, J., Mitchelson, M. and Burridge, A. 2012. *Beyond walls and cages: prisons, borders, and global crisis.* Athens: University of Georgia Press.

Luibheid, E. 2002. *Entry denied: controlling sexuality at the border.* Minneapolis: University of Minnesota Press.

Luibheid, E. and Cantu, L. eds. 2005. *Queer migrations: sexuality, US citizenship, and border crossings.* Minneapolis: University of Minnesota Press.

Marston, S. 2000. The social construction of scale. *Progress in Human Geography* **24**(2), pp. 219–42.

Martin, L. 2011. The geopolitics of vulnerability: children's legal subjectivity, immigrant family detention and US immigration law and enforcement policy. *Gender, Place & Culture: A Journal of Feminist Geography* **18**(4): 477–98.

Martin, L. 2012a. 'Catch and remove': detention, deterrence, and discipline in US noncitizen family detention practice. *Geopolitics* **17**(2), pp. 312–34.

Martin, L. 2012b. Governing through the family: struggles over US noncitizen family detention policy. *Environment and Planning A* **44**(4), pp. 866–88.

Massaro, V. and Williams, J. 2013. Feminist geopolitics: redefining the geopolitical, complicating (in)security. *Geography Compass* **7**(8), pp. 567–77.

McDowell, L. 2004. Work, workfare, work/life balance and an ethic of care. *Progress in Human Geography* **28**(2), pp. 145–63.

Mitchell, K., Marston, S. A. and Katz, C. eds. 2004. *Life's work: geographies of social reproduction*, Malden: Blackwell Publishing.

Mountz, A. 2010. *Seeking asylum: human smuggling and bureaucracy at the border.* Minneapolis: University of Minnesota Press.

Mountz, A. 2011. The enforcement archipelago: detention, haunting, and asylum on islands. *Political Geography* **30**(3), pp. 118–28.

Mountz, A. 2012. Mapping remote detention: dis/location through isolation. In: Loyd, J., Mitchelson, and M., Burridge, A. eds. *Beyond walls and cages: prisons, borders and global crisis.* Athens: University of Georgia Press, pp. 91–104.

Mountz, A., Coddington, K., Catania, R. T. and Loyd, J. M. 2012. Conceptualizing detention: mobility, containment, bordering, and exclusion. *Progress in Human Geography* **37**(4), pp. 522–41.

Mountz, A. and Hiemstra, N. 2012. Spatial strategies for rebordering human migration at sea. In: Wilson, T. and Donnan, H. eds. *A companion to border studies.* Malden: Blackwell Publishing, pp. 455–72.

Mountz, A. and Hiemstra, N. 2014. Chaos and crisis: dissecting the spatiotemporal logics of contemporary migrations and state practices. *Annals of the Association of American Geographers* **104**(2), pp. 382–90.

Nevins, J. 2010. *Operation Gatekeeper and beyond: the rise of the 'illegal alien' and the remaking of the US-Mexico boundary.* New York: Routledge.

Prendergast, C. 2014. Central American minors flood into BP's Nogales Station. *Nogales International* [Online]. Available from: www.nogalesinternational.com/news/central-american-minors-flood-into-bp-s-nogales-station/article_8c68d790-edd9-11e3-8d02-001a4bcf887a.html [Accessed 1 September 2015].

Puar, J. 2007. *Terrorist assemblages: homonationalism in queer times.* Durham: Duke University Press.

Rygiel, K. 2008. Protecting and proving identity: the biopolitics of waging war through citizenship in the post-9/11 era. In: Hunt, K. and Rygiel, K. eds. *(En)gendering the war on terror: war stories and camouflaged politics.* Burlington: Ashgate, pp. 145–68.

Sakuma, A. 2014. Feds greenlight huge immigrant family detention centre in texas. *Associated Press* [Online]. Available from www.msnbc.com/msnbc/feds-green-light-huge-immigrant-family-detention-centre-texas [Accessed 13 July 2015].

Sawicki, J. 1991. *Disciplining Foucault: feminism, power, and the body*. New York: Routledge.

Segura, D. and Zavella, P., eds. 2007. *Women and migration in the U.S.-Mexico borderlands: a reader*. Duke University Press Books.

Sharma, N. 2008. White nationalism, illegality and imperialism: border controls as ideology. In: Hunt, K. and Rygiel, K. eds. *(En)gendering the war on terror: war stories and camouflaged politics*. Burlington: Ashgate, pp. 121–43.

Smith, S. 2012. Intimate geopolitics: religion, marriage, and reproductive bodies in Leh, Ladakh. *Annals of the Association of American Geographers* **102**(6), pp.1511–28.

Sparke, M. 2004. Belonging in the PACE land: fast border crossing and citizenship in the age of neoliberalism. In: Migdal, J. ed. *Boundaries and belonging: states and societies in the struggle to shape identities and local practices*. Cambridge: Cambridge University Press, pp. 151–83.

Sparke, M. 2006. A neoliberal nexus: economy, security, and the biopolitics of citizenship on the border. *Political Geography* **25**(2), 151–80.

Trevizo, P. 2015. Communication still a challenge for indigenous border crossers. *Arizona Daily Star* [Online]. Available from: http://tucson.com/news/local/border/communication-still-a-challenge-for-indigenous-border-crossers/article_b80a0a9e-4e26-5592-b90d-b41723e67d28.html [Accessed 13 July 2015].

Tyler, I., Gill, N., Conlon, D. and Oeppen, C. 2014. The business of child detention: charitable co-option, migrant advocacy and activist outrage. *Race & Class* **56**(1), pp. 3–21.

Urbina, I. 2014. Using jailed migrants as a pool of cheap labor. *The New York Times* [Online]. Available from: www.nytimes.com/2014/05/25/us/using-jailed-migrants-as-a-pool-of-cheap-labor.html [Accessed 15 July 2015].

US Border Patrol. 2014. *Family unit and unaccompanied alien children (0–17) apprehensions FY 14 compared to FY 13* [Online]. Available from: www.cbp.gov/newsroom/stats/southwest-border-unaccompanied-children/fy-2016 [Accessed 12 May 2016].

US Border Patrol. 2015. *US Border Patrol Southwest Border family unit and UAC apprehensions (FY 2015-FY 2016)* [Online]. Available from: www.cbp.gov/newsroom/stats/southwest-border-unaccompanied-children/fy-2016 [Accessed 12 May 2016].

Varsanyi, M. 2008. Immigration policing through the backdoor: city ordinances, the 'right to the city', and the exclusion of undocumented day laborers. *Urban Geography* **29**(1), pp. 29–52.

The White House. 2014. *Fact sheet: emergency supplemental request* [Online]. Available from: www.whitehouse.gov/the-press-office/2014/07/08/fact-sheet-emergency-supplemental-request-address-increase-child-and-adu [Accessed 29 November 2015].

Women's Commission for Refugee Women and Children and Lutheran Immigration and Refugee Service. 2007. *Locking up family values: the detention of immigrant families* [Online]. Available from: www.refworld.org/docid/49ae507a2.html [Accessed 13 July 2015].

Yuval-Davis, N. 1998. *Gender and nation*. London: Sage.

7 On exterior and interior detention regimes

Governing, bordering and economy in transit migration across Mexico

Mario Bruzzone

Introduction: the *hielera* and the bar

In 2013, three migrants to the United States sued US Customs and Border Protection (CBP), alleging mistreatment in immigration detention. They contended that they were fed only once per day, denied communication with their family members, denied access to showers and toothbrushes, and said that their cells were so overcrowded that detainees had to take turns lying down. One plaintiff testified that, after apprehension, 'for six days she wore the same pants, shirt and undergarments she had on when apprehended. During three of the six days … she was menstruating. Because she had no way to clean herself, she smelled bad and was very ashamed that she was unable to properly clean herself.' None of the migrants had yet been determined to be legally removable, and nominally the immigration detention system is one of civil confinement (*Americans for Immigrant Justice v. Customs and Border Protection*, 2013).

The migrants described the site of their detention as a '*hielera*'. *Hielo* is the Spanish word for ice, and a *hielera* is anything that holds ice or is equivalently cold: a freezer, an icebox, a cooler or here, a jail cell. The word was used by guards and prisoners alike. One deposition alleged that:

> The temperature in the *hieleras* was so cold that [the detainee] observed that the lips and fingers of other detainees had turned blue. [She] experienced pain in her ears from the extreme cold. The cold also caused her face to turn red and her lips to chap and split. Because of the cold, she and the other detainees would huddle together on the floor for warmth. The cold temperature made it very difficult to sleep. … She and other detainees repeatedly asked that air conditioning be turned off but the CBP officers would simply laugh at these requests and the cells remained freezing.

Sites of detention combine material infrastructures of confinement, legal regimes of categorisation and exercises in subjectification. The *hielera* marks one extreme on a continuum of detention practices. In it, a punitive orientation toward migrants is produced alongside those conditions described in the complaint: confinement, overcrowded cells, inadequate warmth and indifference to bodily needs and bodily functions. While often obscured, sites such as the *hielera* open many opportunities to actualise power, including establishing the conditions for intimate and 'internal micro-economies' to emerge (Conlon and Hiemstra, 2014), the disruption of social belonging and/or legal rights (Coutin, 2010), and the reinscription of racialised difference (Boyce, Marshall and Wilson, 2015). For migrants not in detention but subject to the US detention regime, the possibility of entering into the carceral system contributes to a fearful atmosphere, often making migrants self-regulating, quiet, even 'docile' (Harrison and Lloyd, 2012; cf. Smith and Winders, 2008; Stuesse and Coleman, 2014). Numerous scholars across disciplines have traced the opportunities for economic accumulation and labour exploitation facilitated and perhaps produced by this system (e.g. De Genova, 2005; Theodore, 2007; Hiemstra, 2010). But other types of detention exist as well.

*

2013 also saw the English-language release of Óscar Martínez's book *The Beast*. Martínez, an excellent storyteller in both the Spanish original and in translation, draws open the curtain on the journeys of Central American migrants through Mexico. Chapter by chapter, moving from the south of Mexico incrementally northward, the book's subjects come to recognise themselves as encumbered by forms of spatial unfreedom. These Central Americans push their ways through Mexico, and Mexico pushes back, socially and through state institutions. Migrants find not only their movements arrested, but also qualitative limitations on their capabilities to even exist within space.

One particularly poignant story involves Erika, a Honduran sex worker in Huixtla, in the southern state of Chiapas. Erika arrived in Chiapas at 14 years old, with the intention of settling somewhere, anywhere, in the US. She never made it. Even at home in Honduras, she says, 'I never had papers. I never had a birth certificate either. I'm like an animal' (Martínez, 2013, 71). 'Like an animal', she is unable to show social membership or legal citizenship by way of documentation. Erika's story is not one of redemption. Nor is it a straightforward tale of victimhood. Rather it is a complex account in which Erika copes with exploitative sex work and, at the same time, manoeuvres her history and situation into one that provides her with material benefits and a degree of agency. When she arrived in Huixtla, she was already pregnant after leaving abuse in Honduras. She sought work in bars, and recalls

> her first days of prostitution with disgust. She'd close a deal with a man at a dive, and they'd go to a motel for half an hour. The room would fill with the smell of beer and sweat and she'd let herself be used. Sometimes it was like these men felt that they owned her for that half hour. … She remembers the many times the sessions ended with what she'd gotten to know so well as a girl: insults and violence.
>
> (Martínez, 2013, p. 75)

By the time Martínez meets her, Erika is 30. Both her world and her circumstances have changed. Sex work provides her an adequate living, enough that she can scarcely imagine her initial goal of migrating to the US. Nor does she want to return to Honduras. Yet she is stuck. The same work that provides her livelihood stigmatises her, and leaves her without clear recourse to other employment with similar pay. The same phenotype that makes her 'sought after' in sex work for her 'fleshier' body and 'lighter skin' (Martínez, 2013, p.76) also makes her stand out and hesitant to travel for fear of detainment and incarceration. Indeed, for undocumented migrants in and undocumented residents of southern Mexico, space is invested with relations of power via ever-present threats of targeted extortion, expropriation and violence. As channelled by Martínez, Erika narrates a confinement to a single small city, a confinement not exactly caused by government but undoubtedly related to state practices. It is a confinement that conditions her choices as well as her subjectivity, what she can do and who she considers herself to be.

*

The *hielera* and the Huixtla bar scene each mark a form of spatial detention for migrants. In this chapter I want to locate them as points toward the extremes of a continuous field of spatial detention practices. Incarceration need not be actualised for detention to become real, as scholars of the state system of immigration detention have long understood. For instance, the devolution of US immigration enforcement to local police and sheriffs since 2001 has led to migrants limiting their use of public space and curtailing their public presence, since even a pretextual police stop can lead to their detainment, the *hielera* and summary deportation (Coleman, 2007; Winders, 2007; Smith and Winders, 2008; Harrison and Lloyd, 2012; Boyce, Marshall and Wilson, 2015). Migrants find themselves circumscribed within communities and very small social worlds. Correspondingly, migrants in transit toward the US also may curtail their public presence, to be less vulnerable to Mexican state 'rescues', extra-legal detention by state agents, kidnapping, forced labour and the extraction of 'rents', 'quotas', or 'tolls'. This list presents additional points on a continuum of migrant detention, and the list of exterior detentions connects to interior policing very deliberately. For 20 years, the CBP has intended to detain and delay overland migrants within Mexico, laid out in its policy of 'prevention through deterrence'. Or rather, the CBP has sought to promote conditions through which migrants are detained and delayed, while leaving such work to others.

Opportunities for accumulation emerge alongside detention practices and detention regimes. In the *hielera*'s 'interior' detention regime, migrant detention may be part of a series of direct state interventions that create and maintain an abject 'unauthorised' population providing cheap sources of labour (De Genova, 2005; Hiemstra, 2010; Conlon and Hiemstra, 2014). Possibilities for accumulation arise 'beyond the overt logic of national security' (Conlon and Hiemstra, 2014, p.335) that legitimates the un/authorised division. So too in the economy of 'exterior' detention present in Erika's story, where her constitution as a labourer occurs outside the US yet in relation to the mechanisms of power that structure practices of state bordering. Erika is one worker in an expansive economy that adheres to migration through Mexico, an economy that includes migrant work en route, the middlemen who may organise migrants' journeys, and the depredations and extortions paid by migrants and their *polleros* (smugglers or guides). Where the 'interior' detention regime orders institutions such as prisons, government bureaucracies and even corporations in order to materialise forms of power on migrants' bodies, the 'exterior' detention regime is comprised of anexact but intentionally produced time-space effects on a territorial exterior. The exterior detention regime enrols complicit actors. In its economy, it substitutes the consistency of punishment – *hieleras* being one example – with the dislocating possibilities of violence and their accompanying physical burdens and intensities.

This chapter argues that the *hielera* and the Huixtla bar exist within a continuous field of forms of spatial unfreedom achieved by political and economic means. I use the term 'spatial unfreedom' analogously to the political-economy term 'social unfreedom'. In political economy 'social unfreedom' charts how people may be juridically free but socially unfree to choose their courses of action – such as juridically free not to work but bound socially to the wage (e.g. Chakrabarty, 2000). I use 'spatial unfreedom' to mark that even juridically 'free' people – those outside legal detentions – may have hindrances on how, where and in what manner they can travel, move, migrate or exist. While the argument proceeds via textual and theoretical strategies, I do so drawing upon a deep involvement with migration in and through Mexico, including a series of ethnographic research trips to central Mexico since 2011; projects attending to incarcerated migrants in the US; nine months working directly in Mexican migrant shelters; and more than 90 formal interviews, and even more informal interviews, with migrants in transit through central and western Mexico.

The terms 'interior' and 'exterior' detention mark state and non-state detentions, while signifying their co-production. In asserting the interconnectivity of forms of detention and state-bordering practices, the first contribution of this chapter is to propose that the external detention regime in Mexico represents an activation of power, rather than a refusal to manage a given territory. Tracing 'prevention through deterrence' as a bureaucratic logic, the following section describes how both interior and exterior detentions are purposeful in their broad contours. Migrants are targeted multiplicatively, and largely without regard for territory, even while that territory conditions state strategies. Reading the recent work of Sandro Mezzadra and Brett Neilson in the context of this external detention regime, the third section examines the generative economic effects of detention. The border regime appears to produce a labour force out of transit migrants. The emphasis on how forms of detention in Mexico are concomitant with migration economies configured by and through the US–Mexico 'border regime' (Mezzadra and Neilson, 2013) comprises the second contribution of this chapter. However, the economic diversity present in Mexico makes Mezzadra and Neilson's analysis incomplete. The fourth section uses J.K. Gibson-Graham's (1996) diverse economies framework to ground more firmly the chapter's economic arguments. Gibson-Graham's work facilitates a reading of the external detention regime as generative of a novel class formation for migrants, one that helps regulate their social and economic integration as labourers, but does so without presuming that they are subsumed by a unified, hegemonic capitalist economy. Taken together, this chapter advocates understanding the exterior detention regime as an accomplishment in which a state invests power in its exterior. The border regime is an inextricable element of the economies that result.

Prevention through deterrence

The interior detention regime of the *hielera* is clearly a state-propelled operation. So too is the exterior detention regime. Since 1993 the US government has implemented a strategy of 'prevention through deterrence' along the US–Mexico border. The strategy demonstrates an active attempt to manage overland migration. No longer may 'unauthorised' migrants cross in the relative safety of urban areas; rather, they must traverse remote, high-risk areas, walking through deserts and mountains, on the hypothesis that this should deter crossing attempts (Doty, 2011; Maril, 2011; De León, 2013). The *Border Patrol Strategic Plan 1994 and Beyond*, which laid out the strategy, states its underlying logic:

> The Border Patrol will improve control of the border by implementing a strategy of 'prevention through deterrence'. … The Border Patrol will increase the number of agents on the line and make effective use of technology, raising the risk of apprehension high enough to be an effective deterrent. Because the deterrent effect of apprehensions does not become effective in stopping the flow until apprehensions approach 100 percent of those attempting entry, the strategic objective is to maximize the apprehension rate.
>
> (United States Border Patrol, 1994, p. 6)

Not only was the risk of apprehension to be raised, but the 'cost' (1994, p. 8) of apprehension as well. Owing to epistemological difficulties in knowing migrants' motivations, the policy describes 'indicators of success', including both a 'shift in flow to other areas in southwest border' than urban crossing points, and 'possible increase in complaints (Mexico, interest groups, etc.)' (1994, pp. 9–10). These among other 'indicators' would signal that the immediate tactics were working. Empirically, little evidence validates prevention through deterrence in reducing undocumented migration nor in reducing the US's undocumented population. Yet other effects have come into force.

This section reads the 'prevention through deterrence' policy in light of its strategic failure, one that contrasts with the significant success of CBP tactics. Realised alongside this failure – indeed, a constitutive part of the policy – has been the production of an exterior space of state management. Since the 1990s, the risks, costs and length of overland migration journeys have increased dramatically. The Central American migrants who today comprise the bulk of the overland flow find themselves vulnerable both to the appropriation of their bodies – as valuables to be kidnapped and ransomed – and to the economic exploitation of their labour (Vogt, 2013; Furlong and Netzahualcoyotzi, 2014). However, harder and more dangerous journeys do not mean 'less likely to be successful' nor 'less likely to occur at all'. That difference invites a closer inspection at the logics and processes of deterrence and detention that produce a state exterior. The strategy here is textual, in order to excavate the avowed intents and instrument-effects that have driven the policy for more than 20 years.

First, the *Plan*'s 'key assumption' that 'a strong interior enforcement posture works well for border control' (1994, p. 5) codes the spatial extent of operations. The 'posture' defines an orientation meant to propagate deterrence effects by both 'agents on the line' and by means of effects visited on, potentially, all unauthorised migrants residing in the US. Via bureaucratic speech-act, activities 'on the line' are made contiguous with those in the territorial interior. 'Border control' may involve activities at the territorial margin and within the territorial interior, but rather curiously is only ever defined via the apprehension rate of those who attempt to cross. The apprehension rate, however, is literally unknowable and incalculable, since population sizes are unknown. One can estimate. But what the lack of definition for 'control' indicates more faithfully is, on the one hand, that border spaces can be variably discursively configured, as 'under' or 'out of' control (1994, p. 7) as bureaucratic priorities warrant; and on the other, that border spaces can be variably extensive, that areas 'under' or 'out of' control can be expanded or contracted, or produced as new spaces requiring intervention.

A second implication of 'prevention through deterrence' is that Border Patrol 'success' derives from a 'shift in flow' of migration. The shift's purpose is anticipatory, to divert routes away from urban crossing points and into a terrain more suitable to Border Patrol priorities. It is not just that urban spaces make it easy for migrants to disappear after crossing, but that Mexican urban spaces can provide vital resources for potential 'entrants'. Rerouting flows lessens migrants' capacities to exploit the resources of urban space. Then, over time, the deterrence effect is to be realised as successive waves of migrants cross the desert and as hazards become increasingly recognised. This spatial reorganisation entails changes on both sides of the border. That is, the policy directs flows through specific configurations of Mexican territory as well as US territory. It signals an intention to effect material changes within Mexico, directly and through the actions of smugglers and others who end up complicit.

Third, the document anticipates not only that physical harm will befall migrants, including violence, but that these harms would become widely known. The indicator that 'complaints' from interest groups and 'Mexico' – a country of over 90 million people in 1994 – marks the work of a logic of differentiation and a geography of subjectivity. In burdening migrants with newly hazardous crossings, the policy produces them as fundamentally distinct from others who are not subject to such dangers. This effect persists even if – even though – the deterrence effect fails. Overland irregular migrants are forced to recognise themselves as differentiated. Even when individuals spatially and socially force their inclusion, they must face that such inclusion is not on the same terms as others. If they succeed and enter the US without inspection, it is at the cost of having to physically submit to a hierarchy of movement, of peril, and of continuing spatial unfreedom. The policy qualitatively differentiates these migrants, and forces them to make choices and recognise themselves through its operations.

Because the exterior effects here occur outside of the US, they are made to appear as at once outside state responsibility, within migrants' (and others') deserts, and as apart from everyday life. 'Prevention through deterrence', in imagining migrants as a legible population who respond to higher migration costs with fewer attempts, tries to produce effects in the borderlands that will change migrants' preferences. Moving migrants to perilous environments operates as part of this bureaucratic logic, and the production of effects on the Mexican side of the border is an intended outcome. In practice, violence, longer journeys and higher costs all detain migrants. In turn, this marks migrants as Other, distinct and yet nevertheless subject to state power. What makes the exterior modes of detention so interesting, however, is the bureaucratic *refusal* of management. The US–Mexico border may have, as Roxanne Doty argues (2011), areas where the US state refuses (moral) responsibility; yet, this does not signal that such areas are outside the state's view, nor outside of its influence. Instead, that refusal marks the active production of an exterior, one that nevertheless is expected to have certain social practices emerge within it – especially migrant exploitation. Those 'unmanaged' formations impress on migrants differential degrees of spatial unfreedom and enable opportunities for accumulation, just as 'managed' formations do.

Border regime as method

Along the US–Mexico border, state management practices consolidate interior and exterior detentions. These management practices, in turn, implicate everyday economic practices and everyday economic life. Moreover, as the effects of management practices at the border spill out into territory far distant from the borderlands, opportunities for accumulation extend outward as well. This means that not only is it possible to study the political economy of the external detention regime in the local spaces of a state's domestic interior, in addition, it strongly suggests that it is in such spaces that the vast majority of a border regime's effects are materialised and felt.

Sandro Mezzadra and Brett Neilson's *Border as Method* (2013) provides a number of essential reference points for understanding how border regimes are structurally and economically embedded in daily life. A critical question animating academic discussions of the political economy of the interior detention regime involves the relations between border regimes and accumulation regimes, between borders and mobility. The mechanisms of the *hielera* – how it is operationalised, how it operates, by whom, and for what ends – present both empirical and theoretical challenges to scholarship. Mezzadra and Neilson's account is compelling and salient because it is equally persuasive in describing the mechanics of interior and exterior detention regimes. This section selectively reads *Border as Method* against the 'prevention through deterrence' policy in order to ground a theoretical analysis of the political economies of both the *hielera* and the Huixtla bar.

Acts of bordering, Mezzadra and Neilson say, are comprised by two essential spatial processes. The first is a process of selection and inclusion. A border excludes by dividing some things from others, but also acts as a device of inclusion by grouping or associating other things. At territorial margins, this process is at work as borders simultaneously filter passage and come to structure affective belonging. Indeed borders operate in a variety of spaces, conditions and knowledge regimes. State borders configure and reinscribe constitutive 'insides' and 'outsides', shifting where and how people make friends and community, people's everyday movements and projects, small-scale business development, large capital investments, cultural rivalries, and of course the validity of legal regimes of militarised border policing. Thus, and consonant with other work (e.g. Nevins, 2010), 'control' of boundaries means less perfect prevention of irregular movements than the sculpting and structuring of the social formations on either side of the border (Mezzadra and Neilson, 2013, p. 55ff.). The second spatial process is differential circulation, in which the border regime conditions not just the possibilities of mobility across the border itself, but also within that which a border separates. This signifies distinct velocities and trajectories within spaces, and also how inclusion itself may be disunified, even incoherent. Differential circulation marks how inclusion may be conditional, even predicated, on subordination to varying degrees of hierarchy, subjugation and social and spatial unfreedom. The material, legal and political conditions of crossing a border alter not just the mobilities nor the routes of migrants within a territory, but also migrants' inclusion as political subjects and/or as embodied labour-power. That is, how they and their labour are permitted to move through space. Importantly, the processes of selection-inclusion and differential circulation are simultaneous; one is not prior to the other.

Mezzadra and Neilson's analytic lens is scaled to the state, with tell-tale markers of World Systems Theory. The *Border Patrol Strategic Plan 1994 and Beyond* reveals a similar scalar imaginary and scalar object. In its 'strong interior posture', it advocates 'closing the loopholes that allow illegal aliens to gain equities in the United States'. Over time, it anticipates, first, a 'change in traditional traffic pattern', second, a 'reduction in use of social services and benefits in the US' – without specifying from or by whom – and, eventually, 'pressure for another "Bracero program" (temporary worker program)' due to 'economic changes in [the] US' (1994, pp. 4, 11–12). As a product of the CBP, the *hielera* participates in the *Strategic Plan*'s ambition to catalyse substantial social and economic changes. More broadly, the document corroborates both selection-inclusion (e.g. the reconstituted 'Bracero' guest-worker program, or migrants' attempts to 'gain equities') and differential circulation (e.g., the traffic pattern, or in the document's emphasis on highway accidents).

The operations the *Strategic Plan* defines, anticipates and orders also mean to alter inclusion and circulation outside US territory. 'Strategic objectives', tactics, 'coordinated actions', and effects are muddled in the document, but key is the conception that full deterrence will only occur by increasing both the risk of apprehension and 'the "cost" to illegal entrants sufficiently to deter entry' (1994, p. 8). Bluntly, the Plan materially establishes a particular political economy in the borderlands: increased economic burdens to migrants, the propagation of a migration economy via increased recourse to *polleros*, altered timings and routes of passage, and proliferating the danger of transit ('Violence will increase as effects of strategy are felt', 1994, p. 4). Crucially, 'prevention by deterrence' must have a spatial extensivity that spills out beyond US territory. The regime of border management affects circulations. In lieu of traveling long-established routes with trusted companions, today migrants employ professional *polleros* both to guide them through and keep them safe in dangerous locations, especially in risky environments (Doty, 2011; Maril, 2011; Boyce, Marshall and Wilson, 2015). It also affects selection-inclusion: migrants are subject to specific economies, such as that of voluntary migrant-smuggling, and to specific forms of violence, including kidnapping and forcible labour (Vogt, 2013; Furlong and Netzahualcoyotzi, 2014). The anticipated 'violence' around the passage is not a 'double effect', but a means to the state's ends, and a mechanism that collectively punishes everyone living near migration routes or in the borderlands.

In the spaces of migration routes such as Huixtla, Mezzadra and Neilson offer an analysis of the interfaces between logics of state power and economic governance. State governance of migrant circulations, Mezzadra and Neilson aver, shifts the 'parameters of time and space' (2013, p. 132) to make hierarchies within labour markets. Erika, as an illegalised labourer in a stigmatised field of employment, hindered in her onward movement as a migrant, perhaps epitomises how labour-power can be made available from an otherwise-mobile body via the continual making and remaking of borders within interior spaces. The twin processes of bordering serve to differentiate her; they direct her into a specific workforce – although this is a tendency rather than an inescapable structure – and constitute her in a class of subjects set apart from unmarked citizens. Erika's constitution as a labourer within exploitative conditions is facilitated by an extralegal regime meant to arrest her movements. Further, this process has deeply subjectivised Erika, who is coerced into staying in Huixtla without testing or probing much the exact boundaries of her spatial unfreedom. Martínez depicts her as deeply self-aware of those identity terms that constitute her difference: as Honduran, as 'older' for her employment, as a sex worker. Even more, her income serves as one of her few bases to claim local inclusion. Set apart bureaucratically by citizenship and culturally by employment, her capacity as a consumer conditions her ability to socially integrate where she lives, as one of the few ways she might 'gain equity' with others. Mezzadra and Neilson term this a species of 'citizenship' (2013, p. 244ff.) whereby governance facilitates some economic formations and forms of economic participation while proscribing others. Thereby, the continuum of economic effects extends between interior and exterior detentions, linked by state-sanctioned processes that govern the terms of inclusion and circulation and yet externalise and elide accountability. Erika, successfully 'deterred', is made or makes herself an economic subject.

The system's complexity indicates the limitations of using geopolitics to understand its political economy. Exterior detention regimes implicate contingent and locally specific, but state-sanctioned, relations between labour and accumulation, and indeed novel class productions alongside increased precarisation. Certainly the ways that states have spatially reoriented border-enforcement activities to their exteriors or to quasi-territorial spaces, the US included, fundamentally concerns economy. A complex calculation occurs as some states attempt to foist off the activities of border enforcement onto others, especially as a foreign aid condition (de Haas, 2008; Hiemstra, 2012; Wahlia, 2013). In addition, the burgeoning scholarship on border externalisation is right to argue that those activities backstop entry and exit enforcement through policing minority and immigrant communities, especially in the United States (Hiemstra, 2010; Conlon and Hiemstra, 2014; Stuesse and Coleman, 2014). Yet externalisation often moves rather than alters interior detention regimes. Exterior detention regimes produce the restructuring of social fields as migrants adapt, are delayed, and have their journeys extended, diverted and impeded. The broad economies implicate duration, violence, subjectification and class conversion.

Class and detention

While Mezzadra and Neilson's work is a key contribution, local application in Mexico may be a challenge. *Border as Method* presupposes the contemporary World System, in that capital and capitalism are its singularly privileged movers. But in Mexico capitalism exists among a diversity of economic formations. An accounting of just those economic forms that involve migrants would include: the commoditisation of migrants through the instrumentality of detention, both by states and by kidnappers (Guillermoprieto, 2011; Sánchez, 2014); neo-feudal conditions that have long physically, socially, forcibly and/or economically detained migrants, especially in agriculture (Chávez, 2012; Marosi, 2014; Ortiz Acevedo, 2014); coerced labour, including the forcible conversion of migrants into minor drug smugglers (Espinoza, 2014); protection rackets orchestrated by local or federal police (Mendoza Aguilar, 2014); share work, for instance in parts of the Mexican fishing industry; forms of work-trade; begging; and the scores of migrant shelters located along common routes that freely give food, water and clothing to migrants. The length of this list only sketches the profound extent that, while the political economy of migrating bodies involves capitalist social relations, capitalist social relations fail to fully explain migration economies.

This incompleteness then poses a challenge. The political economy of the Huixtla bar is misrepresented if reduced solely to capitalism. Erika's choices are configured but not determined by the border regime, which also facilitates the conversion of certain bodies into labourers. More generally, if migrants in Mexico are not exploited for specifically capitalist accumulation, but for 'diverse' modes of accumulation, what economic logic can cohere migration economies? This section uses Mezzadra and Neilson's too-brief encounter with the work of J.K. Gibson-Graham as a point of departure, tentatively proposing that the exterior detention regime is one that attempts to cohere migrants as a class. To the extent that Erika's detention in Huixtla locates a point within a continuum of detention practices, Gibson-Graham's conception of class – as a relation to surplus value – can more firmly ground the ways that detention implicates economy, for individuals and within broader analytic framings. Where previous sections argued for a continuum of state bordering practices and a continuity of economic effects across detention regimes, this section attempts to specify one way in which the subjects of exterior detention regimes are cohered to each other. The invocation of the language of class here is, avowedly, not meant to flatten difference. On the contrary, drawing from feminist economic geography, the goal is to give a proposal for how difference is created and put to work, and subsequent to this production how it may generate opportunities for exploitation.

Gibson-Graham's major and celebrated contribution in *The End of Capitalism (as We Knew It)* hinges on the separation of the 'economically differentiated and complex' social world (1996, p. xl–xli) from the hegemonic discourse that capitalism is the inescapable condition of contemporary life. Diverging from economistic accounts that posit a global capitalism determining the social, Gibson-Graham argue that any given capitalist practice (e.g. factory work, in their example) is overdetermined by processes, events, situations, institutions, relations of power and so forth that are exterior to it (1996, p. 16). Where theorists like David Harvey might view the varying forms of violence and exploitation in Mexico as along a continuous gradation of capitalist, precapitalist and 'ancient forms of labour process' (1992, p. 153), Gibson-Graham's 'diverse economy' refuses any easy teleology. Instead, Gibson-Graham anchor a notion of plural economic space and the coexistence of multiple economic formations. Discourses of hegemonic capitalism serve to obscure but not obviate such formations.

In a key moment, Gibson-Graham reimagine the location and ontological status of class. While Mezzadra and Neilson do operate with a nuanced and complex understanding of class in both its technical composition (the relation to the means of production) and its political composition (class as a subjective and affective relation), in their work class iterates fundamentally from struggles between labour and capital over surplus (Mezzadra and Neilson, 2013, p. 98ff.). That presumes the primacy and hegemony of capital in determining the form and landscape of the social world. By contrast, Gibson-Graham's work retains class as a processual relation, but to the creation, distribution and appropriation of surplus value. Gibson-Graham's terms elaborate how multiple class positions, across a diversity of economic formations, may not only be present within a given site but also how multiple positions may be held by a single individual. A factory worker may be classed through wage labour in the workplace and an appropriator of surplus value produced in a (feudalistic) home structured by patriarchal gender roles. Similarly, migrants in Mexico may be simultaneously exploited and appropriators of surplus value produced by others, they may occupy class positions outside of the wage relation, but most importantly they often occupy a position with regards to exploitation and distribution of surplus that has not only been configured specifically for their political, social and subjective control but that is exclusive to those subjectified as 'migrants'.

Erika's story is once again exemplary, and through it we might trace how a configuration of forces produces her as a migrant. The circumstances of her trip placed her in Huixtla. Her journey was slowed first by an inability to board an airplane – a cheaper, faster and more secure form of transport than the overland journey. Sex work presented itself as one of but few options for work available to her, and her need to work within Mexico has clear relation to the conditions of passage to and across the US–Mexico border. Erika's lack of mobility as much as the inclusion her income allows – that, while stigmatising, sex work pays much better than any other option she can conceive of in Mexico – condition her decision to remain, that is, essentially to give up her onward migration to the US. Border 'enforcement,' together with the production of her exterior detention, may be understood as a technique conjoining state power, bordering and economy. Erika finds herself economically subjectified within this network of relations, produced both qualitatively as a migrant (having less or no claim on the state, in its view) and as the bearer of labour-power.

Gibson-Graham's language of class provides a means to extend and deepen the relation between the identitarian work of bordering and the production of migrants as bearers of labour-power. The intimate economies of Erika's story – the complex relations that comprise the production and division of work and wealth in, through and articulated with everyday, embodied experience – represent a convergence of myriad social forces. Erika's national origin, her life on the streets prior to migration, violence and patriarchy within and without sex work, exploitation, the underdevelopment of Honduras, and poverty all weigh in her situation. They serve as inextricable elements of that situation. She finds herself multiply marginalised, via her irregular immigration status, through her lack of any documents to demonstrate identity or origin, and by her legal vulnerability as a worker in a criminalised economic sector. Her sector itself may even differentiate her, as migrants are sought for the work (Martínez, 2013, p. 76). Because Erika's relationship to the creation, appropriation and distribution of surplus is configured inextricably from her economic participation and inclusion as a migrant, 'migrant' can be said to be a class position. While Erika retains much of the income from her labour, some is appropriated by the bar where she works, and she had no say in its distribution. Following Gibson-Graham, this is not to present a totalising view. Neither is this class relation Erika's only position nor is it the unique way of comprehending the class relations of her story. What Erika shares with fellow migrants similarly classed, however, is the combination of everyday forces that align and push them towards certain forms of economic inclusion while excluding them from others. They share the conditions of possibility for movement and work.

Conclusion: detention at the interface of state and economy

Reading Gibson-Graham's work alongside Mezzadra and Neilson's reveals the close – or intimate – connections between economic life and exterior detention regimes. Forms of spatial unfreedom, articulating through class processes, subjectify migrants traversing Mexico. Where a political economy produces migrants as bearers of labour power, the designation of a body as a migrant's body – and the recognition of a subject as a migrant – enables multiple and differential exploitation of that newly accessible labour power. Mezzadra and Neilson argue that the proliferation of migrant-detention apparatuses worldwide is 'less a means of excluding migrants than of regulating the time and speed of their movements into labour markets' as wage-labourers (2013, p. 132). Whether or not wage-labour is the *ne plus ultra* of detention, both interior and exterior detention regimes make for class-formation projects. From the perspective of a state, the proliferation of detention helps to order how migrant-subjects will enter into their management, and likewise accounts for one way in which states 'profit' from both organised and disorganised border violence.

From the perspective of a migrant, subjectification appears as varying forms of 'time-space expansion', as a series of delays, deferrals and detentions avoided, or a series of delays, deferrals or detentions endured. This chapter has argued for a continuity of forms of migrant detention from state detention facilities to the production of exterior forms of detention. The *hielera* and the Huixtla bar represent points towards the extremes of this continuity. My argument has been that this continuity is, in the US–Mexico border regime, consolidated through the CBP policy of 'prevention through deterrence', that it is productive of and reinforced by the migration economies that have emerged alongside the state project. Further, I have proposed that this political economy, as it attaches to migrants individually, configures them by means of their difference in relation to the creation, distribution and appropriation of surplus.

In this argument, my hope is to present one way of connecting literatures on carceral geographies and border studies, which have in many ways been discrete. One area where they have had fruitful collaboration, in work on the externalisation of border controls, has largely focused on interior modes of detention that are outsourced (cf. Collyer and King, 2015). From the critical perspective offered here, such outsourcing does not convert externalised controls into exterior detention regimes, even while the spatial effects are numerous and important. Rather, the labour of my argument is to recognise those exterior detention regimes in areas where a state attempts management but disclaims influence.

In focusing on political economy, the argument may further extend to future work looking to how detention beyond incarceration serves as an 'interface' between state and economy (cf. Gilmore, 2007, pp. 11–2). State coercion of bodies often occurs in organised ways outside of but in concert with a textual legal regime. As I complete this chapter, Mexico is in the midst of a deep militarisation of transit-migration governance. Nearly all of Mexico's border-enforcement practice is legally extra-textual, in that it is in flagrant, intentional and open contradiction to Mexican law (Morales Vega, 2012; Castilla Juárez, 2014). The effects of this produce an interior detention regime of significant size within Mexico – more than 180,000 detentions in the initial 11 months of 2015 (SEGOB 2015, pp. 122–23) – but also an exterior detention regime within Mexico configured by actions of Mexican state agents. The ambiguity of whether the militarisation and deportations are inside or outside the law indicates that legal texts may not be the primary producers of state detention, nor the difference alone between interior and exterior detentions. What legal documents – and, here, an operational document – can corroborate is the state intent to produce exteriorised effects. For scholars, the important point is that the US and Mexico produce both interior and exterior detention regimes, but that the terms signify not a relation to bordered territory so much as a geography of the spatial extent of state practices. And the internal and external detention regimes may only ever work simultaneously. The consolidation of occasional practices of detention into the dependability of a detention regime also constitutes that regime's outside. I suggest here, then, that research on border studies and incarceration may be 'incomplete' as a field without attention to this interconnection. As to the present moment in Mexico, in which the stability of detention remains elusive, we can locate neither an empirical internal nor empirical external detention, but the co-presence of both, attesting to their multiplicity, continuity and complicity for subjectifying those in transit.

Acknowledgements

I am indebted to the editors, Keith Woodward, Sarah Moore and my parents. Several contributors to this volume, including Jill Williams and Malene Jacobsen, provided insightful comments on a very early version of this work (given as a paper talk). I further thank the UW–Madison Department of Geography and the Trewartha Fund for their support.

References

Americans for Immigrant Justice v. Customs and Border Protection. 2013. 1:14-cv-20945.
Boyce, G.A., Marshall, D.J. and Wilson, J. 2015. Concrete connections? Articulation, homology and the political geography of boundary walls. *Area* **47**(3), pp. 289–95.
Castilla Juárez, K. A. 2014. Ley de migración mexicana: algunas de sus inconstitucionalidades. *Migración y desarrollo* **12**(23), pp. 149–81.
Chakrabarty, D. 2000. *Provincializing Europe: postcolonial thought and historical difference*. Princeton, N. J: Princeton University Press.
Chávez, S. 2012. The Sonoran Desert's domestic bracero programme: institutional actors and the creation of labour migration streams. *International Migration* **50**(2), pp. 20–40.
Coleman, M. 2007. Immigration geopolitics beyond the Mexico–US border. *Antipode* **39**(1), pp. 54–76.
Collyer, M. and King, R. 2015. Producing transnational space: International migration and the extra territorial reach of state power. *Progress in Human Geography* **39**(2), pp.185–204.
Conlon, D. and Hiemstra, N. 2014. Examining the everyday micro-economies of migrant detention in the United States. *Geographica Helvetica* **69**, pp. 335–44.

Coutin, S. B. 2010. Confined within: national territories as zones of confinement. *Political Geography* **29**(4), pp.200–8.

De Genova, N. 2005. *Working the boundaries: race, space, and 'illegality' in Mexican Chicago.* Durham, N. C: Duke University Press.

de Haas, H. 2008. The myth of invasion: the inconvenient realities of African migration to Europe. *Third World Quarterly* **29**(7), pp.1305–22.

De León, J. 2013. The efficacy and impact of the Alien Transfer Exit Programme: migrant perspectives from Nogales, Sonora, Mexico. *International Migration* **51**(2), pp. 10–23.

Doty, R. L. 2011. Bare life: border-crossing deaths and spaces of moral alibi. *Environment and Planning D: Society and Space* **29**(4), pp. 599–612.

Espinoza, L. 2014. Ciudad Acuña: válvula de escape para migrantes. *Zócalo Saltillo* [Online]. 10 June. www.zocalo.com.mx/seccion/articulo/ciudad-acuna-valvula-de-escape-para-migrantes-1412619603 [Accessed 2 May 2016].

Furlong, A. and Netzahualcoyotzi, R. 2014. Migración, trata e infancia en el Plan Mesoamérica. *REBELA – Revista Brasileira de Estudos Latino-Americanos* **3**(1), pp. 47–64.

Gibson-Graham, J. K. 1996. *The end of capitalism (as we knew it): a feminist critique of political economy.* Minneapolis: University of Minnesota Press.

Gilmore, R. W. 2007. *Golden gulag: prisons, surplus, crisis, and opposition in globalizing California.* Berkeley and Los Angeles: University of California.

Guillermoprieto, A. ed. 2011. *72 migrantes.* Oaxaca de Juárez, Oaxaca: Almadía.

Harrison, J.L. and Lloyd, S.E. 2012. Illegality at work: deportability and the productive new era of immigration enforcement. *Antipode* **44**(2), pp. 365–85.

Harvey, D. 1992. *The condition of postmodernity: an enquiry into the origins of cultural change.* Oxford. Cambridge, MA: Blackwell.

Hiemstra, N. 2010. Immigrant 'illegality' as neoliberal governmentality in Leadville, Colorado. *Antipode* **42**(1), pp. 74–102.

Hiemstra, N. 2012. Geopolitical reverberations of US migrant detention and deportation: the view from Ecuador. *Geopolitics* **17**(2), pp. 293–311.

Maril, R. L. 2011. *The fence: national security, public safety, and illegal immigration along the US Mexico border.* Lubbock, TX: Texas Tech University Press.

Marosi, R. 2014. Desperate workers on a Mexican mega-farm: 'They treated us like slaves'. *Los Angeles Times.* 10 December [Online]. Available from: http://graphics.latimes.com/product-of-mexico-labor/ [Accessed 26 February 2015].

Martínez, O. 2013. *The beast: riding the rails and dodging narcos on the migrant trail.* London: Verso.

Mendoza Aguilar, G. 2014. 'Atorados': de migrantes a mendigos. *La Opinión.* 9 March [Online]. Available from: www.laopinion.com/noticiaslatinoamerica/article/20140309/Atorados-de-migrantes-a-mendigos [Accessed 12 August 2014].

Mezzadra, S. and Neilson, B. 2013. *Border as method, or, the multiplication of labor.* Durham: Duke University Press.

Morales Vega, L. G. 2012. Categorías migratorias en México. Análisis a la Ley de Migración. *Anuario Mexicano de Derecho Internacional* XII, pp. 929–58.

Nevins, J. 2010. *Operation Gatekeeper and beyond: the war on 'illegals' and the remaking of the US Mexico boundary.* New York: Routledge.

Ortiz Acevedo, L. 2014. Mujeres migrantes padecen explotación y hacinamiento: reportaje - esclavitud de jornaleras en campos de Sinaloa. *CIMAC Noticias.* 20 January [Online]. http://www.cimacnoticias.com.mx/node/65430 [Accessed 2 May 2016].

Sánchez, L. 2014. Tijuana: deportados, entre la miseria y la extorsión. *El Universal.* 22 October [Online]. Available from: www.eluniversal.com.mx/estados/2014/tijuana-deportados-entre-la-miseria-y-la-extorsion-1048038.html [Accessed 18 January 2015].

Secretaría de Gobernación (SEGOB), Unidad de Política Migratoria. 2015. *Boletín Mensual de Estadísticas Migratorias 2015.* Mexico City: Secretaría de Gobernación, Subsecretaría de Población, Migración y Asuntos Religiosos.

Smith, B.E. and Winders, J. 2008. 'We're here to stay': economic restructuring, Latino migration and place-making in the US South. *Transactions of the Institute of British Geographers* **33**(1), pp. 60–72.

Stuesse, A. and Coleman, M. 2014. Automobility, immobility, altermobility: surviving and resisting the intensification of immigrant policing. *City & Society* **26**(1), pp. 51–72.

Theodore, N. 2007. Closed borders, open markets: immigrant day-laborers' struggle for economic rights. In: Leitner, H., J. Peck, and E. S. Sheppard. eds. *Contesting neoliberalism: urban frontiers*. New York: Guilford Press, pp. 250–63.

United States Border Patrol. 1994. *Border Patrol strategic plan 1994 and beyond: national strategy*. Washington, D.C.: US Border Patrol.

Vogt, W. A. 2013. Crossing Mexico: structural violence and the commodification of undocumented Central American migrants. *American Ethnologist* **40**(4), pp. 764–80.

Wahlia, H. 2013. *Undoing border imperialism*. Oakland, CA: AK Press.

Winders, J. 2007. Bringing back the (b)order: post-9/11 politics of immigration, borders, and belonging in the contemporary US South. *Antipode* **39**(5), pp. 920–42.

Part II
Exposing intimate economies

8 Captive consumers and coerced labourers

Intimate economies and the expanding US detention regime

Nancy Hiemstra and Deirdre Conlon[1]

Introduction

Upon arrival to the Essex County Correctional Facility, staff strip every immigrant detainee of his or her possessions, including personal clothes, jewellery – except a wedding band – and any money on his or her person at the time. Detainees are then issued two sets of uniforms (prison jumpsuits), two sheets, a pillow and pillowcase, mattress, blanket and towel (Essex County, 2013, p. 13). They are also provided with a small number of personal hygiene items such as a toothbrush, toothpaste, comb and soap. Beyond this 'standard issue' detainees are permitted to keep only a limited number of items in their cell at any one time, including six pairs of socks and underwear, respectively, two commissary sweatshirts, a maximum of two pieces of any one toiletry item, and a maximum of fifty commissary items, which range from sugar packets and stamps to prayer rugs, radios and footwear (Essex County, 2013, p. 13). The Essex County Correctional Facility, located in Newark, New Jersey, is one in a cluster of immigration detention facilities in eastern New Jersey that includes two privately operated, designated immigration detention centres and four county jails that hold migrant detainees in addition to criminal justice system prisoners. Intake procedures at Essex County are more or less indicative of the procedures at any one of the approximately 250 facilities detaining immigrants in the United States.

While rules on the items detainees are allowed to have in their possession signal detention's austere environment, detention centre commissaries thrive. Among the top selling commissary items are ramen noodle soups, beef pouches, high carbohydrate cereal bars and an array of toiletries. Even more noteworthy is the fact commissaries sell most of these items at substantially higher prices than markets charge in surrounding communities. In the Essex County facility, for instance, a single serving of ramen noodles costs a detainee $1.03 (£0.72) in contrast to an approximate price of $0.19 cents (£0.13) per serving at a supermarket.[2] A proprietary brand of pain relief tablets (two-pack) retails for $0.44 at the Essex County jail, contrasting with a per pill cost of $0.12, or four times less expensive, at retailers such as Walmart. There are myriad other examples of exorbitantly priced items within detention facilities. In this chapter, we call attention to these and related, seemingly mundane, facets of everyday life in detention in order to argue that profit making on the backs of detained migrants is deeply embedded within the infrastructure and workings of immigration detention. Put differently, we suggest that attending to the intimate economies of immigration detention starkly illustrates the multiple scales at which circuits of exploitation and wealth accumulation exist within the US detention system.

The expansion of immigration detention in recent years is linked to government policy, privatisation and the lobbying efforts of actors who benefit from detention (Lahav, 1998; Fernandes, 2007; Golash-Boza, 2009; Doty and Wheatley, 2013; Menz, 2013; Sorensen and Gammeltoft-Hansen, 2013; Conlon and Hiemstra, 2014; and see Lowen, this volume; Martin, this volume). Indeed, in the United States a Congressional mandate ensures that Immigration and Customs Enforcement (ICE), the agency within the Department of Homeland Security (DHS) responsible for the detention and deportation of migrants, keeps 34,000 'beds' available at all times (Detention Watch Network, 2015a).[3] A growing body of journalistic accounts and scholarship highlights the role of privatisation as a driver of this remarkable detention turn (e.g. Detention Watch Network, 2015b; Flynn and Cannon, 2009), particularly the roughly $164 per day that ICE pays to detain an immigrant (Detention Watch Network, 2015c). For example, there has been significant attention to the influence of the 'immigration industrial complex' – various individuals, companies and entities that benefit from the criminalisation of immigrants – on the continued growth of detention capacity (Golash-Boza, 2009; Doty and Wheatley, 2013).

While privatisation and the 'per bed' rate are certainly of critical importance, this chapter focuses instead on the economic geographies of money *inside* detention facilities. We draw on David Harvey's discussion of accumulation by dispossession, which he characterises as a key feature of capital under neoliberalism (Harvey, 2005). It is clear that the prison system operates to dispossess in this manner (Gilmore, 2007; Mitchelson, 2014). Here, we illustrate that accumulation by dispossession operates in immigration detention as well, and we contend that detention exemplifies the intimate scales at which processes of dispossession occur. By tracing the micro-scale economies of detention occurring in and through the bodies of detained migrants, we see how the accumulation of wealth through detention goes far beyond the amount ICE pays a facility. Wealth is also extracted directly from detained migrants via processes that operate at intimate scales: dispossession of liberty, generation of discomfort and extraction of labour. Through a focus on the widespread availability of both commissary systems and 'Voluntary Work Programmes' in US detention facilities, we argue that in the intimate spaces of detention, detainees are spatially fixed as both captive consumers and coerced labourers in ways that generate important transfers of wealth via processes of dispossession and accumulation.

Our focus on the intimate economies of detention illuminates the complex relations that gird everyday existence for detainees. In doing so, the chapter contributes to deeper understanding of the driving forces behind the expansion of detention regimes in the United States. By asking who is being dispossessed of wealth and how, and who is accumulating wealth and how, we can better trace the overlapping, extended networks of individuals and entities who rely on immigration detention as a source of income. Furthermore, our approach illustrates a need to move past a narrow focus on *privatisation* as the principal driver of the growing detention estate, to a broader consideration of ways in which detainees are *commodified*.

Accumulation by dispossession in the intimate spaces of detention

In this section we introduce concepts that inform our analysis. We first explain our conception of detention space as exemplifying intimate economies. Next, we present a brief overview of the ideology and rationale that frame the growth of privatised immigration detention. We then outline how accumulation by dispossession (Harvey, 2008) provides an apt framework for understanding the complex relations and intimate scales through which detainees become commodities and profits accumulate for a striking array of institutions and actors.

Our understanding of intimate economies of detention is grounded in feminist interventions on 'intimacy'. Key among these are perspectives registering intimacy as inferring the familiar and, in the context of our analysis, this refers to a process of scrutiny at close range, akin to the kind of fine-grained attention that familiar, intimate connections afford (see Berlant, 2000). We therefore subject elements of detainees' everyday lives – such as what they can buy and routine working conditions – to careful scrutiny. In doing so, we draw upon a related conception of intimacy that is equally important to our analysis. In critiquing dominant representations of scale in geopolitics (the city, region, state and so on), feminist geographers have called attention to how everyday life and embodied experience represent scales that influence geopolitics, too. These intimate scales intersect, influence and are altered by other realms, including political, economic and social spheres (see Hyndman and Mountz, 2006; Pratt and Rosner, 2012). In this chapter we identify some of the ways that detainees' bodies, mundane everyday activities of social reproduction, and labour practices are bound up with the accumulation strategies of a range of economic and political actors. Finally, following Wilson (2012), we take intimate economies to mean aspects of life that are typically excluded from considerations of 'the economic', yet are linked to processes of production and exchange in complicated ways and relationships. Collectively, these definitions of the intimate push us to ask what spaces, scales, processes and actors are left out of existing scholarship on the privatisation of detention. Furthermore, by framing our analysis of these intimate spheres vis-à-vis accumulation by dispossession, we consider the complex relations between privatisation in detention and detainee coercion and commodification.

In the United States, the expansion of immigration enforcement through legislation and policy changes that shift the geography of border and immigration enforcement has been crucial in bolstering the role of private corporations in immigration detention (Mountz et al., 2013; Conlon and Hiemstra, 2014). Other factors, too, have been instrumental. In the 1980s the move to divest government funds from detention – and subsequently from prison space more broadly – was welcomed in an era marked by tight fiscal budgets and the burgeoning embrace of neoliberalism that was initiated under the Reagan administration. Neoliberalism, which refers to the now dominant 'institutional framework characterised by strong private property rights, free markets, and free trade' (Harvey, 2005, p. 2), was embraced in the immigration detention sector (Menz, 2013) as it fosters a view of detainees as commodities (Doty and Wheatley, 2013). Neoliberal ideology thus helped facilitate private investment in detention facilities. In turn, privatisation was rationalised, at least in part, with the view that private corporations deal with less cumbersome procurement processes than government entities and therefore offer greater flexibility and efficiency than state or federally operated carceral institutions when it comes to the building, operations and management of detention facilities. Writing about the privatisation of immigration controls in the context of Europe, Lahav (1998) observes that privatisation allows states to be more flexible while also permitting them to generate greater legitimacy as responsive actors in the face of problematic waves of immigration. Similarly, writing about the United States, Barry (2009, p.2) reports that the Bureau of Prisons (BOP), which operates contracts with private corporations to hold 10,000 immigrant detainees, justifies the use of private contractors on the grounds that 'privatization provides the BOP with flexibility to meet population capacity needs in a timely fashion' (see also Martin, this volume).

David Harvey, following Marx, describes the political economy of capitalism as characterised by the ongoing circulation of 'spatial fixes' that rely on 'accumulation by dispossession' (2008, p. 34). This is the process whereby the growth of capital necessitates the privatisation of what ought to be universal rights, rights that were once insured by the state but are less and less guaranteed today. In this process, members of the broad public are stripped of wealth generating resources, which is to say, they are dispossessed; meanwhile, increasingly, capital becomes centralised in the hands of a powerful elite. In other words, a minority elite group accumulates by dispossessing the majority public. As part of the process of wealth transfer and capital accumulation, social groups that are deemed unruly are displaced. This thesis on the workings of capital has been useful in accounting for a range of issues including gentrification (Harvey, 2003; Hodkinson and Essen, 2015), slum clearance (Harvey, 2008) and youth insurrection (Gibson, 2011). In our analysis, we suggest that accumulation by dispossession also operates in detention and, more specifically, within micro-level, intimate economies of immigration detention.

Extending Harvey's conceptualisation, Fine and Ruglis (2009) argue that capital accumulation operates through 'circuits of dispossession' where multiple systems of dispossession and the apportioning of individual responsibility entwine to produce complex consequences that eviscerate rights. These systems eventually disappear society's marginalised minority groups, who, to use Harvey's language, are regarded as 'unruly' in the dominant social order, while profits for private companies soar. As an example, Fine and Ruglis point to under-resourced public schools in New York City, in which minority students are dispossessed of an environment where education is the primary focus, while security and surveillance technology companies accumulate wealth. In an example more closely aligned to immigration detention, circuits of dispossession are clearly evidenced in projects of mass incarceration in the United States, in which racialised populations are criminalised through the creation of new laws and targeted by skewed law enforcement procedures (Davis, 2003; Gilmore, 2007). Prisoners are dispossessed of liberty and their families and communities are stripped of valuable social capital, while prison corporations and politicians they support benefit in increased money and power.

Of particular significance in Fine and Ruglis' (2009) analysis is their fine-grained attention to the ways accumulation by dispossession course through communities, involving multiple actors and producing overlapping effects. What we see in attending to the intimate economies of migrant detention are circuits of accumulation and dispossession that have precisely these consequences for detained migrants. Undocumented migrants – who are always racialised – symbolise the 'unruly' in immigration enforcement. Whereas in Harvey's discussion of the 'spatial fix', the community or neighbourhood from where unruly groups are displaced becomes the site for capital investment, in the case of immigration detention, undocumented migrants are expunged from their communities when they are detained and, in this process, they are stripped, or dispossessed, of resources and networks that family and community provide. Simultaneously, detention centres become sites of capital accumulation. Accumulation occurs at the macro level, with wealth generated for private corporations through the government's payment of $164 per day per detainee bed space, as previously noted. Also, as we highlight in this chapter, additional circuits of accumulation operate at the micro level, in the intimate spheres of day-to-day existence in detention. Corporate as well as government wealth is generated in connection with mundane practices of social reproduction such as eating, bathing and leisure activities. As detainees are dispossessed of the ability to adequately meet basic dietary needs they are compelled to rely on commissaries in order to supplement their food intake. This, in turn, generates profit for companies that operate commissaries in detention centres. A further, related circuit of accumulation by dispossession also occurs in detainee work programmes where, in the effort to meet basic human needs, detainees labour to secure a wage that will help them pay for commissary items. And while detainees are subjected to exploitative wages and exercise few rights as workers, private and public entities save or profit from detainee labour. Attention to the intimate economies of detainees' daily realities, then, shows immigration detention to exemplify capital accumulation's 'circuits of dispossession'.

Project and methods

This chapter draws primarily on an ongoing research project we are conducting on the 'internal economies' of immigration detention in the greater New York City area. The project seeks to identify the multiple components of and participants in the operation of detention facilities, as well as who benefits and how from operations. In addition, the project scrutinises how different models of ownership affect on-the-ground facility operations. Detention facilities can be owned and operated by ICE, by a state or county government contracted by ICE, by a private company, or by some combination of the above. Of the over 400,000 immigrants detained per year (441,000 in 2013) by ICE in approximately 250 facilities, 67 per cent are detained in county- or state-owned facilities, 17 per cent in privately owned (contract) facilities, 13 per cent in ICE-owned facilities, and 3 per cent in Bureau of Prison Facilities (US ICE, 2011; Simanski, 2014) (note: percentages are from 2011 source). All facilities, including those that are ICE-owned, contract out at least some components of their operations to private entities (Doty and Wheatley, 2013; Meissner and Kerwin, 2009). Endeavouring to represent a range of owner-ship models, we selected nine detention facilities that house immigrants taken into ICE custody in the greater New York City area (see Table 8.1).[4]

In order to identify and scrutinise the internal economies of these nine facilities, we have pursued two principal methods. One is document review and analysis. We have collected news accounts, non-governmental organisation reports and publicly available government documents and reports regarding these facilities. We also submitted government freedom of information requests, at the federal level (Freedom of Information Act, or FOIA, requests) to ICE and at the county level in New Jersey (Open Public Records Act, or OPRA, requests) in which

Table 8.1 Location and operation of detention facilities included in project

Facility Name	Location	Operated by
Bergen County Jail	Hackensack, New Jersey	County government
Buffalo Federal Detention Facility	Batavia, New York	ICE
Delaney Hall Detention Facility	Newark, New Jersey	County/Private
Elizabeth Contract Detention Facility	Elizabeth, New Jersey	Private
Essex County Correctional Facility	Newark, New Jersey	County
Hudson County Correctional Facility	Kearny, New Jersey	County
Monmouth County Correctional Institution	Freehold, New Jersey	County
Orange County Correctional Facility	Goshen, New York	County
Varick St. Service Processing Center	Manhattan, New York	ICE

we asked for (1) all contracts between ICE and other federal agencies, county governments and private entities regarding these facilities; (2) all sub-contracts pertaining to the operation of and provision of services within the facilities, such as those to do with food, commissary, medical care, transportation, security, communication and cleaning; and (3) documents internal to facilities, such as commissary records, budgets, schedules and detainee handbooks. While some of the information requests have yet to be filled (in violation of the legal guidelines for fulfilment) and many of the documents received were heavily redacted, we have so far received over 2000 pages of documents to review.

Our second method is conducting interviews with individuals who have access (or come into contact with those who have access) to these detention facilities. We have, thus far, conducted fifteen interviews with lawyers, volunteers with visitation programmes and members of activist organisations working to improve detention conditions or end detention. Perhaps for obvious reasons, the most challenging population to reach has been detainees; most detainees are eventually deported, and those who are not may be reluctant to discuss their experience. To date, we have conducted only two such interviews: one with a detainee and another with a former detainee. To address this gap, in this chapter we also draw on research conducted in Ecuador by Hiemstra in 2008–9 with deportees from the United States. In that project, Hiemstra interviewed forty migrants previously detained in and deported from the United States, asking (among other questions) about the conditions of US detention facilities (Hiemstra, 2012, 2013, 2014). Because approximately 70 per cent of Ecuadorians in the United States reside in the greater New York City area, many of Hiemstra's interviewees were detained at some point in the facilities that are the subject of the present study.

Captive consumers: the commissary system

Here we first outline how commissaries operate, and we then discuss how detention facilities and private sector actors profit from the commodification of daily life. By triangulating documents such as detainee handbooks, facility schedules and commissary lists with interviews with detainees and advocates, we identify how the commissary system exemplifies accumulation by dispossession. We highlight how ordinary and intimate (i.e. personal) activities of daily living, including access to food and laundry facilities, alongside ambient conditions in detention facilities, ultimately deprive detainees of the ability to fulfil basic needs without resorting to purchasing commodities. As part of this process, the companies that operate facility commissary stores accumulate wealth as they are guaranteed to profit from the purchases that detainees are compelled to make. Detainees must often depend on commissaries to address intimate aspects of daily life. Activities of daily living, from hygiene to recreation, are commodified and made (semi)public in ways that life outside detention does not require. This manufactured dependence also illuminates intimate economies in the sense of entangled connections and broader networks involved in economic gain: we see that private, subcontracted entities as well as detention facilities caress one another as they grease the wheels of capital accumulation (see Katz, 2005).

While some detainees are able to turn to family or volunteer visitors to supply or supplement their basic needs, for most the only option is the commissary system. All facilities have a commissary through which detainees may make purchases. Most facilities offer similar items. The Essex County commissary list, for example, contains seven general categories: food, beverages, medicine, personal hygiene items, clothing, footwear and miscellaneous. While operations and procedures vary, generally detainees must indicate desired purchases on a list, submit it on a designated day, and – if they have sufficient funds in their facility account and the requested items are available – their purchases arrive five to seven days later. We compared the prices charged by the Essex County commissary with the same or similar items at Walmart, the multinational retail chain known for its low prices,[5] and found that commissary prices were routinely two to seven times more expensive.[6] Despite these inflated prices, most detainees purchase items through the commissary if they have the funds. The conditions of detention create a persistent sense of privation, or what we suggest can be understood as the dispossession of livability and comfort, that turns detainees into willing – desperate, even – consumers. To exemplify, we turn to the commodification of food, clothing and personal items in detention.

Food

In our research as well as a number of reports (e.g. Curcio et al., 2012; Freeman and Major, 2012), the provision of food is a constant source of complaint among detainees. A primary issue is that facilities do not provide enough food, and that what is provided is of poor quality. As a result, detainees are often hungry. For example, Ecuadorian deportee Jorge B reported that he lost 15 pounds in detention. He noted that in most places he was detained, 'not even a dog would eat what they gave us' (Interview with Hiemstra, April 14, 2009).[7] Data also show that the ways in which meals are scheduled aggravates hunger issues. A New Jersey lawyer we interviewed explained:

> Something we heard repeatedly, [... is] that the food is particularly bad that they offer, the hours of meals are very challenging, so time between dinner and breakfast the next day is very long. ... The feeling among a lot of detainees is that that's done on purpose so you're forced to go to commissary and at commissary you're charged exorbitant prices.
>
> (Interview with Conlon, July 18, 2013)

Meal times listed in the Elizabeth Detention Centre Detainee Handbook (Corrections Corporation of America, 2013), for example, are 6:45 am, 11:45 am and 4:45 pm; this means a fourteen-hour gap between dinner at night and breakfast the following morning. Another interviewee, José Carlos, complained that the times allotted for eating were very short: 'They give you five or six minutes to eat and whether or not you got a chance to eat you had to finish' (Interview with Hiemstra, March 27, 2009). What's more, as stated in all detainee handbooks we reviewed, the only food facilities allow in dormitories is that which can be purchased from the facility's commissary.

Clothing and personal items

As described in the chapter's Introduction, clothing and other personal items are distributed sparingly to detainees. While rules vary according to facility, use of laundry services is generally allowed only once every three days and some hand-books specify that clothing may not be washed by hand in the bathrooms. This means that detainees often must wear an item multiple times before it is washed. Commissaries, however, do sell additional clothing. In our research, detainees also expressed that they were often cold in detention and needed to buy additional layers of clothing in an effort to stay warm; such items can only be attained through the commissary. Many detainees also purchased non-prescription medications and personal hygiene items. One interviewee, Saira, explained that she had to purchase items like shampoo and toothpaste because the quantities issued were insufficient (Interview with Hiemstra, April 7, 2009).

The limited routines of detention and the resulting boredom drive other purchases. Clemente, a former detainee from Ecuador, said that if one tired of watching television, a recourse was to purchase recreational items: 'There are games and such but everything you have to buy. The commissary sells cards, other things, dominoes … they won't even give you a pen unless you buy it' (Interview with Hiemstra, May 4, 2009). These examples demonstrate that the conditions of detention set detainees up to be dispossessed of basic comforts at almost every turn and thus to have to resort to spending their own money at facility commis-saries in an effort to make detention conditions more tolerable (see Conlon and Hiemstra, 2014, for additional examples).

Close scrutiny shows that there are circuits of accumulation and dispossession operating within the commissary system. Private companies and local governments accumulate wealth while detainees are dispossessed of the monetary resources they have. Commissaries bring in considerable monies. For example, one document we obtained listed the revenue of the Buffalo facility commissary for eight months (January to August 2013) as $190,262.[8] In addition, numerous entities are receiving portions of commissary income. No facility in our study runs its own commissary; this service is (sub)contracted out to private entities. Keefe Commissary Network (KCN) operates commissaries in a number of the facilities we are studying in New Jersey. Even though commissaries are contracted out, they still generate income for facilities. Indeed, the home page on KCN's website promises clients it will 'be a source of revenue generation at your facility'. The contract between Essex County and KCN shows that the county receives 48.2 per cent of commissary revenues. Furthermore, numerous companies that supply products to commissaries clearly target the incarceration industry. For example, Essex County's facility commissary sells medicine from Medique Products, which, on its website, lists 'Correctional Health' as one of the markets it targets. The Essex County contract with Keefe Commissary also stipulates that Keefe must provide proof of insurance before being allowed to operate in the facility; therefore the insurance industry is another entity that cashes in on immigration detention. Here, we see Essex County, KCN, product supply companies and insurance companies profiting in various ways from the operation of commissaries.

Through our close (intimate) scrutiny of the commissary system, which operates at a different scale than macro-level indicators of privatised profit in immigration detention, we see that multiple circuits of accumulation by dispossession are in play. Migrant detainees are stripped of many of the comforts that imbue social reproduction, such as feeling satiated with a decent meal or experiencing a comfortable ambient temperature. Dispossessed of these familiar and intimate aspects of everyday life, detainees must resort to commissaries to compensate or fulfil basic needs, and, in this process, they are further dispossessed of their monetary resources. In turn, a plethora of actors benefit from the revenue that is generated from the commodification of detainee everyday life, including county and state governments, manufacturers and private commissary operators. In this sense, commissaries exemplify one of the circuits where wealth accumulation has become an intimate and complex part of the infrastructure of migrant detention.

Examination of this internal economy raises a further, intersecting question: how do detainees who are captive consumers obtain the funds to make commissary purchases? Some individuals have money on their person when they are detained. This is seized and placed in a personal commissary account created for the detainee. Additionally, family and friends can deposit money into the detainee's account; however, this process is also subject to accumulation as there are surcharges on any deposits (Clifford and Silver-Greenberg, 2014). Alternatively, detainees turn to a 'black market' economy within the facility to secure needed items. This system represents a further, deeper instantiation of exploitation as detainees enter into an exchange relation among themselves. Absent these options, detainees may seek any opportunities to earn money while detained. It is here that detention facility labour programmes play a role. We scrutinise these programmes in the next section.

Coerced labourers: 'voluntary' work programmes

Many detention facilities offer some type of labour 'opportunities' to detainees, through what are called 'Voluntary Work Programmes'. It is important to note that work programmes are used throughout the detention system, by all types of detention facilities: ICE run, local government run, and privately run. The Essex County ICE Detainee Handbook (Essex County, 2013, p. 39), for example, states that 'All individuals who are detained at Essex County Correctional Facility are eligible on a voluntary basis for available ICE Detainee Worker openings.' The Handbook details strict requirements for workers and presents work as 'a privilege that may be rescinded for not reporting to work, appearing in an unsanitary condition, or performing unsatisfactorily'. The jobs available include such tasks as cleaning, kitchen food preparation and clean-up, laundry and maintenance.

In exchange for one eight-hour shift, a detainee typically receives one dollar, or roughly thirteen cents an hour. This rate of pay was set when Voluntary Work Programmes (VWP) were established by a 1950 law. One dollar at that time is worth roughly $9.80 at the time of writing, in 2015. Nonetheless, the rate of one dollar per day was upheld in court in 1990 after being challenged under the Fair Labor Standards Act (FLSA); the court ruled that because the FLSA was intended to cover American industry and labour, it did not extend to immigrant detainees (Urbina, 2014). The rate is slightly higher at some facilities; for example, in Essex County, detainees make $1.50 per day, and $3 per day for 'Special Work Details', such as barbering.

According to an investigative article by Ian Urbina (2014), 55 of the 250 facilities that detain immigrants in the United States participate in the Voluntary Work Programme, 'employing' approximately 5,500 detainees per day (of the 34,000 in detention at any given time). Of these, private companies run 34 and local governments operate 21 programmes (Urbina, 2014). In addition, many other facilities have detainees engage in labour but do not compensate them with money; instead they 'pay' them with extra food or privileges like free time (Urbina, 2014). Jacqueline Stevens has estimated that over 135,000 immigrants may be participating in the programmes per year (quoted in Urbina, 2014, n.p.). As Carl Takei of the ACLU (quoted in Urbina, 2014, n.p.) observes, 'This in essence makes the government ... the single largest employer of undocumented immigrants in the country.'

Despite the paltry wage, in our research we have found that many detainees were grateful, even anxious, for the opportunity to earn small amounts of money, to then spend it in the commissary. Though Ecuadorian deportee José Carlos first laughed when speaking of the pay rate and said, 'What can you even do with one dollar!' he continued, 'But there, there when you are in need, when you do not even have money for a water, then one dollar is useful' (Interview with Hiemstra, March 27, 2009). Additionally, detainees often 'welcome the opportunity to work as a way to endure the stress and boredom of incarceration' (Sinha, 2015, p. 33; Urbina, 2014). These 'voluntary' jobs can be so coveted that there is often not enough work to fill detainee demand. One interviewee, Saira, recalled that she and some other detainees had filled out work requests, but they were denied. Javier said he was never offered the opportunity to work, but wished he had been; he said he 'survived' and got through hunger with gifts from other detainees who could buy from the commissary. After working two weeks, Johnny opted to allow other folks desperate for money to make phone calls work: 'There were a lot of people with no money who wanted to communicate [with family] ... as my family already knew I was detained, I let others get the work' (Interview with Hiemstra, April 30, 2009). Amidst this desperation, in some facilities systems develop for determining who receives available assignments. Sinha (2015, p. 35) discusses 'discrimination in the administration of the VWP' in how work assignments are decided, and several of Hiemstra's interviewees reported that facility guards had established systems for deciding who worked, or claimed that only guard favourites were rewarded with positions.

Conversely, there is also evidence that though these jobs are presented as a 'privilege', and though participation is cast as 'voluntary', some detainees are forced to work (Urbina, 2014; Prendergast, 2015; Sinha, 2015). There have been reports of detained migrants being threatened with or experiencing solitary confinement, physical abuse or other punishments if they refuse to work (ACLU, 2012; Urbina, 2014; Prendergast, 2015; Sinha, 2015). That work is not always completely voluntary is evident in the detainee handbooks that we examined. For example, the Essex Detainee Handbook lists refusing to work as a minor violation, with punishment options including loss of privileges and confinement for up to four hours (Essex County, 2013). In the Elizabeth Detention Centre's Handbook, '[e]ncouraging others to participate in a work stoppage or refuse to work' (Corrections Corporation of America, 2013, p. 126) is categorised as a 'highest offense', punishable with, among other things, disciplinary transfer, disciplinary segregation of up to 60 days or loss of privileges. Whether or not detainees are forced to work under threat of punishment, the conditions of detention produce a degree of coercion even for the most willing workers. Sinha (2015) thus argues that Voluntary Work Programmes are in violation of the Thirteenth Amendment of the U.S. Constitution, which prohibits 'slavery and involuntary servitude'.

What are we to make of this system that exploits detainees as it facilitates the operation of detention facilities? It is clear, from our research, that detainees are captive labourers, willing and often desperate to work. Coinciding with this desperation, detainee labour provides opportunities to offset running costs and for wealth accumulation in detention facilities. According to Jacqueline Stevens (quoted in Urbina, 2014, n.p.), 'private prison companies and the government may be avoiding paying more than $200 million in wages that outside employers would collect'. One human rights organisation employee we interviewed estimated that one 187-bed facility may save between five and six million dollars per year through detainee labour. Calculations made from our data (using submitted work schedules) suggest that just one facility, the Buffalo Federal Detention Facility, could be saving roughly $45,000 per week in wages.[9] In addition, the federal government reimburses the 55 facilities officially participating in the federal Voluntary Work Programme for the money that they pay detainees (Urbina, 2014). What's more, though Programme guidelines specify that detainees are supposed to only work in jobs that directly support operation of the facility, there is evidence that this is not always the case (Urbina, 2014; Sinha, 2015). Detained migrants have been found, for example, preparing meals to be served in other (non-detention) facilities run by the same operator (Urbina, 2014). In sum, what is revealed in all this is a glimpse of the complex circuits of accumulation by dispossession – for private companies, subcontractors, governments and facilities themselves – that attach to utterly ordinary needs that detainees have, such as the need for food and warmth or the need to communicate with family and friends. We also see how these circuits operate in association with the exploitation of detainees' labouring bodies, and extend beyond the confines of detention into communities and lives outside.

Conclusion

This chapter has illustrated that processes of dispossession operate at the individual scale of detainee bodies and their day-to-day lives in detention while the effects of these processes reverberate far beyond the individual scale, exposing and implicating a multitude of actors and institutions as beneficiaries of the immigration detention system. The chapter expands Harvey's (2005) concept of accumulation by dispossession by putting it in conversation with a feminist approach to intimacy. In particular, attention to the intimate economies of detention reveals the generation of *circuits of dispossession* (Fine and Ruglis, 2009) that allow us to understand distinct yet critically related practices. Captive consumers and coerced labourers are produced in a violent cycle of privation, manufactured demand, consumption and labour. The conditions of detention are such that detainees are willing to purchase items at inflated prices from facilities' commissaries to make life more bearable. However, as many detained migrants do not have money, one of the few recourses is to work in the facility. Outside of detention, detainees might regard the amount of money they can earn in detention with disdain, but inside the facility, they often covet the available jobs. Then, the wages that detainees earn come right back to the detention providers through the commissaries. In the intimate spaces of detention, meal timings, facilities' cleaning needs and overpriced snacks are all linked, as the mundane activities of social reproduction are monetised in ways that are grossly asymmetrical with regards to wages and prices of basic goods.[10]

From this examination emerges a complex picture of the intricate relations that drive and sustain detention and its large-scale expansion in the United States as well as globally. By scrutinising the intimate economies of exchange that operate in detention, we better understand the voracious demand for and investment in detention over and above political ideology or the lobbying efforts of macro-level actors, such as incarceration-focused corporations. Our analysis indicates that, in contrast to some of the popular critiques of detention, large-scale private corporations are not alone as beneficiaries of detention. Circuits of dispossession are ubiquitous and thrive in facilities regardless of whether they are private, public or some combination of the two. Indeed, our focus on processes of dispossession suggests that immigration detention becomes a realm in which public and private actors become interdependent in their activities and interests to mutual benefit. In a discussion about the privatisation of security in general, Leander (2010, p. 210) observes: 'the commercialization of security reflects a deep blurring and even hybridization of the public/private sectors for the seeking of new markets and creating new commodities.' In contrast to the refrains of 'small government' and 'market-based solutions' advanced by pundits of neoliberalism, then, privatisation merely changes the role that government plays in immigration detention. In addition, the provision of detention becomes an area through which all entities involved magnify mechanisms of authority and control. In connection with the immigration industrial complex, Doty and Wheatley (2013, p. 428) see the state as 'increasingly mobile and fluid, often blurring boundaries between public and private sectors and in the process increasing the power of both'. These symbiotic relationships also contribute to the relentless expansion of detention (see Martin, this volume, for a discussion of specific processes through which private and state entities codify relationships with each other in the provision of detention).

The identification of circuits of dispossession embedded in the intimate, everyday spaces of detention also suggests an urgent need to move beyond an emphasis on the role of *privatisation of detention provision* in critical analyses. We suggest that recognition of the *commodification of detainees* illuminates additional driving forces behind the expanding global detention landscape. As detention facilities put in place systems that extract value at every step of the detention process, including and perhaps especially at intimate scales, detainees themselves become commodified in processes that generate additional opportunities for accumulation.[11] This commodification of detainees augments the privatisation of detention facilities and their operation, by facilitating the investment of more and more individuals and entities – be they private or public – in the expansion of detention regimes. The conversion of everyday spaces of social reproduction into spaces for the production of extra value further discourages critical questioning of the rationales behind and actual consequences of detention. The incarceration of those mobile bodies who do not neatly fit into particular national imaginaries is normalised, and the broader logics governing punitive approaches to immigration and border enforcement are solidified. Identifying and scrutinising the intimate circuits of dispossession through which detainees themselves are commodified, therefore, calls into question the actions of *all* entities involved and, in so doing, has the potential to disrupt the expansion of global detention regimes.

Acknowledgements

The authors would like to thank all participants in the two research projects discussed in this chapter. Thanks also go to Marlene Ramos for critical research assistance and analysis, and to Lindsay Stemke for data analysis. Finally, the authors express deep gratitude to Kate Coddington and Lauren Martin for their thoughtful comments and edits on an earlier draft of this chapter

Notes

1 Both authors contributed equally in the writing of this chapter.
2 $1.00 (US) = £0.69 GBP, calculated with exchange rate for 5 February 2016.
3 Since the implementation in 2009 until 2014, this 'bed mandate' was interpreted to mean that all 34,000 beds had to be *filled* at all times. Beginning in the spring of 2014, the Department of Homeland Security began to interpret this as 34,000 beds had to be *available* at all times (Lee, 2015).
4 As there are no immigrant detention facilities in New York City and Long Island (part of the state of New York, to the east of New York City), immigrants apprehended

there are moved immediately to facilities in eastern New Jersey or other parts of New York State. (Varick Street in Manhattan is for temporary holding only.)

5 Walmart is known for less than reputable labour practices and for its negative impact on local economies. We include it here as comparison because of the widespread distribution of Walmart stores across the United States.

6 Interestingly, items that were actually less than at Walmart included bibles and Spanish-English dictionaries.

7 All interviewee names included in this chapter are pseudonyms.

8 The Buffalo facility has a guaranteed minimum detainee population of 400 (Detention Watch Network, 2015a).

9 Based on calculations from time sheets at the Buffalo Federal Detention Facility for a period of one week in August 2013.

10 Our thanks to Lauren Martin for articulating this point.

11 Our thanks to Kate Coddington for articulating this point.

References

ACLU. 2012. *Prisoners of profit: immigrants and detention in Georgia* [Online]. Available from: www.acluga.org/files/2713/3788/2900/Prisoners_of_Profit.pdf [Accessed 20 September 2014].

Barry, T. 2009. The new political economy of immigration. *Alternet* [Online]. Available from: www.alternet.org/story/127471/the_new_political_economy_of_immigration [Accessed 20 September 2014].

Berlant, L. 2000. *Intimacy*. Chicago: Chicago University Press.

Clifford, S. and Silver-Greenberg, J. 2014. In prisons, sky-high phone rates and money transfer fees. *New York Times*. June 26 [Online]. Available from: www.nytimes.com/2014/06/27/business/in-prisons-sky-high-phone-rates-and-money-transfer-fees.html?_r=0 [Accessed 29 January 2016].

Conlon, D. and Hiemstra, N. 2014. Examining the everyday micro-economies of immigrant detention in the United States. *Geographica Helvetica* **69**, pp. 335–44.

Corrections Corporation of America. 2013. *Elizabeth Detention Center detainee handbook*. Essex County, New Jersey [on file with authors].

Curcio, L., Joshi, A., Mackler, C., and Mandel, M. 2012. Expose and close – Hudson County Jail, New Jersey. Detention Watch Network [Online]. Available from: www.detentionwatchnetwork.org/ExposeAndClose [Accessed 29 January 2016].

Davis, A. Y. 2003. *Are prisons obsolete?* New York: Seven Stories Press.

Detention Watch Network. 2015a. Banking on detention: local lock-up quotas and the immigrant dragnet [Online]. Available from: www.detentionwatchnetwork.org/sites/default/files/Banking_on_Detention_DWN.pdf [Accessed 29 July 2016].

Detention Watch Network. 2015b. The influence of the private prison industry in the immigration detention business [Online]. Available from: www.detentionwatchnetwork.org/privateprisons [Accessed 7 July 2015].

Detention Watch Network. 2015c. About the US detention and deportation system [Online]. Available from: http://www.detentionwatchnetwork.org/resources [Accessed 15 July 2015].

Doty, R. L., and Wheatley, E. S. 2013. Private detention and the immigration industrial complex. *International Political Sociology* **7**, pp. 426–43.

Essex County. 2013. *Essex County Correctional Facility ICE detainee handbook*. Department of Corrections. Essex County, New Jersey [on file with authors].

Fernandes, D. 2007. *Targeted: homeland security and the business of immigration*. Seven Stories Press: New York.

Fine, M. and Ruglis, J. 2009. Circuits and consequences of dispossession: the racialized realignment of the public sphere for U.S. youth. *Transforming Anthropology* **17**(1), pp. 20–33.

Flynn, M. and Cannon, C. 2009. The privatization of immigration detention: towards a global view. *Global Detention Project* [Online]. Available from: www.globaldetentionproject. org/fileadmin/docs/GDP_PrivatizationPaper_Final5.pdf [Accessed 7 July 2015].

Freeman, S. and Major, L. 2012. Immigration incarceration: the expansion and failed reform of immigration detention in Essex County, NJ. [Online]. Available from: www.afsc.org/ sites/afsc.civicactions.net/files/documents/ImmigrationIncarceration2012.pdf [Accessed 16 February 2016].

Gibson, N. 2011. London calling: Fanon, spontaneity and the English insurrections. *Pambazuka News*. 6 September, Issue 546 [Online]. Available from: http://pambazuka .org/en/category/features/76058 [Accessed 7 July 2015].

Gilmore, R. W. 2007. *Golden gulag: prisons, surplus, crisis, and opposition in globalizing California*. Berkeley: University of California Press.

Golash-Boza, T. 2009. The immigration industrial complex: why we enforce immigration policies destined to fail. *Sociology Compass* 3(2), pp. 295–309.

Harvey, D. 2003. *The new imperialism*. Oxford: Oxford University Press.

Harvey, D. 2005. *A brief history of neoliberalism*. Oxford: Oxford University Press.

Harvey, D. 2008. The right to the city. *New Left Review* **53**, pp. 23–40.

Hiemstra, N. 2012. Geopolitical reverberations of US migrant detention and deportation: the view from Ecuador. *Geopolitics* **17**(2), pp. 293–311.

Hiemstra, N. 2013. 'You don't even know where you are': chaotic geographies of U.S. migrant detention and deportation. In Moran, D., Gill, N., and Conlon, D. eds. *Carceral spaces: mobility and agency in imprisonment and migrant detention*. Farnham Surrey: Ashgate, pp. 57–75.

Hiemstra, N. 2014. Performing homeland security within the US immigrant detention system. *Environment and Planning D: Society and Space* **32**, pp. 571–88.

Hodkinson, S. and Essen, C. 2015. Grounding accumulation by dispossession in everyday life: the unjust geographies of urban regeneration under the private finance initiative. *Journal of Law in the Built Environment* **3**(1): 72–91.

Hyndman, J. and Mountz, A. 2006. Feminist approaches to the global intimate. *Women's Studies Quarterly* **34**(1/2), pp. 446–63.

Katz, C. 2005. Partners in crime? Neoliberalism and the production of new political subjectivities. *Antipode* **37**(3), pp. 623–31.

Lahav, G. 1998. Immigration and the state: the devolution and privatisation of immigration control in the EU. *Journal of Ethnic and Migration Studies* **24**(4), pp. 675–94.

Leander, A. 2010. Commercial security practices. In Burgess, P. J. ed. *Handbook of new security studies*. London and New York: Routledge, pp. 208–16.

Lee, M.Y.H. 2015. Clinton's inaccurate claim that immigrant detention facilities have a legal requirement to fill beds. *Washington Post*. May 15 [Online]. Available from: www.washingtonpost.com/blogs/fact-checker/wp/2015/05/15/clintons-inaccurate-claim-that-immigrant-detention-facilities-have-a-legal-requirement-to-fill-beds/ [Accessed 7 July 2015].

Lowen, M. this volume. Intimate encounters with immigrant criminalisation in Arizona.

Martin, L. this volume. Discretion, contracting, and commodification: privatisation of US immigration detention as a technology of government.

Meissner, D. and Kerwin, D. 2009. *DHS and immigration: taking stock and correcting course*. Migration Policy Institute [Online]. Available from: www.migrationpolicy.org/ pubs/DHS_Feb09.pdf [Accessed 29 January 2016].

Menz, G. 2013. The neoliberalized state and the growth of the migration industry. In Gammeltoft-Hansen, T. and Sorensen, N. N. eds. *The migration industry and the commercialization of international migration*. New York: Routledge, pp. 108–27.

Mitchelson, M. L. 2014. The production of bedspace: prison privatization and abstract space. *Geographica Helvetica* **69**, pp. 325–33.

Mountz, A., Coddington, K., Catania, R. T. and Loyd, J. M. 2013. Conceptualizing detention: mobility, containment, bordering, and exclusion. *Progress in Human Geography* **37**(4), pp. 522–41.

Pratt, G. and Rosner, V. eds. 2012. *The global and the intimate: feminism in our time.* New York: Columbia University Press.

Prendergast, A. 2015. GEO lawsuit alleging forced labor of immigrant detainees moves forward. *Westword.com*, 8 July [Online]. Available from: www.westword.com/news/geo-lawsuit-alleging-forced-labor-of-immigrant-detainees-moves-forward-6886851 [Accessed 29 January 2016].

Simanski, J. F. 2014. Immigration enforcement actions: 2013. U.S. Immigration and Customs Enforcement, Department of Homeland Security [Online]. Available from: www.dhs.gov/sites/default/files/publications/ois_enforcement_ar_2013.pdf [Accessed 29 January 2016].

Sinha, A. 2015. Slavery by another name: 'voluntary' immigrant detainee labor and the Thirteenth Amendment. *Stanford Journal of Civil Rights & Civil Liberties* **XI**(1), pp. 1–44.

Sorensen, N. N. and Gammeltoft-Hansen, T. 2013. Introduction. In Gammeltoft-Hansen, T. and Sorensen, N. N. eds. *The migration industry and the commercialization of international migraton.* New York: Routledge, pp. 1–23.

Urbina, I. 2014. Using jailed migrants as a pool of cheap labor. *New York Times*, 24 May [Online]. Available from: www.nytimes.com/2014/05/25/us/using-jailed-migrants-as-a-pool-of-cheap-labor.html?_r=0 [Accessed 29 January 2016].

US ICE. 2011. *Detention management.* Department of Homeland Security [Online]. Available from: www.ice.gov/factsheets/detention-management [Accessed 15 July 2015].

Wilson, A. 2012. Intimacy: a useful category of transnational analysis. In Pratt, G. and Rosner, V. eds. *The global and the intimate: feminism in our time.* New York: Columbia University Press, pp. 3–56.

9 Intimate economies of ambiguity and erasure

Darwin as Australia's 2011–2012 'capital of detention'

Kate Coddington

Introduction

Darwin, Australia is a place often characterised by excess. Located on the *northernmost* edge of the continent, one of the *most remote* and *most isolated* urban areas in all of Australia, the capital of the Northern Territory (NT) is often imagined as too different, too Asian, too hot, too *other*. National newspaper columnist Nicholas Rothwell (2007, p. 51) describes Darwin this way:

> It is growth and wild luxuriance. ... It is the palms swaying against the harbour, purple nightfalls, frangipani blossoms, smoke plumes filling a hazy sky. But it is also the smell of rotting vegetation and decay, wet season thunder, cyclones, rain falling from lead banks of cloud. It is Paradise and Inferno cohabiting; grand hotels, plaques and war memorials at every turn, a marble parliament big enough for a superpower; and, close by, corrugated iron shacks, musty backpackers' markets, wrecking cranes, an endless empire of second-hand car yards.

Darwin is a community of about 125,000 people (in 2013) (Australian Bureau of Statistics, 2013). It is the only major urban centre of the NT, closer in miles to Jakarta than to Melbourne. Darwin was known as Australia's 'Gateway to Asia' for many years and continues to occupy the Australian imagination as a '"strategic military outpost" on the northern frontier' as well as 'a focal point for (post) colonial struggles over mineral resources and space' (Luckman et al., 2009, p.73). Darwin's ethnic makeup also differs from southern Australian cities in association with Asian migration, which began in the 1870s, and because it has the highest proportion of Aboriginal residents of any Australian city.

However, during 2011–12, Darwin also became known as Australia's 'capital of detention'. At that time, it was the site of three immigration detention centres that could house as many as 3,200 asylum seekers. In this chapter, I use the framework of the 'intimate economy' to explore Darwin's role in networks of detention. I argue that logics of detention are geographically situated within a global historical and geopolitical context, yet are also more deeply rooted in certain communities like Darwin than in others. I suggest that detention took root in Darwin so readily because of tendencies towards isolation, ambiguity and erasure that were already present in Darwin community life. These processes of erasure combined with isolation and jurisdictional ambiguity to produce a site where detention flourished.

I begin by outlining a framework for intimacy, a particular vantage point well suited to examining the global, yet locally situated, processes of immigration detention. I next turn to the history of mandatory immigration detention in Australia, detailing how by 2011, Darwin had become Australia's 'capital of detention'. I explore how isolation and jurisdictional ambiguities as well as colonial processes of erasure shaped Darwin as an inviting place for detention. I conclude by considering the productive possibilities of ambiguity and erasure. Rather than illustrating a process of exceptional abandonment by the state, erasure and ambiguity produce an *excessive* state presence in Darwin, a place overrun by the state.

A framework for intimacy

Ara Wilson was one of the first scholars to frame analysis in terms of intimate economies. For her (Wilson, 2012), the use of intimacy is a liberating concept that opens space for analysis that situates global processes like globalisation, neo-colonialism and capitalism within spheres of life related to feeling, relationships and the biopolitical. Wilson (2004, p. 11) writes that intimate economies refers to aspects of people's lives that 'have come to seem noneconomic', and the term has been taken up by others who want to examine the blending of scales and aspects of economic life that are revealed by analysing small places, close relationships and tactile aspects of life (Mountz and Hyndman, 2006; Pratt and Rosner, 2012; Stoler, 2006). Stoler's (2006) documentation of the obsessions of colonial authorities with race, gender, sexuality and other intimate relationships demonstrates the power of intimacy as a framework for analysis to disrupt the smooth flows of global capital, both in the past and the present. Analysing intimacy in relation to global processes combats some of the problematic aspects of pairings such as public/private, global/local, and macro/micro that scholars, particularly feminists, have challenged as being masculinist, disembodied and essentialised (Mountz and Hyndman, 2006). Joining intimacy with the plural, hybrid and overlapping econom*ies* which constitute contemporary relations among individuals and global capitalist processes adds layers of complexity and nuance to scholarship.

The framework of intimate economies is well-suited to the study of immigration detention, which represents a process both global and intimate, enmeshed in global economic processes, transnational xenophobia and the daily realities of indefinite imprisonment. Immigration detention is mobile political strategy, connected to the increasing global mobility of practices of incarceration and deportation (Flynn and Cannon, 2009). Immigration detention is often analysed at the scale of global trends in criminalisation of mobility (Ashutosh and Mountz, 2011), national policy development (Khosravi, 2009) or the embodied scale of the detained migrant suffering physical and psychological trauma (Gill, 2009). Yet as Hyndman and Mountz (2006) write, the global and the intimate represent not two separate hierarchical scales, but instead are co-constitutive, drawing from a feminist epistemology that emphasises the multiple scales (Marston, 2000) and everyday practices (e.g. Smith, 1987) at which global processes like detention take place. Immigration detention operates through a contingent, relational concept of scale: the impact of local activities can 'jump scale' to the national or global level and vice versa (Cope, 2004, p. 71). Conceptualising detention as a process occurring at multiple interconnected scales makes visible power that moves across and through different types of spaces (Mountz et al., 2012).

Yet even as the framework of intimacy envisions connections across places, it is also important to take up the embedded, situated and grounded nature of intimacy in particular places. The site of the community provides a unique glimpse into the overlapping scales and economies through which detention is constructed, maintained and endured. Within this chapter, I employ the concept of intimacy in a variety of ways – as an embodied closeness, as a claustrophobic sense of isolation, as a concept tied to individualised processes of erasure and forgetting – in order to explore the connections between Darwin's intimate historical relationships with erasure and ambiguity, and how those dense webs of connections resurface in the present through practices of immigration detention. I argue that the community and its complex history *is itself* an intimate economy that structures contemporary detention. It is important to understand why legacies of detention continue in places such as Darwin and to situate them within 'global disciplinary strateg[ies]' for mobility and transnational economic networks (Reid-Henry, 2007, p. 627).

Darwin as Australia's 2011–2012 'capital of detention'

Policies of mandatory detention for asylum seekers in Australia date back to 1991, but resonate with a much longer history in Australia of immigration and imprisonment, including quarantine stations, internment camps during the world wars and Aboriginal reserves (Bashford and Strange, 2002). In 1991, Australia opened a 'Reception and Processing Centre' in Port Hedland for asylum seekers from Cambodia, and in 1992 the Migration Amendment Act mandated detention for all asylum seekers arriving by boat. Asylum seekers arriving by boat in Australia were subject to indefinite detention as their refugee claims were processed. By the late 1990s, long stays in the prison-like environments of remote detention centres in Woomera and Baxter prompted asylum seekers from Afghanistan, Iraq and Iran to participate in incidents such as riots, fires, mass escapes, suicide attempts and hunger strikes (Whyte, 2003). Policies detaining asylum seekers firmly entered the public eye in Australia in August 2001, when Prime Minister Howard refused to let asylum seekers rescued at sea disembark on Australian territory. The crisis of the *M.V. Tampa* represented a political opportunity for the prime minister, who threatened the Norwegian captain who rescued the asylum seekers with human-smuggling charges.

During the standoff with the *M.V. Tampa*, the parliament passed a new Border Protection Bill. The new legislation retroactively excised offshore territories for the purposes of migration claims; authorised both the interception of asylum seekers arriving by boat by the Australian military and their diversion to Pacific island nations for processing as part of the 'Pacific Solution'; and established a dual system of asylum processing, where boat arrivals went through a truncated refugee claims process and had limited access to legal services or judicial review (Perera, 2002). The terrorist attacks of 9/11 heightened anxieties about asylum seekers arriving by boat to Australia, and negative portrayals of asylum seekers in the media, escalating government rhetoric against asylum seekers, and the interception and turning back of boats headed for Australia all combined to produce an increasingly toxic political climate towards refugees. Even after Prime Minister Howard left office in 2007, detention remained a mainstay of Australian policy towards asylum seekers arriving by boat.

In this chapter, I portray a snapshot of Darwin in 2011–12. In 2011, I arrived in Darwin to conduct ethnographic field research for my PhD. I spent the next six months in Darwin conducting semi-structured interviews with residents, advocates, members of community organisations and academic researchers. In order to protect the confidentiality of the participants who conducted interviews for this project, I have generalised their role in the community and refrained from using specific, possibly identifying information. I combined these interviews with participant observation at two different community organisations, one dedicated to Aboriginal justice, the second to asylum seeker support and advocacy. I visited asylum seekers at all three Darwin-area detention facilities that I describe below. Together, the field research was designed to capture the experience of Darwin as Australia's capital of detention, a title it maintained until policy shifts in August 2012 led to the reopening of offshore detention facilities on Nauru and Manus Island, Papua New Guinea.

Darwin in 2011–12 was home to three detention facilities, the Northern Immigration Detention Centre (NIDC), the Darwin Airport Lodge (DAL) and the Wickham Point Immigration Detention Centre (WPIDC), with capacity to house 3,200 asylum seekers, more than any other place in Australia. The DAL was a former airport hotel located in the urban centre that had been transformed into a low-security facility housing families with children, as well as single men and women. WPIDC was constructed in 2011 on a site 45 miles from Darwin under a US$140 million (£91 million) lease agreement with a private developer, using modular components similar to shipping crates to form a maximum-security facility to house single men. NIDC was sited within a Darwin military base and housed single men. Conditions at NIDC were so appalling that, in a discussion, a mental health professional who worked with patients there referred to it as 'hell on a stick', a site designed to 'manufacture mental illness' and self-harm. Darwin's central role as a site for the detention of asylum seekers prompted its nickname during 2011–12 as 'Australia's Capital of Detention'.

While this chapter focuses on the 2011–12 period, Darwin's intimate relationships with detention have continued. By 2014, exemplifying the fluid landscape of Australian migration and detention policies, Darwin housed two detention centres. In 2013 a new site housing families with children was constructed along-side WPIDC called Bladin, while inadequate facilities, overcrowding and a push to direct asylum seekers towards offshore detention facilities led to the closure of NIDC and DAL in 2014. Combined, the two facilities can house 2,180 asylum seekers, representing 25 per cent of the capacity of Australia's onshore detention network.

Isolation and jurisdictional ambiguity

In this section, I begin to explore how the intimate setting of Darwin – as a community with a complex history, distinct geography and paradoxical relationship to other communities within Australia – affects contemporary practices of immigration detention in Darwin. I argue that Darwin's history of isolation and its ambiguous governance have shaped the character of the community, producing a place where people have become accustomed to looking the other way and feeling disempowered by federal government practices, which now include the siting of detention facilities. Focusing on the *community* as an intimate space constructed through complex relationships over time highlights the unusually close relationship between isolation and federal intervention, and the cosiness between controversial detention practices and a community where ambiguity has become normalised.

Many different residents of Darwin I interviewed measured the community's attributes by its *differences* from southern Australian cities. The climate extremes, natural disasters, defence and resource industries and the indigenous population all contrasted greatly with population centres like Melbourne and Sydney. Part of Darwin's 'otherness' stems also from its historical and geographic proximity to Asia. Darwin represented Australia's earliest 'Gateway' to Asia, and was the site of a Chinese migrant labour population influx in the late 1800s, the attack on Darwin's harbour by Japanese bombers during World War Two, the landing of Vietnamese refugee boats in the mid-1970s, and the groundswell of resident sup-port for their 'neighbours' in East Timor during that nation's civil war in the 1990s. Many Australians remain anxious about these historical connections to Asia, which add to Darwin's perceived 'differences'.

People I interviewed collectively agreed that Darwin was isolated within Australia. 'For people down south, Darwin is another world', one local advo-cate told me (Interview January 16, 2012). 'People don't notice Darwin: out of sight, out of mind!' another long-time Darwin resident confirmed (Interview March 2, 2012). Geographic isolation from other parts of Australia is attractive to many residents of Darwin, who noted that Darwin became an 'end of the road' destination – where Australians who did not fit in elsewhere settled (Interview February 15, 2012). Yet the isolation also, to many, explained the profusion of detention sites in Darwin. Detention centres were located in Darwin, according to one migrant advocate, because it is an 'isolated community that won't give trouble' (Interview December 29, 2011). Indeed, as Wickham Point Detention

Centre opened in late 2011, government officials giving advocates a tour of the facility acknowledged its isolation, saying, 'we've nothing to hide out here' (Interview November 30, 2011).

Isolation and remoteness have characterised Australian migrant detention sites over the past twenty years, and locating detention facilities in sites such as Woomera or Christmas Island, far from the southern population centres, restricts the abilities of advocates or legal representatives to access detained migrant populations (Whyte, 2003). Yet I argue that federal authorities may have seen Darwin as an ideal combination of remote yet 'serviceable'. Paradoxically, it was the Darwin community's *intimacy* with the federal government that may have encouraged the siting of detention facilities in the community (Interview January 27, 2012). As I outline in the remainder of this section, despite its literal distance from Australia's political centres and symbolic connections to Asia, the community and the Northern Territory as a whole are centrally embedded in Australia's economic relationships, military geostrategic calculations and priorities of the federal government. The disproportionate influence of the federal government in Darwin led to what I call 'jurisdictional ambiguities', the ambiguous and unusual relationship between a powerful federal authority and weaker local and Territory-level governments. Jurisdictional ambiguities resulted from this power imbalance, leaving residents accustomed to the federal government intervening in community life without accountability. Migrant detention thus becomes part of a familiar pattern within a community deeply *intimate* with practices of federal intervention.

Darwin's prominence in the Australian economy derives from its centrality to the increasingly profitable mining industry and proximity to markets in China and Japan. While the mining industry only makes up 3.5 per cent of the NT's workforce (Australian Bureau of Statistics, 2011), it has a large presence in Darwin. Many mining employees are fly-in, fly-out workers who reside in other parts of Australia, but the rhythms of the two-week mining shifts cause the community's mood to fluctuate as people transition in and out of shifts. Gold, manganese and uranium make up most of the revenue derived from mining, although liquefied natural gas and crude oil are also found in the NT (Australian Bureau of Statistics, 2011). Uranium has been an especially controversial product of NT mines since it was first discovered south of Darwin in 1949. Today, uranium mining has become a focus of struggle over NT lands and communities. Community health problems near the Jabiru mine in the east part of the NT, for example, intimately embody the connections between uranium mining and the local Aboriginal community living there, and Aboriginal communities have protested plans to site a radioactive waste dump in the Muckaty Land Trust.

Darwin is also a strategic location for the Australian military. Darwin has the best port site of any in Northern Australia and one of the two best airfields. It currently hosts the Australian Navy, Air Force and Army, as well as the offices of the Northern Command (NORCOM) (Wran, 1995, p.173). As the geopolitical importance of Asia, particularly China, continues to increase, Darwin is poised to play a larger role in national defence, as well as international partnerships (see Ansley, 2012). Because of its strategic location and loyal military partnerships in places like Iraq and Afghanistan, Australia already hosts major US satellite, communication and training facilities (Maclellan 2011, p. 18). Australia's remote bombing ranges have been especially important to this partnership as other long-term bombing sites, such as those on Puerto Rico and Hawaii, have been closed due to political pressure from local residents (Maclellan, 2011). President Obama's visit to Darwin in November 2011 served as a reminder of the strategic and geopolitical importance of Northern Australia for Australian and US interests in Asia, and his announcement of the deployment of 2,500 US Marines to Darwin was a tangible show of his administration's attempted 'pivot' toward Asia (Calmes, 2011).

The federal government controls much of the Territory's mining industry and the military deployed in Darwin. This political and economic intimacy with Darwin extends to general administration. Unlike much of the rest of mainland Australia, the NT has never been granted statehood. After 1978, the Australian federal government granted the Territory many of the rights of statehood yet continued to control Aboriginal land, National Parks and uranium mines (Carment, 2009). As a Territory, the NT does not have equal parliamentary representation in the Australian federal government, and decisions about the Territory repeatedly occur at the federal level (Carment, 2009). Darwin was therefore unique, a resident explained, because of its reliance on federal funding and the history of federal decision-making taking priority within the Territory, especially in the case of mining concessions, military operations and Aboriginal policies (Interview January 16, 2012).

Aboriginal support for remaining a Territory – under which jurisdiction Aboriginal corporations retain greater power than they do in neighbouring states – was important for the rejection of statehood referenda in 2007 (Carment 2009, p. 20). In 2011, the campaign for statehood was resurrected, buoyed by frustration at the federal government's plans to establish the nuclear waste dump at the Muckaty Land Trust, as well as a 2007 policy package directed at NT Aboriginal residents called the NT Emergency Response. However, campaigns for statehood were put on hold indefinitely after the 2012 Territory General Election.

The federal government's power in Darwin is accompanied by the ineffectiveness of local and regional governance. The history of federal control over Aboriginal, military and mining issues sets precedents for the Territory's relative powerlessness. As one local environmental advocate told me, the federal government can 'override all our decisions, like create a nuclear waste dump whether we like it or not' (Interview January 16, 2012). Other residents like this migrant advocate agreed; the community has a history of 'outsiders telling people what to do' (Interview January 21, 2012). For example, another leader within a migrant advocacy group explained that immigration detention centres in the Territory neglected to do environmental impact assessments or similarly mandated tasks because the NT government 'posed no opposition' (Interview January 27, 2012).

He indicated that the NT government actually benefited from their perceived weakness; because they were assumed to be overrun by federal government projects, they assumed 'no political liability' for unpopular projects like detention centres (Interview January 27, 2012). In addition, local governments throughout the NT have long suffered from accusations of incompetence, cronyism and scandals, according to many people with whom I spoke.

Even as Darwin thus appears psychologically distant from southern Australia, it retains practical closeness with federal government operations in Canberra. Disproportionate federal influence in the Territory leads to disproportionate federal intervention. Indeed, during semi-structured interviews for this project, several residents of Darwin attributed the siting of three detention centres for asylum seekers in the area to the disproportionate power of the federal government. Contentious policies such as mandatory detention flourish in places where sovereignty and influence converge, where threatening populations face 'a concentration of executive powers and heightened surveillance' (Billings, 2011, p.272). Such places – like Darwin – become more susceptible to detention and its associated logics and less likely to contest the embeddedness of such practices.

Contradictory and overlapping levels of governance lead to jurisdictional ambiguity. Layers of jurisdictions litter the NT, making it extremely difficult to determine exact responsibilities for projects like detention centres. Aboriginal Development Corporations, Land Councils, newly proposed Territory hub towns, newly installed government business managers, the NT government and the federal government all assume different responsibilities in overlapping territories. Jurisdictional ambiguity erodes protections from the legal system. For Peter Billings (2011, p. 272), geographical and legal sites of exception, such as detention centres or offshore excised places, are created through exactly such processes. As the government suspends, withdraws or erodes the rule of law, it results in concentrated federal power over and surveillance of asylum seekers and Aboriginal populations.

Ambiguous authority is exacerbated by weak constitutional protections for those on the margins of Australian society. Australia lacks constitutional recognition for Aboriginal residents, as well as a functioning Bill of Rights, circumstances that legal scholars I interviewed suggest lead to weakened protection for human rights, although other scholars contest this interpretation (The Australian, 2009). These various overlapping political and legal jurisdictions within the NT lend ambiguity to political projects like mandatory detention, allowing the logics of detention to flourish in their uncertain margins.

Colonialism and processes of erasure

Immigration detention also has taken root in Darwin because of the community's intimacy with processes of historical erasure. Intimacy can be tracked by Canberra's influence in Darwin, but intimacy can also be measured through absence, silences and things forgotten. Here, I employ various meanings of intimacy – as embodied, as closeness, as personal – in order to explore how processes of remembering and forgetting are also involved in siting detention facilities in Darwin. For Sargent (2012, p. 1), landscapes of erasure are sites of intentional destruction, like mountaintops destroyed through mining, or river valleys flooded through the construction of dams. Yet I argue that landscapes of erasure are also more intimate constructions, built upon the ruins of old buildings, the priorities of transient arrivals and the forgotten legacies of colonial injustice. In this section, I describe how Darwin has become a central and active space of erasure, where the built landscape, legacies of colonisation and historical memory are all subject to destruction. The material impacts of erasure for asylum seekers in Darwin include a transient advocacy population unable to draw connections between past mobilisations and contemporary social justice issues, a community dominated by the loud voices of recent arrivals and the constant theatre of new construction. Such intimate relationships with forgetting and erasure allow practices of detention to flourish.

Some of the most significant processes of erasure that destroyed Darwin's built landscape were not under community control. Repeated cycles of disaster and rebuilding have characterised Darwin's history: during the twentieth century, Darwin was destroyed by fire, two different cyclones and bombing by the Japanese military during World War Two (Luckman et al., 2009, p. 74). After Cyclone Tracy demolished the town in 1974, southern newspapers even worried, 'Do we need a Darwin?' (Shevill, 1975). In each case, the city was rebuilt, its growth influenced strongly by post-disaster federal government intervention. Darwin has been quick to rebuild, however, even without a disaster to prompt it. Prominent buildings – the Darwin Hotel, the former hospital – were razed to the ground without recognition (Interview February 21, 2012). One resident told me, 'Darwin wipes out its history, that's what it does' (Interview January 12 and February 21, 2012). Whether prompted by disaster or the whims of Darwin's cyclical redevelopment schemes, the cycle of razing and rebuilding suggests the economic underpinnings of processes of erasure. Indeed, Darwin's incessant rebuilding is a form of creative destruction, the old built environment sacrificed in a constant attempt to provide capital with room for expansion and re-creation.

While bombing and cyclone experiences reflect Darwin's unique geography, its tendency to 'wipe out its history' reflects wider Australian trends towards historical erasure embedded firmly within the process of colonisation, which, as Hall (2008, p. 279) writes, 'relies on forced forgetting and erasure'. Indeed, belief in Australia as *terra nullius*, or the empty continent, underscored white settlers' disregard for Aboriginal life, and the economic benefits of having a 'clean slate' for settlement and new economic development (Veracini, 2007). Stories of settler violence and Aboriginal histories continued to be silenced, in what pioneering Aboriginal historian W. E. Stanner called 'a cult of forgetfulness practiced on a national scale' (quoted in Harris, 2003, p. 72).

In Darwin, the trend toward erasure is particularly exacerbated in sites important to the Aboriginal history of the area. Destruction of Aboriginal histories in

Darwin reflects, of course, wider histories of Aboriginal erasure in Australia. Erasure consists of practicalities, such as the ease with which the 'fabric heavy' heritage of settler courthouses and homesteads replaces the 'fabric light' presence of Aboriginal people living lightly on the land (Byrne, 2003, p.172). Erasure also consists of politics, however, as well: the 'levelling of Aboriginal topography', including places, names, stories and memories, is part of Australia's racialised and violent history (Byrne, 2003, p. 176). For example, the former Darwin hospital, now bare ground, once was the Kahlin Compound, where Aboriginal 'half-caste' children were separated from parents and confined. Darwin's former Retta Dixon Home, a later incarnation of an Aboriginal housing and educational facility, now is bare earth alongside a busy thoroughfare. Neither of these sites was publicly commemorated in any form at the time of my visit to Darwin in 2012. Similar exercises of erasure take place in Darwin's archives, local historians told me (Interview February 21, 2012). There are 'archival silences about Aboriginal people, who are still being written out of the story' of Darwin (Interview February 21, 2012).

Destruction of the built environment has been accompanied by the erasure of historical memory within the community. Transience, always central to Darwin's chaotic demographics, has become more pronounced since the 1970s, exacerbating the process of erasing Darwin's history. Indeed, the Darwin economy is underpinned by government activities, military bases and resource extraction, which together form an unusually transient local economic structure. Many residents described Darwin community life as 'transitory' due to the turnover in government jobs (Interview January 27, 2012). 'Career progress [in these type of jobs] means not being caught in local issues', one advocate told me (Interview January 27, 2012). 'We're a military town', another advocate suggested, and 'less likely to engage in social activism because of it' (Interview January 27, 2012). Employees of the mining, oil and gas industries, other key employers in Darwin, are similarly transient and unlikely to advocate for change in their temporary new home. 'Newer residents arrived with different goals than past groups', as one city employee explained (Interview February 15, 2012). High salaries and temporary positions meant that new residents had little interest in the background or history of the community. As these recent populations put pressure on policy-makers to accomplish their goals, the interests of longer-term residents fade in comparison. Recent changes to the built landscape, exemplified by the new Darwin waterfront, and the expensive housing ringing Myilly Point adjacent to the bare grounds of the former hospital and Kahlin Compound, are physical reminders of the community's priorities.

The processes of erasure upon the Darwin landscape as well as community memories are not only interwoven with settler colonial legacies, but also reflect the racialised violence of Australia's colonial present. As Hage (quoted in Haggis, 2004, p. 560) writes, Australia is both an 'unfinished Western colonial project as well as a land in a permanent state of decolonisation'. Erasure is not a neutral process; it is produced by and is productive for the *continuing* imbalance of racialised power and privilege in Darwin, as well as Australia as a whole

(Haggis, 2004; Amoamo, 2013). Erasure is bound up in local economic priorities and wider circuits of capital demanding new sites for development, new opportunities for extraction and always rapacious growth. The paradox in Darwin that combines disproportionate federal control over Darwin's built environment and economic generators with dismissal of the community as 'remote' and 'peripheral' reflects a continued process of 'spatial erasure', where Darwin's central importance for detention and other aspects of Australian governance is minimised (e.g. Amoamo, 2013).

Contemporary and ongoing forms of erasure in Darwin include the campaigns to police the Aboriginal 'long-grass' communities who camp in Darwin's open spaces. Named for the long spear grass common throughout the Darwin area, long-grass campers are Aboriginal people who have established long-term camping arrangements in sites throughout the city. Portrayed in local media as drunken 'itinerants' and 'fringe-dwellers', these campers have been subject to repeated campaigns by local police and anti-social behaviour task forces that use illegal camping and trespass laws in order to police campers and force them to move (Day, 2012). While people's reasons for being in the long-grass are complex and camping conditions often pose risks for health and safety, campaigns to eradicate the long-grassers from public spaces reflect contradictory community values that at once celebrate Darwin's Aboriginal arts and heritage, while erasing particular Aboriginal communities from public view (Fisher, 2012).

Active processes of erasure similarly affect advocacy efforts for asylum seekers, who are constructed as hypervisible through sensationalised depictions by media and federal authorities, yet also obscured once they reach detention sites in Darwin, subject to photo prohibitions and media blackouts. In Darwin, transient populations and a community intimately bound up in practices of erasure mean that historical advocacy movements tend to be forgotten, such as the galvanising community movements supporting East Timorese refugees in the 1990s. One advocate from that time said that activism was 'smooshed' by local authorities after that point, while others suggested Darwin was unable to retain dedicated advocates due to the high cost of living (Interview January 11, 2012). Activism in Darwin, one advocate said, 'has never been a story' (Interview December 29, 2011). Darwin has neither a strong student community nor an active branch of the national Green party, two groups that strengthen advocacy movements in southern Australia. 'The pool [of advocates] is so small and people who are ambitious just leave', another advocate explained (Interview December 29, 2011).

Fewer potential advocates make for less protest and less advocacy in the community, and the long-term nature of social issues in Darwin such as Aboriginal justice encourage 'apathy to protest', a local historian suggested (Interview February 21, 2012). 'What is the rationale for people in advocacy here?' another asked (Interview December 29, 2011). 'People aren't going to make trouble' (Interview January 2, 2012). One long-time community activist intimately embodied the erasure of these advocacy movements by showing me a poignant collection of his old advocacy t-shirts, which ranged from support for Vietnamese refugees arriving in Darwin in 1975 to Aboriginal land claims and legal battles throughout the 1970s and 1980s to promoting the causes of East Timorese refugees in the 1990s (Interview January 19, 2012). In each case, the Darwin community had undertaken more vigorous and concerted advocacy efforts than appear possible today; in each case, the memories of these successes were disappearing as rapidly as the t-shirts disintegrated in the tropical air. The embeddedness of detention in Darwin can be attributed to this apathy and lack of historical memory, according to advocates with whom I spoke. Without memory of previous campaigns for community change, residents lacked confidence that advocacy could be effective today.

The prevalence of erasure within Darwin community life reflects the community's embeddedness within processes of settler colonialism. A community with silenced archives, razed structures and forgotten movements is a community that has greater difficulty drawing on histories of difference and resistance to combat detention projects. The destruction of the built environment, community memory and community members themselves creates patterns of erasure that linger, constructing a tolerance for absence, for forgetting, that outlives particular buildings or anti-social behaviour campaigns.

Erasure thus ushers an invitation to new forms of racialised violence that build on colonial logics of enclosure such as detention. *Ongoing* settler colonial practices of marginalisation, of disproportionate imprisonment of Aboriginal residents, of violence against Aboriginal community members, and of family separation all resonate today with the treatment of asylum seekers in Australia, yet the intimate relationship of the Darwin community with the 'amnesia' of colonialism protects these other forms of violence as well (Hall, 2008). Both Aboriginal populations and asylum seekers suffer from Darwin's conflicted embrace of difference: even as Darwin's 'multiculturalism' attracts tourists and foreign investment, the community obscures the Aboriginal residents and asylum seekers who are a less visible part of Darwin's diversity. The collective amnesia towards the racialised violence of the past allows for such figurative – and even literal – forms of violence in the present, as the Australian public becomes accustomed to a lack of protest to federal intervention in Darwin. Always, too, violence is connected to the networks of capital accumulation that cross the Northern Territory, as asylum seekers languish in profit-generating detention centres and restructured community governance programmes cut services and benefits for Aboriginal residents. Processes of erasure cannot be viewed as 'neglect' by those in power (Amoamo, 2013) but must be understood as productive of racialised power, a power enmeshed within global networks of capital. The invisible, as Haggis (2004) writes about whiteness, is also located in a specific place of power and privilege.

Conclusion

> The confusing figure of the mask is helpful only so long as, instead of trying to rip it off, we recognize and even empathize with its capacity to confuse, which means we take stock of the fact that what's important is not that it conceals but that it makes truth.
>
> (Taussig, 1997, p.184)

In Darwin, processes of historical erasure entangled in ongoing colonial relationships combine with jurisdictional ambiguities and disproportionate federal influence to produce a community where detention flourishes. One interpretation of these processes of erasure, destruction of the built environment and historical memory, is that Darwin has been abandoned by the Australian state. Analyses of processes of erasure often portray them as neglect (e.g. Amoamo, 2013), which could be compounded by Darwin's perceived geographic and psychological isolation and disconnection from southern Australia. I argue instead for erasure and ambiguity as *productive* processes, not evidence of neglect. In this chapter, I have detailed the excessive federal presence that produces jurisdictional ambiguity in the NT, and the national preoccupation with historical erasure that accompanies settler colonialism. Ambiguity and erasure must be understood as the traces of an *excessive* state presence, the 'mask', as Taussig writes, that makes the 'truth' of ongoing processes of racialised violence in the form of immigration detention legible.

Detention practices proliferate without opposition in places like Darwin because they incorporate Australian fears about national identity. While processes of erasure and ambiguity may *exacerbate* Darwin's intimacy with detention, they nevertheless represent intensification, rather than a contrast, from the rest of Australia. Darwin should not be held in opposition to the imagined tolerance of difference in the rest of Australia; the logics that encourage detention exist everywhere. Darwin represents a microcosm of the fear of difference within Australia, fear that advocates I spoke with traced back to 'old fears' from the time of colonisation (Interview January 27, 2012). 'Australia never came to terms with indigenous people', one advocate explained, and 'the repeated patterns of oppression' sit heavily on Australians' consciousness (Interview January 31, 2012). Policies toward asylum seekers are so contentious, another resident of Darwin suggested, because 'people are all afraid that Australia is going to turn into a foreign place' (Interview February 13, 2012). As another advocate argued, 'People in Australia are not filled with hate, but fear mongering policies are attractive to people who get frightened easily' (Interview March 2, 2012).

The history of Darwin also suggests the multiple scales of economic activity that together inform community life. From the extractive beginnings of settler colonialism to the transient oil and gas work today, Darwin has been a site of temporary, recurring economic exploitation. Cycles of boom and bust, disaster and rebuilding, razing and redevelopment suggest the continued role of Darwin as a site of creative destruction, where new opportunities for capital must constantly be re-created. Furthermore, the economic drivers of Darwin community life are imbued with its violent history, and contemporary policies such as the 2007 Northern Territory Emergency Response that allow corporate access to Aboriginal land and restructure community work programmes have been violently enacted alongside the profitable, privately operated migrant detention facilities that have become centres of self-harm and psychological violence.

The Darwin community's intimate relationship with federal intervention and processes of historical erasure highlights community dynamics that invite detention practices to flourish, yet the resonances between detention, disproportionate federal authority and settler colonialism also suggest the utility of intimacy as a framework for 'jumping scales' of analysis. Intimacy is at once close, tactile, embodied, the decay of old t-shirts or the cosy reliance on federal funding. Yet it also allows for the braiding together of a dense array of connective strands of analysis, connecting geostrategic global processes of migrant enforcement, national levels of policy and financial debate, and community proclivities towards silence, erasure and forgetting with the embodied practices of migrants like Habiburahman (his real name), who spent over two years in Darwin's detention centres, where, 'my nights are sleepless and my days have no light'(Habiburahman and Ansel, 2012, pp. 323–4). Intimacy, as I have argued throughout this chapter, is an important framework for shedding much-needed light on the experiences of migrants like Habiburahman, trapped within the multi-scalar networks of global immigration detention.

Acknowledgements

The author gratefully acknowledges the careful, thoughtful and considerate editing by Nancy Hiemstra and Deirdre Conlon, who added much to this piece and sharpened the arguments throughout. Thanks also to the Darwin residents who gave their time and energy towards this project, especially Justine Davis, Emma Murphy, Peter Robson and the Darwin Asylum Seeker Support and Advocacy Network. Their dedication to social justice in Australia despite everything is inspirational.

References

Amoamo, M. 2013. Empire and erasure: a case study of Pitcairn Island. *Island Studies Journal* **8**(2), pp. 233–54.
Ansley, G. 2012. NZ, Australia to tighten security ties. *Otago Daily Times* 29 January.
Ashutosh, I. and Mountz, A. 2011. Migration management for the benefit of whom? Interrogating the work of the international organization for migration. *Citizenship Studies* **15**(1), pp. 21–38.
Australian Bureau of Statistics. 2011. *Northern Territory at a glance 2011*. Canberra: Australian Bureau of Statistics.
Australian Bureau of Statistics. 2013. *Census 2013*. Canberra: Australian Bureau of Statistics.
Bashford, A. and Strange, C. 2002. Asylum-seekers and national histories of detention. *Australian Journal of Politics and History* **48**(4), pp. 509–27.
Billings, P. 2011. Juridical exceptionalism in Australia: law, nostalgia and the exclusion of 'others'. *Griffith Law Review* **20**(2), pp. 271–309.
Byrne, D.R. 2003. Nervous landscapes: race and space in Australia. *Journal of Social Archeology* **3**(2), pp. 169–93.
Calmes, J. 2011. Obama addresses troops at final stop in Australia. *The New York Times* 17 November.
Carment, D. 2009. History and statehood in Australia's Northern Territory, 2003–2008. *Journal of Northern Territory History* **20**, pp. 19–31.
Cope, M. 2004. Placing gendered political acts. In Staeheli, L.A., Kofman, E. and Peake, L.J. eds. *Mapping women, making politics*. Routledge: New York, pp. 71–86.
Day, W. 2012. *Aboriginal people of Darwin: the Longgrass People*. Darwin: Self-published.
Fisher, D. 2012. Running amok or just sleeping rough? Long-grass camping and the politics of care in northern Australia. *American Ethnologist* **39**(1), pp. 171–86.
Flynn, M. and Cannon, C. 2009. *The privatization of immigration detention—Towards a global view: Global Detention Project Working Paper No. 1*. Geneva: GDP [Online].

Available from: www.globaldetentionproject.org/fileadmin/docs/GDP_Privatization Paper_Final5.pdf [Accessed 11 February 2016].

Gill, N. 2009. Longing for stillness: the forced movement of asylum seekers. *M/C Journal* [Online] **12**(1). Available from: http://journal.media-culture.org.au/index.php/mcjournal/article/viewArticle/123 [Accessed 10 Februrary 2016].

Habiburahman and Ansel, S. 2012. *Nous, les innommables. Un tabou birman [We who cannot be named: a Burmese taboo]*. Paris: Steinkis.

Haggis, J. 2004. Thoughts on a politics of whiteness in a (never quite post) colonial country: abolitionism, essentialism and incommensurability. In Moreton-Robinson, A. ed. *Whitening race: essays in social and cultural criticism*. Canberra: AIATSIS Aboriginal Studies Press, pp. 48–58.

Hall, L.K. 2008. Strategies of erasure: US colonialism and native Hawaiian feminism. *American Quarterly*, **60**(2), pp. 273–80.

Harris, M. 2003. Mapping Australian postcolonial landscapes: from resistance to reconciliation. *Law Text Culture* 7, pp. 71–97.

Khosravi, S. 2009. Sweden: Detention and deportation of asylum seekers. *Race and Class* **50**(1), pp. 38–56.

Luckman, S., Gibson, C. and Lea, T. 2009. Mosquitoes in the mix: how transferable is creative city thinking? *Singapore Journal of Tropical Geography* **30**(4), pp. 70–85.

Maclellan, N. 2011. Australia and the global re-alignment of US military forces. *Dissent*, **Summer**(1), pp. 18–22.

Marston, S.A. 2000. The social construction of scale. *Progress in Human Geography* **24**(2), pp. 219–42.

Mountz, A., Coddington, K., Catania, R. T. and Lloyd, J.M.. 2012. Conceptualizing detention: mobility, containment, bordering, and exclusion. *Progress in Human Geography* **37**(4), pp. 522–41.

Mountz, A. and Hyndman, J. 2006. Feminist approaches to the global intimate. *Women's Studies Quarterly* **31**(1/2), pp. 446–63.

Perera, S. 2002. A line in the sea. *Australian Humanities Review*, **September**, pp. 1–8.

Pratt, G. and Rosner, V. eds. 2012. *The global and the intimate: feminism in our time*. New York: Columbia University Press.

Reid-Henry, S. 2007. Exceptional sovereignty? Guantanamo Bay and the re-colonial present. *Antipode* **39**(4), pp. 627–48.

Rothwell, N. 2007. *Another country*. Melbourne: Black, Inc.

Sargent, P.L. 2012. Landscapes of erasure: the removal—and persistence—of place. In Ellsworth, E. and Kruse, J. eds. *Making the geologic now: responses to material conditions of contemporary life*. Brooklyn: Punctum Books, pp. 106–10.

Shevill, I. 1975. Do we need a Darwin? *Sydney Morning Herald*, 6 January, A6.

Smith, D.E. 1987. *The everyday world as problematic: a feminist sociology*. Boston: Northeastern University Press.

Stoler, A. 2006. *Haunted by empire: geographies of intimacy in North American history*. Durham: Duke University Press.

Taussig, M. 1997. *The magic of the state*. New York: Routledge.

The Australian. 2009. No bill, just rights. *The Australian*. August 31, Opinion section.

Veracini, L. 2007. Historylessness: Australia as a settler colonial collective. *Postcolonial studies* **10**(3), pp. 271–85.

Whyte, J. 2003. We are human beings: the Woomera breakout. In Notes from Nowhere. ed. *We are everywhere: the irresistible rise of global anticapitalism*. London and New York: Verso, pp. 430–37.

Wilson, A. 2004. *The intimate economies of Bangkok: tomboys, tycoons, and Avon ladies in the global city*. Berkeley: University of California Press.

Wilson, A. 2012. Intimacy: a useful category of transnational analysis. In Pratt, G. and Rosner, V. eds. *The global and the intimate: feminism in our time*. New York: Columbia University Press, pp. 31–56.

Wran, N. 1995. *The Committee on Darwin Report*. Canberra: Commonwealth of Australia.

10 Pocket money

Everyday precarities in the Danish asylum system

Malene H. Jacobsen

Introduction

Usually, the term *pocket money* describes a small amount of money that parents give to their children. It connotes an allowance for non-essential or frivolous spending. Yet, in relation to the Danish asylum system, the term *pocket money* refers to asylum seekers' 'cash allowance', the primary source of governmental support they receive from the state for basic essentials like food, clothing and personal hygiene items. So while the term *pocket money* carries with it the idea of non-essential spending, within the Danish asylum system it serves a very different purpose. In this chapter, I examine how the cash allowance system permeates asylum seekers' everyday lives in intimate ways. I argue that this system puts into motion a range of mechanisms that construct a relationship of dependency between the Danish State and the asylum seeker, exacerbate and deepen asylum seekers' financial vulnerability, and shape their spatiality.

Existing literature on migration management has focused on the systemic macro-level state regimes of Western migration management, such as the temporal and spatial expansion of border control (Coleman and Kocher, 2011), new technologies of biometric surveillance (Amoore, 2006), the growth of detention and deportation (Mountz et al., 2013; De Genova and Peutz, 2010; Bloch and Schuster, 2005), and the frequent transfer of detainees (Gill, 2009). Although, this body of research offers important insights into the character of Western migration management practices and how these create new geographies (Mountz, 2011), it tells us little about the micro aspects and day-to-day operations of Western migration management. Scholars' recent focus on the effects of detention and border crossings on migrants' lives (Bosworth, 2014; Conlon and Gill, 2013; Hall, 2012; Hiemstra, 2012; Conlon, 2011a; Gill, 2009) have begun to address this gap in the literature on migration geographies. For instance, scholars have illustrated how waiting has become an essential part of refugees and asylum seekers' daily lives (Conlon, 2011b; Hyndman and Giles, 2011; Mountz, 2011; Schuster, 2011). Building on this emerging body of research, I use the analytic of the everyday in order to examine the intimate economies of the cash allowance. I argue that this analytic provides crucial insights into the ways Western migration management permeates asylum seekers' lived realities and shapes their conduct. By paying attention to the mundane and often neglected aspects of asylum seekers' lives, I first make visible the intimate nature of the cash allowance system and second highlight the deeply felt experiences and daily frustrations with this system.

This chapter draws on fieldwork conducted in Denmark between May and August 2012. The primary methods were participant observation, in-depth qualitative interviews, and archival research. I volunteered three to five days a week in a user-driven cultural house in Copenhagen maintained for and by asylum seekers and others interested in migration policy. The house is an independent organisation with no affiliation to any Danish state institutions involved with asylum and migration management. Conducting interviews in this space allowed asylum seekers to speak freely about their experiences with the Danish asylum system and about their daily lives in the asylum centres. I spent most of my time participating in the weekly house meetings, talking informally over coffee with forced migrants from Middle Eastern and African countries and other volunteers, and lending a hand where I could. I formally conducted eleven semi-structured in-depth interviews and mental mapping exercises with asylum seekers from the Middle East and Africa about their everyday life in Danish asylum centres.[1] I also made several visits to different asylum centres. Finally, I conducted an extensive analysis of policy documents and newspaper articles related to the Danish Immigration Law in the period 1983–2012.

The chapter is organised as follows. First, I explain how 'the everyday' as an analytic enables us to reveal the ordinary and intimate dimensions of migration management practices, such as the cash allowance system. Second, I provide a brief description of the Danish cash allowance system. Third, I use asylum seekers' narratives to examine how this system shapes and embodies asylum seekers' everyday lives. Through a series of four vignettes based on asylum seekers' experiences, I illustrate the intimate nature of the cash allowance system and how it places asylum seekers in a situation of precarity. In conclusion, I return to the concept of the everyday to discuss its potential contribution to furthering debates on migration management.

The everyday and the intimate

'The everyday' occupies an often overlooked and taken-for-granted aspect of life. It consists of ordinary and repetitive practices such as cooking, eating, shopping, walking, working and commuting (de Certeau, 1998). Yet, it is more than this. Feminist geographers emphasise that 'everyday life' serves as an important analytic lens to examine how asymmetrical power relations are structured and experienced on a day-to-day basis through ordinary activities and social interactions (Flint, 2002; Dowler and Sharp, 2001). 'The everyday offers a way of grounding political geography and geopolitics' (Kofman, 2008, p. 527). The everyday provides a critical vantage point for analysing the operation of quotidian statecraft. State practices can be conceptualised as the practices through which the state becomes involved in daily life (Painter, 2006). As such, routine practices including confinement and frequent detainee transfers (Moran et al., 2013; Martin, 2012; Darling, 2011) can be seen as institutional mechanisms through which the state is present and stateness is (re)produced (Mitchell, 1991). Through these practices the state (re)produces migrants' spaces and subjectivities (cf. Foucault, 2009).

In relation to migration management practices, attention to the everyday can reveal the routinised and often unheeded forms of violence these practices include. For example, by focusing on undocumented migrants' everyday lives, Coutin (2000) has illustrated how 'being' undocumented is a label that is not experienced at all times. Often, some migrants who are labelled 'undocumented' or 'illegal' live among and in intimate proximity to other migrants and citizens who are not labelled as such. Although these labels may be irrelevant on a day-to-day basis, they can unexpectedly enter into daily life, often in highly disruptive ways. For instance, in the United States, 'undocumentedness' is increasingly a lived reality for migrants. As policing and surveillance of public spaces, roads and workplaces intensifies, undocumented migrants' vulnerability is reinforced (De Genova, 2002).

Attention to the everyday scrutinises migration management practices by illustrating the highly *intimate* nature of their routinised workings. Originating from the Latin *intimus* ('innermost'), the realm of the intimate captures the 'deeply felt orientations and entrenched practices that make up what people consider to be their "personal" or "private" lives and their interior selves' (Wilson, 2012, p. 32). The everyday and the intimate overlap because intimate practices (love, sex, personal relationships, identities and family life) are sustained through everyday routines. Both terms also capture the mundane yet often neglected aspects of people's lives. In this chapter, I situate the intimate as a dimension of the everyday that is invisible to an outside observer; it is only apparent to the individual (Pratt and Rosner, 2012). I draw on Wilson's (2004) term 'intimate economies' and this collection's title to highlight the intimate nature of the Danish cash allowance system. While it appears to be a banal impersonal economic practice, I show how the cash allowance system operates through intimate relations and interventions. A focus on the intimate economies of this system helps reveal its unseen ramifications. The system can be seen as a *micro*economic practice in a double sense; it operates in the form of tiny sums of cash and through subtle ritualised interactions.

The cash allowance system

In this section, I provide a brief overview of the Danish cash allowance system to illustrate its mundane technicalities. At the time of my research, migrants making an asylum claim in Denmark were prima facie required to live in an asylum centre while their case was being processed. During the day asylum seekers were free to move in and out of the centre. Nevertheless, their mobility was constrained because the majority of the asylum centres were located in remote areas far from major cities like Copenhagen, Aarhus or Odense. While each asylum centre was organised in a slightly different way, they all had similar features such as shared bedrooms, common bathroom facilities, common kitchens and various outdoor facilities. Asylum seekers were not allowed to carry out paid work.[2] To cover expenses for food and other daily essentials, they were instead given a biweekly cash allowance at their respective asylum centres, provided by the Danish Immigration Service.

The Danish government introduced the cash allowance system together with a contract system and Adult Education & Activation reform in 2003, policies that remain in force today. The two new systems and the reform were part of a rhetorical shift towards asylum seekers in Denmark. In the 1980s, Danish politicians broadly perceived asylum seekers as a vulnerable group of people who needed assistance, protection and legal rights (Gammeltoft-Hansen and Whyte, 2011). However, during the 1990s this attitude began to change, notably at a time when the Danish state also began its transition from a welfare state to a workfare regime (Torfing, 1999). Politicians began to argue that asylum seekers could no longer *just* live in asylum centres and receive benefits from the state without 'giving back', and thus, multiple reforms were introduced including the cash allowance system.

The cash allowance system works in tandem with the contract system. In other words, the asylum seeker's cash allowance can be withdrawn if she does not honour her contract. All asylum seekers over eighteen years old must sign an individual contract with the administrator of the asylum centre. The contract stipulates which *aktivering* duties and educational courses the asylum seeker has agreed to participate in and what consequences will result if the asylum seeker is deemed to have violated the contract. *Aktivering* (activation) is a socio-political labour market strategy that refers to a wide range of policies applied within the public benefits system. Usually, the term describes state-mandated activities that seek to increase unemployed people's skills and qualifications and encourage labour-market participation. Within the Danish asylum system, however, *aktivering* typically consists of daily duties such as cooking, cleaning, maintenance of buildings and outdoor areas, childcare, assistance with language translation, and participation in social, cultural and leisure activities (Udlændingestyrelsen, 2012a, 2012b).

The cash allowance consists of two types of allowances: *Basic Allowance* and *Supplementary Allowance*. All asylum seekers receive *Basic Allowance* (USD 9 per day). According to the Danish state, this money is intended to cover expenses for food and personal hygiene items. Asylum seekers can also receive *Supplementary Allowance* (USD 1.50 per day) if they co-operate with Danish authorities and meet the conditions stated in their contract. Finally, the *Supplementary Allowance* increases to USD 5.25 per day if the state decides to process an asylum seeker's case in Denmark (see Table 10.1).

The combination of an asylum seeker's willingness to co-operate with state authorities, her ability to honour her contract, and her state-defined immigration status determine the amount of cash she receives. For example, a single asylum seeker who honours her contract and whose case is being processed in

Table 10.1 Danish cash allowance calculation (2011)

Basic Allowance	USD 9 per day per adult
Supplementary Allowance	USD 1.50 per day per adult
	USD 5.25 per day per adult (if the Danish state decides to process the asylum case in Denmark).
Caregiver Allowance	USD 10.50 per child per day (1st and 2nd child).
	USD 14.25 per child per day (if the Danish state decides to process the asylum case in Denmark).
	USD 7.50 per child per day (3th and 4th child)

Denmark will receive USD 126 (basic allowance) and USD 73.50 (supplementary allowance) for a total of USD 199.50 biweekly. As I will illustrate below, critical attention to this cash allowance system as a seemingly insignificant practice itself shows how migration management takes place through mundane everyday routines.

Everyday precarities

Through examining asylum seekers' narratives about their daily lives, this section highlights the intimate nature of the Danish cash allowance system. In what follows, I use a series of four vignettes to capture asylum seekers' experiences of the cash allowance system and thereby demonstrate the ways in which its operation permeates and conditions their everyday lives, habits, expectations, routines and social relations. I argue that the intimate operations of the system create a multilayered fabric of precarity. While migration scholars have used the concept of precarity to describe the conditions of migrant labourers who experience severe labour exploitation (Lewis et al., 2015; Waite et al., 2014), I use the term to understand the intimate economies of detention, which often exist outside the traditional labour market. Berlant's (2011, p. 192) definition of precarity becomes helpful here. She conceptualises precarity as a condition of uncertainty, instability and – most importantly – as a condition of dependency (see also Waite, 2009). The cash allowance creates a precarious situation for asylum seekers who involuntarily become dependent on the Danish State and are unable to change their financial situation as a result. Asylum seekers are at once under the 'protection' of the Danish State yet simultaneously at its mercy. The cash allowance system creates a relationship of dependency, where asylum seekers are supposed to be grateful for the state's help even when the resources provided are glaringly inadequate to cover basic needs. Their economic precarity is experienced as a daily condition, with broader uncertainties about the status of asylum claims hanging in the background.

Every other Thursday

Through my daily work at the cultural house in Copenhagen, I slowly became aware of the extent to which the cash allowance system structured asylum seekers' lives. Located at one of Copenhagen's small cobblestone-covered side streets, the house was usually buzzing with people coming in and out to meet with friends, participate in language classes or see a lawyer. The smell of sweet pastry donated from a local bakery, strong coffee and *za'atar* would waft out of the kitchen as laughter and conversations in numerous languages filled the different spaces of the house. Yet on pocket money day (every other Thursday), the cultural house was almost empty and very quiet because all the asylum seekers were at their respective asylum centres in order to collect their cash.

The routinised distribution of the cash allowance shapes asylum seekers' spatialities. Every other Thursday shortly before 1:00 pm, asylum seekers gather in a specific building at their asylum centre. They line up to collect their cash allowance in a building guarded by the local police. In order to receive the cash allowance, a Red Cross staff member first checks the asylum seeker's ID card to verify her identity. The asylum seeker then signs an official document to confirm her presence in the asylum centre. Finally, the asylum seeker receives her allowance in cash. The entire process typically takes several hours and interrupts their daily practices and obligations such as cooking, cleaning, sleeping, social interactions and communicating with family and friends in other countries. As part of this ritual, asylum seekers spend a long time waiting in line before they can collect their cash allowance. Principally, asylum seekers in Denmark wait for a ruling of their case. Yet, waiting is also present in less obvious aspects of asylum seekers' lives. They wait for Internet access. They wait for a letter from the Immigration Service or their lawyer. They wait in line to use the bathroom. They wait to start educational classes. Thus, waiting in line for pocket money every other Thursday is just one among many practices where asylum seekers experience the arduousness of waiting to sustain their most basic needs.

Further, these monetary 'allowances' are handed out in cash, which means that asylum seekers often end up carrying the money on their bodies because they lack access to a safety deposit box or bank account. Many of the asylum seekers told me that carrying the cash on their bodies made them feel more vulnerable. An alternative was to hide the cash in their bedroom, though the majority did not see this as a real alternative as many did not trust their roommates. In this way, the pocket money itself became a source of vulnerability once it was in asylum seekers' possession and thereby contributed to exacerbating their sense of everyday precarity.

It is not enough

Here, I illustrate how the woefully inadequate amount of money asylum seekers receive places them in a financially vulnerable situation, which, in turn, affects their daily practices and eliminates their ability to change their everyday life. This discussion also calls attention to the intimate relation between the Danish State and the asylum seekers constituted by the cash allowance system, which makes the asylum seeker dependent on the state in order to survive.

The cash allowance is supposed to cover all basic living expenses such as food, communication, transportation, clothes and personal hygiene. Yet, the USD 9 per day (basic allowance) falls well below Denmark's official poverty line, which was set at USD 18,362 in 2013 after tax per year (USD 1530 per month / 765 biweekly). In fact, the biweekly USD 199.50 maximum amount for an asylum seeker whose case is being processed (and who meets all the conditions) is less than half the sum an unemployed Danish citizen on welfare would receive (approximately USD 493.50 biweekly). These numbers illustrate the stark disparity between what a basic living wage in Denmark is and what asylum seekers actually receive.

As my interviewees stressed, the cash allowance was simply not enough to cover their expenses. Hadi, a young man, who had been in the Danish asylum system for two years at the time of our interview, emphasised: 'they give me money, every two week[s], and then … it is not enough.' Another interviewee, Tamir, similarly stated: 'they give you this very little salary, you can only afford food, so that you survive.' Echoing Hadi and Tamir's statements, Vitus and Nielsen (2011) found that asylum seekers faced difficulty making ends meet in their study of children's conditions in Danish asylum centres. In a report on asylum seekers' ability to cover their need for a sufficient and balanced diet plus acceptable hygiene conditions, the Danish Institute for Human Rights similarly concluded that for many asylum seekers it is simply not possible to make all the necessary purchases with the money they receive (Institut for Menneskerettigheder, 2009). As a form of 'don't die survival' (Hyndman and Giles 2011, p. 362), the cash allowance provides asylum seekers with insufficient financial resources to sustain basic needs.

The meagre nature of the cash allowance has consequences for asylum seekers' daily habits such as smoking, calling family and friends by phone or Skype, inviting friends for dinner, and visiting friends outside the centres. Several asylum seekers explained how they need to plan their budget very carefully in order to make ends meet and potentially have some money for a trip outside the centre to see friends and to buy new clothes or afford cigarettes. In explaining his daily routine, Tamir told me that he would go online to check his Facebook and connect with family and friends as soon as he woke up. Yet, this was difficult and very time consuming because of the limited access to computers and slow Internet connection at the centres. With a tone of sarcasm in his voice Tamir explained:

> [In the centre] we have eight laptops and four of them work. Then you have to line up for using the Internet in the camp. Or otherwise you have to sit for eight years in the asylum system in Denmark and save 100 kr. for every month and then you can buy [one] and then you can think about buying this thing [USB] for the Internet (…) maybe after eight years… maybe a miracle will happen.

Tamir then started laughing, well aware that saving any portion of the allowance was nearly impossible. The sheer inadequacy of the allowance serves to constrain asylum seekers' ability to exercise power over their own lives.

As the asylum seekers I interviewed further emphasised, there was no room for their voices or opinions to be heard about whether or not they want to receive financial support or want to earn their money themselves. The state made the decision that the cash allowance system was in their best interest (Barnett, 2012), notably without their consultation. Asylum seekers were well aware of this paternalism and the forms of passive dependency that the cash allowance system brings into being, and they openly expressed their frustration with this condition of imposed dependency. As Mustafa explained, he aspired to be able to take care of himself by working to become more self-sufficient as he waited for his case to be processed:

> I would really prefer to find a small job to gain a little bit of money because I am smoker and I spend half of my salary on smoking and spend the rest on food. [...] In the end you always think about this unstable situation that you are in and even the economic situation for you is not stable, you will always worry about money. So I would like to have something [a job] so I could make some money.

The inability to work, he stressed, made it impossible for him to address his vulnerable and dependent financial situation. However, there was nothing he could do about it.

Sometimes they are cutting from your salary

In this subsection, I illustrate how conditionality enables the cash allowance system to operate in intimate ways, seeking to self-discipline asylum seekers. Asylum seekers' precarious situation can be further jeopardised by their performance and ability to meet the stipulations set out in their contracts. Through the principles of conditionality, the cash allowance system seeks to function as a technique to observe, measure and regulate asylum seekers' everyday activities.

An asylum seeker's cash allowance is conditional upon on her ability to show up at the centre every other Thursday at 1:00 pm. On a sunny afternoon in early August, Sarah and I sat down in the cultural house's kitchen to have a conversation about how she experienced the cash allowance system. She explained that due to mental health issues she sought to spend as much time as possible outside the asylum centres. Yet, in order to receive her allowance she, like all other asylum seekers, had to be at the asylum centre every other Thursday at 1:00 pm. One Thursday, Sarah was with her family in Copenhagen and was not able to make it back to the centre that day. Sarah therefore called the centre to ask if she could get her allowance the following day. As she recounted, when a police officer answered the phone and she explained her situation, the officer said: 'Do you know that you are not allowed to leave the camp?' Sarah told me that when the officer asked for her name 'at that moment I... I hung up. I did not tell her my name or anything, because I was afraid that she would do something to me.'

Sarah's fears were not unfounded. Indeed, if asylum seekers are unable to be at the centre to collect the money for any reason, they are very likely to lose their biweekly allowance. Yet, in an interview, a former Red Cross staff explained to me that she had seen several examples of the staff trying to hold on to the allowance for an extra day or two if an individual asylum seeker had not shown up at 1:00 pm. But this can be difficult because the Danish Immigration Service requires a balanced budget from the administrator of the centre that includes asylum seekers' signatures and the allowances that have not been picked up after the allowances have been distributed. These budgets were due no later than the Friday following allowance day. However, as Sarah's narrative illustrates, the possibilities of getting the allowance later depends on the relationship between staff and individual asylum seekers.

Prior to implementing the cash allowance system in 2003, asylum seekers received food from cafeterias in the asylum centres three times daily. The cash allowance system might be seen as an improvement as it enables asylum seekers to determine their own needs and the best way to meet these needs. Nevertheless, the cash allowance system functions according to the principles of conditionality because it is tied to the *aktivering* contract. If the administrator of the asylum centre determines that an asylum seeker has violated her contract or is not cooperative, the Danish Immigration Service reduces her cash allowance. Mirroring conditional cash transfer programmes used by governments in the global South (Ballard, 2013) and in United Nations operations to encourage poor people to invest in their own human capital through healthcare, nutrition and education (UNHCR, 2012), the biweekly allotments of cash from the Danish State to asylum seekers continues only if the individual asylum seeker routinely meets the conditions stipulated in her contract and cooperates with the state authorities on her case. As Conlon (2010) suggests, such day-to-day practices serve to self-discipline asylum seekers. If asylum seekers do not cooperate or observe the contract – i.e. do not behave in the 'proper' way – the state can punish them financially.

The system impacts asylum seekers by increasing their sense of vulnerability as indicated by Maysan, another of my interviewees. After she had accomplished her *aktivering* duties for the morning, Maysan and I met in a small park in Copenhagen to talk about how she experienced her everyday life in the Danish asylum system. Maysan's *aktivering* consisted of activities such as cleaning the asylum centre's corridors daily and assisting with language translation. As we talked about *aktivering*, Maysan explained to me that she was not always successful. When I asked her what she meant by this, she explained that if she did not complete her *aktivering* duties, her pocket money would be reduced. As Maysan and other asylum seekers put it, if their allowances were reduced to the basic allowance their money would be even more 'scarce'. Because Maysan and other asylum seekers' cash allowances are conditional, the Danish state has created a situation where asylum seekers' ability to receive the already inadequate allowance depends on their capability to complete their *aktivering*. Therefore, it exacerbates their experience of precarity.

The conditional nature of the cash allowance system, including the possibility of receiving less money and importance of asylum seekers' ability to perform, operates in intimate ways on and through asylum seekers' bodies. One might argue that asylum seekers can just complete their *aktivering* and their financial situation will not be placed in jeopardy. Several asylum seekers, however, explained to me how their money had been reduced without explanation or how they had not received their allocated supplementary allowance when the Danish State decided to process their asylum case. For example, for Maysan it took the state more than six weeks to update her information, which meant that three of her cash allowances did not include the increased supplementary allowance to which she was entitled. Maysan explained that she got some of her money back but only after she made a fuss: 'I started to let them feel that it should not have been in this way and only then they give me the money back. (…) If they are nice people [then they say], "okay okay we are sorry" but sometimes they are saying, "no you are lying". But you are not lying, and this happened to me.' Abdul similarly explained, 'when you go to the office and tell them you are cleaning but they are cutting from your salary, they would say: oh that is a mistake, but they do not correct it so you keep losing this 135 kr.' In an attempt to demonstrate against this, asylum seekers stopped cleaning the kitchen, which was part of their *aktivering*. While Maysan and Abdul's narratives illustrate how asylum seekers actively try to deal with the injustice, asylum seekers in general find it difficult to challenge the practices within the asylum centres as they fear that it might hurt their chances of getting asylum. The conditionality adds another layer to asylum seekers' precarity as it opens the possibility of receiving a reduction in the amount of the allowance.

I need to take a bus and then the train

The cash allowance system in combination with the geographically remote location of the asylum centres effectively constrains asylum seekers' spatiality and ability to make decisions about their own lives. Everyday practices like going to the grocery store, selecting the groceries and cooking become time consuming and labourious. Asylum seekers are reminded daily of their precarious situation and often find it impossible to create a meaningful life.

While publically rationalised in Denmark as a form of assistance and humanitarian protection, the practice of housing asylum seekers in asylum centres located in remote areas, in effect, constructs a space where asylum seekers are geographically isolated from Danish society. This mirrors other states' use of geography to strategically exclude forced migrants (Mountz, 2011). Limited access to public transportation further intensifies asylum seekers' sense of isolation. This is a feeling that many asylum seekers are reminded of on a daily basis as they wait for an infrequent bus or walk the long distance to the train station in order to reach a city where they can buy food.

This geographical isolation adds yet another dimension to asylum seekers' financial precarity. Because asylum centres are located in remote areas without grocery stores nearby, asylum seekers need to make the journey to the city in order to buy food and other necessities. The cost of public transportation is prohibitively expensive. For example, the USD 9 an asylum seeker receives in basic allowance per day does not even buy her a bus or train ticket to one of the bigger cities. In my interview with Abdul, who at the time of our meeting had only been in Denmark for a couple of months, he described how baffled he was by the cash allowance system. He had arrived to Denmark with a small amount of savings, which he was able to use when his pocket money ran out. In a frustrated tone, he explained to me how people in the asylum centres end up spending a lot of their allowance on public transportation to the city: 'I was thinking about that I got to go to Roskilde because I had money and I got to buy my food because I have money. And I was thinking about these people who don't have money, how should they or how could they buy their food if they arrive one week before the pocket money.' As a consequence, Abdul thought about sharing his food with other asylum seekers. But by the end of my time in the field, Abdul's thoughts increasingly turned to his own predicament. He told me his savings were running out and it became increasingly difficult for him to afford train tickets.

Similar to Abdul, Tamir was frustrated with the precarious situation he and other asylum seekers were forced into by the cash allowance system. When I asked Tamir to describe how the cash allowance system influenced his daily life, he explained how the meagre nature of the allowance together with the remote location of the asylum centres structured his daily life in ways that made it impossible to create a meaningful life. He noted:

> I need to take the bus and a train, because I need to go to the cheap places to buy things. And they [the Danish State] are very good at occupying people and keeping them away from actual life, and actual activities. Because you need to take the bus and then the train and buy your stuff and the busses are not running that often. You may spend five hours just to get the ingredients and then spend more time on making the bread and other things from milk – from scratch you know – and then you eat and then you sleep. You are outside of the life, you do not have a life, you do not have a social life, you are just very occupied doing these very basic things to survive.

In a more sarcastic, though equally frustrated tone, Tamir stated that for him the way the Danish system violently structures asylum seekers' daily lives is in some ways more 'clever' than how the state does it in his home country, a country known for its dictatorial and unelected government. In short, he suggested that the Danish system operates in subtle ways that remain obscured from view.

Conclusion

Since the end of the Cold War, Western states have viewed migrants as a threat to their national security and territorial integrity (Walters, 2010). Consequently, state policies and geopolitical practices established by Western governments attempt to securitise and strategically govern displaced and mobile subjects (Bialasiewicz, 2012; De Genova and Peutz, 2010; Feldman, 2011; Topak, 2014). As defining features of contemporary geopolitics (Nagel, 2002; Hyndman, 2012), migration management practices such as remote detention centres, deportation and frequent detainee transfers create new spaces and geographies. Scholars have pointed out that these new practices, spaces and geographies have serious implications for forced migrants' access to asylum protection (Mountz, 2010), the life of migrants' families across borders (Hiemstra, 2012), and incarcerated asylum seekers' connections to asylum advocates (Gill, 2009). With notable exceptions (Bosworth, 2014; Hiemstra, 2012, 2014; Peutz, 2010; Staeheli and Nagel, 2008), however, these studies rarely tease out how migrants themselves experience, embody or even challenge the changing geopolitical landscape of migration management (Noxolo, 2014). Indeed, due to the difficulties of gaining access to migrants, their own stories and representations have played a limited role in theorising the state. Yet, migration management practices are experienced and negotiated by migrants as they move through them, are caught up within them, and attempt to negotiate or even evade them.

In the first part of this chapter, I argued that paying attention to the everyday and the intimate is crucial in order to better understand the quotidian operation of migration management and the forms of violence to which it gives rise. In this conclusion, I return to the concept of the everyday to discuss the broader implications of my analysis and findings. Specifically, I call attention to the importance of migrants and asylum seekers' accounts of the system when we seek to understand how the practice of migration management is carried out.

This chapter puts forward a feminist analysis of Denmark's cash allowance system that places the ordinary, the intimate, and the minute workings at the forefront of thinking about migration management. I have illustrated how the cash allowance system permeates asylum seekers' everyday lives in myriad ways. In the minutiae of its operation, the cash allowance system forces asylum seekers into multilayered situations of precarity. Asylum seekers experience and cope with this precarity as their daily routines and basic needs are constrained. They further struggle with an inability to change their situation. The analytic of the everyday has enabled me to make the intimate nature of the cash allowance system more visible and its ramifications for asylum seekers' lives more knowable. My focus on the everyday has provided insights into an otherwise abstract microeconomic system through which money is distributed.

If we seek to understand the current management of migrants in a comprehensive manner, a focus on the everyday provides a useful analytic. Because much of the literature on securitisation of migration and migration management relies on theoretical understandings of state power through the sovereign (Bosworth,

2014), it often ends up representing the state as a monolithic entity acting upon migrants from a distance (Gill, 2010). In doing so, migrants appear as silenced subjects of state power, rather than as agents who experience, negotiate and challenge relations of power. The everyday, I argue, enables us to re-conceptualise the state and sovereign power through very ordinary, mundane, *ad hoc* and messy practices of statecraft. In the case of Denmark's cash allowance system, attending to the everyday reveals the textures of migration management practice that are obscured from the world at large and often only apparent to the individuals who experience and navigate the system.

Asylum seekers' resistance to the cash allowance system has not been the main focus of this chapter. However, I conclude by reflecting on how the analytic of the everyday might enable us to engage with migrants' lived realities in ways that eschew the easy binaries of domination and resistance. The everyday enables us to illustrate how migrants and other marginalised groups are 'sites of performance in their own right rather than nothing more than surfaces for discursive inscription' (Dowler and Sharp, 2001, p. 169). I argue that the lens of the everyday holds the potential to reveal complexities in how migrants resist and cope with repressive state practices, such as the cash allowance system. Within critical debates about migration management, the view 'from above' generally overlooks migrants' voices altogether. And when it finds them, they are expressed through protests and hunger strikes (Rygiel, 2012). Here migrant voices are only 'audible' when they are spectacular and risky but silenced at all other times. In other words, if we are not 'up close' the only actions of migrants we hear about are overtly political acts. The value of the everyday, as this chapter shows, is its ability to reclaim a realm of mundane and repetitive activities, including ways of dealing with and getting by in the face of repressive practices. These activities are necessarily ambivalent; they cannot be 'read' as either acts of silent passivity or resistance (Harker, 2011) and must be understood, through a focus on the everyday, in all their complexity.

Acknowledgements

I am grateful to the cultural house and the people who were willing to share their stories. A special thanks to my interpreter; without her I could not have done this work. Thanks to Patricia Ehrkamp, Rhys Machold, Marita Murphy and this book's two editors, Deirdre Conlon and Nancy Hiemstra, for their constructive comments on earlier drafts.

Notes

1 Due to confidentiality, I use pseudonyms and I do not reveal the interviewees' nationality.
2 In the fall of 2012, the Danish government introduced a new law that allows some asylum seekers to live and work outside the asylum centres. This research was conducted before the law was implemented and thus I do not engage with how this law influences asylum seekers' everyday life. On January 26th, 2016, the Danish parliament repealed the law that allowed asylum seekers to live outside the asylum centres.

References

Amoore, L. 2006. Biometric borders: governing mobilities in the war on terror. *Political Geography* **25**(3), pp. 336–651.

Ballard, R. 2013. Geographies of development II: cash transfers and the reinvention of development for the poor. *Progress in Human Geography* **37**(6), pp. 811–21.

Barnett, M. N. 2012. International paternalism and humanitarian governance. *Global Constitutionalism* **1**(3), pp. 485–521.

Berlant, L. 2011. *Cruel optimism*. Durham: Duke University Press Books.

Bialasiewicz, L. 2012. Off-shoring and out-sourcing the borders of Europe: Libya and EU border work in the Mediterranean. *Geopolitics* **17**(4), pp. 843–66.

Bloch, A. and Schuster L. 2005. At the extremes of exclusion: deportation, detention and dispersal. *Ethnic and Racial Studies* **28**(3), pp. 491–512.

Bosworth, M. 2014. *Inside immigration detention*. Oxford: Oxford University Press

Coleman, M. and Kocher A. 2011. Detention, deportation, devolution and immigrant incapacitation in the US, post 9/11. *The Geographical Journal* **177**(3), pp. 228–37.

Conlon, D. 2010. Ties that bind: governmentality, the state, and asylum in contemporary Ireland. *Environment and Planning D: Society and Space* **28**(1), pp. 95–111.

Conlon, D. 2011a. A fractured mosaic: encounters with the everyday amongst refugee and asylum seeker women, *Population, Space and Place* **17**(6), pp. 714–26.

Conlon, D. 2011b. Waiting: feminist perspectives on the spacings/timings of migrant (im) mobility. *Gender, Place & Culture* **18**(3), pp. 353–60.

Conlon, D. and Gill, N. 2013. Gagging orders: asylum seekers and paradoxes of freedom and protest in liberal society, *Citizenship Studies* **17**(2), pp. 241–59.

Coutin, S. B. 2000. *Legalizing moves: Salvadoran immigrants' struggle for U.S. residency*. Ann Arbor: University of Michigan Press.

Darling, J. 2011. Domopolitics, governmentality and the regulation of asylum accommodation. *Political Geography* **30**(5), pp. 263–71.

de Certeau, M. 1998. The practice of everyday life. Berkeley: University of California Press.

De Genova, N. P. 2002. Migrant 'illegality' and deportability in everyday life. *Annual Review of Anthropology* **31**(1), pp. 419–47.

De Genova, N. P. and Peutz, N. 2010. *The deportation regime: sovereignty, space, and the freedom of movement*. Durham, NC: Duke University Press Books.

Dowler, L. and Sharp, J. 2001. A feminist geopolitics? *Space and Polity* **5**(3), pp. 165–76.

Feldman, G. 2011. *The migration apparatus: security, labor, and policymaking in the European Union*. Stanford, CA: Stanford University Press.

Flint, C. 2002. Political geography: globalization, metapolitical geographies and everyday Life. *Progress in Human Geography* **26**(3), pp. 391–400.

Foucault, M. 2009. *Security, territory, population: lectures at the Collège de France 1977–1978*. Translated by Graham Burchell. New York: Picador.

Gammeltoft-Hansen, T. and Whyte, Z. 2011. Dansk Asylpolitik 1983–2000. In: Vitus, K. and Nielsen S.S. eds. *Asylbørn i Danmark*. Copenhagen: Hans Reitzels Forlag.

Gill, N. 2009. Governmental mobility: the power effects of the movement of detained asylum seekers around Britain's detention estate. *Political Geography* **28**(3), pp. 186–96.

Gill, N. 2010. New state-theoretic approaches to asylum and refugee geographies. *Progress in Human Geography* **34**(5), pp. 626–45.

Hall, A. 2012. *Border watch: cultures of immigration, detention and control*. London: Pluto Press

Harker, C. 2011. Geopolitics and family in Palestine. *Geoforum* **42**(3): 306–15.

Hiemstra, N. 2012. Geopolitical reverberations of US migrant detention and deportation: the view from Ecuador. *Geopolitics* **17**(2), pp. 293–311.

Hiemstra, N. 2014. Performing homeland security within the US immigrant detention system. *Environment and Planning D: Society and Space* **32**(4), pp. 571–88.

Hyndman, J. 2012. The geopolitics of migration and mobility. *Geopolitics* **17**(2), pp. 243–55.

Hyndman, J. and Giles, W. 2011. Waiting for what? The feminization of asylum in protracted situations. *Gender, Place & Culture* **18**(3), pp. 361–79.

Institut for Menneskerettigheder. 2009. *Afviste Asylansøgere Og Andre Udlændinge i Udsendelsesposition i Danmark* [Online]. Available from: http://menneskeret.dk/ udgivelser/afviste-asylansoegere-andre-udlaendinge-udsendelsesposition-danmark [Accessed 10 February 2016].

Kofman, E. 2008. Feminist political geographies. In: Nelson, L. and Seager J. eds. *A companion to feminist geography*. Malden: Wiley-Blackwell, pp. 519–33.

Lewis, H., Dwyer, P., Hodkinson, S. and Waite L. 2015. Hyper-precarious lives: migrants, work and forced labour in the Global North. *Progress in Human Geography* **39**(5), pp. 580–600.

Martin, L. 2012. 'Catch and remove': detention, deterrence, and discipline in US noncitizen family detention practice. *Geopolitics* **17**(2), pp. 312–34.

Mitchell, T. 1991. The limits of the state: beyond statist approaches and their critics. *The American Political Science Review* **85**(1), pp. 77–96.

Moran, D., Gill, N. and Conlon, D. eds. 2013. *Carceral spaces*. Surrey: Ashgate.

Mountz, A. 2010. *Seeking asylum: human smuggling and bureaucracy at the border*. Minneapolis: University of Minnesota Press.

Mountz, A. 2011. The enforcement archipelago: detention, haunting, and asylum on islands. *Political Geography* **30**(3), pp. 118–28.

Mountz, A., Coddington, K., Catania, T. and Loyd J. M. 2013. Conceptualizing detention: mobility, containment, bordering, and exclusion. *Progress in Human Geography* **37**(4), pp. 522–41.

Nagel, C. 2002. Geopolitics by another name: immigration and the politics of assimilations. *Political Geography* **21**(8), pp. 971–87.

Noxolo, P. 2014. Towards an embodied securityscape: Brian Chikwava's Harare North and the asylum seeking body as site of articulation. *Social & Cultural Geography* **15**(3), pp. 291–312.

Painter, J. 2006. Prosaic geographies of stateness. *Political Geography* **25**(7), pp. 752–74.

Peutz, N. 2010. 'Criminal alien' deportees in Somaliland. In: De Genova, N. and Peutz, N. eds. *The deportation regime*. Durham: Duke University Press Books, pp. 371–409.

Pratt G. and Rosner V. 2012. *The global and the intimate: feminism in our time*. New York: Columbia University Press.

Rygiel, K. 2012. Politicizing camps: forging transgressive citizenships in and through transit. *Citizenship Studies* **16**(5-6), pp. 807–25.

Schuster, L. 2011. Dublin II and Eurodac: examining the (un) intended(?) consequences. *Gender, Place & Culture* **18**(3), pp. 401–16.

Staeheli, L. A. and Nagel, C. R. 2008. Rethinking security: perspectives from Arab-American and British Arab activists. *Antipode* **40**(5), pp. 780–801.

Topak, Ö. 2014. The biopolitical border in practice: surveillance and death at the Greece–Turkey borderzones. *Environment and Planning D: Society and Space* **32**(5), pp. 815–33.

Torfing, J. 1999. Workfare with welfare: recent reforms of the Danish welfare state. *Journal of European Social Policy* **9**(1), pp. 5–28.

Udlændingestyrelsen. 2012a. Kontrakt mellem Udlændingestyrelsen og Røde Kors. Copenhagen: Udlændingestyrelsen.

Udlændingestyrelsen. 2012b. Asylansøgeres vilkår [Online]. Available from: www .nyidanmark.dk/dadk/Ophold/asyl/asylansoegernes_vilkaar/asylansoegernes_vilkaar .htm [Accessed 11 April 2012].

UNHCR. 2012. *An introduction to cash-based interventions in UNHCR operations, March 2012* [Online]. Available from: www.unhcr.org/515a959e9.html [Accessed 10 February 2014].

Vitus, K. and Nielsen, S. S. 2011. *Asylbørn I Danmark*. Copenhagen: Hans Reitzels Forlag.

Waite, L. 2009. A place and space for a critical geography of precarity? *Geography Compass* 3(1), pp. 412–33.

Waite, L., Valentine, G. and Lewis, H. 2014. Multiply vulnerable populations: mobilising a politics of compassion from the 'capacity to hurt'. *Social & Cultural Geography* 15(3), pp. 313–31.

Walters, W. 2010. Migration and security. In: Burgess J. P. ed. *The handbook of new security studies*. London: Routledge, pp. 217–28.

Wilson, A. 2004. *The intimate economies of Bangkok: tomboys, tycoons, and Avon ladies in the global city*. Berkeley: University of California Press.

Wilson, A. 2012. Intimacy: a useful category of transnational analysis. In: Pratt, G. and Rosner, V. eds. *The global and the intimate: feminism in our time*. New York: Columbia University Press, pp. 31–56.

11 Health and intimacies in immigration detention

Nick Gill

> Sana called *The Observer* in 2011. Her voice trembling but resolute, she went methodically through the chain of events in which she claimed she had been sexually assaulted by a healthcare worker at Yarl's Wood in Bedford, Britain's biggest immigration detention centre for women.
>
> (Townsend, 18 May 2014)

In these words Mark Townsend, the Home Affairs editor of the British national newspaper *The Observer*, reported the alleged abuse of Sana (a pseudonym), a 29-year-old woman from Pakistan. The reason for the delay between Sana's first call (in 2011) and the news report (in 2014), according to Townsend, was because Serco, the giant private company that runs Yarl's Wood, fought hard to keep details of the allegations out of the public domain by deploying 'reputation management lawyers' (Townsend, 2014, p. 8). Serco had conducted an internal inquiry as a result of cases that Sana had brought against Serco, the Home Office and the police regarding her treatment. The outcome was an internal report, which recounted 'her claims of how a healthcare worker, whom she had approached with problems of headaches and dizziness, allegedly told her "she did not need medication but needed his penis"' (Townsend, 2014, p. 8). The man then allegedly sexually assaulted her – the third time he had allegedly assaulted her over a five-week period. Sana, who had experienced forced marriage and abusive relationships, left and told a female guard 'I am not safe here' (Townsend, 2014, p. 8). The guard was quoted in Serco's report as saying it is 'just so difficult not to believe that this [the allegation] is true' (Townsend, 2014, p. 8). Later however, the same guard would be criticised in the report for failing to see that Sana's story could be fabricated: senior officers concluded that the guard required guidance in order to become more objective. It was this conclusion that Serco had sought to keep out of the public realm.

Sana's story raises a series of disturbing issues in relation to immigration detention involving detainees' vulnerability, the abuse of power, the health effects of detention conditions and the role of profit-seeking private corporations in obfuscating (mal)practices of control. Taking 'intimate economies' to refer to scrutiny of the economic realm at close range with attention to its effects and ramifications at the individual as well as broader scales, the lens of the intimately economic offers useful purchase onto the set of issues at play in Sana's story. The striking reluctance of Serco to undergo close scrutiny characterises the 'politics of hiding' (Jones et al., 2014) of immigration detention: it is Serco's aversion to one type of intimacy, in the sense of close observation of, or public intimacy with, its affairs, that undergirds the events in Sana's case. This aversion is also closely related to problematic relations between economics and intimacy in detention. As Wilson (2012, p. 42) argues, contrary to hegemonic discourses and understandings, there is often significant overlap between intimate life and economic forces, to the extent that dislodging 'the universality of capitalism … involves advancing an alternate vision of the nexus of intimacy and the global economy'. Immigration detention centres are global sites of profit making that inevitably 'affect, and are shaped by, intimate relations' (Wilson, 2012, p. 42) in profound ways because detention centres render their inhabitants reliant on profit-motivated relationships for their most personal and intimate needs. In immigration detention aspects of lives that should be independent from profit-motivated activities, including important elements of individuals' healthcare and safety, are drawn into relationships of production and exchange in complex ways.

Alongside the relationship between economies and intimacy, in recent years scholars have become increasingly interested in the politics of intimacy, especially in relation to negative, sometimes violent, influences over personal integrity and bodily well-being that often contravene the wishes of subjects (Pain and Staeheli, 2014). In this vein Sana's story conveys not only Serco's distaste for public exposure, but also other forms of reluctance indicative of the presence of power and domination within the context of the blurring of intimacy and economy that Wilson (2012) has identified. First, and most obviously, taking intimacy to euphemistically refer to sexual encounters, it is the healthcare worker's alleged sexualising of Sana without her consent that has resulted in these alleged assaults. Second, if we take intimacy to mean close familiarity or friendship in a non-sexual sense, then it is the placing of individuals like Sana outside their spheres of intimacy, without friends, family and medical services she can trust, once more against their wishes, that makes them vulnerable. The presence of one form of intimacy in combination with the absence of another produces a terrifying and dangerous landscape. What emerges is the importance of taking account of *various intimacies*, as well as the contingencies and combinations of their relations, in understanding the experiences of women like Sana, as well as other potentially vulnerable groups, in immigration detention.

Mary Bosworth points out the many rules and stipulations that should protect immigration detainees' health in detention in Britain. For instance, 'Detention Centre rules stipulate that detainees should be seen by a member of the health-care team within 24 hours of arrival' (Bosworth, 2014, p. 111). Indeed there are various procedures designed to protect the mental and physical health of detainees in detention, embodied in the *Detention Centre Rules* (Immigration and Nationality Directorate, 2001) that Bosworth makes reference to, including (under 'Rule 35') stipulations for the detection and removal of torture survivors from detention.

Yet in practice these procedures are often either not adhered to or they are simply inadequate to safeguard the health of detainees. As Bosworth observes in reflecting upon her extended ethnographic fieldwork in British immigration detention centres:

> Healthcare ... was widely criticized. ... Sometimes the problems were simply practical ones [like not being able to find medication]. Often, however, they were more serious. In all centres, for example, detainees complained that, no matter what their aliment, they were just given 'paracetemol'. There was also a widely held belief that the medical team did not believe what they were told. [One detainee from Jamaica suggested that] 'They possibly think that because they are in detention they fake their complaints'.
>
> (Bosworth, 2014, p. 132)

Alongside this sort of neglect runs the over-valorisation of the imperative to save costs by cutting corners. Francis Webber, a British immigration solicitor with over 30 years' experience, describes how a test case in 2006 brought by two torture survivors revealed that for years the private medical services providers in detention centres in the UK had not carried out routine screening for evidence of torture within 24 hours of a detainee's arrival 'because the Home Office regarded it as unnecessary and inappropriate and refused to pay for it' (Webber, 2012, p. 138). Webber surmises that 'immigration detention fosters a culture of inhumanity, in which suicide attempts, self-harm and hunger strikes are dismissed as "attention-seeking"' and concludes that immigration detention 'is a dangerous place to be' (2012, p. 139).

After years of criticism by the Prisons Inspectorate, the Royal Medical Colleges, the courts, medical charities and Members of Parliament, the responsibility for healthcare in immigration detention was shifted from the Home Office and the security companies in charge of detention centres to the National Health Service (NHS) between September 2014 and April 2015, raising hopes of improvements in healthcare in immigration detention (Miller and Sambrook, 2014). These hopes were dashed, however, when it became clear that the NHS had no intention of providing services itself, but would simply act as a commissioner of private companies to do the work, raising the possibility that the NHS's good reputation has been co-opted in an effort to legitimate an essentially unsafe and unhealthy environment. In September 2014 for instance, contracts to provide healthcare in four detention centres were awarded to G4S by NHS England, causing outrage among activists who pointed to G4S's health record in immigration detention such as their involvement in the death of Jimmy Mubenga, a 46-year-old father of five who died after heavy restraint by three G4S guards on a British Airways plane during an attempt to deport him to Angola in 2010.[1] One of the centres in which G4S is now responsible for healthcare services is Yarl's Wood, the centre where Sana was held. In December 2014 *The Telegraph*, a national newspaper, reported continuing problems with medical treatment even after the NHS had taken over the responsibility for commissioning healthcare services in detention (Sanghani, 2014). These included month-long periods without insulin for Type 1 diabetes sufferers, staff preventing detainees from calling an ambulance when a detainee had collapsed and a wheelchair user being told they had to 'crawl' to their wheelchair (Sanghani, 2014).

In this chapter I ask how thinking about intimacy can help us to understand threats to detainees' health in immigration detention. I argue, following Wilson (2012), that the health of detainees is regularly compromised by their presence in immigration detention owing to the often unacknowledged mingling of economic and intimate life that takes place there. This is compounded by private corporations' resistance to intimate public scrutiny of their affairs. I examine the consequences of these phenomena in the next section, focusing in particular on neglect, disbelief and abuse. Recognising the different forms of intimacy at work in Sana's story though, I also argue that the threat, the fear and sometimes the advent of unwanted intimacy, understood as sexual relations at the scale of the body and in the context of power and exchange in immigration detention, forms an important additional part of women's experiences of detention centres in the UK (while I focus on women the chapter is equally relevant to other potentially vulnerable groups in detention such as transgender groups and non-heteronormative groups more broadly). In the third section I therefore use the unique perspective afforded by thinking about intimacy in terms of and in relation to economy and exchange, to explore the utility of considering this type of intimacy for understanding the health consequences of immigration detention. Furthermore, non-sexual intimacy with friends and supporters, which may be desired but is confiscated in detention, constitutes an additional form of intimacy that affects immigration detainees through its absence, as Sana's case illustrates. In the fourth section I discuss how this lack of intimacy impacts on detainees' health. Through the course of the chapter then, I explore the ways in which different types of intimacy – their presence, their absence and their combination – can help us to understand threats to the health of detainees. I conclude that deployment of multiple understandings of related but distinct intimacies is likely to be most productive in working out how immigration detainees' health, detention centre economies and intimate life intersect.

Intimate economies and scrutiny

In this section I show that the mingling of economic and intimate life puts detainees' health at risk in immigration detention in various ways. The imperative to reduce costs, protect reputations and guarantee the operational functioning of detention centres with minimal disruption undermines the attention that is given to concerns of an emotional or personal nature, which ultimately nurtures the neglect, disbelief and abuse of detainees. What is more, these effects would not be publicly accepted if they were plainly visible. A perspective that takes seriously *both* the relationship between the economic and the intimate, *and* the lack of public intimacy with this relationship, is therefore required.

Here and throughout the chapter I draw on three related research projects that constitute a programme of research that began in 2003. The first project was doctoral research[2] that aimed to explore the challenges facing immigration decision makers in the United Kingdom from the perspective of both decision makers themselves and asylum seekers in their care. Thirty-seven interviews were conducted, including with former detainees and detention centre employees (see Gill, 2009). The second project[3] examined the challenges and mitigating strategies of asylum support groups in the UK and United States. This project involved a survey of over 100 asylum support groups in the US and UK, two focus groups, and interviews with more than 40 activists, volunteers and support group workers (see Gill et al., 2014). The third project, which is ongoing at the time of writing, examines the asylum appeal process in England and Wales[4] and has involved the observation of immigration detainee bail hearings as well as interviews with people who have been detainees. In what follows I draw on both primary material in the form of interviews with activists and detainees, and secondary material such as activist publications and Internet sites, giving particular attention to sources in which detainees describe detention in their own words.[5]

Neglect

The root cause of what has been called the 'institutional medical abuse' (Webber, 2012, p. 141, quoting Doctor Frank Arnold) of detainees in detention is the reduction of the detainee to a mere 'body', a 'what' rather than a 'who', whose identity is subsumed in systems of bureaucratic management which reduces them to little more than a unit and a number (Hall, 2012). This dehumanisation of detainees (Hiemstra, 2014) is abundantly clear from the testimonies of detainees and former detainees themselves. Detainees make mention of neglect both in terms of the conditions of detention and the treatment of detainees.

In terms of the conditions in detention, a key consideration is the cleanliness of the centres. One detainee, who issued a statement in protest against his detention in 2006, described uncleanliness as a central characteristic of his internment:

> There are about five cleaning staff for the whole centre. They are here to be presented to visitors. How they clean the surroundings, ranging from the kitchen to the toilets is better seen than imagined. They only clean the entrance and passages. The toilets and bathrooms are left to the detriment of the detainees. Hence [security firm] and visiting staff have their own separate facilities. Most of the detainees contract diseases through the toilets because they are being used by every detainee, and no disinfectant is used in washing and cleaning them. Sometimes the passage stinks. You can always perceive the odour while passing through.
>
> (Garcia et al., 2006, p. 41)[6]

Other detainees draw attention to the lack of adequate ventilation in the centres:

> The most alarming problem facing the detainees is their susceptibility to a hazardous and unhealthy environment … every single window in all the rooms in the various wings of Harmondsworth are sealed. Communicable diseases are therefore likely to be transferred from one detainee to another. … The rooms most times are always very hot and uncomfortable. … We are not breathing normally and are usually very weak. We are gradually suffocating to death. What a degrading condition.
>
> (Garcia et al., 2006, pp. 15-17)[7]

In terms of the treatment of detainees, one medical doctor who had visited many detainees in detention explained that detainees can sometimes be apprehended during routine visits to police stations and therefore may not have medicine that they need with them. Yet medical staff in detention centres are often slow to respond when health issues arise. 'I've seen people with HIV infections on antivirals denied their antiviral phials for weeks' he attests, 'and that surely carries the risk of acquisition of resistance to first line drugs. Second line drugs are definitely not available in most of the countries from which they come.'

Detention companies are paid a fixed sum for the care of detainees (around £100 per detainee per day[8]), and since 'the maximisation of profit is their raison d'être' (Webber, 2012, p. 141) this can create an incentive to underinvest in their care. Although the companies themselves would defend their healthcare provision, it is the squeezing of the provisions for the safe care of detainees that ultimately intrudes upon their intimate lives. The activities that they should be able to carry out in private, individually and independently, such as using the toilet, eating, washing and breathing clean air, become sites and occasions of subjection, shame and exposure to health risks.

Disbelief

The notorious 'culture of disbelief' (Souter, 2011) that pervades Britain's asylum system exacerbates these risks. There are various economic motivations to not take claims of medical problems seriously in detention, including (1) the cost of dealing with any problems that arise, (2) aversion to confronting the moral challenge that sick people pose in a detention regime that is focused on generating profits, (3) a perception among security staff that detainees will lie about their medical conditions in order to gain immigration status, which will cost the British taxpayer money, and (4) the risk of costly media exposure if medical neglect comes to light.

These economic considerations nurture a lethal brand of scepticism surrounding detainees' claims of ill health, pain and medical needs. The consequences manifest in private, embodied sensations such as discomfort and pain, as well as emotions like frustration, anger and shame. One detainee in the mid 2000s recalled that:

> Their health-care was/is just there for the sake of the name because we did not get the right treatments and were treated like animals. If I say animals

that would make it better because animals are treated better in this country. Most of time we were told to drink lots of water to cure stomach ache, throat or any kind of pain. If you go back that is when you'll be given paracetemol tablets and mostly we were told that we are attention seekers just going to the health care so that we can be allowed to stay in their country. So the best solution there was to sleep in our rooms rather than to be told off, and yet you felt the pain.[9]

At other times serious risk of compound mental or medical injury can result, when torture survivors and sick people are disbelieved. Although victims of torture should not be incarcerated, only 9 per cent of doctors' reports of evidence of torture lead to the detainee being released (Phelps, 2014, citing United Kingdom Border Agency, 2011). And even having evidence of torture recognised by centre doctors is not assured. In my research one doctor told me: 'I have seen patients where the doctor has written no scars and I counted 15.' He continued:

I have over and over again seen the comment in the notes, quote 'claimed to be epileptic on treatment', 'claimed to be HIV positive on treatment', 'claimed to be diabetic on insulin'. ... I have on frequent occasions seen utter failure to make any effort to find out whether this 'claim' is true or not. ... The problem here is this. If you start from the proposition the patient is lying for secondary gain it is impossible to establish an adequate clinical relationship.

Abuse

A further feature of British immigration detention is the frequent allegations of abuse of detainees at the hands of centre staff, ranging from verbal and psychological abuse to serious beatings. 'I have witnessed several cases of torturing carried out by these ill-educated staff swearing and insulting older people twice their age, old enough to be their dads' one detainee in Harmondsworth detention centre stated.[10] Others allege different, subtle ways (that will not leave a mark that could later form evidence of abuse) to suppress and mistreat detainees. 'They can take you to segregation and leave you there for days to break you' one detainee who I interviewed in 2014 observed before going on to say:

And most of the time they do succeed. Because the rooms, you say 'boy I cannot even breathe in there,' they set the ventilation so you cannot breathe. ... This is a torture, a torture, they won't touch you to hurt you, but they will shut down the vent so you won't get any, any air in your room ... if they don't like you for whatever reason, the colour of your skin, your face, the way your beard grows, you're in trouble. This is control mechanism and a torture chamber ... people don't understand, they don't want to think about what is exactly happening. ... But you are managed, tortured by the air. It goes on.

Another source of discomfort is extremes of temperature. Detainees have reported that showers are sometimes too hot to wash properly, with inevitable implications for sanitation. Others have reported abusive exposure to very cold conditions. One male Angolan detainee in 2004, for example, alleged his intentional exposure to extreme cold that affected his health:

> I was sleeping in my room when an officer woke me up [to take] me to London Airport. I asked the officer if I can change before we go because it was cold. They said 'no'. I asked the manager why I can't change and he replied 'I'm the manager and I can do whatever I want; I am the one who gives the orders.' In the same moment ten big strong men came in and put me to the van. I also asked these men if I could go to my room and change – the men also refused. I begged them if I could at least put a jumper on because it was cold and I was shaking. They refused once again and acted like they didn't care whether I was cold or not. We went to the van and headed down to London. ... I was very cold and afraid I was going to die because of the cold. In the van I begged the guards to give me clothes or something to put on because I couldn't handle the coldness any longer – I was shaking with cold. ... When I arrived in Manchester I asked for clothes and the officers there also refused. ... When I arrived at [my final destination] I got sick because of the cold I was feeling during the journey.[11]

This account is in keeping with other allegations from detainees about how abuse operates to undermine their health in immigration detention. One statement issued by a group of detainees from the Democratic Republic of Congo in 2006 from within the British detention estate alleged that '"Escort officers" use ... excessive force; serious beating while handcuffed is so rampant. Most of us have scars and some have sustained physical injuries from handcuffs to our hands during the beating.'[12]

In a high profile study, Medical Justice (2008), a registered UK charity, reported almost 300 cases of alleged assaults against asylum deportees, including against pregnant women and minors. The allegations ranged from being beaten, choked, kicked, gagged, overzealously restrained via the use of handcuffs, dragged about, knelt on or sat on, and sexually abused. The alleged results ranged from bruising and swelling to fractures, dislocations, cuts, bleeding and head, neck and back pain. A former chief inspector of prisons, Lord David Ramsbotham, wrote in reaction to the report that 'our national reputation is not something to be treated lightly or wantonly, and ... if even one of the cases is substantiated, that amounts to something of a preventable national disgrace' (Medical Justice, 2008, p. 1).

If disbelief and neglect both derive from the economic imperatives of immigration detention, abuse is perhaps harder to understand. Rather than simply economic in origin, abuse can be seen as a form of pathology that could result from the vicarious traumatisation of staff, the withdrawal of staff from the human consequences of their work towards a 'state of denial' (Cohen, 2001) that they are dealing with human beings with feelings and moral worth, and the positioning of staff in situations of extreme and unaccountable power over others in which sadism and cruelty are likely to flourish (Zimbardo, 2007; Milgram, [1974] 2005). Whatever its cause though, it is clear that if abusers do lurk within British detention centres, they will be particularly keen to avoid the close scrutiny that public intimacy with their activities entails.

The accounts of neglect, disbelief and abuse in immigration detention reveal the ways in which economics intrudes upon intimacy in this environment by turning activities that should be private into sites and occasions of shame, violence and suffering. It also reveals the reliance of this intrusion upon a lack of scrutiny. As a result we can see how two different forms of intimacy – as the ordinarily private activities of personal life, and as close observation – are implicated in detention centres in disturbing ways, and combine to produce unacceptable results.

Unwanted intimacy

I now explore how sexual identity and sexual relations operate within an economy of power. I show how the fear and economy of sexual encounters overshadow much of the experience of detainees in detention. I also explore the effects of a lack of privacy for detainees in the context of the often overtly heterosexual and masculine culture of the detention centre. In doing so I demonstrate how sexual intimacy is also drawn into the subjection of detainee populations, and how it is set within a context of economic utility and malfunctioning public scrutiny.

Returning to Sana's allegations of sexual abuse, Serco settled Sana's claims for what Townsend describes as a 'modest sum' (Townsend, 2014, p. 8). Her claims of abuse at Yarl's Wood are not isolated though. Allegations of inappropriate behaviour, including unwanted sexual intimacy, date back to 2007 according to Townsend. Although he recognises that efforts have been made to improve things since that time, Townsend reports that at times in Yarl's Wood '[a] perception appeared to have evolved among detainees that if they flirted or slept with guards their case might be treated more favourably' (Townsend, 2014, p. 8). One woman, Leah (a pseudonym), who Townsend quotes in his article, alleged that '[t]he guards would flirt with the detainees. I spoke to some ladies who were in proper relationships with the guards. They used to give these women the impression that if you sleep with me I'll put in a good word for you' (Townsend, 2014, p. 8). Another woman, Sharon (also a pseudonym) explains that, 'small essentials like nice soap, nice hair products … they thought if they gave in to demands they would get these things in return. […] The girls would put on their hot pants and dance closely with these guards like in a nightclub, grinding and winding' (Townsend, 2014, p. 8).

In 2014, *Women for Refugee Women,* an organisation that seeks to raise awareness of the experiences of women in immigration detention, published a research report that examined the treatment of women claiming asylum in Britain's detention estate (Girma et al., 2014). They interviewed 46 women, many of whom had experienced arrest and imprisonment, prostitution and forced marriage, violence from soldiers, police or prison guards, torture and rape in their home countries or *en route* to the UK. Eighty per cent said they had been tortured or raped. Yet they also frequently reported that detention centre staff had verbally abused them (50 per cent), that staff had been racist towards them (22 per cent), they had been guarded by a solitary male member of staff (87 per cent) and that this had made them feel uncomfortable (70 per cent of these). Sixty-seven per cent said they did not trust medical staff in detention, and many reported mental health problems, suicidal ideation and poor healthcare available in detention.

Townsend's evidence and the Women for Refugee Women report highlight the sexualised hostility that permeates immigration detention. Economy invades intimacy in such a setting: staffing with female staff only or providing additional training and monitoring for all staff would cost more at the expense of profit making. Sexual identity as a private and ordinarily domestic matter thus becomes laden with power relations and, as the bartering for sexual favours reveals, also apparently commodified, with obvious risks of subjection and exploitation.

These risks are compounded by a striking lack of privacy in the centres. Female detainees report that '[there are] cameras in your room. You don't know if there are perverts using the cameras for their own use' and they make reference to 'the stress of being locked up, having cameras everywhere and not being able to make and receive calls.'[13] Others object to the lack of discretion among guards, which results from a configuration of power and control that apparently makes some of them feel that social norms that typically function to convey respect for others can be disregarded. 'There is no privacy' one female detainee complained. 'Male officers come and enter your room without knocking and go through your underwear during room searches.'[14] Women have to collect sanitary products from the main office in Yarl's Wood whenever they have their periods. 'Sometimes there are just men on the desk, so I'll wait for hours until there's a woman,' one detainee told *The Telegraph* in 2014 (Sanghani, 2014, n.p.). 'I can't ask a man' she continued, 'I'm not used to talk (sic.) about these things with men. I don't see why they can't just give us … the products' (Sanghani, 2014, n.p.).

This lack of privacy intersects dangerously with health issues. The doctor mentioned earlier, for example, describes how the use of same-language detainees for interpretation during medical examinations, as a tactic to save money spent on professional interpreters, can 'be problematic when you are dealing with highly confidential information which might then spread all the way round the detention centre' such as information on HIV or sexuality. This is especially problematic for gay men in a predominantly, and sometimes aggressively, heterosexual environment. 'Gay people [are] vulnerable' one healthcare worker revealed in an exit letter after over five years of working in a British detention centre, explaining how the centre manager they had worked with was unwilling to house known gay men separately from the rest of the centre for their own protection despite the risks of bullying by a powerful homophobic group of Jamaican detainees there. This resulted in substantial numbers of individuals within the centre reporting harassment.

The absence of intimacy

So far in this chapter I have explored the effect of the presence, absence and combination of various forms of *negative* intimacy, expressed in terms of 'scrutiny', 'reluctance' and 'intrusion' for instance. In this section I turn to a more positive understanding of intimacy as close and trusting friendships or relationships with others to argue that the deprivation of this positive form of intimacy is just as important to understanding detainees' experiences. I argue that the confiscation of supportive intimate relationships with familiar others constitutes another way in which the economy of detention interacts with intimacy in the subjection of detainees.

It is clear that many of the health risks that detainees face are exacerbated by their isolation. It is well known that immigration detention can lead to mental health problems (Steel et al., 2006; Robjant et al., 2009), that the longer one is detained the more acute these problems are likely to become (Bull et al., 2012) and that the consequences are likely to persist for many years after release (Coffey et al., 2010). One of the reasons for this is the excision of detainees from their communities and relationships of support (see Mountz, 2013).

The Women for Refugee Women report explicated the importance of intimate and trusting non-sexual relationships and friendship to women in detention. Lydia Besong is one of the authors of the report and a former detainee in Yarl's Wood. She writes in the forward to the report that

> [T]he thing that kept me going [in detention] is that I received many, many Christmas cards from my supporters. … Every time I opened a card I felt very emotional to know that many people were thinking of me. … But in Yarl's Wood there were many women who did not receive one card. I met one girl who was only 18 who had come here seeking asylum from Nigeria because of the harm she has suffered in her traditional community. Nobody knew she was in detention. She was totally alone. She was crying all the time.
>
> (Girma et al., 2014, p. 2)

When detention deprives detainees of their networks and confidantes, the risk of ill health, both mental and physical, is exacerbated. For Lydia Besong '[o]ther people act like a pillar – if you feel you are going to fall they keep you standing' (Girma et al., 2014, p. 2). That is why isolation in detention is so damaging.

The transfer of detainees from centre to centre often acts to exacerbate their isolation (see Gill, 2009, 2016). One former detainee who I interviewed in 2014 reflected on why he thought he had been moved frequently from centre to centre during his three and a half year confinement:

> The only thing I could think of is that they didn't like for me to be settled in any place. When I get to stay in one place I get to make friends, everything is nice for me, I have friends. And the movement affects your health. I had lots of problems in the hospital. ... I arranged visits to a local hospital because the health care in the centre is not up and running, but they would bring me, [to a different centre] and the doctor would say he doesn't want to see me.

Others also claim that transfers to different centres have been arranged to coincide with appointments to see medical personnel, constituting medical abuse by withholding medical care. Appointments have been missed and detainees have been left feeling as though this was a premeditated outcome. An activist passed on the following testimony from a detainee of over a year to me in 2013:

> Many times they are moving me always because of my independent doctor appointment in order to frustrate me and they don't want an outside doctor to assess so that there can be clear evidence to my medical problems and situation. ... I had a referral to [a charity], it was stopped by UKBA. Also an appointment with [a different charity] was also stopped by the UKBA. After that I made another rescheduled appointment with [the second charity] to visit me at the centre, that was the reason the UKBA moved me to [detention centre]. Now because of my upcoming appointment ... they moved me because they don't want it to happen. Obviously the UKBA knowing full well I have medical problems.

One long-time activist and senior figure in a group that supports people in detention and campaigns against its excesses, expresses similar concerns with respect to immigration detainees:

> People with serious mental illness [are] being transferred around the detention estate with the explicit purpose of, and you can see on the file, of upsetting them. They are too comfortable in their detention, let's move them somewhere else so that we can upset them and break them so that they agree to move back [to their country of origin].

When detainees are moved from centre to centre, there is a heightened risk that they will be separated from their medical notes or their medication. Movement and transfers therefore undermine not only general contact networks and legal supports, but also medical networks that play an important part in protecting the health of detainees. If we understand the accounts above to be accurate representations of detainee experience, they illustrate the complex ways in which yet another form of intimacy, medical intimacy, is drawn into the system of power, exchange and control that immigration detention exhibits.

Conclusion

This chapter has revealed the array of intimacies that are implicated in immigration detention as well as their relevance to detainee health. Some intimacies that would be helpful to immigration detainees are notably absent, such as the close scrutiny that might hold the private companies that run the centres and provide the healthcare to account, as well as intimacy with friends and loved ones that might provide valuable emotional support. Other intimacies inhere, but are drawn into relationships of commodification and exchange, illustrating the ways in which ordinarily private and personal matters such as daily self-care and sexual identity are colonised by economic imperatives, business concerns and the self-interest of staff and managers. The health consequences of these intimate economies are acute. Detainees who are well are at increased risk of becoming sick, and detainees who are already sick appear to be at greater risk of compound illness and injury. This applies to both mental and physical health problems; indeed immigration detention can be seen as an independent mental health risk in its own right, quite apart from its tendency to aggravate pre-existing conditions (Phelps, 2014).

Work influenced by feminist scholarship is increasingly adopting the lens of the intimate because it offers a way to break free from established categories that reify relationships and attachments, such as identity, kinship and nationalism (Pratt and Rosner, 2012; Wilson, 2012). The intimate offers a productive intellectual opening, partly because of its elasticity. It is not overly *against* some opposite, nor is it committed to a specific scale, but rather functions as a 'placeholder in critical analyses of global life [that] resist[s] ideological reifications [and] forms of knowledge that perpetuate global inequality' (Wilson, 2012, p. 48). As such, the lens of intimacy is self-consciously complex, layered and textured in ways that dominant discourses, which separate global from local and economic from private, are not.

In this chapter I have embraced this complexity by calling attention to the multiple forms of intimacy that circulate in immigration detention and influence detainees' health. Thinking about intimacies in the plural promises to lend plasticity and agility to discussions of intimate life, which acts as a valuable guarantee against the settling of intimacy as an intellectual perspective into a specific mould, scale, ideology or politics. Immigration detention usefully illustrates not only the multiplicity of intimacies that link the global to the personal, but also the relationships between intimacies, some of which facilitate and complement each other, others of which share contingent or substitutive relationships.

Although the picture painted of migrant health in immigration detention is bleak in this chapter, the complexity and agility of the lens of intimacy can also highlight ways to work against the detention regime. Activist groups who monitor and publicise the happenings within immigration detention for instance are instrumental in cracking open the intimacy of dangerously closed and obfuscated spaces. *The Detention Forum*, for example, is a well-organised group of activists working to end immigration detention and resist its most objectionable consequences. It has been instrumental in prompting and organising submissions to a Parliamentary Inquiry into Immigration Detention in the UK – the first of its kind (All Party Parliamentary Group on Refugees & the All Party Parliamentary Group on Migration, 2015). The report from the inquiry has given unprecedented public prominence to the deficiencies in healthcare in immigration detention (although whether real change comes about as a result remains to be seen).

What is more, where there may be a temptation for detainees to organise their resistance, re-working or resilience (see Katz, 2004) within detention around settled identities such as national groups or by grades of immigration status, a focus on the intrusions of detention centre life into intimate health concerns foregrounds the ways otherwise disparate groups might unite around common struggles and experiences. The recognition of similarity over difference offers grounds to build empathy and solidarity. The very ambiguity of intimacy, then, offers a chance to unify differently positioned but universally vulnerable groups that are affected by uneven economies and unjust power relations (see Wilson, 2012). Intimacy offers not only a useful critical lens in this context, but also a resource that refuses unhelpful divisions.

Acknowledgements

Thanks first to the research participants. I would also like to acknowledge funding support from the Economic and Social Research Council (ESRC), grant numbers PTA-030-2003-01643, RES-000-22-3928-A and ES/J023426/1, and my co-investigators and researchers on these projects. I am also grateful to participants in a series of seminars on the theme of immigration detention funded by the ESRC, grant number ES/J021814/1, which has given rise to many discussions and presentations that have informed my argument.

Notes

1 In 2014 the three guards who had restrained Jimmy Mubenga for half an hour while he audibly protested that he could not breathe were acquitted of manslaughter, despite the overtly racist text messages that two of the three of them had exchanged before Mubenga's death.
2 Funded by the Economic and Social Research Council (ESRC) of the UK at the University of Bristol, UK (grant number PTA-030-2003-01643).
3 Funded by the ESRC, grant number RES-000-22-3928-A. For this project I was assisted by two co-investigators, Drs. Deirdre Conlon and Imogen Tyler, as well as a researcher, Dr. Ceri Oeppen.
4 The project focuses specifically on first tier appeals, meaning appeals made by appellants to an immigration judge in a tribunal against an initial decision taken on their application by a government official. There are higher tier appeal options open to appellants whose first tier appeal is unsuccessful, although in practice these are difficult to access.

The project is funded by the ESRC, grant number ES/J023426/1. For this project I have been assisted by Ms. Jennifer Allsopp and Drs. Melanie Griffiths, Andrew Burridge, Rebecca Rotter and Natalia Paszkiewicz.

5 One activist source I draw on extensively is a pamphlet entitled 'Voices from Detention II' (Garcia et al., 2006) which reports on detainees' experiences of detention in the UK and Australia in their own words.

6 Nigerian male detained in the mid 2000s in Campsfield House immigration detention centre, Oxfordshire, quoted in 'Voices From Detention II'.

7 Statement of 61 detainees in Harmondsworth immigration detention centre, issued in January 2006 in response to the tragic suicide of Bereket Yohannes, found hanged in a shower block in Harmondsworth on 19 January 2006. Statement reprinted in 'Voices From Detention II'.

8 HC Deb, 17 January 2014, c721W. Note: the 'HC Deb' in this reference refers to a House of Commons Debate. The debate in question took place on 17 January 2014 and details can be accessed from Hansard, the edited verbatim report of proceedings of both the House of Commons and the House of Lords. Hansard can be accessed here: http://www.parliament.uk/business/publications/hansard/ (accessed 30 September 2015). The 'W' denotes that the source is a written answer, and the 'c721' indicates that the column number is 721.

9 Zimbabwean woman detained in the mid 2000s in Yarl's Wood immigration detention centre, Bedfordshire, quoted in 'Voices From Detention II' (Garcia et al., 2006, p. 12).

10 Nationality, age and gender not given, quoted in 'Voices From Detention II' (Garcia et al., 2006, pp. 15–17, 20).

11 Quoted in 'Voices From Detention II' (Garcia et al., 2006, p. 24).

12 Quoted in 'Voices From Detention II' (Garcia et al., 2006, p. 21).

13 Zimbabwean woman detainee, mid 2000s, quoted in 'Voices From Detention II' (Garcia et al., 2006, p. 10).

14 Zimbabwean woman detainee, mid 2000s, quoted in 'Voices From Detention II' (Garcia et al., 2006, p. 10).

References

All Party Parliamentary Group on Refugees & the All Party Parliamentary Group on Migration. 2015. *The report of the inquiry into the use of immigration detention in the United Kingdom* [Online]. Available from: https://detentioninquiry.files.wordpress.com/2015/03/immigration-detention-inquiry-report.pdf [Accessed 20 March 2015].

Bosworth, M. 2014. *Inside immigration detention.* Oxford: Oxford University Press.

Bull, M., Schindler, E., Berkman, D. and Ransley, J. 2012. Sickness in the system of long-term detention. *Journal of Refugee Studies* **26**(1), pp. 47–67.

Coffey, G. J., Kaplan, I., Sampson, R. C. and Tucci, M. M. 2010. The meaning and mental health consequences of long-term immigration detention for people seeking asylum. *Social Science & Medicine* **70**(12), pp. 2070–79.

Cohen, S. 2001. *States of denial: knowing about atrocities and suffering.* Cambridge: Polity Press.

Garcia, J., Nasho, E.-K. and Peretz, L. eds. 2006. *Voices from detention II: a collection of testimonies from immigration detainees in the United Kingdom and Australia in their own words.* Oxford: Barbed Wire Britain.

Gill, N. 2009. Governmental mobility: the power effects of the movement of detained asylum seekers around Britain's detention estate. *Political Geography* **28**(3), pp. 186–96.

Gill, N. 2016. *Nothing personal? Geographies of governing and activism in the British asylum system?* Oxford: Wiley-Blackwell.

Gill, N., Conlon, D., Tyler, I. and Oeppen, C. 2014. The tactics of asylum and irregular migrant support groups: disrupting bodily, technological, and neoliberal strategies of control. *Annals of the Association of American Geographers* **104**(2), pp. 373–81.

Girma, M., Radice, S., Tsangarides, N. and Walter, N. 2014. *Detained: women asylum seekers locked up in the UK*. London: Women for Refugee Women.

Hall, A. 2012. *Border watch: cultures of immigration, detention and control*. London: Pluto Press.

Hiemstra, N. 2014. Performing homeland security within the US immigrant detention system. *Environment and Planning D: Society and Space* **32**(4), pp. 571–88.

Immigration and Nationality Directorate. 2001. *Detention Centre Rules, SI 2001/238*. London: HMSO [Online]. Available from: www.legislation.gov.uk/uksi/2001/238/pdfs/uksi_20010238_en.pdf [Accessed 18 March 2014].

Jones, R., Robinson, J. and Turner, J. 2014. *The politics of hiding, invisibility, and silence: between absence and presence*. London: Routledge.

Katz, C. 2004. *Growing up global: economic restructuring and children's everyday lives*. Minneapolis: University of Minnesota Press.

Medical Justice. 2008. *Outsourcing abuse: the use and misuse of state-sanctioned force during the detention and removal of asylum seekers* [Online]. Available from: www.medicaljustice.org.uk/images/stories/reports/outsourcing%20abuse.pdf [Accessed 26 June 2014].

Milgram, S. [1974] 2005. *Odedience to authority*. London: Pinter & Martin.

Miller, P. and Sambrook, C. 2014. The national shame that is healthcare in UK immigration detention. *Open Democracy* [Online]. Available from: www.opendemocracy.net/ourkingdom/phil-miller-clare-sambrook/national-shame-that-is-healthcare-in-uk-immigration-detention [Accessed 7 July 2015].

Mountz, A. 2013. Mapping remote detention: dis/location through isolation. In Loyd, J., Mitchelson. M. and Burridge, A. eds. *Beyond walls and cages: prisons, borders, and global crisis*. Athens & London: The University of Georgia Press, pp. 91–104.

Pain, R. and Staeheli, L. 2014. Introduction: intimacy-geopolitics and violence. *Area* **46**, pp. 344–47.

Phelps, J. 2014. A crisis of harm in immigration detention. *Open Democracy* [Online]. Available from: www.opendemocracy.net/5050/jerome-phelps/crisis-of-harm-in-immigration-detention [Accessed 6 July 2015].

Pratt, G. and Rosner, V. eds. 2012. *The global and the intimate: feminism in our time*. New York: Columbia University Press.

Robjant, K., Hassan, R. and Katona, C. 2009. Mental health implications of detaining asylum seekers: systematic review. *The British Journal of Psychiatry* **194**, pp. 306–12.

Sanghani, R. 2014. Inside Britain's 'worst' immigration removal centre at Christmas. *The Telegraph* [Online]. Available from www.telegraph.co.uk/women/womens-life/11308434/Yarls-Wood-Inside-Britains-worst-immigration-removal-centre-at-Christmas.html [Accessed 6 July 2015].

Souter, J. 2011. A culture of disbelief or denial? critiquing refugee status determination in the United Kingdom. *Oxford Monitor of Forced Migration* **1**(1), pp. 48–59.

Steel, Z., Silove, D., Brooks, R., Momartin, S., Alzuhairi, B. and Susljik, I. N. A. 2006. Impact of immigration detention and temporary protection on the mental health of refugees. *The British Journal of Psychiatry* **188**(1), pp. 58–64.

Townsend, M. 2014. MPs to probe Serco over sex assault claim at asylum centre. *The Observer*. 18 May 2014 [Online]. Available from: www.theguardian.com/uk-news/2014/may/17/mps-serco-yarls-wood-centre-sex-assault-claim [Accessed 3 February 2016].

United Kingdom Border Agency. 2011. *Detention Centre Rule 35 Audit*. London: Home Office [Online]. Available from: www.gov.uk/government/uploads/system/uploads/attachment_data/file/257174/det-centre-rule-35-audit.pdf [Accessed 24 September 2015].

Webber, F. 2012. *Borderline justice: the fight for refugee and migrant rights*. London: Pluto Press.

Wilson, A. 2012. Intimacy: a useful category of transnational analysis. In Pratt, G. and Rosner, V. eds. *The global and the intimate: feminism in our time*. New York: Columbia University Press, pp. 31–56.

Zimbardo, P. 2007. *The Lucifer effect: understanding how good people turn evil*. New York: Random House.

12 Intimate encounters with immigrant criminalisation in Arizona

Matthew Lowen

Inside Operation Streamline, Part 1

A man from Mexico stands before a Judge in Tucson's Evo A. DeConcini Federal Courthouse. He is the last of 70 people that day who have all just pleaded guilty to the petty misdemeanour charge of 'illegal entry'[1] under Section 8 of the United States Code (8 U.S.C.) § 1325. Every weekday a different group of up to 70 immigrants is paraded before a Judge in the same manner, facing the same fate in federal criminal court proceedings colloquially called Operation Streamline.

On this day, the man before the Judge, like the previous 69 others, has been sentenced to between 30 and 180 days in federal prison, following which he will be deported with a criminal record. He is from Mexico and the entire proceeding has been translated between Spanish and English for all 70 of the Latin American defendants. The Judge asks if he has anything else he would like to say for the record, anticipating no response as there have barely been any so far, and he is the final defendant of the day. But this time the cadence to the legal process is interrupted and he answers 'si' – 'yes' – and continues with: 'Yo creo que ningún ser humano es ilegal.' The translator follows quickly: 'I believe that no human being is illegal.'

The man's words hang in the courtroom air as the Judge takes in what was just said. Usually the only deviation in the bureaucratic monotony of these proceedings is something as simple as a faulty translator headset worn by the immigrants as they wait handcuffed and shackled to enter their guilty plea before the federal court. At this point in the proceedings the same series of questions has been asked and answered by each of the 70 immigrants and a bureaucratic rhythm of sorts has been achieved. But on this day the deviation in question is a succinct and political rebuke of the entire process, not simply a hiccup in the mundane mechanics of legal process.

I am there as an observer, having accompanied a group of students who are learning about United States (US) and Mexico border issues. My work with the American Friends Service Committee (AFSC) in Tucson, Arizona on criminalisation, mass incarceration and private prisons places the daily proceedings of Operation Streamline directly at the intersection of those issues and I am frequently asked to contextualise the public Streamline hearings in Tucson's Federal Court for various groups of students and educators learning about border issues. The criminal prosecutions of immigrants such as Operation Streamline is a critical part of the deterrence tactics employed by Customs and Border Patrol (CBP), and always one of the more memorable parts of any tour of the border region and the surrounding mechanisms of enforcement.

This verbal challenge is more than a minor distraction from the now routine slog of guilty pleas that Operation Streamline turns out each day in Tucson's Federal Court. The phrase itself, 'no human being is illegal', is a pointed critique of a governmental system that is criminalising immigrants simply for being in the country and considers them 'illegal'. This phrase has been widely popularised by immigrant rights organisations (the AFSC among others) in an effort to galvanise immigrant and allied communities and critique the criminalisation practices of the US government, while problematising the use of 'illegal' in legal and quotidian parlance. It can be found on signs and bumper stickers and heard in protests and demonstrations around the country. It elicits a significant history of immigrant rights activism that suggests a more complex experience with federal immigration policies than the limited narrative of this man's life in relation to the US and Mexico border, as presented in Streamline proceedings – one that for the federal government only begins with his apprehension by CBP and ends the second he walks out of the courtroom on his way to a federal prison sentence.

It is impossible to fully know the motivations behind this man's challenge to the legal process to which he was subjected, but this momentary glimpse into one man's intimate encounter with the US system of immigrant criminalisation points to larger themes that always already exist beneath the veneer of crisp, clean legal proceedings. However, even as I situate Operation Streamline as representative of immigrant criminal prosecutions in Arizona and throughout the country, the power of this example lies in the accessibility to the proceedings themselves. As others have critically argued (Borderlands Autonomous Collective, 2012), Operation Streamline is but one facet of a continuum of harsh immigration enforcement policies.

This chapter makes three main arguments. First, practices such as Operation Streamline serve to criminalise vast numbers of immigrants, unnecessarily bloat federal and private prison populations and budgets, and are critical to unpacking a broader 'border regime' that is maintained along the United States' border with Mexico. Secondly, understanding the political and economic realities behind these criminalising practices is key to unlocking possibilities for a world where immigrant criminal prosecutions are a thing of the past. And finally, individual and collective actions aimed at confronting criminalising practices such as Operation Streamline have been, can and must continue to highlight the damaging societal costs of this broader border regime.

In line with these three arguments, the chapter is organised into three main sections: *Contextualising criminalisation* offers a brief history of Operation Streamline and how it figures into immigrant criminal prosecutions writ large. *Private prisons and political connections* presents political and economic linkages between anti-immigrant legislation, the for-profit private prison industry and mass incarceration; and the final section, *Confronting criminalisation*, details critiques of Operation Streamline as it functions in Tucson, Arizona as well as collective actions against it and criminalisation as a whole.

The intersection of these three themes – immigrant criminalisation, its political and economic context, and the critiques and resistance to both the practice and the context of immigrant criminalisation – is profoundly evident in the judicial space of Operation Streamline. It is by its very nature an intimate space where the politics of criminalisation are buttressed by the economic incentives of incarceration, and alternately complicated by even a casual observer's critique. The intimacy is both obvious in the cramped physical spaces of legal procedure, and palpable in the vulnerable interactions each immigrant has with the various personifications of the federal government, be it the Judge, court staff, CBP agents or US Marshals who are effectively the police force for the federal government. That a massive system of criminalisation can be momentarily highlighted so clearly in an afternoon proceeding has vaulted Operation Streamline proceedings to a certain level of national recognition and as such is the connective tissue of the remainder of this chapter.

Contextualising criminalisation

Operation Streamline as an enforcement project of the US Customs and Border Patrol (CBP), on the face and due in part to its name, appears to be an organised set of practices that one might imagine takes place all along the border. This is both true and misleading. In all of the six different locales where Streamline takes place, the number of defendants, approach of the judge and the representation by defense counsel is distinct and apparently determined separately from each other courtroom along the southern US border. This chapter will focus on Operation Streamline in Tucson, Arizona, as it convicts the largest number of undocumented immigrants and has been made the subject of political grandstanding by Arizona Senators McCain and Flake (Flake, 2015) and included by name in efforts to pass immigration reform. I will outline how and when Streamline was established, where it fits within CBP's strategic plan, and discuss the financial costs and consequences of this massive buildup of criminalisation and incarceration of immigrants.

In Tucson, Arizona, Operation Streamline essentially gives immigrant defendants a 'choice' between two very unsatisfactory options. Initially each defendant is criminally charged with both 'illegal entry' (a misdemeanor, 8 U.S.C. § 1325) and 'illegal re-entry' (a felony, 8 U.S.C. § 1326). The proceeding that plays out each day in court is a plea hearing where each person agrees to plead guilty to the misdemeanour charge of 'entry' and in exchange the government drops the 're-entry' felony charge which carries a maximum sentence of five years in federal prison. For the defendants who are unlucky enough to have been selected by CBP to go through Streamline proceedings, taking the plea agreement is almost certainly the quickest way through a system that is stacked against them.

These charges are rarely challenged with a not-guilty plea by their court-appointed contract defense attorneys, who are usually representing between six and eight immigrants in one proceeding.

The act of pleading guilty carries significant unintended consequences that will likely forever impact future options for documented re-entry into the US, whether that be a temporary visa of any kind, permanent residence or citizenship. Not only is a criminal record an automatic disqualifier for legal presence in the US of any kind, all recent immigration reform efforts have made it abundantly clear that criminal records are but one factor in limiting undocumented immigrants' eligibility in seeking legal status of any sort. In this way, the criminalisation of immigrants through processes such as Streamline has essentially guaranteed the permanent separation of thousands of families, as the vast majority of people returning to the US without documentation are doing so as a result of family ties. By criminalising these people, the government of the United States has sided with incarceration over families under the guise of immigration enforcement.

First implemented in Del Rio, Texas in December 2005, Operation Streamline was conceived as a CBP effort to deter future border crossing simply by making the consequences of undocumented border crossing more painful by adding criminal charges on top of deportation for a certain number of immigrants. The decision to try groups of immigrants through criminal court rather than civil proceedings or with simple deportation was a departure from previous CBP practices and paved the way for the ongoing mass criminalisation of immigrants that has led to unprecedented numbers of incarcerated immigrants, and federal courts being overwhelmed with criminal cases against immigrants (Libal, 2015).

As outlined in CBP's 2012–16 Strategic Plan, as part of the Consequence Delivery System, Operation Streamline criminalises immigrants for their mere presence in the US, imprisons them for up to half a year, and only then follows through with the already assumed deportation (US Customs and Border Protection, 2012). Another CBP practice of so-called immigrant deterrence includes lateral repatriation which intentionally deports immigrants to different points along the US and Mexico border from where they are originally apprehended. This practice is intended as a further disincentive for attempting to cross again, but the reality is that it isolates and endangers immigrants by placing them in circumstances where they have no social or economic connections (Slack et al., 2013).

As a whole, CBP's Consequence Delivery System is simply a present-day policy reminiscent of failed past enforcement practices that assume that making the immigration experience more difficult will impact the decision to migrate in the first place (see also Bruzzone, this volume). Earlier CBP enforcement tactics such as Operation Gatekeeper, which was first implemented in 1994, caused a shift in immigration patterns farther away from population centres. As a result, Operation Gatekeeper was responsible for thousands of migrant deaths after migration routes moved further into the remote desert and mountain areas (Nevins, 2010).

Like Operation Gatekeeper before it, practices such as Operation Streamline and others aimed at making undocumented immigration a more painful prospect completely miss the economic, social and political realities in Latin America that are driving migration in the first place. Nearly US$18 billion annually of federal tax revenue is currently being invested in these failed efforts under the guise of border security and immigration deterrence. More money is now spent on border enforcement than all other federal law enforcement agencies combined (Meissner et al., 2014). However, recent research demonstrates the futility in such efforts, and at best only delays future attempts at re-entry into the US (Slack et al., 2013).

Since Streamline was enacted, the number of immigrant criminal prosecutions across the country has skyrocketed. In 2013 over 90,000 people were prosecuted for either misdemeanour entry or felony re-entry, compared to just over 12,000 total prosecutions in 2002 (Grassroots Leadership, 2014). While Streamline is a significant part of this prosecutorial explosion, it is also important to remember that it is but one example of a broader system of criminalising immigrants.

The Tucson Sector, which covers all but the westernmost part of Arizona and is one of nine CBP sectors located along the US/Mexico border, adopted Streamline protocols in January 2008. Currently the Tucson Sector prosecutes more immigrants through Streamline than any other CBP sector on the southern U.S. border. Through FY2012, over 200,000 people have been prosecuted through Streamline. As the Office for Congressional Affairs points out, that is '45 percent of the 463,051 immigration-related prosecutions in Southwest border districts during this period' (Seghetti, 2014, p. 8).

The CBP process and criteria for referring detainees to Tucson Streamline proceedings is largely a mystery. All indications point to a relatively random process based on a selection of up to 70 immigrants each day to Streamline court with the only known criteria being that the immigrants speak Spanish, and that they have been recently apprehended by CBP for at least the second time so they can be charged with 're-entry'. Given that Operation Streamline has evolved differently in the various CBP Sectors where it is used, and as a result of a perceived need to more quickly process large numbers of immigrant detainees, it is not surprising that the criteria remains loose and enigmatic. The difficulties and procedural confusion associated with rapid growth of poorly planned programmes such as Streamline have been found elsewhere with immigration enforcement expansion such as with the 287(g) and Secure Communities programmes that gave wide-ranging authority to local law enforcement agencies (Coleman, 2009).

The financial costs of Operation Streamline in the Tucson Sector alone are staggering. Estimates by former Tucson Federal Public Defender Heather E. Williams conservatively put the annual cost of Streamline hearings in Tucson and subsequent incarceration of defendants at $96 million (2008). With the costs to the federal government for incarceration of a single immigrant at $161 per person per day according to the American Civil Liberties Union (2014), the economic burden of these criminalisation tactics has the potential to dramatically climb should numbers and/or sentences increase.

Not factored in to these overwhelming costs of criminalising immigrants are the social and economic costs to the people being convicted and deported, as well as their families who are also left in limbo as their family ties are disrupted and fragmented. The reasons for cross-border immigration into the US without the proper documentation are many, nearly all of which are related to economic necessity. Whether the family of the Streamline defendant is in the US or abroad, the economic necessity of the work for which s/he is migrating will only increase with criminalisation, deportation and the likelihood of future debt from multiple attempts to cross the border. These societal costs to the families and individuals who end up prosecuted, though impossible to calculate, are enormously impactful on the social and economic fabric of families here and abroad, and must be considered when describing the costs of a criminalisation program such as Streamline (Slack et al., 2015).

In many ways, Operation Streamline is simply the most visually jarring example of the criminalisation of immigrants. With some 400,000 deportations each year under President Obama's guidance (Gonzalez-Barrera and Krogstad, 2014), there is no more obvious demonstration of the overwhelming numbers of immigrants becoming needlessly ensnared in the judicial system resulting in their eventual deportation than Streamline. The face of immigrant criminal prosecutions has become the daily *en masse* proceedings of Operation Streamline.

Inside Operation Streamline, Part 2

The hearing is drawing to a close, the courtroom nearly empty save for the final defendant who still stands before the Judge. His lawyer, and only a handful of officials from the various agencies and the courthouse remain. Only one hour earlier the clinking chains of 70 disheveled and exhausted immigrants facing prison time and eventual deportation had made the high-ceilinged courtroom feel crowded. Now the US Marshals are beginning to pack up, the rotating translators cleaning the last of the headsets, and all but the last few defense attorneys have departed. However, following the man's declaration that 'no human being is illegal', all remaining eyes in the Streamline proceedings are on him.

The Judge leans forward and asks for him to repeat himself, perhaps surprised by any response at all. Once again the man says, 'Yo creo que ningún ser humano es ilegal.' And the translator repeats the words again, 'I believe that no human being is illegal.' The Judge responds by thanking him for his courage to speak up and acknowledges that it must not have been easy to do so. She says these things with what appears as sincerity, but goes on to point out that 'unfortunately the federal government disagrees with you'. Indeed it does. Considering the congressional mandate that ICE maintain 34,000 immigration detention beds at all times, there exists all but a guarantee that the presence of undocumented immigrants will continue to be treated as criminal behaviour and punishable by a prison sentence and deportation (Carson and Diaz, 2015).

Private prisons and political connections

Beyond the detention bed quota there are several intersecting factors that lie just beneath the surface of the Judge's characterisation of the US government's disagreement with the notion that an entire class of people cannot be 'illegal'. Those reasons are deeply intertwined in the political economies of mass incarceration, political manoeuvering and financial incentives. This section will unpack how the for-profit private prison industry uses its lobbying and political influence on elected officials for their own benefit, including maintaining a revolving door between lobbying and political positions. I will also outline examples of how the influence of the industry has further created a dependence and similarly a willingness to continue economic reliance on for-profit private prison companies. These examples will highlight the role of political influence and lobbying in laws and practices with specific focus on recent legislative efforts at passing immigration reform. Finally, this section will collectively demonstrate the linkages between mass incarceration and scenes of immigrant criminalisation such as those taking place in Streamline proceedings each day.

The economic benefits of criminalising immigrants for the private prison industry run deep. As the previous section mentions, $18 billion dollars of federal spending is dedicated to immigration enforcement. Much of the enforcement work that the federal government engages in is actually handled by for-profit private companies, which automatically creates a situation where expanding enforcement of immigration policies, especially those that criminalise immigrants, is incentivised by the possibility of new federal contracts for any number of detention, transportation, security or other service contracts (Feltz and Baksh, 2012).

There are currently over 250 immigrant detention facilities across the US; 62 per cent of these facilities are run by for-profit private prison companies such as Corrections Corporation of America (CCA) and GEO Group (Carson and Diaz, 2015). From 2005 to 2011 the federal government increased the annual amount spent on immigrant detention as a result of criminal prosecutions from just under $600,000,000 to over $1 billion for a combined total of more than $5.5 billion during the same time period. In 2011 overall spending on federal detention exceeded $1 billion for the first time (Grassroots Leadership, 2012). CCA alone brings in 44 per cent of its annual revenue thanks to contracts with the federal government – right around $750 million (Law, 2014).

With payouts this high, one need not look too far to find a trail of lobbying money and campaign donations to key political players. From US Senators making immigration policy, to political advisors and elected officials in Arizona defending laws that further ensnare immigrants in the criminal justice system, the ties to the private prison lobby are powerful and growing stronger.

Recent efforts at national immigration reform have been enlightening as to the important position that criminal prosecution programmes such as Operation Streamline occupy. Legislation passed by the US Senate in 2013 with the Corker-Hoeven amendment included specific requirements for the three-fold expansion of Streamline in the Tucson Sector alone (United States Senate, 2013).

Though ultimately failing to pass in the House of Representatives, all indications are that any similarly styled immigration reform legislation will include significant increases in border security spending and programmes. In public statements, Arizona Senators McCain and Flake have stated their unwavering support for the continuation and expansion of Operation Streamline in CBP enforcement and deterrence practices (Fox News Latino, 2014). Senators McCain and Flake have even introduced a legislative resolution aimed at ensuring programmes like Streamline have no limitations placed on them (Flake, 2015), even though there is no indication of any desire by the Obama administration to do so.

In recent years, Arizona has established itself as ground zero for inflammatory, racist and anti-immigrant laws, many of which have been replicated, introduced and enacted in other states. The anti-immigrant reputation that Arizona lawmakers have garnered is rightfully earned thanks to a wide range of hostile legislation that has passed since Jan Brewer became Governor in 2009 after Janet Napolitano was tapped to run the Department of Homeland Security under President Obama. Some of the laws that Arizona has passed include establishing English as the official state language, thus putting public services conducted in Spanish at risk; requiring that employers use the flawed government programme, E-Verify, to check employment eligibility; making it difficult if not impossible to obtain a driver's license as an undocumented immigrant; and charging out-of-state tuition to undocumented college students even when they have lived in Arizona for years at a time. These reactionary bills, and others, were solely aimed at making life more difficult for immigrant communities throughout Arizona.

Most famously, in an effort to outdo the federal government's policies of mass deportation and criminalisation of immigrants, Arizona lawmakers passed Senate Bill (SB) 1070 in 2010, which required police officers to check the papers of anyone who presents 'reasonable suspicion' – a term that was never properly defined and has no legal precedent – that she or he is in fact an immigrant. While all but a few components of this bill have been successfully challenged in court on constitutional grounds for violations of Fourth Amendment protections from improper search and seizure, the impacts of a law that sanctioned racial profiling were felt throughout the country thanks to other states mimicking Arizona's actions. In 2010–11 alone, there were some 48 different SB 1070 copycat laws introduced in other states, five of which were made into law (Gordon and Raja, 2012).

In 2013 bi-partisan leadership in the US Senate established the 'Gang of Eight', a group of eight Senators who were tasked with crafting a comprehensive immigration reform bill that could theoretically pass the Senate and hopefully be adopted and passed by the House as well. Notably, Arizona Senators John McCain and Jeff Flake were two of those eight members. All but one of the Gang of Eight Senators received campaign contributions from for-profit private prison companies. Senator McCain alone had over the course of several years, including during his failed presidential run, collected a combined $71,000 from CCA and GEO Group (Isaacs, 2014a).

It is hardly surprising that political advisors to now former Arizona Governor Jan Brewer had a long history with the for-profit private prison industry. Corporations have literally made a business out of insinuating themselves into political arenas for the sake of future prison contracts with local, state and federal agencies. But rarely have the benefits of such arrangements been so obvious. For example, Paul Senseman served as Brewer's spokesman and helped to defend SB 1070 alongside the bill's author, then State Senator Russel Pearce, after it was signed into law. Before working at the Governor's office, Senseman was CCA's head lobbyist for the state of Arizona during the years leading up to the eventual passing of the law. Similarly, Highground Consulting was enlisted to work on behalf of the state during both the drafting of SB 1070 and the time following it being signed into law. Meanwhile the owner, Charles Coughlin, was acting as Governor Brewer's campaign manager and advisor (Hodai, 2010).

When it comes to private prison political influence and back scratching, it is not only political lobbying and campaign donations, as Chris Kirkham uncovered in his exposés into the financial underpinnings of one county in Arizona (2012). Pinal County, home to the towns of Florence and Eloy, both of which are dominated by state prisons, federal detention facilities and private prisons, has its own special monetary kickbacks thanks to the financial entrenchment of CCA in the economic fabric of the community. CCA operates six prison and detention facilities between Florence and Eloy, and local politicians have vociferously pointed out the necessity of CCA operations to the financial viability of the County at this point. One of the Florence facilities that CCA runs pays into the Pinal County general budget $2 per day per person held in their facility. This arrangement results in anywhere between $700,000 and $1.4 million in extra annual revenue, most of which goes directly to the discretion of Pinal County Sheriff Paul Babeau, who has very publicly demonstrated his support for cracking down on undocumented immigrants even though Pinal County is still over an hour and a half drive from the border with Mexico (Kirkham, 2012).

Arizona's recent election cycle in 2014 saw Mark Brnovich elected as Attorney General. Brnovich has worked for CCA in a number of capacities, first as a Senior Director of Business Development and then as a CCA lobbyist in Utah. He was also appointed to the Governor's Commission on Privatisation and Efficiency under Brewer, which subsequently recommended the privatisation of K-12 education in Arizona. Brnovich's ties to prison privatisation extend further than his own personal history. His spokesman Matt Benson, a former Governor Brewer staff member, also has experience with the lobbying firm, Veritas LLC, which, not coincidentally, worked on behalf of GEO Group (Isaacs, 2014a). The political and financial tradeoffs between companies like CCA and GEO Group with lawmakers is certainly cause for concern, especially when considering the potential benefits that the for-profit private prison industry will inevitably see following any federal comprehensive immigration reform efforts that would also include increased enforcement practices. Such benefits would inevitably include larger and a greater number of federal contracts to detain immigrants on either immigration or criminal grounds for private prison companies. Additionally, as contributions to this volume show, many of the same companies that build and manage prisons have subsidiary companies that provide transportation, security, monitoring and other imprisonment-related services that would also be positioned to obtain new federal contracts.

The for-profit private prison industry is not content to focus solely on prisons and detention beds. As certain private prison sectors have begun to slow their expansion (i.e. state prison bed contracts), and many states have at least begun to consider alternatives to incarceration, as well as adjusting previously extreme sentencing laws, the private prison industry has taken notice by diversifying. In response, for-profit private prison companies long ago made moves to expand into transportation, security and health care, but more recently have begun expanding into areas of treatment, alternatives to incarceration and even probation (Isaacs, 2014b).

So while widespread attention has been rightly given to the ties between the private prison industry and US immigration policies, the bottom line for these companies is to secure new contracts regardless of the government agency that is on the paying end. In this way, efforts to confront both the criminalisation of immigrants and mass incarceration find obvious and ripe common ground in private prison companies who are making enormous profits off all forms of mass incarceration. This of course presents both opportunities and challenges in confronting immigrant criminalisation. On one hand linking campaigns working on mass incarceration and immigration concerns – or simply identifying how these efforts are already linked – offers the chance to learn and develop new strategies and partnerships. On the other hand, the financial entrenchment of private prison companies in communities such as Pinal County, Arizona presents challenges to efforts aimed at closing detention and prison facilities alike, even though the realised economic benefits for rural communities like this remain minimal at best when reliant on prison economies (Bonds, 2009). The possibilities for theoretical and concrete linkages are tremendous, as long as these efforts attend to the goal of ending mass incarceration in all forms rather than attempting to halt only the prison profiteers.

Inside Operation Streamline, Part 3

As the man walks away from the Judge, the chains around his hands and feet jingle as he moves. The few remaining functionaries in the courtroom are already packing up as he leaves the room to be bussed to prison for his assigned sentence prior to his deportation. His small but poignant rebuttal of the systematic criminalisation of immigrants that had broken the monotonous rhythm of rehearsed legal proceedings is now passed and the courtroom is readied for tomorrow's hearing.

Was this man's familiarity with the phrase thanks to news media and word of mouth, or had he lived for some time in the United States and become acquainted with the immigrant rights movement? It seems fair to assume that at the very least this man's willingness to stand before a Judge in federal court and calmly recite such a specific political phrase grows out of a personal experience with the culture and history associated with the immigrant rights movement. Whatever this man's experience, it is a critical reminder that the women and men who are daily herded through Operation Streamline in Tucson, Arizona have much more complex lives than the court creates space for, even as the process itself categorises and criminalises them without regard for those same complexities.

Confronting criminalisation

Any discussion of the criminalisation practices aimed at immigrants in the United States can easily become overwhelming and unwieldy due in part to the lack of tangible, consistent spaces where criminalisation takes place. Operation Streamline in Tucson, Arizona presents one such space and as such has become a point of contention for community activists and politicians alike. Following the previous section's attention to political and economic interests vis-à-vis enforcement tactics, this section deals with the community response to Streamline's daily *en masse* criminal prosecutions of immigrants. Both grassroots community action and legal responses are explored here, as well as a discussion of the outcomes and effectiveness of these two styles of strategy.

Critiques of Operation Streamline are abundant, as are the community actions to confront the mass criminalisation of immigrants that these proceedings represent (Gipe, 2014). In Tucson, Arizona, a coalition group with roots in the sanctuary movement calling itself the End Streamline Coalition has coalesced around efforts to confront Operation Streamline and criminal immigrant prosecutions writ large. Citing a broad number of concerns regarding the care, treatment and legal representation and processes for immigrant defendants, the End Streamline Coalition and other community and immigrant rights organisations have rallied to publicly challenge the notion that immigrant criminalisation is inevitable and serves any purpose. Through staged protests outside the Federal Courthouse, letter-writing campaigns to the participants of Streamline proceedings, accompanying groups to witness Streamline proceedings, and daily monitoring of the hearings themselves, the profile of Operation Streamline and the criminalisation practices exemplified therein have been thrust into the national spotlight in a way that was previously ignored.

Most notably, on the morning of October 11, 2013, Tucson community members intercepted two buses carrying the 70 Streamline defendants to the federal courthouse and surrounded the buses while protestors locked themselves around the wheels, thus halting their arrival to the Streamline proceedings. Meanwhile at the federal courthouse, another group of protestors locked themselves across the gate where the buses would normally pass through. Both groups remained positioned until the afternoon and were arrested following their actions (Corella, 2013). Not only did this protest effectively shut down Tucson Streamline proceedings for the day, the October 11th action was the first in a long series of nationwide protests coordinated by the National Day Labor Organising Network (NDLON) in front of Immigration and Customs Enforcement (ICE) offices, federal detention centers and other federal courthouses calling for an end of immigrant criminal prosecutions. The 70 immigrant defendants who were en route to the federal courthouse in Tucson never made it there and were instead simply deported – as would have been the case regardless – but in this case, without federal criminal convictions and months in federal prison.

In the months following the bus stopping action, those arrested used the opportunity to further their public criticism of Streamline proceedings during their own trials (Taracena, 2015), during sentencing (Ingram, 2015), publicly through press releases and opinion pieces (Schivone, 2015), as well as with public demonstrations of support. One clear and impactful goal of all their advocacy was to remain focused on the immigrants being apprehended and forced through Streamline rather than on themselves or whatever sentencing outcome they received.

Community responses such as those in Tucson are not the only source of criticism aimed at the use of Streamline proceedings. Various tactics have been used to disrupt the logics of criminal immigrant prosecutions. Federal Public Defenders have challenged Streamline protocols on behalf of immigrant clients, charging that due process violations were taking place during the en masse processing. On two separate occasions these legal challenges have been ruled on by the US Court of Appeals for the Ninth Circuit, in San Francisco, California. The Ninth Circuit has jurisdiction over most of the western United States including Alaska and Hawaii, and only the US Supreme Court has higher legal authority. The first ruling put limitations on the then-common practice of asking all 70 defendants at once to respond in unison to the Judge's questions, as well as to plead guilty together. In practice this resulted in smaller groups of defendants being addressed at once. Citing similar due process concerns for the lack of individual attention to each defendant, this was also challenged and resulted in the current arrangement of proceedings where the Judge addresses each individual defendant separately regarding her or his circumstances of apprehension and subsequent guilty plea (Robbins, 2010). It remains alarming that these challenges were necessary in the first place, especially considering the life-long consequences against one's chances at documented re-entry and/or residency in the US after receiving a criminal conviction in Streamline proceedings.

Legal recourse can be a useful tactic for establishing precedent and ensuring legal protections for defendants, but unfortunately can be both incremental and slow to realise any results. Rather than suggest that the above-mentioned important but nonetheless minor changes to Streamline proceedings have alleviated concerns, it would seem that the success of such challenges highlights ongoing systemic issues with criminal prosecutions of immigrants. It also draws attention to the slow pace that can accompany legal strategies aimed at systemic change. In this case, critiques levied at Operation Streamline by the End Streamline Coalition and the group of bus stoppers from Tucson are not aimed at making the criminal prosecutions of immigrants a more legally clean process, but rather at ending the practice altogether. When thousands of immigrants are given criminal convictions and prison sentences for their mere presence in the United States, the systems that are ensuring their prosecution and incarceration must be ended rather than improved.

To illuminate that sentiment, in addition to ongoing concerns for the lack of sufficient due process in Streamline proceedings, there are other important procedural matters that are regularly raised by groups like the End Streamline Coalition (Carlson and Wolf, 2015). There are regular examples of ineffective counsel by the contract defense attorneys who are tasked with representing immigrant defendants, such as failure to identify potential asylum and other claims for remaining in US, failure to identify and ask for appropriate translation services for immigrants whose first language is not Spanish or English, but rather an indigenous language, or simply ensuring that their clients fully understand the legal proceedings going on around them. For this reason, legal remedies that purport to make Streamline kinder and gentler will not significantly impact the systemic criminalisation of immigrants even as those challenges are an important piece to the overall critique. Similarly, the elimination of Operation Streamline in Tucson or anywhere is only one piece of the systemic criminalisation of immigrants. Nonetheless, through linking a plethora of efforts aimed at confronting mass incarceration, immigrant criminalisation, and for-profit prison privatisation, it seems clear that gains have and can continue to be made.

Conclusion

The intimate economies hinted at by *en masse* hearings such as Operation Streamline and the for-profit private prison contracts they subsidise, I argue, must be situated within the broader context of mass incarceration. It is not enough to object to the visually available shock of Operation Streamline, nor is it enough to be offended by the exorbitant costs of immigrant prosecutions, detentions and deportations. While understandable and even vital to the overall critique of mass incarceration in the United States, activists and scholars alike must be wary of a singular focus on these specific issues or risk eliding the root issues of systemic disenfranchisement and criminalisation.

As Operation Streamline is but one part of a broader border regime that includes all levels of the securitisation of the border regions, criminal prosecutions, detention and deportation (Borderlands Autonomous Collective, 2012), I suggest that Streamline is critically useful in understanding and confronting criminalisation of immigrants. Additionally, any critique and confrontation must include the for-profit private prison industry and political collusion that both conspire towards the strengthening of systemic modes of oppression and categorisation where criminality is commodified into political and economic benefits. Within these analyses and efforts are a multitude of opportunities for collaborations between immigrant rights activists and critics of mass incarceration to learn from one another and continue to join forces.

While individual challenges to a systemic criminalisation of immigrants such as the lone individual proclaiming to the judge that 'no human being is illegal' may not dramatically alter or change the realities facing immigrants and their communities, it offers a critical reminder of the inherent necessity to do so, as well as to remain focused on the actual lives of those directly impacted. These brief snapshots of immigrant criminal prosecutions vis-à-vis Streamline are intended to continue a conversation among advocates for immigrant rights and those fighting mass incarceration, while infusing a critique of the for-profit prison industry. The intimate ties found in Tucson's Federal Courtroom, between economic forces of the for-profit private prison industry, border enforcement strategies of the government, mass incarceration, and failed immigration policies, are laid bare by the human faces of the 70 immigrants who are quickly shuffled through a plea hearing towards prison doors and eventual deportation. Never have the two spectres of deportation and imprisonment been so closely aligned, and never has it been so critical to fight back.

Acknowledgements

I am indebted to the commitment and hard work of Tucson's End Streamline Coalition. I am moved by the collective efforts of those many dedicated people who beautifully shut down Operation Streamline on October 11, 2013. And I am humbled by the everyday struggles of immigrants, their families and the community who daily demand dignity and human rights in the face of criminalisation and injustice.

Note

1 The terms 'illegal entry' and 'illegal re-entry' are deeply problematic legal terms in the United States Federal Code, and are used every day, repeatedly in the courtroom. In no way is this meant to justify the vernacular use of 'illegal' as an appropriate way to describe undocumented immigrants in the United States.

References

American Civil Liberties Union. 2014. Alternatives to immigration detention: less costly and more humane than federal lockup [Online]. Available from: www.aclu.org/aclu-fact-sheet-alternatives-immigration-detention-atd [Accessed 7 July 2015].

Bonds, A. 2009. Discipline and devolution: constructions of poverty, race, and criminality in the politics of rural prison development. *Antipode: A Radical Journal of Geography* 41(3), pp. 416–38.

Borderlands Autonomous Collective. 2012. Resisting the security-industrial complex: operation streamline and the militarization of the Arizona-Mexico borderlands. In: Lloyd, J., Mitchelson, M., and Burridge, A. eds. *Beyond walls and cages: prisons, borders and global crisis.* Athens: University of Georgia Press, pp. 190–208.

Carson, B. and Diaz, E. 2015. *Payoff: how Congress ensures private prison profit with an immigrant detention quota* [Online]. Available from: http://grassrootsleadership.org/reports/payoff-how-congress-ensures-private-prison-profit-immigrant-detention-quota [Accessed 8 July 2015].

Carlson, L. and Wolf, D. 2015. Correcting the record on Operation Streamline. 6 July. *Arizona Daily Star* [Online]. Available from: http://tucson.com/news/opinion/column/guest/correcting-the-record-on-operation-streamline/article_bf92bf98-9971-51c2-9b69-16ceffa96693.html [Accessed 7 July 2015].

Coleman, M. 2009. What counts as the politics and practice of security, and where? Devolution and immigrant insecurity after 9/11. *Annals of the Association of American Geographers* **99**(5), pp. 904–13.

Corella, H. 2013. Activists block Tucson courthouse, immigration hearings canceled for the day. 11 October. *Arizona Daily Star* [Online]. Avalilable from: http://tucson.com/news/local/activists-block-tucson-courthouse-immigration-hearings-canceled-for-the-day/article_884dc9da-3287-11e3-918e-0019bb2963f4.html [Accessed 6 April 2016].

Feltz, R. and Baksh, S. 2012. Business of detention. In: Lloyd, J., Mitchelson, M., and Burridge, A. eds. *Beyond walls and cages: prisons, borders and global crisis.* Athens: University of Georgia Press, pp. 143–51.

Flake, J. 2015. *Senator Jeff Flake's website* [Online]. Available from: www.flake.senate.gov/public/index.cfm/press-releases?ID=8F1CE69C-9817-43A8-9453-09A1BCB149D4 [Accessed 19 May 2015].

Fox News Latino. 2014. Feds quiet on Arizona program that guarantees jail time for undocumented immigrants. 20 September. *Fox News Latino* [Online]. Available from: http://latino.foxnews.com/ [Accessed 8 July 2015].

Gipe, L. ed. 2014. *Operation Streamline: an illustrated reader.* Tucson: University of Arizona.

Gonzalez-Barrera, A. and Krogstad, J. 2014. *U.S. deportations of immigrants reach record high in 2013* [Online]. Available from: www.pewresearch.org/fact-tank/2014/10/02/u-s-deportations-of-immigrants-reach-record-high-in-2013/ [Accessed 7 July 2015].

Gordon, I. and Raja, T. 2012. 164 anti-immigration laws passed since 2010? A MoJo analysis. *Mother Jones Magazine* [Online]. Available from: www.motherjones.com/politics/2012/03/anti-immigration-law-database [Accessed 9 January 2015].

Grassroots Leadership. 2014. *Shadow Report of Grassroots Leadership and Justice Strategies to The International Convention on the Elimination of All Forms of Racial Discrimination Regarding Criminal Prosecutions of Migrants for Immigration Offenses and Substandard Privately Operated Segregated Prisons* [Online]. Available from: http://grassrootsleadership.org/shadow-report-grassroots-leadership-and-justice-strategies-international-convention-elimination-all [Accessed 7 July 2015].

Grassroots Leadership. 2012. *Operation Streamline: costs and consequences* [Online]. Available from: http://grassrootsleadership.org/OperationStreamline [Accessed 7 July 2015].

Hodai, B. 2010. Ties that bind: Arizona politicians and the private prison industry. 21 June. *In These Times* [Online]. Available from: http://inthesetimes.com/article/6085/ties_that_bind_arizona_politicians_and_the_private_prison_industry [Accessed 8 July 2015].

Ingram, P. 2015. Judge finds Operation Streamline protestors guilty. 14 April. *Tucson Sentinel* [Online]. Available from: www.tucsonsentinel.com/local/report/041415_streamline_protesters_guilty/judge-finds-operation-streamline-protesters-guilty/ [Accessed 8 July 2015].

Isaacs, C. 2014a. Crony capitalism: for-profit prison corporation influence in Arizona's Attorney General race. 7 October. *AFSC Arizona* [Online]. Available from: https://afscarizona.org/2014/10/07/crony-capitalism-for-profit-prison-corporation-influence-in-arizonas-attorney-general-race/ [Accessed 7 July 2015].

Isaacs, C. 2014b. *Treatment industrial complex: how for-profit prison corporations are undermining efforts to treat and rehabilitate prisoners for corporate gain* [Online]. Available from: http://afsc.org/resource/treatment-industrial-complex-how-profit-prison-corporations-are-undermining-efforts-treat-a [Accessed 7 July 2015].

Kirkham, C. 2012. Private prisons profit from immigration crackdown, federal and local law enforcement partnerships. June 7. *The Huffington Post* [Online]. Available from: www.huffingtonpost.com/2012/06/07/private-prisons-immigration-federal-law-enforcement_n_1569219.html [Accessed 8 July 2015].

Law, V. 2014. What do private prisons have to do with the upcoming election? 28 October. *Truthout.com* [Online]. Available from: www.truth-out.org/news/item/27068-what-do-private-prisons-have-to-do-with-the-upcoming-election [Accessed 7 July 2015].

Libal, B. 2015. *Written statement of Grassroots Leadership before the United States Commission on Civil Rights.* January 30, Washington D.C. [Online]. Available from: http://grassrootsleadership.org/blog/2015/01/bob-libal-testify-us-commission-civil-rights [Accessed 7 July 2015].

Meissner, D., Kerwin, D. M., Chishti, M. and Bergeron, C. 2014. *Immigration enforcement in the United States: the rise of a formidable machinery.* Migration Policy Institute [Online]. Available from www.migrationpolicy.org/research/immigration-enforcement-united-states-rise-formidable-machinery [Accessed 7 July 2015].

Nevins, J. 2010. *Operation Gatekeeper and beyond: the war on 'illegals' and the remaking of the U.S.-Mexico boundary.* New York: Routledge.

Robbins, T. 2010. Border Patrol program raises due process concerns. 13 September. *National Public Radio* [Online]. Available from: www.npr.org/templates/story/story.php?storyId=129780261 [Accessed 7 July 2015].

Schivone, G. 2015. Activists put on trial for defending immigrants. 15 March. *Arizona Daily Star* [Online]. Available from: http://tucson.com/news/opinion/column/guest/activists-put-on-trial-for-defending-immigrants/article_1c078ca8-55d9-56ff-8c07-268636e36c01.html [Accessed 8 July 2015].

Seghetti, L. 2014. *Border security: immigration enforcement between ports of entry* [Online]. Available from: www.fas.org/ [Accessed 7 July 2015].

Slack, J., Martínez, D.E., Whiteford, S. and Peiffer, E. 2015. In harm's way: family separation, immigration enforcement programs and security on the US-Mexico border. *Journal on Migration and Human Security* 3(2), pp. 109–20.

Slack, J., Martínez, D.E., Whiteford, S. and Peiffer, E. 2013. *In the shadow of the wall: family separation, immigration enforcement and security.* The Center for Latin American Studies: The University of Arizona [Online]. Available from: https://las.arizona.edu/mbcs [Accessed 7 July 2015].

Taracena, M. 2015. Operation Streamline immigration activists acquitted of all but two charges. 7 March. *The Range, Tucson Weekly* [Online]. Available from: www.tucsonweekly.com/TheRange/archives/2015/03/17/operation-streamline-immigration-activists-acquitted-of-all-but-two-charges [Accessed 8 July 2015].

United States Customs and Border Protection, United States Border Patrol. 2012. *2012–2016 Border Patrol Strategic Plan, Mission: Protect America.* Available from: www.cbp.gov/border-security/along-us-borders/strategic-plan [Accessed January 8, 2015].

United States Senate. 2013. *Senate Bill 744* [Online]. Available from: www.congress.gov/bill/113th-congress/senate-bill/744 [Accessed 31 January 2015].

Williams, H. 2008. *Written Statement of Heather E. Williams, First Assistant Federal Public Defender, District of Arizona – Tucson, Before the United States House of Representatives Subcommittee of Commercial and Administrative Law.* June 25, Washington, D.C. Available from: http://judiciary.house.gov/ [Accessed 7 July 2015].

13 Intimate economies of state practice
Materialities of detention in Finland

Anitta Kynsilehto and Eeva Puumala

Introduction

Migrant detention in the Nordic countries has been examined relatively little when compared to research carried out on these practices elsewhere, for example the United Kingdom (e.g. Malloch and Stanley, 2005; Gill, 2009; Hall, 2010; but see Khosravi, 2009 on detention in Sweden). This chapter focuses on migrant detention in Finland, thus far a completely ignored country case in detention studies. In our view, there are two main reasons for this: firstly, Finland is often mapped with other Nordic countries willing to be seen as operators of human-faced migration management yet tough on border control, and second, the number of migrants and refugees in the country has been extremely low as compared to other European and Nordic countries. The young and still developing Finnish detention system is at an important crossroads both legislatively and in terms of the organisation of migrant detention. This chapter documents an ongoing change in the detention landscape in Finland. At the same time, it analyses the significance of a difference in the logic along which detention is organised in Finland as compared to other European countries where migrant detention is increasingly privatised.

On matters of migration, Finland is bound by European Union (EU) legislation, including the Dublin regulations[1] (European Parliament and Council of the European Union, 2013), which indicate that asylum seekers must file a claim for refugee status in the first state they enter into within EU territory, and the EU Returns Directive, which stipulates the maximum length of detention (European Parliament and Council of the European Union, 2008). Also, political discourse and the ensuing legislative process follow largely similar lines as elsewhere in Europe, despite low numbers of migrant arrivals in Finland until 2015.[2] The distinguishing factor that sets the Finnish case apart from most other countries is that Finland cannot be regarded as an example of a country where detention has been organised according to neoliberal principles of marketisation where private companies play a significant role in providing detention 'services'. There is a different logic regarding intimate economies of detention at play in Finland, where the whole system of receiving, accommodating, returning and deporting migrants has been organised to meet the economic interests of the state. It is a system in which migrants are regarded as a liability to the state, a costly population that needs to be controlled efficiently so that the migration 'flows' can be 'managed' and contained, and the supposed economic strain produced by the arrival of migrants can be kept to a minimum. At least until the present day, Finland has sought to keep as close a record of the population as possible, including migrants, in order to provide some kind of welfare services to the population. At the same time, it has upheld policies that are intended to make Finland appear a non-desirable country in which to seek international protection and where strict migration policies are efficiently put into practice.

The chapter sets out to (1) contextualise the use of migrant detention in Finland and (2) through this contextual framing create a theoretical approach through which we examine the consequences of detention in terms of intimate personal experience. The first part of the chapter outlines the central legislation that frames detention, and highlights the major ways in which the logic of organising detention has differed from the ways in which migrant detention is practised in many other countries. These include, for example, employment of public social work professionals for the major part of operations in the detention units. This practice could, at least at the outset, suggest a more human-focused than securitarian (Mainwaring, 2012) or privatised (e.g. Rodier, 2012; Tyler et al., 2014) way of organising detention. Moreover, detention is largely used to maintain the assigned goals of an effective return policy, be that within the intra-European removal system for the purposes of 'responsibility-sharing' (so called Dublin transfers) or deportation/removal to third countries (Schuster, 2005). The effective return policy entails that people who receive a negative decision to their asylum request, and who are denied a residence permit on any other ground, are returned by the police to their country of origin. Also, those applicants who can be returned on the basis of the Dublin regulations are accompanied by the police to the country of first entry. Asylum applicants are accommodated in 'open' centres the functioning of which is, however, highly regulated. Indeed, a close record is kept of the applicants' whereabouts despite the freedom of movement within the country during the asylum process. This practice aids the location and possibly the detention of those applicants who have received a negative decision in order to, firstly, prevent them hiding from the police, and, secondly, to enact removal. Most detainees in Finland are, in fact, awaiting deportation or removal from the country.

Through the example of detention, we discuss ways in which sovereign practices become manifested in space and on bodies and what kinds of politico-economic relations are involved. We build theoretically on the idea that the act of detention inscribes culpability, illegitimacy and susceptibility on the mobile/immobilised body. Such a stance envisages borders and the organisation of political space in intimate, corporeal and ambivalent terms (see Johnson et al., 2011). Detained bodies become the battlefields of border practises, which define the 'mezzanine spaces of sovereignty' (Nyers, 2003, p. 1080) in which those bodies can exist (see Perera, 2002; Rajaram and Grundy-Warr, 2004, 2007).

Detention is merely one example of such spaces; others include, for example, reception centres for asylum seekers, airports, waiting-zones and refugee camps. Through the notion of mezzanine spaces of sovereignty, we examine intimate economies related to and enacted within the detention infrastructure by relying on ethnographic data that Eeva has collected at the Metsälä detention unit. The notion of intimate economies is interpreted through those material and corporeal relations that become visible in the act of detention – and the often-following act of deportation or removal. Indeed, in Finland, an effective return policy is considered a way to discourage the arrival of asylum seekers and it reflects well the economic stance on migration that characterises Finnish asylum and migration policies.[3] The Finnish case, thus, is an example of the economic logic of cost effectiveness with respect to migration. Our interest in this chapter is to scrutinise how that logic undergirds the broader scale of the organisation of the Finnish detention infrastructure and what its effects and ramifications are at the individual level.

The notion of mezzanine spaces of sovereignty provides an analytical tool with which it is possible to highlight how the policy of effective returns materialises both on the detained person and in the way detention is organised in Finland. In our examination, we are particularly interested in the detained body and its capacity to enact political agency (Edkins and Pin-Fat, 2005; Puumala et al., 2011; Conlon and Gill, 2013; Puggioni, 2014; Puumala and Kynsilehto, 2015), and in the ways in which the Finnish focus on minimising migrants' economic impact shapes detainees' experiences.

Receiving and detaining migrants in Finland

It was only in the early 1990s that Finland started to receive people seeking asylum, with Somalian nationals as the first group of 'spontaneous arrivals' (i.e., as asylum seekers, not within the resettlement quota). Since then, and until 2015, Finland has received 1,000–6,000 asylum applications annually; this is a very low number compared to most European countries, and much less than in the other Nordic countries, apart from Iceland. The largest nationality groups lodging asylum claims over the years have been nationals from Afghanistan, Bulgaria, Iraq, the Russian Federation and Somalia. Favourable decisions on asylum amount to a very small percentage (approximately five per cent) of overall applications annually, which is, however, increased by a somewhat larger percentage (approximately 30 per cent) of accorded residence permits for the need for protection or for a strong humanitarian reason. One reason for which a person may be denied asylum in Finland is related to the intra-European 'responsibility-sharing' mechanism, that is the Dublin regulations, according to which the person will be sent back to the country of first arrival (i.e. her or his fingerprints are found in the EURODAC). Staying after a failed asylum claim, expiry of a tourist visa or an existing residence permit, or a change of status for which the residence permit has initially been accorded are paths through which a person may become undocumented. As elsewhere, estimations concerning the number of persons without a valid residence permit vary considerably. Currently the number of undocumented persons is estimated to fall somewhere in between 2,000 and 4,000 persons, most probably closer to the lower estimate than the higher one.[4]

Migrant detention is used for two primary purposes in Finland: during the phase when the person's identity is being examined, or when the person has received a deportation or removal order and is waiting for the removal to be enacted, if there are grounds to believe that s/he would hinder the removal process.[5] Hence, a person's asylum process may start in detention – the first phase of identity examination – and it may end in detention – as he or she is awaiting removal/deportation. Therefore we emphasise that migrant detention is closely entwined with the practices of receiving asylum seekers, whether it refers to a person whose identity verification is undertaken before the asylum process proper, or in the case of a negative decision where her/his removal is pending. Both of those reasons are connected with the prevailing economic stance on asylum as detention is used to maintain and increase the effectiveness of the identification and removal processes. Further reasons for detaining a foreigner as stated in law 815/2015 are grounds to believe that the person will commit a crime in Finland or if, upon individual assessment, the person is considered as a security threat. These latter reasons directly and in the above two slightly less explicitly attest to the state's quest to appear as the protector of the society (Malloch and Stanley, 2005; Hiemstra, 2014; Trubeta, 2015).

As to the detention infrastructure, there are two types of centres for accommodating people without a valid residence permit: reception centres that host people during the asylum process, and detention units that are deployed for the two primary purposes for migrant detention described above. This distinguishes Finland from some other European countries, such as Greece (Trubeta, 2015) and Malta (Mainwaring, 2012), where detention is systematically imposed on any person arriving irregularly in the country (even though that practice contradicts the European Returns Directive guidelines), or the UK, where asylum seekers are regularly detained for unlimited periods (e.g. Malloch and Stanley, 2005; Gill, 2009; Griffiths, 2012). The main difference between these two forms of assigned residence is that reception centres are open centres whereas detention units are closed, carceral spaces. Throughout the years since the early 1990s when Finland began to receive asylum seekers in any substantial numbers (approximately 4,000 per year), reception centres have been established and closed on an ad hoc basis depending on the fluctuating number of arrivals. Asylum seekers are dispersed to different locations around the country and are often situated in remote areas of the countryside. This dispersal across the extended and scarcely populated territory of the country, from the countryside of Ostrobotnia in the West, close to the Russian border in Karelia in the East, to Finnish Lapland in the North, and circular trajectories within which asylum seekers are moved from one centre to another work in a way that it becomes increasingly difficult to maintain relations with and integrate into the local community (see Mountz, 2011; Mountz et al., 2012; Conlon, 2013; Hiemstra, 2014). Indeed, it is not far-fetched to claim that through such a practice of 'churning' (see Gill, 2013) the accommodation and detention systems are connected to regional policy as municipalities where facilities for hosting asylum seekers are located receive monetary support from the state to cover the costs of organising health, social and educational services for asylum claimants. With declining population rates in remote areas, this practice bolsters the ability of the given municipality to provide these services also to permanent residents. The Finnish practice of churning is an example of how intimate economies operate locally, even at the level of a singular body, yet they have impacts on entire municipalities and regions in association with governmental subsidies. What changed in September 2015 in terms of organising the reception of asylum seekers was that private companies were, for the first time, allowed to operate reception facilities due to the sudden increase in the need for accommodation. There are as yet no indications that this privatisation will be extended to migrant detention.

Up until 2014, there was only one detention centre in Finland, Metsälä detention unit, located on the outskirts of the capital Helsinki. In October 2014, a new detention unit was opened in Joutseno, in the renovated premises of the former Konnunsuo prison. The capacity in Metsälä has been for years just 40 places, which has been insufficient for lodging the number of people assigned with administrative detention orders. The average number of detainees per year is around 1,500 persons. After the opening of the new facility, the overall official capacity of Finnish detention centres rose to 70 persons. The practice of detention is, however, far more common in Finland than the accommodation capacity of the centres would lead us to think. Migrants are held in police custody when the distance between the reception centre and the detention unit is long or when the units are full. Migrant detention in Finland has been operated by public authorities and the detention units are administered by social work professionals, not by private security companies as is the case in some other countries across Europe, such as in the UK, and elsewhere globally. Unlike Metsälä, which is administratively placed under the social and health services of the municipality of Helsinki, the detention unit in Joutseno is operated by the Finnish Immigration Service (Migri), a state office that operates under the Ministry of the Interior. This indicates a change of logic in organising detention from social services to a security-driven branch of administration.[6]

The ethnographic data we rely on was collected in the Metsälä detention unit as a part of a larger project which explored the corporeal manifestations of the logic of sovereignty and the political agency of (failed) asylum seekers (see Puumala and Pehkonen, 2010; Puumala, 2012, 2013). For the purposes of the larger project, ethnographic work was conducted in three different reception centres for asylum seekers as well as the detention unit, in addition to which legal representatives, state officials, mental health professionals working with asylum seekers and staff from each facility were interviewed. The period of data collection took place from August 2006 to June 2008, which means that the ethnographic data used in this chapter is somewhat dated. However, as the focus of the interviews with detainees was on the experience that the detention aroused and the connections between people within the detention unit and outside, the data are still valid as the operational logic and organisation of the unit remain the same. All interviews with detainees, totalling six semi-structured in-depth interviews, were arranged by the unit staff in accordance with a certain profile: people who had been detained after receiving a negative asylum decision or people who were waiting for removal or deportation from the country. In addition, the director and leading counsellor of the unit were interviewed. What emerges out of all these interviews is that the lived experience of living in detention is ambiguous. The function of the interview data presented in this chapter is not to make claims of who detainees 'really' are and how they should be represented, but instead reflect on how the status of detainee affects their self-conceptions and relations to others, how the everyday is lived, the past remembered and the future planned beyond their current status. An analysis of the local, embodied space(s) of detention reveals the intimate economies that stretch throughout the system and that arise from the economic logic governing migration in Finland.

Intimate economies, daily materialities, and the detained body

In our analysis of the empirical data, we will discuss the logic organising detention in Finland, and the change that seems to be underway. Before a more detailed analysis of the intimate economies and daily materialities that become enacted during detention, it is useful to describe the material surroundings within the unit.

As one would perhaps expect, security measures play a significant role in the detention unit. The yard of the brown two storey brick building – formerly an office and since transformed to serve the current purpose – is surrounded by a high fence topped with barbed wire and surveillance cameras. The fenced yard is small. The staff always supervises the scheduled hour-long daily outings that are announced through speakers. In Metsälä detainees are not locked in their rooms, which allows for various forms of agency and relationality in the daily interactions of detainees.[7] However, inside the unit movement is restricted: detainees can access their own room, toilet and bathroom facilities, Internet booths, dining area at times when food is served, the TV room and the lobby. The rooms for men and women are separated from one another, and there are also two isolation rooms that are located in a different corridor from other living spaces. In addition, there is a playroom for children and a couple of tiny rooms where detainees can receive visitors. For visitors, access to the centre is restricted to certain times of the day, and they have to pass through a metal detector before being admitted. As for the detainees, they can buy prepaid calling cards from the staff, play ping-pong and games with a console, read, stay out of their rooms during scheduled times, surf the Internet (with restricted access) and watch television. There are bars on the room windows and opening the windows – apart from the small ventilation windows – is strictly prohibited. In the staff office there are multiple closed-circuit television screens through which the situation in different parts of the unit as well as outdoors can be observed.

Detention reflects a situation where the sovereign border thickens to the extreme and becomes almost impenetrable. As such, detention represents a 'mezzanine space of sovereignty' (Nyers, 2003, p. 1080), a space of in-between-ness where the detainees are neither fully inside nor fully outside the territory of the state, meanwhile they are kept separate from and deprived of the rights of regular residents. The political character and effects of detention as a mezzanine space of sovereignty is reflected in Isin and Rygiel's (2006, p. 193) notion of a 'zone'. They conceive zones to be spaces where the rules of freedom have been suspended – sovereign politics has taken a hold of the human body (cf. Agamben, 1998). The zone works internally (see Squire, 2009, pp. 154–5) and renders people placed in those spaces invisible and inaudible.

If one is to conduct research in places like detention units, the material conditions need to be accepted to an extent. Yet at the same time, the role that the researcher must adopt and that is expected from the officials needs to be renegotiated with detainees if one is actually going to carry out the research project. The ordering of space and the measures that come with it do not always support the researcher's endeavours:

> The staff has to find an alternative place for my interview with Ahmed[8], a young man from Somalia, as the children's play room – where my interviews thus far have taken place – is occupied. Salla, the counsellor who was assigned to help me, leads us to the room where the Immigration Service conducts asylum interviews. The room is divided in half with Plexiglas. The interviewing migration officer customarily sits on one side of the glass and the asylum seeker on the other. I ask to sit on the same side as Ahmed, as he is looking a bit suspicious of the nature of the interview. I'd rather talk with him somewhere else, but the options in the unit are limited. A mobile phone has already been given to me and now Salla advices me to press the emergency button on the phone should I feel myself threatened. She also shows the buzzer on the wall, so that I can let them know when we are finished and want to be let out. Then we are locked inside: we can exit the room, but not the corridor that separates the interview room from the lobby. Ahmed and I sit on opposite sides of the small room – some 1.5 meters separate us. He sits down and leans against the wall looking at me, while I face the table in order to be able to write.
>
> (Eeva's research journal, May 29, 2007)

This excerpt from Eeva's research journal illustrates how the interaction of bodies is ordered within the carceral space of the detention unit. The spatial organisation of the centre creates distinctions between detainees and the staff through the multiply locked doors and hallways. Interaction between the immigration officer and the migrant takes place through Plexiglas, separating the two parties from one another in concrete terms. The whole facility, in fact, relies on separating bodies from one another, and inscribing power on certain bodies while other bodies are stripped of it. There is very little space in between these positions and the hierarchy both between the staff and detainees and among the staff itself is clear.

The material surroundings are indicative of the relations between various subjectivities within the centre and, as such, they provide an excellent example of how the state and its economic and governmental interests become practised and put into operation (cf. Darling, 2014, p. 484). This, again, relates back to the notion of 'mezzanine spaces of sovereignty', where sovereign ambitions and regulations extend to detainees' experiences of their capacity for action, maintenance of relations and their daily experiences. The regulation of movement, scheduled daily rhythm of life and numerous institutional rules and bans that limit the daily lives of detainees have corporeal ramifications and evoke a response. In order to analyse that aspect of the daily materialities of detention, we now draw on the interviews themselves, which give insight into the ways in which detainees themselves perceive their situation.

> In jail ... No, it's never good. To be in jail. And I haven't done wrong, because I am an asylum seeker. [...] But to put me in jail, whereby I haven't committed any crime, because I'm seeking help from you, and you tell me that you don't give it to me, then you put me in jail. You cheat me. [pause] It's a cheat. [...] You know, I feel self-pity about myself. [...] You know this place makes me remember all the time my story, because why do I leave, why don't I have the access to see the natural sun, to talk to people like the way I used to do. I really live like in a cage. I don't like it. [...] So, it worries me that I'm not outside and I am not a criminal, but I'm living, you know, in a place whereby they see you as something different.
>
> (Interview with Benjamin from Ghana)

The interview with Benjamin illustrates that categorisations have concrete corporeal consequences, which take form through the state's efforts to figure out who is entitled to what kind of international protection and who does not fill the pre-requisites of any protection. Detention and the logic of accommodating asylum claimants can be thought of as practices that both abstract the body as a case number in a bureaucratic process, but simultaneously bear an inevitably material dimension (Puumala and Kynsilehto, 2015). As a specific tool in efficient migration management, migrant detention in Finland serves the purpose of regulating, not ending, corporeal mobility by containing bodies in assigned spaces (see also Mountz et al., 2012). In the interview quote, Benjamin reflects on his feelings of being caged, contained in a space where contact with others is limited and where his identity may be under scrutiny, but at the same time who he is does not matter – he is seen as someone or some*thing* different.

The idea of the zone suggests that in some cases the act of crossing a border, sometimes even arriving at the space of the border (for example, at an airport or transfer zone), can annihilate one's identity and make one a susceptible body without identity in the eyes of the receiving state. Borders, therefore, are not simply geographical markers, or even sets of policies or governmental practices; they are carnal sites in which certain political and socio-economic relations are enforced and where desire, fear, hope and desperation intertwine. Being detained reflects an experience of living in an assigned space that, through its material organisation, labels the detained body with a specific marker. As Benjamin's interview quote shows, this phase of being jailed is a waiting period for a next phase across globally mobile circuits. As the following quote illustrates, the circuits are global and the Dublin regulations have resulted in the development of an EU-wide system of migrant churning:

> The police say I don't have identity. So they are accusing me of misidentification. Now they are telling that they had got my identity, but they want to send me back to Lithuania, because it's the first European country that I entered. But they are giving this decision that my wife can stay here. They are making separation. I'm quite dissatisfied because we came here together, me and my wife. Now we seek asylum together. But the police made the decision that she can stay here, but I have to go back. There is disparity, in my opinion. Why do you try to separate us? And another thing, the lawyer told us that if I go back, no problem, because later I can come. ... It is impossible to come here from Nepal. I spent 6,500 euros, and I don't have anything else now. If I can come later, why can't I stay now? She is under-aged and they cannot deport her.
>
> (Interview with Shiva from Nepal)

While the extracts from the meeting with Ahmed and the interview with Benjamin were indicative of the daily materialities that come into operation in a detention centre, Shiva's account reflects the intimate and personal ramifications that are related to the operation of an effective return policy.

Shiva also described the way in which two very different types of 'businesses', human smuggling and accompanied involuntary return, intertwine. Shiva and his wife had sold all their property in order to organise their travel to Europe. They had not envisaged seeking asylum in Europe, but Shiva had intended to study journalism at a university. He had relied on human smugglers to organise the documents, permits and travel route only to find out in Lithuania that what he had been told by the smuggler was untrue: the study fees had not been paid. As a result the couple became asylum claimants. The EU-wide aspiration to control migration has led to a flourishing form of shadow economy that risks the life and limb of many migrants. The permit system, with its complicated bureaucratic processes and the many different grounds on which one can obtain legal residence in Finland, seemed utterly incomprehensible to Shiva. Yet, Shiva's story illustrates perfectly how a focus on everyday life, the intimate details of asylum seekers' lives and minute decisions are linked to broader economies that include border practices and the mezzanine spaces of sovereignty, which, once again, have material consequences.

Shiva's account sheds light on another peculiarity of the Finnish detention system. While in many other European countries unlimited and prolonged detention times are one of the most pressing problems, in Finland detention times have remained relatively short, from a couple of days to three months. Thus, in the Finnish case, the ramifications and effects of the economic realm are perhaps most visible with regard to return and deportation policy, not in the detention infrastructure, as it has remained in the hands of public authorities. Indeed, it could be asked – as the detention unit has been run by social services – whether the ethos of care that might be presumed is at all visible in the daily lives of detainees, or whether the staff have been co-opted by the logic of sovereignty so that their work forms a part of the shadow state.

Acts of solidarity, political advocacy and the future prospects of detention

Despite the isolated nature of detention, detainees are not fully cut off from others, but seek to connect with actors outside the unit in various ways. Those expressions of solidarity that critique the practice of detention and the political advocacy around detention are the focus of this last part of the chapter.

Detainees have very few possibilities for arguing their cases in public, but people more favourably positioned with regard to the national body politics have brought cases into the public realm. NGOs and activist groups such as Free Movement have organised demonstrations outside the detention facility, which have addressed both the personal struggle of a detainee and the overall practise of detention. Detainees have participated in these demonstrations by opening windows in their rooms, despite the unit rules that forbid doing so. That way they have been able to talk and interact with the demonstrators outside the facility by, for example, reaching their hands towards them through the bars. These acts and events are concrete representations of solidarity. They also testify to the corporeal limitations that characterise detention and illustrate how mezzanine spaces of sovereignty are related to daily materialities, such as people's capacity to articulate their cases, to interact with others and to gain any visibility outside the framework of detention. They also testify to the ongoing politico-corporeal struggle that the very practice of detention represents and sometimes they can function as engines of legislative change or at least political debate around detention.

Turning now to political advocacy, recently national and international organisations' access to detention centres was codified in law 1216/2013, which came into effect at the beginning of 2014. The law grants NGOs and INGOs access to detention 'in accordance with the consent of the detention unit' (this clause of course bears the potential of hampering access), and unlimited access to the Ombudsman for minorities to visit and talk to detainees in private. Access to detention is an important aspect of monitoring the situation and the subject of campaigns by civil society organisations in Europe and worldwide (as Caroline Fleay's contribution to this volume attests). Located on the outskirts of the capital city, the Metsälä detention unit has been easily accessible to organisations and activist groups.

However, the situation is less promising as regards the Joutseno facility. After its fact-finding visit to Finland in October 2014, the European Committee for the Prevention of Torture and Inhuman or Degrading Treatment or Punishment (CPT) criticised the remote location of the Joutseno unit and equally noted that it resembles a prison (Reinboth, 2014). This facility is indeed a former prison, though it has been designed to host vulnerable detainees, including families with children. From an administrative perspective, the location of the second detention unit is connected to the overall organisation of the asylum seeker reception system in Finland. Municipalities hold a position of autonomy in Finland, which means that the state cannot decide to open either reception centres or detention units without agreement from the municipality. It is more lucrative for municipalities that are more peripherally situated to host centres, as the received economic subsidies are often used to remedy economically stressed municipal governments. However, activist networks have questioned whether there were other interests at work in the choice of Joutseno, a place that is practically cut off from any potential physical contact to the outside, including family and friends as well as visitors from anti-detention advocacy groups.[9]

At the time of writing this chapter, two legislative changes had just been enacted that may produce significant shifts in the overall detention landscape in Finland. Firstly, the laws regulating detention were modified: the Finnish Aliens Act (Act 30.4.2004/301) and the law governing treatment of detained foreigners and detention units (Act 15.2.2002/116). Importantly, article 51 of the Aliens Act that regulates the granting of a temporary residence permit to persons who cannot be deported/removed to their country of origin was modified to emphasise 'voluntary return'. Also, a requirement was added that such individuals facilitate their own removal. These modifications have been widely criticised in that they are likely to make 'voluntary return' obligatory for those who have received a negative decision on their asylum claim, but who cannot be returned to their countries of origin (see Kynsilehto, 2014). Under the earlier legislation they have received a temporary residence permit, the so called 'B-permit' that has been mainly given to nationals of Afghanistan, Iraq and Somalia. This permit is far from an ideal solution, and it has been much criticised due to the continuous state of liminality its issuance has denoted for permit holders (see Puumala, 2012). However, many Finnish non-governmental organisations have pointed out that the modifications will in practice make the situation more difficult for those who lack other grounds for a residence permit. It is likely to produce a new group of people in an irregular situation, which may lead to more people being detained in the future. Coupled with the important increase in the number of migrant arrivals and parallel updates of country of origin information concerning Afghanistan and Iraq in autumn 2015 in order to make fewer people eligible for asylum in Finland, the number of those without a migration status may increase considerably from 2016 onwards.

Furthermore, some of the approved legislative changes illustrate contradictions within the making of Finnish policy on detention. For example, the proposed modifications included a statement prohibiting the detention of unaccompanied minors who seek international protection.[10] However, the laws continue to include grounds for child detention,[11] and alternatives to detention remain limited. Subsequently, different interlocutors who had been consulted during the legislative process, for example the Finnish Red Cross and Amnesty Finland, raised the criticism that non-governmental organisations were 'heard but not listened to' (Kumpula and Johansson, 2014). In reply to this criticism, the Minister of the Interior (2011–15), Päivi Räsänen, promised to end child detention and pointed to the strict time limits for detaining youths (15–18 years) included in the proposed law. Yet, she reminded advocates of the difficulties experienced in other countries in finding alternatives to detention, which, according to her, has complicated the exploration of these options in the case of Finland (Räsänen, 2014). In the end, detention of unaccompanied minors younger than 15 years was forbidden altogether, as well as the use of police custody for detaining unaccompanied youth (15–18 years). However, children with their families continue to be detained. Indeed, the emphasis on 'vulnerable groups' in the opening of the detention facility in Joutseno already indicated that child detention is a practice to be continued in Finland.[12] What these developments do suggest, in any case, is that the topic of materially reorganising the distribution of unwanted migrants within the country – as well as their deportation – continues to be on the table.

As the year 2015 illustrated in many ways, both the Finnish system of receiving asylum seekers and the practice of detention are undergoing critical changes. In the field of reception, a rapid privatisation of parts of the reception centre network took place. As regards detention, the legislative changes and the overall discussion of effectively removing those who do not receive a reception permit suggest that new practices and guidelines are likely to develop. For instance, there is ongoing discussion of the need to introduce more tightly controlled centres – yet not proper detention facilities – for those waiting for removal. These developments resonate closely with the idea of mezzanine spaces of sovereignty where sovereign practices and border control take place within the sovereign territory and follow a logic of exceptionalism.

Conclusion

In this chapter, we have discussed migrant detention in Finland as an example of a situation whereby the reception and detention of migrants is ordered foremost by the economic interests of the state. We have used the notion of 'mezzanine space of sovereignty' to analyse ways in which politico-economic logic bears concretely on individual bodies and experiences. We have illustrated corporeal materialities at play both in the macro-spatial, countrywide organisation of detention and other forms of assigned residence, and spatial dimensions within a detention facility through an ethnographic approach.

The detention landscape is in the process of undergoing multiple changes in Finland. Firstly, the opening of the Joutseno facility in a former prison, administered by the Interior Ministry, suggests a change of logic from a social work approach to a more security-driven detention practice. Moreover, designing the interior spaces of the premises to suit the needs of children and families is at odds with the government's stated goal to put an end to child detention altogether; 'beautifully decorated walls don't turn a detention unit into a day-care centre,' as one activist recently put it. Secondly, the laws that regulate detention and allocation of residence permits to people whose deportation to their countries of origin is de facto impossible have been revised. These changes are likely to produce a larger number staying irregularly who will, thereby, become deportable and, hence, detainable persons in Finland according to the dominant logic and the way in which detention has been practiced in the country. Furthermore, as many civil society organisations have highlighted, the new laws on detention may make it more difficult for advocacy organisations to access detainees. In addition, as the numbers indicated in this chapter suggest, the use of police custody for detaining migrants is likely to continue in many parts of the country. This is problematic as people who have not committed any crime are closed into the carceral spaces of local police stations. Adding to the problem is the fact that these police stations are dispersed across the country, which makes it yet again very difficult for civil society organisations and other activists to monitor the situation, and for family members and friends to maintain relations with the detainees.

The Finnish case is an example of the state's quest to minimise the economic impact of seeking asylum rather than a system that is driven by private interests. Nonetheless, it illustrates the way in which the economic realm intertwines with people's lives and bears corporeal and material consequences. Through our theoretical engagement with the issue, it becomes obvious that in Finland the whole question of detaining migrants is deeply imbricated with state practice and the building of a national community that retains a particular conception of who can be accommodated in the Finnish society and for whom this possibility is effectively foreclosed. Furthermore, as our analysis of the ethnographic data, the logic of organising detention and ongoing political debate around the issue shows, there are, acting simultaneously, multiple and overlapping practices of governance at work. Sovereignty is far from an abstract concept. It is a set of (spatial) practices that has concrete corporeal, material and intimate effects.

Notes

1   The Dublin regulations date back to the Dublin convention of 1990 that entered into force in 1997, followed by the Dublin II regulation from 2003, and the most recent one replacing the earlier agreements, referred to as Dublin III regulation, from 2013.
2   In 2015, 32,476 asylum applications were filed in Finland. This figure signifies an almost ten-fold increase to the annual numbers over earlier years. Moreover, for the first time Finland became one of the most attractive countries for people seeking international protection in the EU.
3   The effects of the dominant economic stance in Finland are blatantly obvious in the number of arriving asylum seekers. In 2014, Finland received 3651 asylum claimants, while the neighbouring country Sweden – whose migration policy is characterised by the principle of humanitarianism – received in the same year 81,301 applications. For detailed statistics, see the Finnish Immigration Service website, www.migri.fi/about_us/statistics/statistics_on_asylum_and_refugees and the Swedish Migrationsverket website, www.migrationsverket.se/English/About-the-Migration-Agency/Facts-and-statistics-/Statistics.html.

4 The numbers given by the police are those of people apprehended without valid documentation for their stay (visa, residence permit), for example 2933 persons in 2014. However, these numbers include persons who lodged an asylum claim upon being apprehended. Different estimations are based on associations' and service-providers' encounters with and other information on people without a valid residence permit or other legitimised basis of stay. The variation depends also on the definition of who is potentially counted as being undocumented (i.e. everyone without a valid residence permit, only non-EU citizens, etc.).

5 In June 2015, the law was modified in accordance with the EU Reception directive with an added category for the person to be detained if s/he lodges an asylum application in detention, if there are grounds to believe that s/he does that only to hinder the removal process. It is not possible to assess the full implications of this modification yet.

6 A somewhat similar change has taken place in organising reception that continues to be administered by the Ministry of Interior, yet reception units are increasingly operated by Migri and the Finnish Red Cross, not by municipalities, as was the case earlier.

7 In the Joutseno detention unit rooms are very small and each is equipped with a television with satellite channels serving all language needs. There are, however, less common spaces and thus the detainees are likely to remain more isolated in their daily life.

8 The names of the research participants have been changed to protect their anonymity.

9 However, it must be said that in the Finnish system there is a laudable degree of openness by the administration to civil society engagement and to academic research (see also Kynsilehto and Puumala, 2013; Puumala and Kynsilehto, 2015).

10 The UN Committee on the Rights of the Child (CRC) has notified Finland several times for detaining unaccompanied minors. Amnesty Finland has been at the forefront of advocating the end of child detention, in line with the global campaign to this end. In 2011, after intensive campaigning by human rights and migrants' rights organisations, the newly composed coalition government included in its work programme the aim of ending child detention and promised to draft a proposal charting alternatives to detention for everyone during the governmental term.

11 Child here is understood as a person under the age of 18 years, as defined in the International Convention on the Rights of the Child, to which Finland is a party.

12 See Tyler et al., 2014 for a critical engagement on child detention and related advocacy in the UK.

References

Act 15.2.2002/116. *Laki säilöön otettujen ulkomaalaisten kohtelusta ja säilöönottoyksiköstä* [Law governing treatment of detained foreigners and detention units] [Online]. Available from: www.finlex.fi/fi/laki/ajantasa/2002/20020116 [Accessed 11 February 2016].

Act 30.4.2004/301. *Ulkomaalaislaki* [Finnish Aliens Act] [Online]. Available from: www.finlex.fi/fi/laki/ajantasa/2004/20040301#L4P51 [Accessed 11 February 2016].

Agamben, G. 1998. *Homo sacer: sovereign power and bare life.* Stanford: Stanford University Press.

Conlon, D. 2013. Hungering for freedom: asylum seekers' hunger strikes - rethinking resistance as counter-conduct. In: Moran, D., Gill, N. and Conlon, D. eds. *Carceral spaces: mobility and agency in imprisonment and migrant detention.* Farnham: Ashgate, pp. 133–48.

Conlon, D. and Gill, N. 2013. Gagging orders: asylum seekers and paradoxes of freedom and protest in liberal society. *Citizenship Studies* **17**(2), pp. 241–59.

Darling, J. 2014. Another letter from the Home Office: reading the material politics of asylum. *Environment and Planning D: Society and Space* **32**(3), pp. 484–500.

Edkins, J. and Pin-Fat, V. 2005. Through the wire: relations of power and relations of violence. *Millennium: Journal of International Studies* **34**(1), pp. 1–24.

European Parliament and Council of the European Union. 2008. Directive 2008/115/ EC on common standards and procedures in Member States for returning illegally staying third-country nationals. Issued by the European Parliament and the Council, 16 December 2008. *Official Journal of the European Union,* 24 December 2008 [Online]. Available from: http://eur-lex.europa.eu/LexUriServ/LexUriServ.do?uri=OJ: L:2008:348:0098:0107:EN:PDF [Accessed 11 February 2016].

European Parliament and Council of the European Union. 2013. Regulation No 604/2013 on establishing the criteria and mechanisms for determining the Member State responsible for examining an application for international protection lodged in one of the Member States by a third-country national or a stateless person (recast). Issued by the European Parliament and the Council, 26 June 2013. *Official Journal of the European Union*, 29 June 2013 [Online]. Available from: http://eur-lex.europa .eu/LexUriServ/LexUriServ.do?uri=OJ:L:2013:180:0031:0059:EN:PDF [Accessed 10 February 2016].

Gill, N. 2009. Governmental mobility: the power effects of the movement of detained asylum seekers around Britain's detention estate. *Political Geography* **28**, pp. 186–96.

Gill, N. 2013. Mobility versus liberty? The punitive uses of movement within and outside carceral environments. In: Moran, D., N. Gill and Conlon, D. eds. *Carceral spaces: mobility and agency in imprisonment and migrant detention.* Aldershot: Ashgate, pp. 19–36.

Griffiths, M. 2012. Anonymous aliens? Questions of identification in the detention and deportation of failed asylum seekers. *Population, Space and Place* **18**(6), pp. 715–27.

Hall, A. 2010. 'These people could be anyone': fear, contempt (and empathy) in a British Immigration Removal Centre. *Journal of Ethnic and Migration Studies* **36**(6), pp. 881–98.

Hiemstra, N. 2014. Performing homeland security within the US immigrant detention system. *Environment and Planning D: Society and Space* **32**(4), pp. 571–88.

Isin, E. F. and Rygiel, K. 2006. Abject spaces, frontiers, zones, camps. In: Dauphinee, E. and Masters, C. eds. *The logics of biopower and the war on terror: living, dying, surviving.* Basingstoke: Palgrave Macmillan, pp. 181–203.

Johnson, C., Jones, R., Paasi, A., Amoore, L., Mountz, A., Salter, M. and Rumford, C. 2011. Interventions on rethinking 'the border' in border studies. *Political Geography* **30**(2), pp. 61–9.

Khosravi, S. 2009. Sweden: detention and deportation of asylum seekers. *Race & Class* **50**(4), pp. 38–56.

Kumpula, K. and Johansson, F. 2014. Säilöönottolakien uudistus on kääntymässä päälaelleen [The renewal of detention laws is turning upside down]. *Helsingin Sanomat*, guest editorial, December 10.

Kynsilehto, A. 2014. Introducing 'forced voluntary return': new prospects for becoming irregular in Finland. *Fahamu Refugee Legal Aid Newsletter* 49 [Online]. Available from: http://rightsinexile.tumblr.com/post/87519885022/introducing-forced-voluntary- return-new [Accessed 10 February 2016].

Kynsilehto, A. and Puumala, E. 2013. Persecution as experience and knowledge: the ontological dynamics of asylum interviews. *International Studies Perspectives* DOI: 10.1111/insp.12064.

Mainwaring, C. 2012. Constructing a crisis: the role of immigration detention in Malta. *Population, Space and Place* **18**(6), pp. 687–700.

Malloch, M.S. and Stanley, E. 2005. The detention of asylum seekers in the UK: representing risk, managing the dangerous. *Punishment & Society* **7**(1), pp. 53–71.

Mountz, A. 2011. The enforcement archipelago: detention, haunting, and asylum on the islands. *Political Geography* **30**(3), pp. 118–28.

Mountz, A., Coddington, K., Catania, R.T. and Loyd, J.M. 2012. Conceptualizing detention: mobility, containment, bordering, and exclusion. *Progress in Human Geography* **37**(4), pp. 522–41.

Nyers, P. 2003. Abject cosmopolitanism: the politics of protection in the anti-deportation movement. *Third World Quarterly* **24**(6), pp. 1069–93.

Perera, S. 2002. What is a camp …? *Borderlands e-journal* **1**(1) [Online]. Available from: www.borderlands.net.au/vol1no1_2002/perera_camp.html [Accessed 10 February 2016].

Puggioni, R. 2014. Speaking through the body: detention and bodily resistance in Italy. *Citizenship Studies* **18**(5), pp. 562–77.

Puumala, E. 2012. *Corporeal conjunctures no-w-here: failed asylum seekers and the senses of the international.* Acta Universitatis Tamperensis 1744. Tampere: University of Tampere.

Puumala, E. 2013. Political life beyond accommodation and return: rethinking relations between the political, the international, and the body. *Review of International Studies* **39**(4), pp. 949–68.

Puumala, E. and Kynsilehto, A. 2015. Does the body matter? Determining the right to asylum and the corporeality of political communication. *European Journal of Cultural Studies.* DOI:10.1177/1367549415592898.

Puumala, E. and Pehkonen, S. 2010. Corporeal choreographies between politics and the political: failed asylum seekers moving from body politics to bodyspaces. *International Political Sociology* **4**(1), pp. 50–65.

Puumala, E., Väyrynen, T., Kynsilehto, A., and Pehkonen, S. 2011. Events of the body politic: a Nancian reading of asylum-seekers' bodily choreographies and resistance. *Body & Society* **17**(4), pp. 83–104.

Rajaram, P.K. and Grundy-Warr, C. 2004. The irregular migrant as homo sacer: migration and detention in Australia, Malaysia and Thailand. *International Migration* **42**(1), pp. 33–64.

Rajaram, P.K. and Grundy-Warr, C. eds. 2007. *Borderscapes: hidden geographies and politics at territory's edge.* Minneapolis and London: University of Minnesota Press.

Reinboth, S. 2014. Suomi saa taas moitteita paljuselleistä [Finland is again notified for using slopping-out cells]. *Helsingin Sanomat*, November 1.

Rodier, C. 2012. *Xenophobie business: A quoi servent les contrôles migratoires?* Paris: La Decouverte.

Räsänen, P. 2014. Lainmuutoksella rajoitetaan lasten säilöönottoa [Modification of the law limits child detention]. Reader's opinion. *Helsingin Sanomat*, December 18.

Schuster, L. 2005. A sledgehammer to crack a nut: deportation, detention and dispersal in Europe. *Social Policy & Administration* **39**(6), pp. 606–21.

Squire, V. 2009. *The exclusionary politics of asylum.* Basingstoke: Palgrave Macmillan.

Trubeta, S. 2015. 'Rights' in the grey area: undocumented border crossers on Lesvos. *Race & Class* **56**(4), pp. 56–72.

Tyler, I., Gill, N., Conlon, D. and Oeppen, C. 2014. The business of child detention: charitable co-option, migrant advocacy and activist outrage. *Race & Class* **56**(1), pp. 3–21.

14   The pleasures of security?

Visual practice and immigration detention

Alexandra Hall

Introduction

Early in my fieldwork at Locksdon[1], an immigration removal centre (IRC) in the south of England, officers discovered a 'body missing' at lunchtime roll check one weekend. A detainee, North African in origin, had simply disappeared. As protocol dictated, the officers conducted a standing roll check, a lock up and full search of the establishment, and they requested extra staff and tracker dogs to scan the buildings. Officers posted around the perimeter fence to watch for the man in case he was still on the premises, and they were only stood down at 6 pm when it was clear the detainee had gone. An escape was a serious incident and 'looked very, very bad on the establishment', as one of the officers told me. 'Someone wasn't doing their job properly.' The disappearance of a person constituted, ultimately, a failure of the watchful security regime under which immigration detainees lived. In the hours and days after the escape, the officers reached a consensus that the detainee must have somehow scaled the razor wire surrounding the Centre buildings and climbed over a roof to drop down in the kitchen area, to then escape on the bread delivery van. How was this possible with the checks on exiting vehicles? The officers tentatively began to blame the OSGs (Operational Support Grade), among whom were several female and older male members of staff who were widely suspected to 'not be up to the job'. Gallingly for Locksdon staff, the visiting investigating team insisted on the possibility that the escapee could still be in the establishment days after the event. Locksdon officers were made to re-search areas again and again. Furthermore, the investigating team (officers thought amazingly) took seriously a dream vision that one of the detainees claimed to have had regarding the escapee, a dream that involved ducks and dirty water. The manhole covers were duly lifted and searched, but to no avail. The overwhelming feeling among Locksdon officers was of having lost the initiative, and of having been 'made to look stupid' by one of the detainees.

*

In this chapter, I argue that *watching* is a visual practice characteristic of securitised detention – a practice which encapsulates anxieties and emotions, and which instantiates and (re)produces gendered, racialised power relations within everyday spaces of detention, reverberating out to (and in from) wider political and economic realms. This visual practice thus exemplifies an intimate economy, one that takes the familiar as the terrain of a global security regime. Feelings – of anger and frustration, humiliation and vengefulness – were important within this terrain, and were frequently expressed at Locksdon, one of four United Kingdom IRCs operated by Her Majesty's Prison Service under contract to the immigration authorities. The officers working with the detainees were trained prison officers. While they broadly acknowledged the fruitlessness of securely detaining hundreds of men at the establishment under immigration law, officers often argued that the detainees in the UK detention estate were unknown, in the sense of lacking identity documents, or the assessments and records that accompanied convicted prisoners within the prison estate. The detainees therefore posed a potential risk: 'we don't know who they are, what they've done' so 'it's better to be too secure than not secure enough.' Importing a retributive disciplinary logic from mainstream prison, the officers subjected the detainees to a suspicious surveillant regime in the name of security. One of the most basic functions of the job, as the officers saw it, was to supervise the detainees closely, maintain good order and prevent escape while immigration adjudications were finalised. An escape like the one described above constituted an embarrassing failure for the officers.

It has become commonplace to suggest that fear is the prevailing affective disposition associated with contemporary projects of international security, of which I take immigration detention to be a part. While 'the looming uncertainty of ill-defined threat' (Massumi, 2005, p. 8) certainly permeates many contemporary international security initiatives, especially the war on terror's pre-emptive strikes, much is taken for granted about the affective dynamics of these initiatives and of the experiential manifestation of emotions. Despite their traditional denigration in the practice and analysis of international politics, emotions clearly play a crucial role in political decision-making, perhaps especially in security. They feature centrally in canonical International Relations texts, for instance, but they have tended to be divided into 'relevant' and 'reasonable' feelings (fear of insecurity, desire for power) and 'unreasonable' others (honour, respect) (see Saurette, 2006). However, a growing body of work on emotions (e.g. Ahmed, 2004; Barbalet, 2001) and on affect (e.g. Berlant, 2004; Gregg and Siegworth, 2010) has done much to dislodge the inherent rationalism conventionally associated with the practice and explanation of politics, exposing the diversity of affective registers within contemporary security (Anderson and Adey, 2012). I argue that the claim that post-9/11 security projects produced a novel kind of affective politics – typically characterised by neurosis, or fear (see Isin, 2004; Massumi, 2005) – might profitably be qualified by a more nuanced account of the situated emergence of particular emotions, whose effect might be discerned at particular sites of security. Within detention, for instance, anxiety and disquiet were certainly part of the officers' range of experience, but so too were irritation, humiliation and contempt.

It is perhaps particularly useful to consider the 'irrational' affective dynamics of security when their economic justifications are considered. Amid ongoing high-profile border crises – from the 2014 'surge' at the US-Mexican border to the chaos surrounding the Channel Tunnel between Britain and France in the summer of 2015 and the desperate ongoing humanitarian disaster of the Mediterranean coast – western states are keen to demonstrate a tough stance towards unauthorised border crossings, while balancing international humanitarian obligations. The vexing question, for states, is how best to secure the border against unauthorised people 'without status', whilst simultaneously facilitating desirable and economically beneficial types of mobility within the demands of neoliberalism. Despite having little or no obvious deterrent effect on illegal immigration, detention is a solution of choice for western states eager to assert control of borders. The ongoing expansion of secure facilities in the UK continues apace, despite the fact that immigration detention is widely acknowledged as an ill-suited and ineffective means of administering vulnerable, desperate and distressed populations (see the Report of the Joint Inquiry by the All Party Parliamentary Group on Refugees and the All Party Parliamentary Group on Migration, 2015). It is a frustrating and puzzling state of affairs. Detention practices, of course, exacerbate the ongoing criminalisation of migration, producing the detainee as a 'culprit' worthy of the 'enforcement spectacle' (De Genova, 2007). Perhaps more than any other feature of this border enforcement spectacle, detention is concerned with securing sovereignty itself, leaving unaddressed the complex reasons for global migration.

Border insecurity, inevitably, offers a golden profit-making opportunity for private global security contractors, whose encroachment into detention is well-documented (Bacon, 2005; Golash-Boza, 2009). Salter and Mutlu (2011) point out that many border security initiatives (their example is post-9/11 spending on the Canadian-US border) are vastly expensive and often lack public support, yet produce little discernible increase in security. Salter and Mutlu (2011) argue that what drives the inexorable border security investment by states simply cannot be captured by models of economic and political activity that privilege rationality, coherence and prudent decision-making about means and ends. Instead, they make the case for placing centrally the affective elements of political initiatives that provide their own, often unconscious, logic. They deploy psychoanalytical theory to understand 'the dynamics between emotion and rationality in decision-making' (2011, p. 181), using the work of Freud and Melanie Klein to argue that border security projects such as those on the Canadian-US border are 'phantastic objects' which encircle, re-enact and revisit the trauma and panic of 9/11, producing a vision of the US, paradoxically, that has no need of border security.

In this chapter I, too, am concerned with examining affective emotional dynamics of security practice and with the unconscious 'motives and forces of which we are largely unaware' (Roazen, 1968, p. ix). I also turn to psychoanalytical theory, to tease apart the relationship between security and affect within immigration detention. More specifically, I use the feminist deployment of psychoanalytical theory to examine *watching* as a practice and instantiation of gendered power within detention. As the escape episode above makes clear, visual practice was a core part of the labour of detention for staff, at least in Locksdon. That is, the officers' visual capacities (to notice, observe, monitor, watch) were a 'layer of the body' (Crary, 1994, p. 22) that became disciplined and trained as part of the effort to secure the detainee population, embodying the generalised suspicion which drives the expansion of securitised detention. The feminist critique, more than anything, has revealed how watching is reflective of hidden pleasures and desires that are fuelled by the unconscious. The feminists are clear that the dark pleasures of visual mastery within spectatorship in particular are inherently gendered, reflecting and reproducing wider power relations. My starting point in this chapter is that our understanding of contemporary practices of security must pay attention to the (hidden) pleasures that they incorporate, and also to their gendered character. This is not because these practices (like immigration detention) do not have horror, fear and violence inscribed in them. Rather, fascination, desire and pleasure have a place within contemporary security that is barely acknowledged, but which nonetheless fuels a burgeoning global security regime. The claims of reasonable and justifiable decision-making that accompany the rise of detention across the west – from its validation within governmental strategies for managing the border and the large-scale investment in facilities, through to the officers' day-to-day securitisation of visual practice within detention – occludes a troubling affective politics. My argument, put simply, is that securitised visual practice within detention, and indeed the inexorable growth of detention itself, is organised as a response to the anxieties of difference, de-masculinisation and loss of control at the border.

My concern is with everyday sociality and experience within detention. I argue that the feelings of anxiety and anger that the Locksdon officers expressed on discovering they had 'lost the initiative' to one of the detained men after the escape are not divorced from some more significant analysis of international security, detention and border control. My focus, then, is on the intimate in the sense that Mountz and Hyndman (2006, p. 451) suggest when they say that the 'body is the finest scale of political and economic space'. As feminist critiques of globalisation have long demonstrated, the intimate and the global are inseparable, whatever the (abstract, masculinized) narratives of global politics might otherwise suggest (Mountz and Hyndman, 2006, p. 448): 'They are neither separate spheres nor bounded subjects. Rather, they co-constitute places such as the border, the home and the body.' Familiar, proximate, physical habits and experiences (the detainee's sense of being surveilled, the officers' watchful gaze) do not bear the imprint of some more important securitised political and economic spheres: these habits and experiences *constitute* the political importance and economic organisation of detention. Put differently, the embodied, intimate relations between staff and detained people at Locksdon, and the affective elements of life within immigration detention, *are productive of* global border security. They are where global border security is manifested and experienced where it matters most – intimately, in individual lives. In what follows, I assume that acts of detention and their political effects on individual lives require an understanding of the ways in which the security regime is produced within daily, even banal, social practices and interactions, which is to say in the intimate spaces and relations of detention.

My discussion proceeds in two parts. The first section considers the seminal work of feminist film theorist Laura Mulvey and her appropriation of psychoanalytical theory. Her argument about power and mastery of the viewed subject offers insights into the watchful and objectifying regime of immigration detention. The second section examines the gendered nature of detention work and the way the prison officers sought to reclaim a (masculinised) sense of control amid what they viewed as a feminisation and de-professionalisation of their skills.

Visual pleasures? Security and visual practice

In her classic 1975 essay, *Visual Pleasure and Narrative Cinema*, feminist film theorist Laura Mulvey deployed psychoanalytical theory as a 'political weapon' to examine the way in which the unconscious of patriarchal society 'structures ways of seeing and pleasure in looking' (2009, p. 14). Mulvey's overall concern is with what she calls the heterosexual division of labour within the conventional narrative structure of classic Hollywood film. The cinema, she argues, crystallises two kinds of visual pleasure. First is scopophilia, or pleasure in looking at the bodies of others as (erotic) objects. Mulvey here draws on Freud, who associated scopophilia with voyeurism: with 'taking other people as objects, subjecting them to a controlling and curious gaze' and with 'watching, in an active and controlling sense' an objectified other (Mulvey, 2009, p. 17). Mulvey also describes a narcissistic process within spectatorship, in which 'curiosity and the wish to look intermingle with a fascination with likeness and recognition' (2009, pp. 17–8). The (male) spectator is invited to identify with the film's hero, so that 'the power of the male protagonist as he controls events coincides with the active power of the erotic look, both giving a satisfying sense of omnipotence' (Mulvey, 2009, pp. 21). The represented (female) form can also become a fetish object, valued for its beauty and on whom the gaze dwells at length. Women in film, Mulvey argues, become passive spectacles for the spectator (understood to be men), who are active 'bearers of the look' (2009, p. 19). Mulvey's coining of the now famous term, 'the male gaze', echoes wider work of the era, work that posits a core relationship between gendered subject position, power and visuality (see Berger, 1972). The point of this feminist critique was that the cinematic experience crystallises the organisation of broader patriarchal society and the differentially ordered subject positions of men and women.

The feminist deployment of psychoanalytical theory draws attention to the problematic *difference* of women, and the neutralisation of that difference within spectatorship. For the Freudians, female bodily difference represents (for the male unconscious) the threat of castration, and de-masculinisation. For the Lacanians, woman's lack of phallus places her in a negative relationship to language, and locates her 'as other (enigma, mystery)' (Kaplan, 2000, p. 120). Mulvey argues that the male unconscious has

> two avenues of escape […]: preoccupation with the re-enactment of the original trauma (investigating the woman, demystifying her mystery) counterbalanced by the devaluation, punishment or saving of the guilty object […];

or else complete disavowal of castration by the substitution of a fetish object or turning the represented figure itself into a fetish so it becomes reassuring rather than dangerous.

(2009, p. 22)

That is, voyeuristic disparagement and festishistic glorification are both reflections of the 'need to annihilate the dread that woman inspires' (Kaplan, 2000, p. 121) – anxiety about difference and loss of masculinity. It is worth making clear at this point that subsequent feminist work has disengaged the male gaze from men, arguing that women can, of course, assume the role of spectator, and men can be gazed upon: the 'gaze is not necessarily male (literally) but to own and activate the gaze, given our language and the structure of the unconscious, is to be in the masculine position' (Kaplan, 2000, p. 130). That is, both male and female spectators can embody the controlling gaze and the passive subject position.

The gendered character of vision that psychoanalysis places centrally has been further supplemented by critical accounts which have emphasised how watching (in film and beyond) is also organised according to racial and ethnic difference (Pratt, 1992) and is bound up with sexual identity. Film theorists have pointed out that the 'imperial gaze', conjured within cinematic representations of racial and ethnic otherness, intersect with the male gaze in troubling ways (Kaplan, 1997). The white male subject, gazing upon a woman or a racialised other, confronts in both a disquieting difference:

They assume power lies with them, with their gaze, and are uneasy when there is an entity which seems to elude their control, to look and perhaps be different. Their discomfort leads to their construction of the primitive/ civilised binary categorisation, so as to defend against difference.

(Kaplan, 1997, p. 62)

It is the fear of difference, and the need to subjugate it, that permeated both the colonial encounter and, argues Kaplan, the classic Hollywood depictions of difference in film. The generalised othering that Said (1978) called orientalism codes political, economic and social boundaries through 'racial' or ethnic markers of difference, in intersection with cultural competences, sexual proclivities, psychological dispositions and cultivated habits (Stoler, 1995). Otherness becomes mapped within what Foucault calls a 'grid of intelligibility' – a hierarchy of distinctions in perception and practice that conflated, substituted and 'collapsed the categories of racial, class and sexual Others strategically and at different times' (Stoler, 1995, p. 11). Both the imperial and the male gaze place centrally the white western male subject, and in both, 'anxiety prevents this gaze from actually seeing the people gazed at' (Kaplan, 1997, p. 78). I will argue that it is anxiety about the loss of (gendered) control, and the threat of de-masculinisation by both female colleagues and detainees that shapes practices of watching and looking within the intimate everyday at Locksdon.

Security at Locksdon was actively produced via multiple visual efforts to maintain control of a disciplined regime. Security, for the officers, meant a smooth-running timetable of activities but also, more importantly, a feeling of mastery and having what the officers called 'the initiative'. Officers embodied a watchful, proactive and alert gaze over the detained men during everyday activities. The practised 'instincts' of the experienced officer produced a scopic regime that took up '[t]he smallest infraction ... with all the more care for it being small' (Foucault, 2007, p. 45). Every encounter, passing glance or chance glimpse provided an opportunity to notice something *specific* about a detainee: something anomalous, suspicious or out of place (see Hall, 2012). The staff 'Obs book' (Observations book) was a written inscription of this ongoing scrutiny, where staff wrote up notes and observations about detainees and events during their shift in chronological order:

> Detainee A caught smoking in corridor. I told him to put it out. Detainee blew smoke in my face, told me I could do nothing if he wanted to smoke. Eventually went back into dorm. Detainee has bad attitude and has shown aggression towards staff. Could pose possible threat of disorder in future.

> Detainee B seen watching perimeter fence out of window and discussing something with Detainee C when I passed. Possible security risk.

> Detainee D seemed very miserable at lunchtime. Friend reported was talking of suicide and refused to eat at lunch and tea.

In the Obs book, the officers' attentiveness became a textual record of vigilance. Observations of mundane transgressions and insolence became 'evidence' of possible security problems. The officers' attentiveness to detail was disciplinary and normalising in Foucault's (1977) sense, making it possible to single out 'troublemakers'. An insolent or disruptive detainee would be moved away from his friends as 'punishment', a violent man would be segregated to 'cool off' and a depressed man would be moved together with his friends, or referred to health care for special attention (see Hall, 2012).

In the literature, the total institution tends to be associated with an authoritative, disinterested sovereign gaze, and with a normalising, calculative examination, which 'manifests the subjection of those who are perceived as objects and the objectification of those who are subjected' (Foucault, 1977, p. 185). My first point, then, is that at Locksdon, rationalising disciplinary power as Foucault described it was entangled with a range of affective dispositions that the officers called 'gut feelings' about when trouble was on its way: 'That's what it's like here. It can be so quiet that you can be lulled into a false sense of security. But underneath it all the tension is mounting up and every once in a while it all goes off.' Officers described their work in the IRC as 'bodywatching' (see Hall, 2012). The term 'body' designated, first, the detainee's body as object within the IRC, to be organised, tracked and surveilled, but also the detainee's body that might betray itself through its movements. It was this body that the officers subjected to a 'meticulous observation of detail' (Foucault, 1977, pp. 181–2). The officers oscillated between positions of stationary spectatorship where their gaze ranged over a given area (for instance in the Visits Hall), and a proactive form of attention on the move (when conducting periodic dormitory searches for weapons or contraband). Bodywatching aimed to fix and order detainee bodies in the classic disciplinary sense, to inculcate an orderly physical circulation and to foster a desired norm of compliant behaviour. It also relied on circulating, interacting bodies to betray future intent. Bodywatching was a culturally learned disposition and an awareness of other bodies in time and space that was *more* than visual. It became, instead, an instinct which registered norms and deviations in proper movement and behaviour, and which directed the officers' gaze accordingly.

My second point is that visual practice within Lockson contained hidden pleasures and anxieties in precisely the way Mulvey describes. The dominant visual mastery of the people detained in Locksdon was an objectifying and ultimately degrading form of watching, resonating with the sadistic and disparaging elements of voyeurism. It was not only that detainees were forced to live in constant exposure, nor that centre routines at the time of my fieldwork regularly included periodic strip searches and intrusive dormitory searches. Rather, the scopic regime of Locksdon was wholly concerned with 'control and domination' (Kaplan, 2000, p. 122), and with a visual objectification of the detainees that refused to properly *see* the detainees as people. The officers' use of the de-individualised term 'body' to refer to men reflected this visual objectification (as in 'we have a body missing' or 'there are two bodies to locate in Reception'). For officers, much of the pleasure of their work came from exerting an active and dominant identity vis-à-vis the detainees. A good day was when all the rules were obeyed, when the officers' active, visual alertness addressed the first signs of indiscipline and when the officers' active (masculine) gaze and the passive (feminised) objectification of the detainees was properly balanced.

The pleasure in 'keeping the initiative' was threatened, of course, by detainees' minor misdemeanours and acts of resistance – from evading roll check and being insolent, to acts of violence and even escapes. During my fieldwork, for instance, after a spate of security incidents (a concealed weapon, an increase in self-harm incidents, confrontations with detainees), Locksdon's manager called for extra prison service staff to join Locksdon officers as a show of strength. He also arranged for detainees who caused trouble to be temporarily sent to a nearby prison establishment where they would be accommodated alongside prisoners. Announcing this initiative to staff, the manager summed up: 'We will maintain control and have the initiative. We will not allow anyone to take the initiative from us.' Later on, one officer summed up the new temporary rules to a colleague: 'We're going to show them that we is the daddy.' The 'troublesome' detainee – who contested the regime, or who protested at his treatment, or who resisted the officers' authority – became for the officers a contravention of the order of domination-subjugation within the centre. It was the officers, not the detainees, who were supposed to embody 'action' via their probing visual habits.

The disruption of proper order could be 'righted' by ever more extreme forms of visual exposure (segregating detainees into a special accommodation and observation cell) or by a concerted show of physical masculine strength (as in the drafting in of extra staff) or by the literal and enforced passivity of the detainee within a violent tussle, when officers would restrain a disruptive detainee using control and restraint (C&R) techniques.[2] As the male officer's masculine identity was performatively brought into being (Butler, 1990) within the physical enactment of C&R techniques, the detainee's capacity for action was annulled. As the officer asserted his strength among colleagues, the detainee's physicality was suppressed. If, after Foucault (2000, p. 340), power is relational, productive and contingent and also resisted – 'an action upon an action, on possible or actual future or present actions' – then the C&R incident was when Locksdon's regime dissolved into pure violence. Violence, as Foucault argues (Foucault, 2000, p. 340) 'acts upon a body or upon things, it forces, it bends, it breaks … it closes off all possibilities.' The C&R incident was when mastery of the detainee moved from a visual to a physical realm – reducing him to an inert, contorted and 'wrapped up' body just as the officer's body was materialised as 'male' in its vigour.

Visual practice at Locksdon, then, was objectifying and concerned with the production of security via the maintenance of a relation between active (officer) gaze and passive (detainee). The gaze that the officers extended towards the detainees tended to view them as wholly 'other'. The officers' rational, disciplined and controlled mastery of the regime was contrasted with the 'emotionality', enforced passivity and undisciplined character of the detainees. Officers' understandings of the detainees drew on stereotyped schema that organised knowledge about men according to notions of skin colour, 'race', cultural difference, national origin and gender. The otherness of the detainees was marked on their bodies via skin colour and manifested through the body and its movements, which in turn produced evidence of detainees' 'different mindset'. The 'Africans', for instance, were often described as having a 'different culture' that was expressed through different physicalities: chanting or 'going into trances' when distressed or angry. Even as officers rationalised that 'it was just their way of being angry' their response was frequently 'not knowing what to do to calm them down'. The controlling gaze that was extended to the detainees viewed them as a threat to security, possibly, but also a threat as Kaplan describes: potentially dislodging a privileged position for white male subjects. It is for this reason that acts of resistance, disobedience and, indeed, active subjecthood among detainees were so troubling for the officers, constituting as they did a disconcerting active return of the gaze. The male/imperial gaze that plays out within the detention centre, and wider border security initiatives, is one which 'refuses mutual gazing, mutual subject-to-subject recognition' (Kaplan, 1997, p. 79). It is for this reason that events such as the escape were so frustrating for the officers, denying them the visual, sovereign mastery they craved. In the next section I show how the masculinised gaze sought to neutralise the 'threat' posed by women within the Centre. The devaluation of prison labour, coupled with the presence of women as workers and the gendered character of watching meant that women, as well as detainees, were viewed as a source of danger at Locksdon.

The danger of women

Locksdon was an overwhelmingly masculine environment. All the detainees, and the majority of officers, were men. I understand gender to be the categorisation of persons within socio-cultural discourses related to the materiality of bodies marked as different through the discourses of 'sex'. Gender also refers to the contextual embodied social performance of identity in relation to these discourses, in intersection with sexuality, age, occupation, class, race and religion (Connell, 1995, Moore, 1994). Gendered discourse delimits what is contextually understood as proper, physical, emotional and social behaviour for a man and a woman, though the dominant discourses are constantly contested (see Connell, 1995). 'The masculine', particularly, has been understood as a contingent and performative identification – 'an uncertain and provisional project' (McDowell, 2001, p. 182) within a set of contested masculine ideals. What Connell (1995) calls 'hegemonic' finds its opposition in the softer, vulnerable and passive feminine body (Grosz, 1994). Gendered power in the West also draws upon post-Enlightenment divisions between nature and culture, bodies and intellect. Intellect, rationalism and culture are associated with masculine forms, while the feminine is associated with the body, emotionality and nature (Moore, 1994). More specifically, 'the affective' becomes mapped across a gendered terrain, with certain emotional experiences and displays being gendered and gendering in turn. Particular kinds of occupation and labour, tasks and expertise have thus become gendered (McDowell, 2001). Emotional labour and the allocation of tasks in the workplace, for example, are gendered and gender in turn (Hochschild, 1983).

For male officers at Locksdon, work in a prison establishment enabled the articulation of a distinctive kind of masculine identity. Crucially, the military formed part of many officers' sense of masculine identity. Many of the officers had previously served in the Armed Forces and would always be interested to find out whether new members of staff 'had served'. Military life is associated with a particular 'heroic male project', in Whitehead's (2002) terms: one of conquest and discipline, privileging physical perseverance, teamwork and bravery. The stories, anecdotes and reminiscences shared by those Locksdon officers who had served in the Forces, however, tended not to recall conflict situations, but instead invoked the (male) sociality of the barracks, pubs and training grounds of Forces life. One man told me that he had enjoyed the army because 'people looked out for one another – we looked after our own'. The nostalgia for the military was for a structured and ordered existence, and also for the affinity of Forces life. The relationships among ex-Forces personnel tended to bind men to other men in the military context while often separating them from 'civvy' men, and from women. As a well-trodden route for ex-Forces staff, prison service work allowed for the continued performance of a disciplined masculine identity for many officers.

There are three points that are important for the purposes of this volume. The first is that many of the more experienced prison officers saw their work as prison officers to have been gradually devalued. One of these changes was the move to a more inclusive, representative prison service recruitment drive to include a wider mix of backgrounds, and a more equal gender balance. As one officer told me, 'They're trying to move away from a Forces background, but it works, so why change it?' The inclusion of women, especially, was deeply problematic for some officers, as I describe below. Another change relates to the privatisation of prison work – both in mainstream prisons and in immigration detention. The officers saw privatisation to herald a loss of professional standards, minimisation of training and devaluing of their expertise. One senior officer told me that the pay was higher in private establishments, frequently attracting management-level staff, but that 'we are the experts in holding people, at looking after people in custody'. He pointed out that after a recently reported disturbance and fire in a private IRC, it transpired that staff did not know the establishment headcount or day's movements, or the number of bodies in the beds. This would never have happened in a prison service establishment he claimed. It is also the case, importantly, that the majority of officers begrudged their labour being co-opted by the immigration authorities. They resented their work being reduced to 'babysitting' the detainees, and frequently compared the dissatisfying work at an IRC with detainees to the more rewarding work with convicts (cons) a 'proper prison'. One officer explained it to me thus: 'I'm so sick of it. You can reason with cons. You can explain why they can't have what they want. With them [detainees] they just expect everything to happen right now.'

In many ways, the disquiet about change that the majority of officers (mostly male, but not exclusively so) articulated was related to the overall feminisation of prison work, and with the privileging of 'softer' feminine skills within a modernised Prison Service. Within Locksdon, the work with detainees did not permit a performance of the masculine in the way that work with hardened convicts did. The officers felt themselves to be transformed into 'social workers' and 'babysitters'. Paradoxically, the stereotypical physicality (indeed, brutality) associated with prison work was understood by officers themselves to require balancing by skills more usually associated with 'the feminine': the ability to negotiate, to demonstrate understanding and empathy. The 'good officer' (male or female) was not 'soft' in dealings with detainees, but had to appreciate the difficulties of being incarcerated. Although they valued compassion (a feminised trait), officers ultimately had to engage in physical struggles with detainees in the name of security. The ability of women officers to do so was always in question. As one officer put it: 'They [management] want us to be social workers, but then, suddenly, we're expected to roll around on the floor with them. You can't have it both ways.'

The second point is that women constituted a problem at Locksdon. Studies of gendered relations within the Prison Service show that the increase in the number of female officers has threatened the traditionally male domain, with men resenting the 'positive discrimination' women are perceived to receive (Farnworth, 1992). The literature about women in traditionally male occupations has consistently demonstrated that women bring ambiguity, danger and uncertainty.

The literature also attests to the limited subject positions that are available to women: they are viewed as needing protection, or as de-feminised pseudo-males, or as dangerous sources of erotic temptation (Crawley, 2004, p. 195; Young, 1991). While women's 'natural' skills of diplomacy are generally viewed as a calming influence on prison establishments, female officers are ultimately seen to be doing a 'man's job' (Crawley, 2004, p. 123). Locksdon's female officers could certainly be regarded by their male colleagues as good officers. In fact, several men professed to prefer them – 'I like working with women. There's none of that macho stuff you get with men. And they can make really good officers. They know how to calm things down.' Nevertheless, 'the girls' (new, inexperienced and unskilled female officers) at Locksdon were seen to lack rigour and professionalism, leading to chinks in the secure regime (like the OSGs who inspected the bread van in the escape described above). These newer female colleagues were not equated with the small number of expert, respected and admired female colleagues. Nevertheless, women in general (female officers and other female staff) were associated (by their male colleagues) with weakness, both in the sense of physical vulnerability and also in the sense of being more emotional.

More specifically, gendered understandings of 'emotion' did not link women with anger, pride or 'machismo', but to sympathy and kindness. This apparently rendered them more susceptible to manipulation by detainees, but also more suited to care of the detainees. As one female officer put it, 'they [male officers] just don't have a clue. When a detainee starts crying, they just freeze and call a nurse.' The task of securing the detainee body via visual mastery and the use of force was the job of the *officers*, while tasks associated with the care of detainees were the prime responsibility of others – education, nursing and religious staff. For the officers, the enactment of feminised 'care' by other staff often undermined the masculine imperative to keep control of the secure establishment. Yet, importantly, the presence of caring (weak) female staff at Locksdon was necessary for the production of meaningful boundaries around the (male) officers' own, more important task of security and protection. Women – both female officers and other female staff – frequently drew forth protective and paternal styles from male officers that created a 'subordinate relation of those in the protected position' (Young, 2003, p. 4). Nurses constantly complained that the officers were overprotective and patronising towards them, as well as expecting them to bear the brunt of the emotional work of the establishment. When a senior male health care professional was appointed to the establishment, nurses were angered by officers telling them that 'Now we won't have to look after you' and that 'You'll feel safer now, won't you?' Officers, on the other hand, complained that the detainees would manipulate the nurses.

Finally, the gaze at Locksdon was thoroughly gendered in precisely the way that Mulvey describes. As an overwhelmingly male environment, where male and female members of staff were highly visible to one another, Locksdon tended to privilege a libidinous male gaze that ranged freely over female colleagues' bodies. Women's bodies were objectified, commented upon, discussed and evaluated by men (officers and detainees alike), whose voyeuristic enjoyment of the female form was scarcely concealed. In Mulvey's words, the male's 'determining ... gaze project[ed] its fantasy onto the female figure' and the female officers were forcibly given 'traditional exhibitionist roles' and imbued with a 'to-be-looked-at-ness' (2009, p. 19). Women were objectified and fetishized as objects of desire, but also as objects of danger. Women, it was acknowledged, could disrupt male loyalties and weaken the masculinised security regime. It was also the case that the presence of women in Locksdon was necessary for the articulation of a particular kind of sexualised masculine identification among male officers. At Locksdon, the casual pursuance of available females (married or not) was a matter of competition among some men: one of life's pleasures, a 'natural' way for men to behave. A small cohort of officers would brag about their sexual exploits with trusted colleagues as a way of expressing, performing and accentuating a certain kind of masculine identity among peers. One officer explained that he was pursuing a clerical staff member as 'an ego boost' as he gleefully recounted his successful seduction to his friends (see Hall, 2012).

In sum, women at Locksdon were at once vilified and objectified, glorified and fetishized. As Mulvey and others have suggested, this oscillating pleasure and denigration can be related to unconscious masculine desires and anxieties. Within Locksdon, the economic, social and cultural changes that have eroded the privileged position of male officers in the creation of 'security' within prison establishments were experienced intimately, countered and neutralised within close-hand relations between colleagues – a disparaging comment, a protective and patronising 'cuddle', a tacit accusation of incompetence. The fear of feminisation of their labour, as well as the instinctual, affective threat that the psychoanalysts attribute to the female body, shaped the male gaze at Locksdon. The intimate encounters of the establishment distilled much wider sets of concerns about the role of men and women within securitised and economic domains (as protector and protected, as object and subject of desire, as watcher and watched), concerns which animate wider security discourses. The experiences and interactions between colleagues and detainees sought to sooth male anxieties while causing unease among women who did not 'fit'.

Conclusion

In this chapter I have argued that affective dynamics within immigration detention are important for understanding the production of border security. More specifically, I have argued that visual practices, justified as reasonable and rational responses to the potentially threatening and 'illegal' detainee within a series of border crises, contained (and were shaped by) complex, unacknowledged *pleasures*. The insight that feminist film critique and psychoanalytical theory offers to a consideration of immigration detention is how voyeuristic and festishistic modes of watching intertwine to 'pursue aims in indifference to perceptual reality, and motivate eroticised phantasmagoria that affect the subject's perception of the world to make a mockery of empirical objectivity' (Mulvey, 2009, p. 19).

There are, simply, no ways of watching that are separate from the pleasures that Mulvey describes. In this way, the scrutiny of the detainees is never simply about the upholding of a disinterested secure regime, nor of the objective recognition of a threat or danger. There is both a festishisation of difference and a voyeuristic delight in extending the (masculine) gaze over the bodies of mastered detainees and disparaged female colleagues. Indeed, securitised visual practice is organised as a response to the anxieties of difference, to a nebulous feeling of loss of control and to a fear of de-masculinisation, anxieties that ricochet from the intimate levels of bodily experience within one IRC to the global expansion of detention.

I have shown that the broader economy of detention (shaped by an encroaching feminisation, privatisation and de-valuing of 'expert' male labour) produces a particular set of anxieties for staff (male and female) who identify with an older set of power relations. The simultaneous glorification and vilification of female colleagues within Locksdon, played out in desiring and belittling spectatorship, encircled the threat women posed: to masculine expertise, to masculine 'protector', to 'irrational' masculine desire. In line with the concerns of this volume, the shifts in the economy and labour market (of which the prison service is a part) are lived at an intimate scale at Locksdon, becoming encapsulated within bodily experience, a libidinous glance or a sexist joke about a female colleague. To be clear, and to return to Hyndman and Mountz's arguments about the 'global intimate', these everyday encounters instantiate the masculinist logic of international security (and border security especially). As Young (2003) argues, the protective masculine role of the security state requires a subservient, grateful and obedient object to protect – a feminised citizenry. Within the male Locksdon officers' disquiet about 'weak' women can be found a distillation of a wider set of concerns about the border as a site of insecurity and threat.

I have also shown that the visual regime at Locksdon was concerned with neutralising the threat of the detainee as a racialized, de-masculinised, vaguely threatening 'other'. It is possible to relate the anxieties of the surveillant regime at Locksdon to what Kaplan calls the imperial gaze, one which seeks to uphold a privileged position for white (male) subjects. The officers' watchful surveillance of the detainees encapsulated wider racialized and criminalised anxieties about migration. This is perhaps especially the case within immigration detention, where the supposed illegality, and unknownness, of the detainees is prominent in officers' minds. Incidents like the escape described at the start of this chapter capture the complex affective dynamics that were in play in Locksdon: the doubt surrounding junior female colleagues' competence, staff humiliation in front of the investigating team from the prison estate at having lost a detainee, and staff anger at the disappearance of a detainee. This detainee, in evading the officers' mastering gaze, inverted the relations of domination and passivity that imbued Locksdon, and wider border politics. Within events like these, the officers' mastery of the establishment crumbled, exposing the extent to which the everyday visual practices at Locksdon were as much to do with constructing an idealised vision of sovereign control as with security per se. As Kaplan argues, voyeurism and festishism 'are mechanisms the dominant cinema uses to *construct* the male spectator in accordance with the needs of his unconscious' (2000, p. 120; italics in original). In sum, it is the unconscious need of the (masculine) sovereign state to reassert itself against a perceived loss of control at the border that drives the expansion of detention, just as the unconscious anxieties of the (masculine) officer shapes everyday life within detention.

Acknowledgements

Thanks to the editors, for their patient, scrupulous and very helpful comments on earlier drafts. Thanks also to Martin Coward, who drew my attention to the work of Laura Mulvey.

Notes

1 Locksdon is a pseudonym. I conducted one year of ethnographic fieldwork among officers at this IRC, the fuller account of which can be found in *Borderwatch* (Hall, 2012)
2 Control and restraint techniques were used to bring violent (or potentially violent) detainees under control. The techniques include arm holds, exerting pressure to parts of the body or holding detainees on the ground.

References

Ahmed, S. 2004. *The cultural politics of emotion*. London: Routledge.
Anderson, B. and Adey, P. 2012. Governing events and life: 'emergency' in UK Civil Contingencies. *Political Geography* **31**(1), pp. 24–33.
Bacon, C. 2005. The evolution of immigration detention in the UK: the involvement of private prison companies. *Refugee Studies Centre Working Paper no. 27* [Online]. Available from: http://repository.forcedmigration.org/show_metadata .jsp?pid=fmo:4343 [Accessed 15 June 2015].
Barbalet, J. 2001. *Emotions, social theory and social structure*. Cambridge: Cambridge University Press.
Berger, J. 1972. *Ways of seeing*. London: Penguin Books.
Berlant, L. 2004. *Compassion: the culture and politics of an emotion*. New York: Routledge.
Butler, J. 1990. *Gender trouble: feminism and the subversion of identity*. London: Routledge.
Connell, R. 1995. *Masculinities*. London: Allen and Unwin.
Crary, J. 1994. Unbinding vision. *October*, **Spring**, pp. 21–44.
Crawley, E. 2004. *Doing prison work: the public and private lives of prison officers*. Devon, UK: Willan Publishing.
De Genova, N. 2007. The production of culprits: from deportability to detainability in the aftermath of 'homeland security'. *Citizenship Studies* **11**(5), pp. 421–88.
Farnworth, L. 1992. Women doing a man's job: female prison officers working in a male prison. *Australian and New Zealand Journal of Criminology* 25: 278-95.
Foucault, M. 1977. *Discipline and punish: the birth of the prison*. London: Penguin.
Foucault, M. 2000. *Essential works of Foucault 1954–1984, Vol. 3: Power*. Edited by J. Faubian, Translated by R. Hurley and others. London: Penguin Books.
Foucault, M. 2007. *Security, territory, population*. Houndsmill: Palgrave Macmillan.
Golash-Boza, T. 2009. The immigration-industrial complex: why we enforce immigration policies destined to fail. *Sociology Compass* **3**(2), pp. 295–309.
Gregg, M. and Seigworth, G. eds. 2010. *The affect theory reader*. Durham: Duke University Press.

Grosz, E. 1994. *Volatile bodies: toward a corporeal feminism.* Indiana University Press: Bloomington.

Hall, A. 2012. *Borderwatch: cultures of immigration, detention and control.* London: Pluto Press.

Hochschild, A. R. 1983. *The managed heart: commercialization of human feeling.* Berkeley, CA: University of California Press.

Isin, E. 2004. The neurotic citizen. *Citizenship Studies* **8**(3), pp. 217–35.

Joint Inquiry by the All Party Parliamentary Group on Refugees and the All Party Parliamentary Group on Migration. 2015. The Report of the Inquiry into the Use of Immigration Detention in the United Kingdom [Online]. Available from: https://detentioninquiry.files.wordpress.com/2015/03/immigration-detention-inquiry-report.pdf [Accessed 15 June 2015].

Kaplan, E. 1997. *Looking for the other.* London: Routledge.

Kaplan, E. 2000. Is the gaze male? In: Kaplan, E. ed. *Feminism and film.* Oxford: Oxford University Press, pp. 119–39.

McDowell, L. 2001. Men, management and multiple masculinities in organisations. *Geoforum* **32**(2), pp. 181–98.

Massumi, B. 2005. The future birth of the affective fact: the political ontology of threat. In: Seigworth, G. and Greg, M. eds. *The affect theory reader.* Durham, NC: Duke University Press, pp. 52–71.

Moore, H. 1994. *A passion for difference: essays in anthropology and gender.* Cambridge: Polity Press.

Mountz, A. and Hyndman, J. 2006. Feminist approaches to the global intimate. *Women's Studies Quarterly* **34**(1/2), pp. 446–63.

Mulvey, L. 2009[1975]. *Visual and other pleasures.* Basingstoke: Palgrave Macmillan.

Pratt, M. 1992. *Imperial eyes: travel writing and transculturation.* London: Routledge.

Roazen, P. 1968. *Freud: political and social thought.* New York: Vintage.

Said, E. 1978. *Orientalism.* London: Routledge and Kegan.

Salter, M. and Mutlu, C. 2011. Psychoanalytic theory and border security. *European Journal of Social Theory* **15**(2), pp. 179–95.

Saurette, P. 2006. 'You dissin' me?' Humiliation and post 9/11 global politics. *Review of International Studies* **32**(3), pp. 495–522.

Stoler, A. 1995. *Race and the education of desire: Foucault's history of sexuality and the colonial order of things.* Durham, NC: Duke University Press.

Whitehead, S.M. 2002. *Men and masculinities.* Cambridge: Polity.

Young, I. 2003. Feminist reactions to the contemporary security regime. *Hypatia* **18**(1), pp. 223–31.

Young, M. 1991. *An inside job: policing and police culture in Britain.* Oxford: Clarendon Press.

Afterword

Intimate economies, anomie and moral ambiguity

Dora Schriro

First afterthoughts

There is little that is civil about 'civil detention' as currently practiced around the world. In the United States and elsewhere, we are as mindful of the conditions our families faced and proud of their difficult journeys from one country to another as we are ambivalent about how to respond to the plight of others fleeing danger and those seeking a better life today. Even when we agree that our borders should be opened, and large numbers of foreign-born individuals accepted, we worry how wise is our welcome, we worry whether we will be safe and if there will be 'enough' left for us.

The number of people in need increases, as governments grow more unstable, violent non-state actors exert more power than do the police or government, more young men and women seek work elsewhere, more children travel unaccompanied by adults to live with relatives in less dangerous locales, and more families cross borders from bad to better places seeking asylum. And, increasingly, countries on every continent are responding to these surges of humanity in strikingly similar and inhumane ways, most notably, the detention of adults and children, the aged and infirm, and the indigent and unrepresented, in converted correctional facilities, temporary camps and abandoned military bases, often for indefinite periods of time. There is little that is *civil* about civil detention.

In the remarkable treatise, *Intimate Economies of Immigration Detention: Critical perspectives*, authors from around the world, each one an expert in his or her own right, have considered various roles and responsibilities that public, private and non-profit actors assume in the provision of immigration detention. At the micro and the macro levels, these interactions, in no small measure economic exchanges, are personal and highly impersonal as well as lucrative in multiple ways. Both for-profit and non-profit organisations own and operate detention facilities at considerable corporate and personal gain. Other actors benefit as well, such as those involved in the provision of related services like health care, food service and electronic monitoring systems. In the United States, for example, actors employed by Immigration and Customs Enforcement and Customs and Border Protection, two agencies within the Department of Homeland Security, also benefit. Individuals benefiting range from federal enforcement agents trained to engage in apprehension, removal and relief activities; to entry level, semi-skilled personnel retained by the public or private sector to guard the detained or monitor facility compliance with government rules and regulations. Even those who volunteer their services, it is posited, derive some benefit, whether personal or professional, from their exchanges with their foreign-born clients.

This text affords policy makers and practitioners alike a unique perspective on civil detention. Civil detention is an economic enterprise. Civil detention is an exceptionally profitable economic enterprise. Civil detention operates at the intersection of national boundaries and interpersonal relationships, somewhat perverse personal and profitable relationships. They are perverse relationships in that the relationships are unequal: both the government and their citizens are in positions of power greater than that of the immigrants, and the position of the detained immigrants is further diminished by virtue of their incapacitated status. And because civil detention is an exceptionally profitable economic enterprise, it is likely to continue to rank high among governments' preferred remedies for and responses to the plight of others fleeing danger and those seeking a better life.

Reflections on detention and anomie

Anomie is a condition of instability. It is caused by a breakdown of standards and values or from a lack of purpose or ideals. Its impetus can be a repressive system of law, one in which the laws are based on a powerful collective conscience or set of social norms, all too often grounded in unconscionable yet strongly held beliefs. No one is immune. We are all susceptible to the impact of anomie on social order. Individuals and groups alike can experience its effects. As the contributions in this book collectively show, immigration law can be both cause and symptom of anomie, of a condition of instability in which the belief that 'our families' migration was urgent but your families' need to immigrate is not' dominates.

The social systems within which we operate consist of interconnected parts, each part influencing and being influenced by the other parts, intending to work together to maintain a state of balance and social equilibrium for the group as a whole. The impact of one part upon another can cause either function or dysfunction and sometimes both. Crime, for example, is detrimental to the group in that it is associated with physical violence, loss of property and fear. Crime is also beneficial to the extent that it creates and sustains an awareness of shared moral bonds and increases social cohesion. So it is with unlawful immigration and mass migrations. An influx in the foreign born is associated with anticipated job losses, terrorist threats and xenophobia. An influx in foreign born also heightens one group's awareness of perceived differences, no matter how small, between us and others, and fortifies our belief in the need to act on those perceptions.

It is striking the extent to which intimate relationships can be infused with anomie, how the physical proximity of one group of persons born in one country, providing goods and services to a group of persons born in another country, can be so acrimonious, cause and contribute to moral ambiguity, and be guided by economic gain instead of by the country's or its citizens' core values. It is also striking how often the close proximity and frequency of the exchanges between the powerful and powerless create barriers. Rather than fostering familiarity, proximity and frequency can affirm the anomie, fueling the beliefs that expand and extend the economic exchanges, tolling both the personal losses as well as the financial gains. Thus anomie limits our ability to see our neighbours as we see ourselves, inhibiting our ability to love and to forgive them as we do our own.

Civil detention, as currently practiced in the United States and other countries, is a blend of civil law and criminal law enforcement policy and practice, fueling and further fostering the impact of anomie, a moral ambiguity within and between those born in that country and elsewhere. In fact, immigration detention is not supposed to be the same as criminal incarceration. As a matter of law, immigration detention is intended to hold individuals only as long as necessary, when necessary, in order to process and prepare detained individuals for removal or relief, whereas criminal incarceration is expressly punitive in its purposes and goals. Thus, well established legal differences between civil detention and criminal incarceration become blurred by civil enforcement systems' adoption of correctional policies and practices, their performance standards, and most notably their utilisation of penal institutions and personnel to manage the many individuals crossing national borders, few of whom have a criminal history, few of whom have been previously incarcerated.

It is remarkable how quickly policies and practices can be put into place, in this instance, policies and practices that give preference to and perpetuate detention; policies and practices that attack the symptoms, but not the source, of the problem; policies and practices whose economic benefits incentivise their entrenchment and expansion.

What to do? Next steps

Economic relationships are not intrinsically bad relationships, and neither are intimate economic relationships. It is the rationale for their formation, formalisation and continuation that is probative, and all too often, problematic.

Few immigrants present the kinds of risk attributed to persons remanded to correctional facilities or placed on electronic monitoring and other forms of close supervision in the criminal justice arena. Most have no criminal history. They are fleeing danger, seeking a better life, asking for asylum. Some cross the borders lawfully, others do not, but in the end, they all want the same thing: citizenship. The premise of a positive intimate economic relationship should be that a government's response to both routine migration and exceptional surges is commensurate with the real risks these people present and consistent with the international community's core values.

In 2009, the US Department of Homeland Security undertook a system-wide governmental study of immigration detention. The study concluded that its detention system was premised upon the principles of criminal, rather than civil, law, when in fact, its foundational precept is that migrants are not to be detained as punishment. Moreover, many in immigration detention who qualified under the law for relief from removal had been denied its protection. In stark contrast, a *civil* system of civil detention would feature policies and procedures and a physical plant governed by the presumption that release to the community is the rule and not the exception, no matter the mix of public, for-profit and non-profit actors acting on behalf of the government. And, in cases where release alone is insufficient, an objective risk assessment would be made and the least restrictive means necessary applied to ensure attendance at mandated immigration proceedings. The 2009 study also determined that measures such as monetary bond and electronic monitoring, neither of which is a minimally restrictive alternative means for ensuring appearance of migrants at their proceedings, was used to excess. The US Government made a number of changes and realised some improvements but the overall system is still fundamentally flawed.

A detention system as envisioned by the 2009 study, and enthusiastically adopted by the Department of Homeland Security as its template for reform, has yet to be realised in the United States, but these precepts can no longer be ignored. By resorting to detention without regard to these foundational principles, indiscriminately labeling most to all migrants as threats to public safety and national security, and refusing to determine and utilise the least restrictive means of achieving compliance with immigration proceedings, the US Government fails to meet its legal obligations and fundamental fairness goal. These failures leave in their wake a growing population that is over-incarcerated and underserved, struggling with the consequences of unnecessary detention and over-supervision. The adjudication of claims has become haphazard and unfair, and the scarce pro bono legal services diverted to address these issues are needlessly depleted.

Looking towards the future, the US Government and others must review and revise their current practices. Reform requires the advanced development, and fair implementation, of viable plans to adhere to these precepts. Detention should be a last resort. Release to the community should be a first resort, but not with excessive supervision requirements. Accelerated deportation proceedings lacking in due process must be avoided. All governments must review and revise their relationships with public, for-profit and non-profit partners. Many of these actors contract with multiple governments, making more ubiquitous the current approach which results in unnecessary detention and over-supervision, both infirm policies characterised by a paucity of corollary health and mental health care as well as social, educational and vocational services.

If we were to pursue something other than the economically advantaged relationships in which we currently engage, then what? Envision migration systems whose rewards and risks are congruent with their peoples' founding principles and consistent with their core values. Here, in the United States, it is this:

> Give me your tired, your poor,
> Your huddled masses, yearning to breathe free,
> The wretched refuse of your teeming shore,
> Send these, the homeless, tempest tossed to me,
> I lift my lamp beside the golden door.[1]

In the United States, a civil system of civil detention would look like this. There would be a presumption against detention. Release into the community would be the rule rather than the exception. The governance of a *civil*, civil system would be embedded with evidence-based practices and not based upon deterrence-based detention policies. The standards of care ascribed to by all government actors would expressly prohibit the application of a penal model. Detention would be used only when required by law, for the fewest number of individuals – particularly not for families, children and asylum seekers – for the shortest time possible. There would be meaningful access to legal information and representation as well as family visitation and communication.

When release alone into the community is insufficient, an objective risk assessment would be employed to identify the least restrictive means, such as community-based supervision, to achieve compliance with attendance at immigration proceedings. More restrictive alternatives to detention, including electronic monitoring and cash bond, would be used only where demonstrably necessary in an individual case. In those cases where a specific flight risk or danger is established and payment of a financial bond is the least restrictive means of addressing those risks, the bond amount would be set at an attainable level based on individual circumstances.

Other components of immigration enforcement would be informed by this alternate vision as well. The management tools and informational systems of immigration enforcement agencies, as well as their continuum of care, would be guided by the commitment to provide care for individuals in their custody and under their supervision, utilising the least restrictive means to achieve compliance, and not to make involved parties' activities more profitable. This alternative vision of enforcement would also encompass independent monitoring for compliance and meaningful federal oversight of detention operations, through on-site presence at facilities of government officials authorised to intercede quickly and as often as necessary, and to ensure that effective complaint mechanisms are in place.

What would a civil system of civil detention, one that balances the nation's costs and benefits and values the worth of all persons, look like in another country, in your country? That is an important question worthy of a careful answer, a question to which we should all turn next.

Note

1 Lazarus, E. 1883. *The new colossus*. New York: American Jewish Historical Society.

Index

For Product Safety Concerns and Information please contact our EU
representative GPSR@taylorandfrancis.com
Taylor & Francis Verlag GmbH, Kaufingerstraße 24, 80331 München, Germany

www.ingramcontent.com/pod-product-compliance
Ingram Content Group UK Ltd.
Pitfield, Milton Keynes, MK11 3LW, UK
UKHW021007180425
457613UK00019B/837